THE FUTURE OF ASIAN TRADE DEALS AND IP

The pulling out of the Trans-Pacific Partnership (TPP) by the US marks a new era for trade deals and potentially for intellectual property (IP). The TPP has evolved to become the Comprehensive and Progressive Agreement for TPP (CPTPP) with the remaining 11 members suspending some of its provisions, over half of which are IP-related. While the TPP excludes the two Asian giants – India and the People's Republic of China (PRC) – the ongoing Regional Comprehensive Economic Partnership (RCEP) negotiations include both of them.

The first part of this edited collection sets out to re-examine some basic principles of trade negotiation, such as choosing the right representatives to negotiate and enhancing transparency as a cure to the public's distrust against trade talks; moreover, it analyses how CPTPP might impact on RCEP's IP chapter and examines the possible norm setters of Asian IP. It then focuses on the PRC's trade and IP strategy against the backdrop of the power games between the PRC, India and the US.

The second part of the book reflects on issues related to investor–state dispute settlement and its relationship with IP, such as how to re-calibrate the balance in international investment arbitration, and whether compulsory license of IP constitutes expropriation in India, the PRC and select ASEAN countries.

The third part of the book questions and strives to improve some of the proposed IP provisions of CPTPP and RCEP and to redefine some aspects of international IP norms, such as: pre-grant patent opposition and experimental use exception; patent term extension; patent linkage and data exclusivity for the pharmaceutical sector; plant variety protection; pre-established damages for copyright infringement; and the restructuring of copyright limitations in the public interest.

The Future of Asian Trade Deals and IP

Edited by
Kung-Chung Liu
and
Julien Chaisse

•HART•
OXFORD • LONDON • NEW YORK • NEW DELHI • SYDNEY

HART PUBLISHING

Bloomsbury Publishing Plc

Kemp House, Chawley Park, Cumnor Hill, Oxford, OX2 9PH, UK

HART PUBLISHING, the Hart/Stag logo, BLOOMSBURY and the Diana logo are trademarks of Bloomsbury Publishing Plc

First published in Great Britain 2019

A catalogue record for this book is available from the British Library.

Library of Congress Cataloging-in-Publication data

Names: Liu, Kung-Chung, editor. | Chaisse, Julien, editor.

Title: The future of Asian trade deals and IP / edited by Kung-Chung Liu and Julien Chaisse.

Description: Oxford ; New York : Hart, 2019. | Includes bibliographical references and index.

Identifiers: LCCN 2019029554 (print) | LCCN 2019029555 (ebook) | ISBN 9781509922772 (hardback) | ISBN 9781509922796 (Epub)

Subjects: LCSH: Intellectual property—Asia. | Foreign trade regulation—Asia.

Classification: LCC KNC370 .F48 2019 (print) | LCC KNC370 (ebook) | DDC 346.504/8—dc23

LC record available at https://lccn.loc.gov/2019029554

LC ebook record available at https://lccn.loc.gov/2019029555

ISBN: HB: 978-1-50992-277-2
ePDF: 978-1-50992-278-9
ePub: 978-1-50992-279-6

Typeset by Compuscript Ltd, Shannon

TABLE OF CONTENTS

PART III
IMPROVING THE IP PROVISIONS OF CPTPP/RCEP AND REDEFINING GLOBAL IP NORMS

LIST OF CONTRIBUTORS

Christoph Antons is Professor of Law at the Newcastle Law School, University of Newcastle, Australia; Affiliated Research Fellow at the Max Planck Institute for Innovation and Competition, Munich; and Senior Fellow at the Center for Development Research, University of Bonn, Germany.

Julien Chaisse is Professor at The City University of Hong Kong, School of Law. He is an award-winning scholar of international law with a special focus on the regulation and development of economic globalization. Dr Chaisse has published numerous well-regarded and widely cited books and articles, such as *China's International Investment Strategy* (Oxford University Press, 2019), *The Regulation of the Global Water Services Market* (Cambridge University Press, 2017) and *International Economic Law and Governance* (Oxford University Press, 2016). In addition to his professorship, Dr Chaisse is a highly experienced arbitrator and a leading consultant to international organizations, governments, multinational law firms and private investors.

Liyu Han is Professor of Law at Renmin University of China Law School, focusing on International Economic Law and WTO Law, Vice President of the China Society of International Economic Law and Vice President of WTO Law Society of China Law Society.

Tomoko Ishikawa is Associate Professor at Nagoya University in Japan. She is a member of the ICSID Panel of Conciliators, appointed by the Chairman of the ICSID Administrative Council and a member of the Legal Advisory Committee of the Energy Charter Treaty.

Su-Hua Lee received her Bachelor of Laws from National Taipei University and Master of Laws (Magister iuris comparativi, M iur Comp) from Rheinischen Friedrich-Wilhelms-Universität Bonn, and earned a Doctor of Laws degree (PhD) from National Taiwan University. Lee has been Professor of Law at National Taiwan University since 2016. Her principal teaching and research interests are in the fields of intellectual property, patent protection of biotechnology and pharmaceutical products, civil law (laws of contract and torts) and competition law.

Han-Wei Liu joined Monash University in January 2018, from National Tsing Hua University where he was Assistant Professor of Law (tenure track). Dr Liu works in the areas of international economic law, law and technology, and international law and global governance. Before academia, he practised with Baker & McKenzie and Russin & Vecchi for several years. Han-Wei earned his PhD, summa cum laude, from the Graduate Institute, Geneva (IHEID)/University of Geneva on Kathryn Davis Scholarship and his master degrees from Columbia Law School and Oxford University on Taiwan Government Scholarship and British Chevening Scholarship, respectively. He received his LL.M. and LL.B. degrees from National Chengchi University. His publications have appeared in leading international law journals, such as *Journal of International Economic Law*, *University of Pennsylvania Journal of International Law*, *Melbourne Journal of International Law* and *Columbia Journal of Asian Law*. Dr Liu has been invited to present his works in conferences held by, among other institutions, Cambridge, Duke, Harvard and Warwick. Dr Liu has held visiting posts at Harvard and Columbia Law Schools. Dr Liu has received several research grants from the Taiwan government and has advised high-tech firms and government-funded think-tanks on regulation of digital communication, cross-border data flow, and technology transfer/export control issues. In addition to his editorial role in 2009 at *Columbia Journal of European Law*, Dr Liu currently sits on the editorial board of *Manchester Journal of International Economic Law* and the *Chinese (Taiwan) Yearbook of International Law and Affairs* and serves as a referee for various journals and publishers.

Kung-Chung Liu is Lee Kong Chian Professor of Law (Practice), founding director, Applied Research Center for Intellectual Assets and the Law in Asia (ARCIALA), School of Law, Singapore Management University. Professor Liu is also Professor at Renmin University of China, as his specialization in intellectual property law and competition law is widely recognized in Asia. He has edited and co-edited 13 books with vision and leadership of thought, which include *Annotated Leading Copyright Cases in Major Asian Jurisdictions* (City University of HK Press, forthcoming 2019), *Annotated Leading Trademark Cases in Major Asian Jurisdictions* (Routledge forthcoming 2019), *Innovation, Economic Development and IPR in China and India – A Study of 6 Industries* (Springer forthcoming 2019), and *SEPs, SSOs and FRAND – Asian and Global Perspectives on Fostering Innovation in Interconnectivity* (Springer forthcoming 2019).

Si-Wei Lu is a PhD student at National Chengchi University. Prior to her Ph.D. studies, she clerked at Taiwan Intellectual Property Office and thereafter earned her master degree in law from National Tsing Hua University. Si-Wei's areas of academic interest include intellectual property law, intellectual property management, international trade law, and law for science and technology.

Yaojin Peng is an associate professor of intellectual property law, biotechnology law, at the Institute of Zoology (IOZ), Chinese Academy of Sciences (CAS), in Beijing, China. He holds a Bachelor's degree in life sciences and a Master's degree in law. He completed his PhD at the Faculty of Law, Maastricht University, the Netherlands.

Prabhash Ranjan is an Assistant Professor of law at the South Asian University, New Delhi, India. he holds a PhD in law from King's College London. He has been a Visiting Fellow at the Lauterpacht Centre for International Law, Cambridge University and a Visiting Scholar at Brookings India. He is the author of the book *India and Bilateral Investment Treaties: Refusal, Acceptance, Backlash* (Oxford University Press, 2019).

Prashant Reddy T is Assistant Professor at National Academy of Legal Studies & Research (NALSAR); External Fellow, Applied Research Centre for Intellectual Assets & the Law in Asia (ARCIALA), School of Law, Singapore Management University (SMU).

Haochen Sun is Associate Professor of Law and Director of the Law and Technology Center at the University of Hong Kong Faculty of Law. He specialises in intellectual property and technology law. His recent scholarship has focused on the theoretical and policy foundations of intellectual property, Chinese intellectual property law, and international and comparative intellectual property law.

Jiaxun Sun is a PhD candidate currently studying at Renmin University of China Law School.

Benjamin Tham holds bachelors' degrees in science and law from the National University of Singapore and the University of Nottingham respectively and is admitted to the Singapore Bar. Benjamin is currently a research associate at the Centre for AI and Data Governance at the Singapore Management University (SMU) and an assistant editor of the Singapore Institute of Arbitrators' Journal. He is a former intern at the Legal Policy and Affairs Division of the Intellectual Property Office of Singapore and a former research associate at the Applied Research Centre for Intellectual Assets and the Law in Asia at the SMU.

Peter K Yu is Professor of Law, Professor of Communication and Director of the Center for Law and Intellectual Property at Texas A&M University in the United States. Born and raised in Hong Kong, he previously held the Kern Family Chair in Intellectual Property Law at Drake University Law School and served as Wenlan Scholar Chair Professor at Zhongnan University of Economics and Law in Wuhan, China.

Haoran Zhang is a PhD student at Renmin University of China.

1

Introduction

The Intersection between Intellectual Property Rights and Free Trade Agreements

KUNG-CHUNG LIU AND JULIEN CHAISSE*

Recent trends in international trade and investment agreements show elements of change with regard to traditional approaches to trade rule making. While overall multilateral regulation of the so-called 'Singapore issues' (investment, competition, transparency in government procurement and trade facilitation) have been taken off the World Trade Organization (WTO) agenda, several prominent WTO Members have recently taken more comprehensive regulatory steps in their free trade agreements (FTAs) by including elements of intellectual property rights (IPRs) regulation – a fundamental component of WTO law. However, traditionally trade law and IP law have been two distinct areas of law, and interaction between the two legal communities remains rare.

In addition, the pulling out of the Trans-Pacific Partnership (TPP) by the United States (US) marks a new era for trade deals and possibly for intellectual property (IP). The TPP evolved into the Comprehensive and Progressive Agreement for TPP (CPTPP) between the remaining 11 members of the TPP by suspending some of its provisions, over half of which are IP-related. While the TPP excludes the two Asian giants – India and the People's Republic of China (PRC) – the ongoing Regional Comprehensive Economic Partnership (RCEP) includes both of them. The PRC, India and Singapore are three of the participating countries negotiating the RCEP, along with members of ASEAN, Japan, New Zealand, Australia and South Korea. Noteworthy is the fact that India has not been able to sign a single major trade deal since joining the WTO Agreement in 1994; the contentious issue

* Dr Kung-Chung Liu is Lee Kong Chian Professor of Law (Practice) Director, Applied Research Centre for Intellectual Assets and the Law in Asia, School of Law, Singapore Management University/ Renmin University of China. Dr Julien Chaisse is Professor at the City University of Hong Kong, School of Law.

has almost always been intellectual property. To date, there has been limited literature that looks at the CPTPP and impending RCEP from Asian perspectives.

This is the context and background considerations for the conference organized by the Applied Research Centre for Intellectual Assets and the Law in Asia (ARCIALA), School of Law, Singapore Management University (SMU) on 'The Future of Asian Trade Deals & Intellectual Property' in December 2017. This conference brought together some 20 academics and experts from both trade law and IP law with strong Asian backgrounds. The present volume is the result of the conference, with one editor working on IP law and the other working on trade law, and 12 chapters in addition to this introductory one.

The main theme that runs through the conference and the book is about re-examining the two important trade deals and their IP Chapters. The book also strives to analyse how and to what extent Asian economies can shed some light on CPTPP, rectify the RCEP IP Chapter, and even redefine some aspects of international IP norms since their two key drivers, namely the US and the European Union, are not part of the CPTPP and RCEP talks. To better achieve its goals, the book has a three-part structure that covers the general development from TPP to CPTPP and further to RCEP, investor-state arbitration and IP, and improving the IP provisions national and regional (CPTPP and RCEP) and redefining some global IP norms.

Part I. From TPP/CPTPP to RCEP

The first part sets out to establish one of the basic principles of trade negotiation, namely choosing the right representatives to negotiate. It then looks into the major actors of trade deals and IP rules in Asia (namely China, India, and the US) by focusing on China's trade and IP strategy against the backdrop of the power games between the PRC, India and the US, and China's evolving IP schemes, in order to shed light on how Asian economies will reconfigure the IPR rules in future negotiations.

Benjamin Tham (**Chapter 2: Selecting the Right Representatives to Participate in Trade Negotiations**) addresses a perennial issue surrounding plurilateral FTA negotiations, ie secrecy, confidentiality and the lack of inclusivity, by first analysing the reasons for and against such a status quo being commonly adopted. He then looks at the consequences arising therefrom and how it affects IPRs by reference to stakeholder involvement models adopted by other trade agreements, the draft Anti-Counterfeiting Trade Agreement, the Transatlantic Trade and Investment Partnership, and the RCEP. The chapter recommends a new model of multi-stakeholder involvement and explains why this new model is necessary from an IPR perspective. Suggestions in relation to stakeholders who should participate in future plurilateral FTA negotiations under this new multi-stakeholder model include involving international organizations, civil society organizations, non-governmental organizations and academics.

Liyu Han and Jiaxun Sun (Chapter 3: Trade Strategies and Power Games between China, the US and India) discuss the trade strategies and power games between the PRC, US and India. The US took a drastic turn from multilateralism to bilateralism and put forward the 'Indo-Pacific dream' in Asia, a system of bilateral agreements and negotiations, which would greatly affect China and India. In addition, the US is rewriting world trade order based on the 'America first' principle and targeting China's alleged unfair trade practices. China's trade policy since the opening up has been joining the WTO, upholding its multilateralism and embracing FTAs. India has an extremely complex relationship with China due to a border dispute and the Tibet and Pakistan issues. Its relations with the US also remain uncertain. The chapter suggests that China should pursue more comprehensive FTAs with more trade issues and deeper commitments, and support the multilateral trading system of the WTO, as this would benefit the whole world; that China and US should give each other space and time to develop trade policies at their own pace; and that the US, India and China should join efforts in building constructive relations to realize the Indo-Pacific dream.

Han-Wei Liu and Si-Wei Lu (Chapter 4: The Future of China's Trade Pact and Intellectual Property Rights) analyse the rise of China as a new global power and its role in shaping international IPRs by both domestic reforms and participation in bilateral and multilateral trade agreements. They offer a historical and contemporary account of China's evolving IPR schemes in the context of international trade in order to enlighten Asian economies' reconfiguration of the IPR rules in future negotiations. This chapter sketches out the changing face of the Chinese IPR regime in the pre-WTO era, revisits China's evolving IPR regime in the post-WTO era, and carefully examines the design of IPR provisions in its FTAs and mega-regional negotiations. China has gradually improved its IPR regime by taking into account external relationships, global norms and its long-term development. Recent initiatives in the context of the One-Belt-One-Road initiative provide new momentum to IP developments not only for China, but also the areas involved, to which policymakers should pay heed.

Peter K Yu (Chapter 5: The RCEP Negotiations and Asian Intellectual Property Norm Setters) closely examines the RCEP negotiations and the Asian countries' recent efforts to set regional IP norms. The chapter highlights the provisions in the draft RCEP IP Chapter, focusing on the four main branches of IP law (copyright, trademark, patent and trade secret) as well as the areas of IP enforcement and pro-development measures. The chapter outlines the role of the five norm setters in the RCEP negotiations – namely, the Association of Southeast Asian Nations (ASEAN), India, Japan, South Korea and China – China being the only one of all of these negotiating parties not having advanced draft negotiating texts. It suggests that the Asian countries' willingness to accept higher IP standards in the RCEP negotiations, or at least their ambivalence towards those standards, shows that these countries have now started to recognize the alignment of the TRIPS norms with their self-interests, and gone are the days when they accepted without questioning those norms that have been established abroad in the developed world.

Part II. Investor-State Arbitration and Intellectual Property

International investment agreements (IIAs) and investor-state dispute settlement (ISDS), which allows private companies to sue states via arbitration, are closely intertwined with the protection of IPRs. The tension between the protection of IPRs and the public interest of the host state manifested in several investment arbitration cases, such as *Philip Morris Asia Limited v. The Commonwealth of Australia* and *Eli Lilly v. Canada*, has given rise to concerns over the ISDS regime. The recent developments in the IIA regime towards greater sensitivity to the public interest of the host state are highly relevant to the future directions of IPR protection. Therefore, Part II examines the ISDS mechanism, which has existed in regional trade agreements such NAFTA and many bilateral investment treaties (BITS) under IIA, and the application of this mechanism.

Tomoko Ishikawa (Chapter 6: Recalibrating the Balance in International Investment Agreements) explores two recent developments in the practice of IIA making, in which the IIA regime exhibits greater sensitivity to the public interest of the host state. One is the inclusion of general exception clauses modelled on GATT Article XX and GATS Article XIV, and the other is the reference to investors' responsibility, in particular corporate social responsibility (CSR). This chapter claims that, while the textual transplant of general exception clauses in IIAs from GATT and GATS entails the risk that it might result in less regulatory flexibility, references to CSR have a potential role to play in rebalancing investment obligations and the public interest of the host state. This chapter also demonstrates the potential effects of including provisions on investor responsibilities in IIAs. Even when a reference to CSR is not addressed to investors, such a reference might still inform the interpretation and application of substantive investment obligations through, for example, the application of the principle of effective interpretation. Given that there is an imbalance between the lack of an effective mechanism to hold transnational corporations accountable for their conduct and the heavy protection of foreign investment in the IIA regime, and that in certain cases investors' activities do have a grave impact on the public interest of the host state, an explicit recognition of internationally accepted standards of corporate responsibility in IIAs would be the direction the future IIA negotiations should take.

Prabhash Ranjan (Chapter 7: Issuance of Compulsory Patent Licences and Expropriation in Asian BITs and FTA Investment Chapters) extends the analysis of ISDS and IPRs interactions by looking at whether the issuance of a compulsory patent licence constitutes indirect expropriation under BITs and FTA investment chapters by India, China, Malaysia and Thailand. The chapter shows that while some investment treaties of these countries exclude issuance of compulsory patent licences from the ambit of expropriation, many treaties do not do so explicitly. If issuance of compulsory patent licences is challenged as expropriation before an ISDS tribunal, the outcome would depend on a number of factors such as the language of the treaty, the interpretative approach that a tribunal may adopt, and the degree of interference caused by the issuance of compulsory patent licence, etc. In order to safeguard regulatory autonomy, these countries may consider adopting a model that excludes issuance of compulsory patent licensing from the ambit of expropriation in the investment treaty. This chapter suggests that India, China, Malaysia, Thailand and the like need to carefully draft their treaties, in order to curb arbitral discretion and provide regulatory space to adopt compulsory patent licensing without worrying about an ISDS challenge.

More recently, the ISDS has found its way into TPP and RCEP. Although, the ISDS formed a central part of America's negotiating strategy during the TPP. It is very likely that any potential ISDS provision in the RCEP will be substantially different, because both India and China are present in the RCEP negotiation and are unlikely to surrender their national sovereignty to ISDS. The RCEP is therefore in a position to redefine the norms on ISDS and IP.

Part III. Improving the National, Regional (CPTPP/RCEP) and Global IP Provisions

Part III offers a selected analysis of some of national and regional IP provisions (CPTPP and RCEP), how they can be improved or better implemented, and their potential to redefine some global IP norms. It first covers the patent provisions with three chapters dealing with pre-grant opposition and experimental use exceptions, patent term extension (PTE), and the mitigation of the patent linkage, respectively. It then discusses, in sequence, provisions on IP in plant material, pre-established damages for copyright infringement and trademark counterfeiting, and copyright limitations.

Prashant Reddy Thikkavarapu (Chapter 8: Will RCEP Redefine Norms Related to Pre-grant Opposition and Experimental Use Exceptions in International Patent Law?) points out the exciting leading role which RCEP could potentially play to redefine norms related to pre-grant opposition and experimental use exceptions in international patent law, although the final text of CPTPP did not incorporate these demands. If the pre-grant oppositions (Article 5.14) and experimental use exceptions (Article 5.3) of the leaked text are in fact adopted by the RCEP, it will be a milestone of sorts, because most international agreements focus only on the rights of IP owners. Safeguards against expansive patent rights like pre-grant oppositions and exceptions like the one on experimental use are almost never the subject matter of discussion at the international negotiation table. Thus, if RCEP incorporates both these provisions it would mark the dawn of a new age, where Asia takes the lead in remolding international patent law norms to better balance the rights and limitations.

Yaojin Peng (Chapter 9: Patent Term Extension in the Pharmaceutical Sector) analyses the role of PTE in the pharmaceutical sector. The PTE system originated in the US, expanded to other jurisdictions in Europe and Asia, and is now being considered by jurisdictions around the world. Interestingly, although based on similar objectives and following the same US model, jurisdictions have set forth slightly different provisions and made diverse interpretations concerning the PTE system. The tailoring of the specific PTE rules and policies in a jurisdiction depends on its domestic pharmaceutical industry. It demonstrates that the conditions for granting a PTE are highly controversial, the PTE systems and case law are still evolving, and there remain plenty of uncertainties to be clarified. This chapter highlights the convergences and divergences among the PTE systems in Japan, Korea and Taiwan, to examine and identify the pros and cons of different approaches taken by these jurisdictions. It provides recommendations for the potential negotiation of the PTE requirement in the context of the CPTPP/TPP and the introduction of the PTE system in China.

Su-Hua Lee (**Chapter 10: Mitigating the Impacts of Patent Linkage on Access to Medicine**) looks at how to mitigate the impacts of patent linkage, demanded only by CPPTT and not by RCEP, on access to medicine. The importance of patent linkage in Asian countries has been rising due to the FTAs with the US and the coming into effect of the CPTPP. This measure might cause negative impacts on public health if the mechanisms in favour of the generics industry are not incorporated when establishing the patent linkage regime. The experiences that Singapore, South Korea and Taiwan have had with patent linkage while striving to improve access to innovative drugs and the competitiveness of the domestic pharmaceutical industry might provide some lessons for members of the CPTPP in striking a proper balance of interests between original and generics companies.

Christoph Antons (**Chapter 11: Intellectual Property in Plant Material and Free Trade Agreements in Asia**) discusses the rise of IPRs in plant material over the last few decades, the expansion of the International Convention for the Protection of New Varieties of Plants (UPOV) since the WTO TRIPS Agreement, and the considerable impact of current FTAs and negotiations on these trends. The chapter identifies those countries that have shown particular interest in upscaling the IP protection of plant material, and focuses on agreements that emphasize cooperation and exceptions to IP protection rather than a further strengthening of the system. It advises developing countries to remain extremely cautious about the expansion of IPRs in this field and to resist pressure to adopt positions and legislative models in FTAs that are potentially harmful to their economic interests or that threaten their agro-biodiversity. Countries with constitutional and treaty obligations towards indigenous and other communities with traditional resource rights should highlight such obligations during international treaty negotiations to achieve the necessary freedom to legislate for the protection of such rights.

Kung-Chung Liu and Haoran Zhang (**Chapter 12: Pre-established Damages for Copyright Infringement and Trademark Counterfeiting**) critically discuss the pre-established damages for copyright infringement and trademark counterfeiting. One of the solutions for the difficulty for IP right holders to prove their actual loss as a result of infringement that arises is statutory damages or pre-established damages. The CPTPP has embarked on this solution on its own initiative for copyright infringement and trademark counterfeiting. After examining the experiences in some Asian jurisdictions and identifying its potential downsides, this chapter suggests that the CPTPP interpret and apply this new regime by following the Japanese regime as a benchmark, and that the RCEP should abandon its current leaked version, which further strengthens, or denatures, pre-established damages for copyright infringement and trademark counterfeiting and, at most, mirror the CPTPP.

Haochen Sun (Chapter 13: Liberalizing Use of the Three-Step Test and Copyright Limitations in the Public Interest) completes the analysis of Part III by looking at the three-step test and copyright limitations. The RCEP's draft IP Chapter comprehensively sets out a host of minimum standards for IP protection in the participating countries and has given rise to a plethora of concerns over negative effects such as the stifling of creativity, innovation, and economic growth. Therefore, this chapter argues that trade agreement negotiators should take limitations on copyright seriously. First, it cautions against the direct inclusion of the three-step test in future trade agreements, including the RCEP. Second, it proposes that the test be altered in a liberal manner to allow it to be interpreted and applied in the public interest under future trade agreements. The chapter suggests that both professionalism and transparency are needed to guide the negotiation process of such agreements.

Acknowledgements

We would like to thank Kent Suárez for checking the English of the volume.

PART I

From TPP/CPTPP to RCEP

2

Selecting the Right Representatives to Participate in Trade Negotiations

A New Model of Multi-Stakeholder Involvement for Future Plurilateral Free Trade Agreement Negotiations

BENJAMIN THAM*

This chapter seeks to address a perennial issue surrounding plurilateral free trade agreement negotiations, ie secrecy, confidentiality and the lack of inclusivity, by first analysing the reasons for and against this approach being commonly adopted. The chapter then looks at the consequences arising therefrom and how these impact on intellectual property rights by reference to stakeholder involvement models adopted by other trade agreements, namely, the Anti-Counterfeiting Trade Agreement, Transatlantic Trade and Investment Partnership and the Regional Comprehensive Economic Partnership, and the lessons to be learned from the negotiations of these trade agreements are examined. Finally, the chapter attempts to make recommendations by way of a new model of multi-stakeholder involvement and seeks to explain why this new model is necessary from an intellectual property rights perspective. Suggestions regarding the stakeholders who should participate in future plurilateral free trade agreement negotiations under this new model of multi-stakeholder involvement will also be made. It is intended that this new model would not only be relevant from a policy perspective but would also be meaningful at the systemic level.

* Research associate, ARCIALA, SMU. (All online information last accessed 15 August 2018.)

I. Secrecy and Confidentiality and Lack of Inclusivity in Trade Negotiations

As François de Callières, French diplomat and special envoy of King Louis XIV, succinctly puts it in his classic work on diplomatic negotiations titled *De la manière de négocier avec les souverains*, 'secrecy is the soul of (diplomatic) negotiations'.[1] Indeed, employing secrecy as a negotiation strategy has been 'a norm'[2] established by diplomats and trade negotiators for centuries.

Consequently, there is no question over the pervasiveness of secrecy entrenched in negotiations for plurilateral free trade agreements.[3] Secrecy in plurilateral free trade agreement negotiations may have originated from earlier multilateral trade agreements such as the General Agreement for Tariffs and Trade (GATT). For example, in Art XXVIII GATT which provides for the 'Modification of Schedules', the 'Interpretative Note *Ad* XXVIII' provides that '[t]he CONTRACTING PARTIES and each contracting party concerned should arrange to conduct the negotiations and consultations with the greatest possible secrecy in order to avoid premature disclosure of details of prospective tariff changes'. This applies even to renegotiations as the GATT Secretariat 'is required to circulate as secret documents all notifications for initiating renegotiations, with the accompanying information as well as the reports on completion of bilateral negotiations and the final report on the conclusion of all negotiations/consultations'.[4]

Before looking into the various justifications (or lack thereof) for secrecy in plurilateral free trade agreement negotiations, it is apposite to first look into what such secrecy generally entails. Maher, in the context of the now defunct Trans-Pacific Partnership trade agreement (TPP), describes the situation regarding secrecy:

> Soon after the US joined the TPP negotiations, the original negotiating states entered into a confidentiality agreement, and New Zealand became the official depository of all documents. This was formalised by an exchange in letters that stated that the negotiating parties agreed to hold the following documents in confidence for four years after the TPP came into force or the last round of negotiations had been completed: the negotiating texts, the proposals of each government, accompanying explanatory materials, emails related to substance of the negotiations, and any other information exchanges in the context of the negotiations.[5]

[1] François de Callières, 'De la manière de négocier avec les souverains', Wikisource http://fr.wikisource.org/wiki/De_la_mani%C3%A8re_de_n%C3%A9gocier_avec_les_souverains.

[2] M Limenta, 'Open Trade Negotiations as Opposed to Secret Trade Negotiations: From Transparency to Public Participation' (2012) 10 *New Zealand Yearbook of International Law* 73, 78.

[3] C Herrmann, 'Transleakancy' in C Herrmann, B Simma and R Streinz (eds), *Trade Policy between Law, Diplomacy and Scholarship: Liber amicorum in memoriam Horst G. Krenzler* (Springer, 2015) ch 5 at 41.

[4] A Hoda, *Tariff Negotiations and Renegotiations under the GATT and the WTO* (Cambridge University Press, 2001) 90.

[5] S Maher, 'Behind Closed Doors: Secrecy and Transparency in the Trans-Pacific Partnership Trade Negotiations' (2016) 13(2) *SITES* 187, 195.

That is, however, not all. Secrecy not only shrouds the documents described above, which are generally shared between member countries, but also similarly envelopes documents which member countries generate for domestic intra or inter-agency use only. Examples of such documents are well illustrated in the case of *Kelsey v Minister of Trade*.[6] Professor Jane Kelsey (an academic with a research interest in the TPP) and seven other groups representing various interests brought an application for a judicial review of the Minister of Trade of New Zealand's decision in which he refused to release certain documents in relation to the TPP negotiations. These include, but are not limited to, "[a]ll papers tabled by New Zealand during the negotiations', '[a]ll proposals for text and amendments to the text tabled by New Zealand during the negotiations', '[b]riefing notes and position papers provided by the Ministry to [the Respondent], to the Cabinet, to other government agencies or to Opposition parties or spokespersons on general or specific matters' and '[a]ny cost-benefit study, impact assessment or similar analysis of the proposed agreement as a whole, of specific provisions, or impacts on particular sectors or policies that have been conducted by or for the New Zealand government'.[7]

Such documents would shed light on the inner workings of a particular member country during the trade negotiations. As explained by Dr David Walker (the then Deputy Secretary of New Zealand's Ministry of Foreign Affairs and Trade (NZ MFAT) and New Zealand's Chief Negotiator for the TPP) in his affidavit, these documents 'provide information to the Government on the state of negotiations and seek approval to negotiate particular parts of the TPP', 'set out New Zealand's "bottom lines" and particular areas of sensitivity for [New Zealand] in the negotiations' and also 'proposals from New Zealand, or [New Zealand's] responses to other negotiating partners' positions, on a variety of issues'. The documents requested would also include '[p]apers and proposals tabled [which] reflect tactics adopted during negotiations and reveal [New Zealand's] underlying negotiating strategy and objectives particularly when considered alongside Cabinet mandates and the advice that the [NZ MFAT] has provided to the [Minister of Trade]'.[8]

Dr Walker justified restricting public access to such information on the basis that 'the documents which are subject to the request are of the utmost sensitivity'. Public disclosure would potentially prejudice New Zealand's negotiating positions and NZ MFAT 'simply could not achieve the best possible outcome for New Zealand in the TPP if our objectives and our means of achieving them were made public'.[9] In other words, member countries to plurilateral free trade agreement negotiations would inevitably want to approach the negotiating table

[6] *Kelsey v Minister of Trade* [2016] 2 NZLR 218.
[7] Ibid [47].
[8] Paragraph 77 of Dr Walker's affidavit adduced in relation to *Kelsey v Minister of Trade* (ibid), cited in the respondent's submissions at para 59, http://tpplegal.wordpress.com/legal-challenge.
[9] Ibid.

keeping certain cards close to their chest, and showing their hand is simply neither practical nor feasible.

It is submitted that, irrefutably, there are benefits to a shroud of secrecy and confidentiality which cloaks the inner workings of a member country, working documents shared between member countries and the entire negotiations as a whole. Similar to negotiations between commercial parties, every party wins some and loses some and the degree of trade-off ultimately depends on one's bargaining power. Consequently, groups which perceive themselves to be 'on the losing end' are bound to voice the strongest opposition to the negotiations. Therefore, secrecy and confidentiality ensure that 'negotiations run more smoothly and efficiently, because they are shielded from external pressures such as opposition from NGOs or civil society groups'.[10]

Further, secrecy and confidentiality of the negotiations allow parties to avoid committing themselves to a particular position(s) prematurely. Member countries can be flexible in their respective negotiating stances adopted at the negotiating table, ie they are able to put forth their respective proposals freely and their ability 'to make concessions and/or to try options before finally settling for an agreement' is unfettered.[11] Since the final outcome will generally be different from what was initially envisaged, negotiators 'are reluctant to anticipate conclusions'.[12] In the absence of such flexibility, it is submitted that parties would face great difficulty in achieving their objectives and/or bridging their differences in order to find middle ground to conclude the agreement. Efficiency will inevitably be compromised.

In addition to efficiency and flexibility, secrecy and confidentiality also ensure mutual trust between trade negotiators. This was recognized by the General Court of the European Union in the case of *Sophie in 't Veld v European Commission*,[13] where a Dutch Member of the European Parliament sought access to all documents relating to the Anti-Counterfeiting Trade Agreement (ACTA). The court held that secrecy and confidentiality are required to 'ensure the effectiveness of the negotiation' by allowing for 'mutual trust between negotiators and the development of a free and effective discussion' because 'any form of negotiation necessarily entails a number of tactical considerations of the negotiators, and the necessary cooperation between the parties depends to a large extent on the existence of a climate of mutual trust'.[14] Therefore, the court concluded that there is a 'legitimate interest in [the European Commission] not revealing strategic elements of the negotiations' because the initiation and conduct of such trade negotiations 'fall, in principle, within the domain of the executive, and that public participation in the procedure

[10] Limenta (n 2).

[11] P Roffe and X Seuba, 'ACTA and the International Debate on Intellectual Property Enforcement' in P Roffe and X Seuba (eds), *The ACTA and the Plurilateral Enforcement Agenda* (Cambridge University Press, 2015) 10.

[12] Ibid.

[13] Case T-301/10 *Sophie in 't Veld v European Commission* EU:T:2013:135.

[14] Ibid [119].

relating to the negotiation and the conclusion of an international agreement is necessarily restricted'.[15]

Even though secrecy and confidentiality are required to ensure the efficiency of negotiations, it is submitted that this is not a desirable state of affairs. First, trade negotiators may come from a narrow range of backgrounds in terms of training and/or experience or they may represent only a narrow range of interests. Consequently, they will not be 'necessarily skilled at anticipating or appreciating the "non-trade" impacts of trade deals, for example in the fields of human rights, environment, and health'.[16] Trade negotiators with experience working only in trade-related state agencies may not be able to fully understand the consequences of a data exclusivity clause on access to medicines, or how clauses on plant varieties may adversely affect farmers. Secrecy and confidentiality further exacerbate this problem by denying access to stakeholders who represent such 'non-trade' interests to the different types of documents described above in relation to the trade negotiations. These stakeholders are therefore unable to participate in any form of fruitful and effective democratic engagement with the respective state agencies involved in the trade negotiations. This is especially so when the outcome of the negotiations in relation to intellectual property rights (IPRs) can potentially have far-reaching effects on various groups of society, as the latter chapters of this book shall demonstrate.

Second, in relation to IPRs, it is not uncommon for IPRs to be used as bargaining chips in plurilateral free trade agreements involving small market economies. When small market economies negotiate with their economically stronger counterparts,

> small market economies have sometimes accepted intellectual property related terms for other trade-related benefits, which if assessed independently of those other supposed benefits would not be economically credible in the small market economy. However, because these intellectual property concessions may bring benefits in other areas, small market economies use intellectual property as a kind of expedient trade-off.[17]

Secrecy and confidentiality prohibit the involvement of various stakeholders who might otherwise act as vital counter-balances in formulating policy decisions vis-à-vis IPRs during negotiations. Therefore, trade negotiators for small market economies may be unable to fully appreciate or calculate the potential long-term consequences of such trade-offs in exchange for other benefits.

Third, consequential to the secrecy and confidential state of affairs surrounding the negotiations of plurilateral free trade agreement negotiations, many vested interests and avenues exist for confidential documents to be publicly leaked online in this modern age of the Internet. It could be argued that this could actually be

[15] Ibid [120].

[16] S Joseph, *Blame it on the WTO? A Human Rights Critique* (Oxford University Press, 2011) 58.

[17] S Frankel, *Test Tubes for Global Intellectual Property Issues: Small Market Economies* (Cambridge University Press, 2015) 23.

desirable as it enables some form of transparency, as leaked documents pierce through the shroud of secrecy and confidentiality, providing non-actors with glimpses to the negotiations in question. It is, however, submitted that leaked documents often do more harm than good because a leak may increase controversy (leading towards potential vitriol) due to its inherent nature. This includes questions on the authenticity of the leaked documents, the state of its relevance at the present state of negotiations in question, whether there has been any malicious tampering of the leaked documents (assuming that it is a legitimate copy), and the motivations behind the actions of the leaker.[18]

Even though secrecy and confidentiality are not desirable because they limit vital involvement by stakeholders representing various interests in plurilateral free trade agreement negotiations, this chapter does not advocate throwing the baby out with the bathwater, as complete transparency is similarly not a viable option because it compromises on the efficiency of the negotiations (notwithstanding the fact that the status quo of secrecy and confidentiality in relation to negotiations is highly unlikely to go away). As one commentator observed, 'simply arguing in favour of open negotiations on the one hand and closed negotiations on the other is misguided'.[19] This chapter argues that the solution to this conundrum can be found via a middle ground approach built on a new model of multi-stakeholder involvement, which will be discussed later in this chapter.

II. Who Sits at the Negotiating Table?

Traditionally, plurilateral free trade agreement negotiations are led by either the trade or foreign affairs ministries of each respective country. For example, Global Affairs Canada is the relevant department in the government of Canada in charge of foreign affairs and international trade.[20] In Malaysia, however, the Ministry of International Trade and Industry led the trade negotiations for both the TPP and the Comprehensive and Progressive Agreement for Trans-Pacific Partnership (CPTPP).[21]

Consequently, it is not uncommon for trade negotiators to come from various backgrounds. For example, Kazuyoshi Umemoto, a diplomat who was Japan's ambassador to Italy, was Japan's Chief Negotiator for the TPP.[22] Trade officials,

[18] Herrmann (n 3) at p 45.

[19] Limenta (n 2) at p 74.

[20] Global Affairs Canada website, http://www.international.gc.ca/gac-amc/priorities-priorites.aspx?lang=eng.

[21] Ministry of International Trade and Industry, Malaysia, website, http://fta.miti.gov.my/index.php/pages/view/71.

[22] T Crowell, 'How the TPP Rose from the Dead', *AsiaSentinel*, https://www.asiasentinel.com/econ-business/trans-pacific-partnership-rose-dead.

such as Ng Bee Kim, who is the Director-General of Trade at Singapore's Ministry of Trade and Industry, was Singapore's Chief Negotiator for the TPP.[23]

As plurilateral free trade agreement negotiations often involve clauses (apart from the usual tariff concession clauses) that may require technical expertise, such as clauses in relation to IPRs, technocrats are often roped in for their respective expertise. For example, Daren Tang, who is the Chief Executive of the Intellectual Property Office of Singapore, handles all international intellectual property (IP) negotiations, which includes free trade agreements (FTAs) such as the TPP and Regional Comprehensive Economic Partnership (RCEP) agreement.[24]

III. Examples of Stakeholder Involvement in Recent Trade Negotiations

Despite all the secrecy and confidentiality surrounding plurilateral trade agreement negotiations, trade negotiators do not operate in a vacuum. Views and opinions from 'primary stakeholders' are often sought. These 'primary stakeholders' generally consist of 'major industries and export interests' and, thereafter, trade advisory committees to the trade negotiators 'primarily consist of the representatives of industries, trade associations and large corporations',[25] ie parties who are able to yield influence in one way or another over the governments of each respective member country. It is thus not uncommon for trade negotiators to conduct frequent consultations with such trade advisory committees over the process of each negotiation round and this often involves providing them with 'greater access to the negotiating documents'.[26]

The examples of the ACTA, the Transatlantic Trade and Investment Partnership (TTIP) and RCEP, discussed below, will show that even though there is a recent promising trend towards seeking involvement from a more diverse group of stakeholders, much room for improvement is still available for the way future trade deals could be conducted.

A. ACTA

The ACTA is a trade agreement 'designed to address the digital realm and copyright interests'.[27] The majority of the ACTA's provisions are focused on 'stronger

[23] Lee Kuan Yew School of Public Policy website, http://lkyspp2.nus.edu.sg%2Fips%2Fevent%2Flunch-with-ms-ng-bee-kim-and-mr-daren-tang-on-the-trans-pacific-partnership&reauth=1.
[24] Ibid.
[25] Limenta (n 2) 90.
[26] Ibid.
[27] S Sell, 'The Dynamics of International IP Policymaking' in D Gervais (ed), *Intellectual Property, Trade and Development* (Oxford University Press, 2nd ed, 2014) ch 3 at 76.

enforcement of intellectual property rights'[28] via both civil and criminal means. For example, the ACTA 'contains extensive obligations with regard to copyright law, which deals with civil remedies, criminal offences, border measures, enforcement of intellectual property rights in a digital environment, technological protection measures and electronic rights management information'.[29] The ACTA effectively requires member countries to introduce a number of TRIPS-plus obligations, ie obligations over and above TRIPS, into their national legislation.

The extent of secrecy and confidentiality surrounding the ACTA negotiations 'was a consistent source of concern'.[30] Prior to the commencement of formal negotiations, the United States (US) requested all other member countries to enter into a confidentiality agreement 'which classified all correspondence between ACTA parties as "national security" information on the grounds that it was confidential "foreign government information"'.[31] Additionally, the initial negotiating rounds were 'held in secret locations, with each participating country offering near-identical cryptic press releases that did little more than fuel public concern about the potential scope of the treaty and the prospect that it might be concluded without public input or review'.[32]

The Office of the United States Trade Representative (USTR) similarly took extensive measures to ensure secrecy over the course of the entire negotiations on their end. Save for the trade negotiators, only selected 'cleared advisors' had access to the negotiating texts and numerous requests made to the USTR to release such documents were rejected on the basis of 'national security'[33]. The majority of such 'cleared advisors' are 'corporate lobbyists'[34] from corporations that are generally owners and/or licensors of multiple IPRs. According to Knowledge Ecology International,[35] these include, for example:

- Senior Counsel for intellectual property at Time Warner Inc;
- Trade Director for Motion Picture Association of America, Inc;
- Divisional Vice President, Global Government Affairs and Policy of Abbott Laboratories, Inc;
- Director, International Government Affairs, Eli Lilly and Company;

[28] M Rimmer, 'Trick or Treaty? The Australian Debate over the Anti-Counterfeiting Trade Agreement' in P Roffe and X Seuba (eds), *The ACTA and the Plurilateral Enforcement Agenda* (Cambridge University Press, 2015) ch 10 at 169.

[29] Ibid 179.

[30] M Geist, 'Slaying the ACTA myths' in P Roffe and X Seuba (eds), *The ACTA and the Plurilateral Enforcement Agenda* (Cambridge University Press, 2015) ch 24 at 346.

[31] Ibid.

[32] Ibid.

[33] Sell (n 27).

[34] J Love, 'Who are the cleared advisors that have access to secret ACTA documents?', *Knowledge Ecology International* (14 March 2009), http://www.keionline.org/20953.

[35] Ibid.

- Vice President, Intellectual Property Policy at Entertainment Software Association; and
- Vice President, International Government Affairs at Johnson & Johnson.

Despite increasing demands for greater transparency, the member countries 'released a joint statement claiming that 'it is accepted practice during trade negotiations among sovereign states to not share negotiating texts with the public at large, particularly at earlier stages of the negotiation'.[36] The negotiating texts were not publicly disclosed until April 2010,[37] several months before the text of the ACTA was finalized in November 2010.[38] The ACTA therefore stands at one end of the extreme, where secrecy and confidentiality is maintained at the highest level and access is only granted to a very select group of 'primary stakeholders' by certain member countries.

B. TTIP

The TTIP is a proposed trade and investment agreement between the European Union (EU) and the US where negotiations commenced in July 2013[39] and are currently ongoing. The TTIP aims to remove 'trade barriers (tariffs, unnecessary regulations, restrictions on investment etc.) in a wide range of economic sectors so as to make it easier to buy and sell goods and services between the EU and the US'.[40]

Even though, strictly speaking, the TTIP is not a proposed plurilateral trade agreement but a bilateral one, it is submitted that the unique circumstances surrounding the TTIP negotiations, where the European Commission has the requisite mandate from the governments of the 28 member countries to negotiate on their behalf, renders the TTIP negotiations analogous to other plurilateral trade agreement negotiations in more ways than one.

For example, similar to most plurilateral trade agreement negotiations, IPRs play a role as a bargaining chip between parties in the TTIP negotiations. In particular, the EU is pushing for further protection for its geographical indications. One of the negotiating objectives of the EU is for the 'provision of a level

[36] Geist (n 30) 347.

[37] L Philips, 'EU, negotiating parties to release ACTA text', *euobserver*, http://euobserver.com/justice/29881.

[38] Joint statement on the Anti-Counterfeiting Trade Agreement (ACTA) from all the negotiating partners of the agreement, *European Commission Press Release Database*, http://europa.eu/rapid/press-release_IP-10-1504_en.htm?locale=en.

[39] European Commission, 'The Transatlantic Trade and Investment Partnership (TTIP) – State of play' (27 April 2016) 2.

[40] European Commission, 'FAQ on the EU-US Transatlantic Trade and Investment Partnership ("TTIP")' (17 June 2013) 2.

of protection that prohibits the use of a [geographical indication] name *even when the consumer is not misled*, i.e. when the true origin of the product is indicated or in translation or accompanied with expressions such as "kind", "type", "style", "imitation" or the like'.[41] (emphasis added) This is not surprising as geographical indication products exported outside the EU 'represent some €15 billion' and the US is 'by far the leading destination country for EU [geographical indications], accounting for 30% of total food and beverage imports from the EU'.[42]

With regard to the TTIP negotiations, Bernd Lange, chair of the European Parliament's Trade Committee, made an ambitious statement after 11 months of negotiations with the European Commission that '[t]he access conditions we have agreed on will increase the transparency of the TTIP process significantly. What we have achieved today will also set a precedent for the transparency of future trade talks'.[43] The European Commission similarly points out that they have 'developed an unprecedented policy of transparency in the TTIP negotiations'[44] which would be achieved in four ways:

(a) public disclosure of selected documents;
(b) engagements with civil society representatives;
(c) formation of a TTIP advisory group; and
(d) holding of citizens' dialogues.

i. Public Disclosure of Selected Documents

The European Commission claims that '[a]ll the EU position papers and negotiating proposals are made public shortly after they are tabled in the negotiations', which consists of 'documents that have already been shared with the Member States and the European Parliament before they are submitted to the US'.[45] Specifically, the European Commission publishes two page factsheets (written 'in plain language'[46]) and negotiating texts provided to US negotiators comprising of EU textual proposals and EU position papers. Textual proposals refer to the EU's 'initial proposals for legal text on topics in TTIP [and] are tabled for discussion with the US in negotiating rounds'.[47] Position papers lay out and describe

[41] European Commission, 'Agriculture and Geographical Indications (GIs) in TTIP – A Guide to the EU's Proposal' (21 March 2016) 9.

[42] Ibid 8.

[43] A Krivade, 'All MEPs have access to all confidential TTIP documents', *European Parliament* (2 December 2015) http://www.europarl.europa.eu/news/en/press-room/20151202IPR05759/all-meps-to-have-access-to-all-confidential-ttip-documents.

[44] European Commission, 'TTIP – State of play' (n 39) 7.

[45] Ibid.

[46] 'EU negotiating texts in TTIP', *European Commission* (14 July 2016) http://trade.ec.europa.eu/doclib/press/index.cfm?id=1230&serie=866&langId=en#rules.

[47] Ibid.

the [EU's] general approach on a particular topic in the TTIP negotiations which 'are tabled for discussion with the US in negotiating rounds'.[48] Additionally, '[d]etailed summaries of all negotiating rounds are published shortly after each round'.[49]

ii. Engagements with Civil Society Representatives

The European Commission claims that it 'regularly engages with civil society representatives and the general public, both in between and during negotiating rounds. In particular, one day of each negotiating week is dedicated to direct engagement between interested stakeholders and the US and EU negotiating teams'.[50] This is done in order to 'ensure that a plurality of interests is taken into account during the negotiations'.[51] The European Commission then publishes a summary of what transpired during these Civil Society Dialogues.

From the Civil Society Dialogue held in relation to the third negotiation round of the TTIP, the following are examples of representatives of the European Commission who participated:[52]

(a) Damien Levie, EU Deputy Chief Negotiator for the TTIP, Head of Unit USA and Canada, Directorate-General for Trade;
(b) John Clarke, Director, International Bilateral Relations, Directorate-General for Agriculture and Rural Development;
(c) Monika Hencsey, Head of Unit, Trade and Sustainable Development, Generalized System of Preferences, Directorate-General for Trade;
(d) Anders Jessen, Head of Unit, Intellectual Property & Public Procurement, Directorate-General for Trade;
(e) Fernando Perreau de Pinninck, Head of Unit Tariff and Non-Tariff Negotiations, Rules of Origin, Directorate-General for Trade; and
(f) Denis Redonnet, Head of Unit, Trade Strategy, Directorate-General for Trade.

Participants from civil society groups involved in the Civil Society Dialogue include:

(a) Humane Society International;
(b) Eurogroup for Animals;
(c) TechAmerica Europe.

[48] Ibid.
[49] European Commission, 'TTIP – State of play' (n 39) 7.
[50] Ibid 8.
[51] European Commission Directorate-General for Trade, 'Expert Group to Advise European Commission on EU-US Trade Talks' (27 January 2014) http://trade.ec.europa.eu/doclib/press/index.cfm?id=1019.
[52] European Commission, 'Civil Society Dialogue: Transatlantic Trade and Investment Partnership (TTIP) – Third Negotiation Round' (14 January 2014) 1.

iii. Formation of a TTIP Advisory Group of Experts

The European Commission also formed a TTIP advisory group of experts, comprising of 'independent experts representing varied interests (business, SMEs, trade unions, consumers, NGOs, public health)'.[53] Through the formation of this advisory group of experts, the European Commission intends to achieve 'close dialogue and exchange with all stakeholders in the TTIP talks, in order to achieve the best result for European citizens'.[54] In order to ensure that the advisory group of experts are enabled 'to provide the best advice possible', the European Commission will share not only 'detailed information about progress in the talks', but also 'for the first time', EU negotiating documents will also be shared when necessary 'in a manner that ensures confidentiality'.[55] The EU Chief Negotiator for the TTIP, Ignacio Garcia Bercero, chairs this advisory group of experts and works directly with them. Details of the meetings are made available on the TTIP website.

Members of the advisory group of experts include, for example:

(a) Monique Goyens, Director-General of the Bureau Européen des Unions de Consommateurs, representing consumer interests;
(b) Monika Kosinska, Secretary-General of the European Public Health Alliance, representing health sector interests;
(c) Pieter de Pous, EU Policy Director of the European Environmental Bureau, representing environmental interests;
(d) Pekka Pesonen, Secretary-General of COPA-COGECA, representing agricultural sector interests;
(e) Luisa Santos, Director of International Relations at Businesseurope, representing business interests; and
(f) Roxane Feller, Head of Economic Department at FoodDrinkEurope, representing food and drink sector interests.

iv. Holding of Citizens' Dialogues

Additionally, the European Commission conducts citizens' dialogues 'held in all Member States with the participation of the EU Commissioner and [Director-General of] Trade'.[56] For example, on 26 February 2018, EU Commissioner Cecilia Malmström participated in a citizens' dialogue in Sofia where 'the current state of the EU/US negotiations on TTIP'[57] was discussed.

[53] European Commission, 'TTIP – State of play' (n 39) 8.
[54] European Commission Directorate-General for Trade, 'Expert Group' (n 51).
[55] Ibid.
[56] European Commission, 'TTIP – State of play' (n 39) 8.
[57] European Commission, 'Citizens' Dialogue in Sofia with Commissioner Cecilia Malmström' (26 February 2018) http://ec.europa.eu/info/events/citizens-dialogues/citizens-dialogue-sofia-commissioner-cecilia-malmstrom-2018-feb-26_en>.

v. Comments and Observations

The European Commission has not only sought extensive consultations but more notably, it has sought to undertake 'broad consultations at an early stage of the process'.[58] For example, in March 2014, it carried out an online public consultation where the key issue concerned 'whether the EU's proposed approach for TTIP achieves the right balance between protecting investors and safeguarding the EU's ability to regulate in the public interest'.[59] This was less than 10 months after negotiations commenced between the EU and the US.

However, the shroud of secrecy and confidentiality nevertheless remains to a certain extent. First, consolidated texts remain classified. Consolidated texts reflect 'the draft compromises between the EU and the US'[60] and 'may contain provisions opposed by one of the parties, which are then used as bargaining chips by the other negotiating party'.[61] The EU's textual proposals and position papers that are publicly disclosed only reveal the EU's official negotiating position in relation to the TTIP negotiations. However, since the US has refused to publish its official positions, because it takes 'the view that releasing classified TTIP documents would impede the negotiations … access to the consolidated TTIP negotiating documents also remains restricted for the general public'.[62]

Second, even though all Members of the European Parliament (MEPs) will have access to the consolidated TTIP negotiating documents,[63] such access is heavily restricted. MEPs can only read the consolidated texts in a 'secure reading room at the European Parliament' and are only permitted to take 'handwritten notes'.[64] Therefore, 'cell phones, laptops or other electronic devices [are not allowed] into the reading room'.[65] This, in one way or another, undermines the MEPs abilities to be able to review the consolidated texts in a productive manner and be able to provide critical and constructive comment in that regard.

Despite this, the EU's efforts in the TTIP is clearly a massive upgrade from ACTA in terms of allowing for multi-stakeholder involvement. As seen above, senior trade officials are involved in engaging with the various stakeholders, ranging from the usual 'primary stakeholders' all the way to the general public. However, it remains doubtful whether the EU's efforts would indeed set the trend

[58] R Meléndez-Ortiz and A Abdel-Latif, 'ACTA: What Lessons for Future Plurilateral Trade Agreements?' in P Roffe and X Seuba (eds), *The ACTA and the Plurilateral Enforcement Agenda* (Cambridge University Press, 2015) ch 26 at 382.

[59] Ibid.

[60] Krivade (n 43).

[61] L Puccio, *TTIP: Access to consolidated texts and confidential documents* (European Parliamentary Research Service, 2016) 2.

[62] Ibid.

[63] Ibid.

[64] Krivade (n 43).

[65] M von Hein, 'TTIP Reading Room: A small step toward transparency', *DW* (29 June 2016) http://www.dw.com/en/ttip-reading-room-a-small-step-toward-transparency/a-19012651 (accessed 2 July 2018).

for future plurilateral trade agreement negotiations especially when there is an absence of parity of bargaining powers between parties, for example where small market economies are involved.

C. RCEP

The RCEP is a proposed plurilateral free trade agreement between the member countries of the Association of Southeast Asian Nations (ASEAN) (which comprises Brunei Darussalam, Cambodia, Indonesia, Laos, Malaysia, Myanmar, Philippines, Singapore, Thailand, and Vietnam) and Australia, China, India, Japan, South Korea and New Zealand. Negotiations commenced in 2013 and are currently ongoing with a view that a substantial agreement could be concluded by end-2018.[66]

In relation to the RCEP negotiations, transparency is far below that achieved by the EU under the TTIP. Everything known with regard to the RCEP negotiations so far has come from leaked negotiating texts. No member countries has released its official negotiating positions nor is there any official release of any consolidated texts at the time of writing. Member countries either do not publish summaries of what transpired during each round of negotiations, or even if they do, such summaries tend to be quite brief in nature without many details (if any) disclosed.

From the 15 October 2015 version of the leaked text available on bilaterals.org,[67] some notable points in relation to the proposed IP Chapter can be discovered.

(a) Section 2 covers copyright and related rights. Art 2.6, which provides for detailed provisions concerning the protection of broadcasts transmitted by wire or over the air as well as against the unauthorized retransmission of television signals on the Internet, suggests stronger and more expansive protection to broadcasters under the RCEP.
(b) Section 3 relates to trade marks. Art 3.10, which provides for the protection of well-known trade marks, shows disagreement over member countries in relation to the extent of protection to be extended for well-known trade marks under the RCEP.

New Zealand is one of the few member countries which publishes summaries of each negotiation round, ministerial meeting and leaders' summit via the

[66] W Sim, 'RCEP on track for substantial agreement by year-end in big win for free trade: Chan Chun Sing' *The Straits Times* (1 July 2018), http://www.straitstimes.com/asia/east-asia/16-countries-to-work-with-greater-focus-to-conclude-regional-trade-pact-by-year-end.

[67] 'RCEP – draft IP chapter (15 Oct 2015 version)', *bilaterals.org* (19 April 2016), http://www.bilaterals.org/?rcep-draft-ip-chapter-15-oct-2015.

NZ MFAT. A summary provided by the NZ MFAT in relation to Round 20 of the RCEP negotiations held in Incheon, South Korea, gave us a brief glimpse of the direct involvement of civil society organizations. The summary states that '[a] series of engagements between negotiators and representatives of civil society organisations were held over the course of the round, with the Working Groups on Services, Investment, Legal and Institutional Issues, E-commerce and the Trade Negotiating Committee/Intellectual Property Working Group all meeting individually with civil society representatives'.[68]

The willingness of the RCEP trade negotiators to engage with representatives of civil society organizations directly is something to be welcomed. Generally, 'public information sessions and briefings often do not amount to the level of formal consultations through which stakeholders, and in particular, civil society groups, can make written proposals and submissions regarding the issues being considered'.[69] Unfortunately, no further light was shed as regards which civil society organizations were involved; how they were selected; the amount of material made available to the civil society representatives to enable a meaningful engagement; the various positions put forth by those representatives during the negotiations; the conclusions from this engagement; whether such engagements will continue to be held on a regular basis; the extent of involvement of the civil society representatives in the negotiations, etc.

IV. A New Model of Multi-stakeholder Involvement: EU (TTIP) + RCEP

Plurilateral free trade agreements have evolved from being 'primarily related to cutting tariff or quotas [or] exchanging tariff concessions' to involving 'non-trade obligations or standards which have far-reaching ramifications behind the borders'.[70] One good example would be that concerning IPRs as exemplified by the ACTA, TTIP and RCEP as shown above.

It is suggested that a possible explanation for member countries' reluctance to actively and meaningfully engage with stakeholders is a general scepticism over the benefits of doing so. Traditionally, 'NGOs and concerned individuals are often perceived to play a role as government antagonists rather than partners in the area of trade negotiations'.[71] 'Primary stakeholders', on the other hand, are instead viewed as 'partners because governments believe they will benefit from business involvement in trade talks'.[72]

[68] 'Round 20, Incheon, October 2017', *NZ MFAT*, http://www.mfat.govt.nz/assets/FTAs-in-negotiations/RCEP/recep-round20-incheon.pdf.
[69] Meléndez-Ortiz and Abdel-Latif (n 58) 381.
[70] Limenta (n 2) 91.
[71] Limenta (n 2) 93.
[72] Ibid.

Unfortunately, even though IPRs have a 'totally different nature and rationale, discussions leading to the adoption of IP norms in the context of trade negotiations have assumed considerations and attitudes proper to tariff deals'.[73] Commentators have thus argued that plurilateral free trade agreement negotiations, which involves IPRs as a bargaining chip, ought to be 'approached from the broad perspective of public policy rather than that of traditional trade negotiations', ie

> [the] bargaining approach should be replaced by a different perspective, focused on the construction of sound and nationally adjusted IP regimes that build, among others, on the objective of TRIPS to 'contribute to the promotion of technological innovation and to the transfer and dissemination of technology, to the mutual advantage of producers and users of technological knowledge and in a manner conducive to social and economic welfare, and to a balance of rights and obligations'.[74]

Therefore, 'new forms of multi-stakeholder involvement' is required, 'especially when working on agreements and laws that impact people's fundamental rights'.[75]

It is suggested that this could be achieved through a new model of multi-stakeholder involvement utilizing a middle ground approach between secrecy and confidentiality to ensure efficiency of the negotiations on one hand and plurality of views on the other. This is constructed by aggregating the positives from the EU (in the TTIP) and RCEP approaches in their respective negotiations. In other words, the EU's model for transparency and multi-stakeholder involvement, as adopted in the TTIP negotiations, plus the RCEP's model, where stakeholders have direct engagement with trade negotiators from all member countries under a confidential setting.

A general framework of this new model will therefore ideally consist of the following features:

(a) Public disclosure of selected documents by a member country. This could include factsheets written in plain language and textual proposals and position papers stating a particular member country's official negotiating proposal ('Feature 1').
(b) Engagements with civil society representatives by a member country ('Feature 2').
(c) Formation of an advisory group of experts by a member country ('Feature 3').
(d) Holding of citizens' dialogues by a member country ('Feature 4').
(e) Direct engagement between stakeholders and trade negotiators from all member countries to the negotiations ('Feature 5').

The benefits of adopting this new model are threefold. First, in addition to the benefits of each Feature as explained above, it is submitted that this framework

[73] Roffe and Seuba (n 11) 10.
[74] Ibid 11.
[75] M Schaake, 'ACTA, a View from the Eye of the Storm' in *The ACTA and the Plurilateral Enforcement Agenda* (P Roffe and X Seuba gen eds) (Cambridge University Press, 2015) ch 19 at p 298.

ensures that secrecy and confidentiality in relation to certain aspects of the negotiation process nevertheless apply (albeit to a reduced extent) in a manner that does not compromise the efficiency of the negotiations severely. One such important aspect would be that of consolidated texts. Similar to the TTIP, there is good reason for consolidated texts and corresponding minutes and notes taken at each negotiating round to remain secret and confidential. In any case, consolidated documents 'are documents that are still in the process of being negotiated, and therefore incomplete and subject to change'.[76] Public disclosure of consolidated texts may, it is suggested, limit the flexibility of trade negotiators in future negotiating rounds, especially when consolidated texts 'may lack provisions that could be added subsequently as last minute compromises are reached'.[77] Therefore, by not compromising the primary concerns of member countries in relation to plurilateral trade agreement negotiations, it is submitted that this new model is a feasible and realistic one.

Second, allowing direct engagement between the various stakeholders and the trade negotiators from all member countries would allow the trade negotiators (especially those representing member countries with larger bargaining powers) to be able to directly listen to, engage and understand the difficulties that encumber the negotiating positions of other member countries (especially the small market economies) straight from the horse's mouth rather than a garbled, second-hand version. This would encourage all member countries to seek win-win solutions insofar as possible.

Third, and perhaps most importantly, adopting this new model would allow for a 'greater degree of compliance'[78] after the negotiations are concluded. Generally, plurilateral free trade agreement become officially binding upon ratification. Similar to multilateral free trade agreements, a member country is legally obliged to 'transform its internal law in accordance with the rules contained in the [particular trade agreement]' upon ratification, ie member countries 'agree to limit their autonomy and to exercise their normative power only in a particular direction'.[79] For example, Art 25.2.2(a) of the CPTPP provides that member countries 'affirm the importance of sustaining and enhancing the benefits of [the CPTPP] through regulatory coherence in terms of facilitating increased trade in goods and services and increased investment between the [member countries]'.[80]

Despite this, it is not uncommon for member countries to face problems in complying with their obligations under international trade agreements for

[76] Puccio (n 61).

[77] Ibid.

[78] Limenta (n 2) 77.

[79] J Chaisse, 'Deconstructing the WTO Conformity Obligation: A Theory of Compliance as a Process' (2015) 38(1) *Fordham International Law Journal* 57, 64.

[80] NZ MFAT website, http://www.mfat.govt.nz/en/trade/free-trade-agreements/free-trade-agreements-concluded-but-not-in-force/cptpp/comprehensive-and-progressive-agreement-for-trans-pacific-partnership-text.

various reasons. Similar to most commercial contracts and agreements, international trade agreements also often contain provisions on dispute settlement in anticipation of such problems.[81] For example, in the initial years after India signed the TRIPS Agreement in 1994, the US brought a complaint to the Dispute Settlement Body of the World Trade Organization against India for not taking the necessary steps to ensure that its domestic intellectual property regime conformed to that under the TRIPS agreement.[82]

It is therefore submitted that consultations with stakeholders coming from various fields and representing different interests, 'coupled with greater transparency, have multiple advantages in terms of strengthening the legitimacy of the negotiating process, enriching the texts being negotiated, addressing public interest concerns and facilitating the implementation of the negotiated outcomes'.[83]

However, admittedly, as pointed out earlier, it is doubtful that the EU's approach in the TTIP would be a feasible model, especially where there is an absence of parity of bargaining power between member countries, which is not uncommon in plurilateral free trade agreement negotiations involving Asian countries. Therefore, a scaled down version of this framework, consisting of only Features 2, 3 and 5, conducted under a confidential setting and where confidential agreements similarly bind the stakeholders involved, may be more practical and realistic as a model for future plurilateral free trade agreement negotiations in such contexts.

Should this new framework (under either the scaled down or the full version) be adopted in future, it is imperative that member countries do not pay mere lip service to its application. For example, sufficient notice and materials ought to be provided to the advisory group of experts prior to each meeting so that adequate preparation could be done to ensure a fruitful and meaningful discussion with the trade negotiators, etc.

V. Lessons to be Learned from the ACTA

As mentioned above, the ACTA stood at one end of the extreme in relation to the shroud of secrecy and confidentiality covering the entire negotiation process. This led to the fuelling of 'opposition to the undertaking and generated an understandable suspicion among governments and economic actors excluded from the discussions, as well as members of civil society at large'.[84] The consequential discontent and dissent culminated into thousands taking to the streets to protests

[81] See eg Chapter 28 of the CPTPP.

[82] S Guennif and J Chaisse, 'Present Stakes around Patent Political Economy: Legal and Economic Lessons from the Pharmaceutical Patent Rights in India' (2007) 2 *Asian Journal of WTO & International Health Law and Policy* 65, 84–85.

[83] Meléndez-Ortiz and Abdel-Latif (n 58) 381–82.

[84] Roffe and Seuba (n 11) 9.

against the ACTA across Europe.[85] The European Parliament claimed that it 'experienced unprecedented direct lobbying by thousands of EU citizens who called on it to reject ACTA, in street demonstrations, e-mails to MEPs and calls to their offices. [The European Parliament] also received a petition, signed by 2.8 million citizens worldwide, urging it to reject the agreement'.[86] Eventually, the public pressure contributed to the European Parliament voting to reject the ACTA. As this point of writing, the ACTA is not yet in force; despite being signed by 11 countries it has only been ratified by Japan.[87]

Several reasons have been proffered for the failure of the ACTA. First, the absence of any meaningful form of transparency meant that it 'undermined trust, particularly among civil society and public opinion and fuelled speculation about the reach and implications of the provisions being negotiated'.[88] As previously mentioned, public disclosure of the negotiating texts only took place several months before the text of the ACTA was finalized. Attempts to address concerns of a lack of transparency, 'particularly in the last stages of the negotiations, were, rightly or wrongly, perceived as being too little, too late'.[89]

Consequently, the shroud of secrecy and confidentiality 'allowed significant misapprehensions to develop, while making it difficult for negotiators to communicate the actual scale and content of what was being achieved'.[90] Such misapprehensions were spread via 'misinformation and fear tactics spread over the Internet, social networks and media platforms'.[91] This even gave rise to misconceptions vis-à-vis IPRs in general as 'media coverage and groups such as Anonymous propagated the view that [intellectual property] is merely a tool for large businesses to take advantage of smaller ones and of consumers'.[92] It is therefore imperative for future plurilateral free trade agreement negotiations 'to address transparency concerns from the start of the negotiating process rather than to adopt a "reactive" and "defensive" posture when the process is more advanced'.[93]

Second, the absence of multi-stakeholder involvement to provide timely feedback played a part in member countries failing 'to appreciate both the level and volume of dissent the inclusion of counterfeiting and piracy over the digital

[85] D Lee, 'Thousands take to streets across Europe', *BBC* (8 March 2012), http://www.bbc.com/news/technology-16999497.

[86] European Parliament, 'European Parliament rejects ACTA' (4 July 2012), http://www.europarl.europa.eu/news/en/press-room/20120703IPR48247/european-parliament-rejects-acta.

[87] NZ MFAT website, http://www.mfat.govt.nz/en/trade/free-trade-agreements/free-trade-agreements-concluded-but-not-in-force/acta.

[88] Meléndez-Ortiz and Abdel-Latif (n 58) 380.

[89] Ibid.

[90] A Kamperman et al, *The Anti-Counterfeiting Trade Agreement (ACTA): An Assessment* (European Parliament Directorate-General for External Policies, 2011) 6.

[91] C Li, 'Lessons Learned from the ACTA Process – An Industry Perspective' in *The ACTA and the Plurilateral Enforcement Agenda* (P Roffe and X Seuba gen eds) (Cambridge University Press, 2015) ch 17 at 280.

[92] Ibid.

[93] Meléndez-Ortiz and Abdel-Latif (n 58) 380.

environment would cause, as well as the discontent stemming from what many viewed as excessive secrecy throughout the negotiations'.[94]

In conclusion, when negotiating future plurilateral free trade agreements, member countries would do well to heed the following caution:

> Ultimately, the ACTA negotiating process showed that the ability of addressing effectively public interest concerns is critical for the successful completion of plurilateral and regional trade negotiations or their failure. This is even more so the case if such agreements deal with regulatory issues which extend deep into the domestic legal regimes of the negotiating parties and, thus, raise concerns, in particular for domestic stakeholders, in terms of the ability of parties to pursue public policy objectives.[95]

VI. Examples of Stakeholders Who Should Participate in Future Trade Negotiations

As seen in the above examples of the TTIP and RCEP, new models of policy making moving in the direction of a greater plurality of views and opinions have been emerging in relation to plurilateral free trade agreement negotiations. As opined by David Held, '[a]lthough governments and states remain powerful actors, they have helped create, and now share the global arena with, an array of other agencies and organizations'.[96] National and state administrations, key international organizations, multinational corporations and various trans-national interest groups and NGOs claim their share in exercising power and influence over international and domestic policy making. In the following sections, examples of stakeholders who should participate and be consulted upon in future plurilateral free trade agreement negotiations under the proposed new model of multi-stakeholder involvement will be examined.

A. International Organizations

International organizations can play a big role in influencing trade negotiators. This is especially so in relation to IPRs clauses in plurilateral free trade agreement negotiations, such as those concerning test data protection which will have an impact on a member country's access to medicines. Having the involvement of such international organizations would greatly assist trade negotiators, especially

[94] B Mercurio, 'ACTA: Anatomy of a Failed Agreement' in P Roffe and X Seuba (eds), *The ACTA and the Plurilateral Enforcement Agenda* (Cambridge University Press, 2015) ch 22 at 336.

[95] Meléndez-Ortiz and Abdel-Latif (n 58) 389–90.

[96] D Held, 'Regulating Globalization? The Reinvention of Politics' (2000) 15(2) *Int'l Sociology* 394 at p 398.

when the negotiations involve member countries such as certain ASEAN member countries, where 'public health and access to medicine is an important issue'.[97]

The first example would be that of the United Nations (UN). Several subsidiary bodies of the UN 'deal with the interface of IP and public health, including the United Nations Conference on Trade Development (UNCTAD), United Nations Programme on HIV/AIDS (UNAIDS) and United Nations Development Programme (UNDP)'.[98] Second, the World Health Organization (WHO), which is 'the leading international organisation focusing on public health issues, has been responsible for a large number of initiatives and studies in relation to access to medicines'.[99] Third, the World Bank, which 'works in collaboration with client countries to improve availability, affordability, acceptability and utilisation of essential medicines through endorsement of good governance and management practices in the pharmaceutical sector' and also 'works in partnership and collaboration with technical agencies such as the [WHO] and procurement specialists like UNICEF to leverage expertise and learning in the pharmaceutical sector across organisations'.[100]

It is submitted that international organizations, such as the examples above, could be influential during their engagements with trade negotiators from all sides of the negotiation table because not only would they be perceived to be more neutral, as they have no vested interest in the trade negotiations, but they would also possess the relevant data, research and technical knowledge and expertise to inform trade negotiators on the possible consequences of various positions should they be eventually adopted. Such international organizations are also likely to be interested in engaging with trade negotiators during the negotiation rounds, as they would be able to play a pre-emptive role instead of assisting countries where the status quo is fixed. The involvement of such international organizations would therefore be greatly valuable in, for example, the RCEP negotiations as it includes member countries that are least developed countries (LDCs) such as Laos,[101] where certain epidemics (such as HIV) still remain a very huge problem.

B. Civil Society Organizations, NGOs and Academics

Similarly, civil society organizations, NGOs and academics can also play a part by engaging with trade negotiators under the proposed new model of multi-stakeholder involvement. This can include, for example, institutions involved in

[97] S Jusoh, 'Free Trade Agreements and Implications on Public Health – An Analysis of FTA of Selected ASEAN Member States' (2009) 4 *AJWH* 187, 215.

[98] L Hsu, *Trade, Investment, Innovation and their Impact on Access to Medicines – An Asian Perspective* (Cambridge University Press, 2016) 27.

[99] Ibid.

[100] World Bank website, http://www.worldbank.org/en/topic/health/brief/pharmaceutical-policy.

[101] Hsu (n 98) 41.

'wider [efforts] including poverty reduction, education, price control, or better national health policies'.[102]

One such example is the Open Source Drug Discovery (OSDD), which 'comprises a community of students, scientists, researchers, academicians, institutions and corporations' committed to discovery of drugs in an open source mode', and has affordability and accessibility of medicines as its very core philosophy. The OSDD's mission is to 'bring openness and collaborative spirit to the drug discovery process by developing an open source model of innovation for tropical infectious diseases with the objective of keeping medicine cost low and developing a web-based platform for collaboration'.[103]

The Access Campaign of the Médecins Sans Frontières is another example. Briefly, the Access Campaign's mission is to 'bring down barriers that keep people from getting the treatment they need to stay alive and healthy' by advocating 'for effective drugs, tests and vaccines that are available, affordable, suited to the people we care for, and adapted to the places where they live'.[104]

The Access Campaign expressed concern with the RCEP IP Chapter in its 'MSF RCEP IP Chapter Technical Analysis' published in November 2016[105] ('the MSF Technical Analysis Report'). Further, on 24 February 2017, the Access Campaign published a letter[106] addressed to all the member countries of the RCEP addressing how the RCEP Investment Chapter 'threaten to restrict access to affordable medicines for millions of people' ('the MSF Letter').

Through both the MSF Letter and the MSF Technical Analysis Report, the Access Campaign suggested recommendations on amendments to the draft RCEP negotiating text. In the MSF Letter, the Access Campaign raises its concerns that

> proposed provisions in the leaked draft investment chapter and its intersection with other proposals on IP could potentially undermine a national government's capacity to implement and execute policies to protect public health and ensure affordable access to medicines for all, especially in developing countries where most of MSF's medical operations are based.[107]

In particular, the Access Campaign, in relation to the draft investment chapter, argues that intellectual property 'should be excluded from the definition of 'Investment' and other proposed definitions, including intangible property and related/other property rights in RCEP'.[108] In the MSF Technical Analysis Report, the

[102] Y Li, 'Intellectual Property and Public Health: Two Sides of the Same Coin' (2011) 6 *AJWH* 389, 418.

[103] OSDD website, http://www.osdd.net/about-us/how-osdd-works.

[104] The Access Campaign website, http://msfaccess.org/about-us.

[105] The Access Campaign, 'Regional Comprehensive Economic Partnership – Intellectual Property Chapter and the Impact on Access to Medicines', http://msfaccess.org/rcep-ip-chapter-analysis.

[106] The Access Campaign, 'RCEP Investment Chapter Presents a Grave Threat to Access to Medicines', http://msfaccess.org/rcep-investment-chapter-presents-grave-threat-access-medicines.

[107] Ibid.

[108] Ibid.

Access Campaign explained why all member countries to the RCEP negotiations ought to reject any proposal to introduce a data exclusivity obligation and patent term restorations.[109]

Therefore, not only do certain civil society organizations, NGOs and academics have a role to play in engaging with trade negotiators under the proposed new model of multi-stakeholder involvement, there are in fact NGOs, such as Médecins Sans Frontières, which have signalled their strong intentions that they would like to engage with trade negotiators if possible. Through initiatives such as the MSF Letter and the MSF Technical Analysis Report, it is submitted that such NGOs certainly have much to contribute to the trade negotiations due to their experience on the ground and their feedback as regards the potential consequences, if certain negotiating proposals were to be adopted, should not be ignored. Neither should such valuable feedback be taken as dissent, nor should such institutions be taken to be a disruptive force by the trade negotiators and the trade negotiations as a whole.

C. Domestic Stakeholders

Domestic stakeholders, such as generic drug manufacturers and collective management organizations, should similarly be allowed to participate in future plurilateral free trade agreement negotiations under the proposed new model of multi-stakeholder involvement so that they are able to express opinions on how a particular domestic industry could be impacted by certain proposals made during the trade negotiations. Input from domestic stakeholders provided to trade negotiators could be helpful as this could include critical empirical data from their respective industries. Also, seeking their feedback at an early stage would allow trade negotiators to carefully calibrate their negotiating positions in such a way as to anticipate possible strong domestic resistance in one way or another subsequent to a member country's ratification of the trade agreement.

VII. Conclusion

IPRs are commonly used as bargaining chips during plurilateral free trade agreement negotiations, especially those involving member countries with small market economies. This is a particular problem in relation to Asian plurilateral free trade agreement negotiations, as small market economies such as LDCs are often involved where issues such as access to essential medicines are especially

[109] The Access Campaign, 'Regional Comprehensive Economic Partnership – Intellectual Property Chapter and the Impact on Access to Medicines' (n 105).

pertinent. One example is the involvement of Laos in the RCEP. The potential far-reaching implications arising from the imposition of onerous obligations involving IPRs due to a lack of consideration of a plurality of views and opinions requires us to reconsider the traditional norms of the shroud of secrecy and confidentiality surrounding plurilateral free trade agreement negotiations.

The lessons learned from previous trade negotiations, in particular the ACTA, and the challenge posed to future plurilateral free trade agreement negotiations, is how can the right balance be achieved between secrecy and allowing a plurality of views, feedback and opinion through multi-stakeholder involvement, ie meeting 'the desire of citizens for greater participation while recognising the prerogative role of governments in conducting negotiations'.[110] It is suggested that this proposed new model of multi-stakeholder involvement would provide good guidance in this regard. Two concluding points will be made, in order to provide further motivation for member countries of future plurilateral trade agreement negotiations to adopt this new model.

First, in relation to the ACTA example, 'the secrecy regarding almost every aspect of ACTA has probably been the worst ally to those wishing it to be a success comparable to that of TRIPS'.[111] Put simply, 'not disclosing what happens in a room is obviously the best way to stimulate speculation on, precisely, what happens in that room'.[112] This is all the more so when such failure to give adequate disclosure 'affects fundamental rights and important economic interests'.[113]

Second, are trade talks really secret in this day and age? In this modern age of the Internet and, in particular, social media, it would be foolish to try to maintain secrecy because it 'is not only doomed to failure but also fails to acknowledge the very nature of the Internet and the major transformation that it has made in the way society perceives transparency'.[114] If it is pointless to maintain absolute secrecy and confidentiality in plurilateral free trade agreement negotiations, would it not be more efficient for the overall negotiations if various stakeholders could be invited to provide suggestions and feedback right from the very beginning?

With the ongoing trade wars, the trend towards the agreement of plurilateral free trade agreements is unlikely to go away, and in fact it could encourage countries to enter into such agreements in order to protect their respective economic interests. In this regard, it is hoped that the suggestions and warnings given in this chapter could, in one way or another, provide some guidance in the future.

[110] Limenta (n 2) 77.
[111] Roffe and Seuba (n 11) 9.
[112] Ibid.
[113] Ibid.
[114] Roffe and Seuba (n 11) 9.

3

Trade Strategies and Power Games between China, the US and India

LIYU HAN AND JIAXUN SUN*

I. Introduction

While it is now especially difficult to predict where the multilateral trade system under the World Trade Organization (WTO) is heading, no one can deny that great changes have taken place in the field of world trade. The WTO, the most effective and powerful international organization dealing with trade, once praised and even worshiped for its 'dramatically improved procedures for settling disputes',[1] has met some tremendous obstacles. Therefore, the trade strategies and power plays of major countries are once again attracting attention.

The United States (US), India and China are all major countries and have complex relationships with each other. These three countries play crucial roles when it comes to trade around the world, especially in Asia. However, their different economic strengths, systems and national ideologies mean that they may not see eye to eye on various issues. India and China are neighbours and members of the BRICS Forum,[2] and have an ongoing territorial disputes.[3] The US is a developed economy, while India and China are developing economies. The US is a typical capitalist economy, and India also chose a path of capitalism, while China claims it has a socialist market economy. The US and India claim they are large democratic countries, whereas China claims it is a socialist democratic country.

* Liyu Han is Professor of law, Renmin University of China Law School. Jiaxun Sun is a PhD candidate, Renmin University of China Law School.

[1] JH Bello, 'The WTO Dispute Settlement Understanding: Less is More' (1996) 11 *American Journal of International Law* 416, 416.

[2] BRICS Forum contains five countries with new international markets: Brazil, Russia, India, China and South Africa.

[3] India and China have had a long, drawn-out dispute over the southern border of Tibet, which has occasionally led to small-scale conflicts.

These differences are all easy targets when one party tries to gain negotiation advantages over the others and achieve its own trade goals. The complexity of these countries and their interactions provide ideal and rich material for academics to explore the role of these major countries' trade strategies and power plays in the context of international trade.

Therefore, section II of this chapter will analyse how the overall world trade order has sunk back to power games. Sections III and IV will discuss the trade strategy of China and the US respectively, from history to the present, and then sort out the trade relations between the three countries. Section V will be dedicated to India and how it has fits into the structure of the US-China conflict. In section VI, this chapter will shed some light on the pattern of power plays in trade, and will look beyond the current situation to the future of international trade.

II. From Rule-based World Trade Order Back to Power Games

A. From Power Games to Rule-Based World Trade Order under US Drive

Before the Uruguay Round,[4] both international politics and trade were dominated by power games. Trade has always been both the purpose and means of politics at the same time, and there were not many comprehensive, systematic and binding rules for world trade besides the constantly declining tariffs between states. It is almost common sense that dismantling and eliminating trade barriers will ultimately benefit the welfare of the whole world. Therefore all the efforts of bilateral, regional and multilateral trade negotiations and agreements have been wholly or partly about lifting trade barriers, one way or the other.

There is no denying that the WTO is truly a phenomenal achievement in maintaining the order of world trade. It is exceptional in two ways. First, the WTO administers a unified package of agreements which creates a system of trade rules that cover a large percentage of world trade. If a society wants to evolve from barbaric and savage to cultured and orderly, rules must exist before they can be obeyed. The WTO achieved that, at least. Second, the WTO also created a strong system to implement the rules, namely the dispute settlement mechanism, which, despite its current limitations, is nonetheless extraordinary. The design of negative

[4] The Uruguay Round is the 8th round of multilateral trade negotiations conducted within the framework of the General Agreement on Tariffs and Trade (GATT).

consensus[5] in the Dispute Settlement Body (DSB) has ensured adjudication and enforcement of every issue brought up to it, which no other international (quasi-) judicial bodies have ever achieved. In this sense, calling the dispute settlement system 'the crown jewel' is not an exaggeration.[6] These two characteristics have laid the foundation of a rule-based world trade order.

With the collapse of the Soviet Union, the US literally became the sole global superpower, and had a lot of say in creating this rule-based system. As a result of being probably the most 'litigious nation on earth',[7]

> US GATT experts felt the United States would benefit from a more legalistic, more American, system of settling disputes. A more judicial approach to the resolution of GATT disputes would promote certainty in commercial trading relations and the international rule of law, of which the United States was the chief champion.[8]

Therefore, the US strongly promoted updating the GATT dispute settlement system.

However, many countries were so used to applying political approaches in solving international disputes that they hesitated to move along, or even objected to doing so. Notwithstanding, the US applied aggressive measures to open up foreign markets rather than waiting for the slow-paced Uruguay Round to materialize, due to the high trade deficit in the 1980s. Under President Reagan's administration, Section 301 of the US 1974 Trade Law was used to its full extent, drawing widespread condemnation from the US's trading partners. As Bello and Holmer put it:

> Section 301's successful application by the United States induced foreign capitals around the world to see GATT dispute settlement procedures in a new light, as a way to discipline U.S. unilateralism. … Ironically, the United States, the chief champion of the international rule of law, succeeded in its advocacy for a stronger, more effective dispute settlement system, based upon the rule of law, because the United States itself was increasingly perceived as an international scofflaw, acting in its own self-interest, without regard to international law, rules, or agreements.[9]

Then came an era of the reign of rules in world trade. For 20 years, in spite of constant doubts and criticisms, the WTO did its job properly. Every state consulted

[5] Articles 6.1, 16.4, 17.14 and 23.7 of Understanding on Rules and Procedures Governing the Settlement of Disputes clearly state that a panel shall be established when requested, a panel or appellate body report shall be adopted, and an authorization to suspend concessions or other obligations shall be granted 'unless at that meeting the DSB decides by consensus not to'.

[6] J Chaisse, 'Deconstructing the WTO Conformity Obligation: A Theory of Compliance as a Process' (2015) 38 *Fordham International Law Journal* 57, 58.

[7] JH Bello and AF Holmer, 'U.S. Trade Law and Policy Series No. 24: Dispute Resolution in the New World Trade Organization Concerns and Net Benefits' (1994) 28 *The International Lawyer* 1095, 1097.

[8] Ibid.

[9] Ibid 1102.

the WTO rules when there was a dispute, rather than holding a political meeting and settling it out of the WTO framework.

B. World Trade Arena has Sunk Back to the History of Power Games

Since then, weakness in the WTO mechanism and accumulated dissatisfaction have led to the world trade order sinking back into power games. As a result, the landscape of the world trade order has started to shift drastically away from the strictly rule-based system. On the one hand, the negotiation to improve WTO rules has completely failed,[10] as the Doha Round[11] has yielded no real results in nearly two decades, and more and more countries are trying to reach their trade goals through bilateral or regional negotiations, one of which is the well-known Trans-Pacific Partnership (TPP).[12] On the other hand, partly due to the 'negative consensus' decision-making mode of the WTO, the Appellate Body of the Dispute Settlement Body has encountered an enormous member shortage problem. Starting with opposing the reappointment of Appellate Body member Seung Wha Chang by the US based on 'the failure to address in a meaningful manner U.S. concerns', the US has blocked the selection of Appellate Body members. This has led to the result that 'the Appellate Body is down to four sitting members. … The number of Appellate Body members could be reduced to three this fall, threatening the continued operation of the Appellate Body.'[13] The US has heavily criticized the Appellate Body for 'disregard for the 90-day deadline for appeals, continued service by persons who are no longer AB members, issuing advisory opinions on issues not necessary to resolve a dispute (too much *Obiter Dicta*), review of facts and review of a member's domestic law *de novo* and its claim that its reports are entitled to be treated as precedent'.[14]

Negotiations in the Doha Round are currently stalled, and the monitoring and surveillance of the implementation of WTO rules have been seriously

[10] See J Chaisse and M Matsushita, 'Maintaining the WTO's Supremacy in the International Trade Order – A Proposal to Refine and Revise the Role of the Trade Policy Review Mechanism' (2013) 16 *Journal of International Economic Law* 1, 2.

[11] The Doha Round, launched in 2001, is the latest round of trade negotiations among the WTO membership. It aims to achieve major reform of the international trading system through the introduction of lower trade barriers and revised trade rules.

[12] After the US pulled out, the remaining 11 countries signed the modified version of TPP as the Comprehensive and Progressive Trans-Pacific Partnership (CPTPP) on 11 November 2017, which accepted and confirmed the core values, rules and commitments negotiated earlier and suspended some provisions relative to the US.

[13] TP Stewart, ' Can The WTO Be Saved From Itself? Not Without A Major Crisis, and Possibly Not Even Then' (2018) 4 *Washington International Trade Association* 1, 2.

[14] Ibid 3–12.

neglected.[15] With the (possibly intentionally caused) failure of the two most important missions of the WTO, most countries are seeking bilateral or regional ways to regulate and encourage trade. Some result in agreements such as TPP, while others simply provide a negotiation platform which comes up with less binding documents, such as statements or announcements. With fewer rules to follow, the negotiation between two or a handful of parties is easier to conclude, which not only means that the arrangements are more custom-made, but also that the comparative power of the parties plays a more important role than the existing rules.

Vowing to reduce the US trade deficit, US President Trump ditched the TPP, renegotiated NAFTA (the North American Free Trade Agreement), among others, and again resorted to Sections 301 and 232, which has greatly shaken the global rule-based system.[16] It is amazing to observe how the world trade arena has sunk back to the history of power games.

III. China's Trade Strategy

A. Joining the WTO and Upholding its Multilateralism

During the Cold War, China sided with the Soviet Union, against the US and was hostile to almost all the Western countries, which meant that China was shut out of international trade. Later, China and the Soviet Union fell afoul of each other, the tension between China and the US slowly thawed, and China adopted the policy of Reform and Opening-up, which included genuine efforts to boost outbound international trade and inbound investment. At first, China was unfamiliar with the world market and took cautious steps when concluding agreements with other states.

Prior to the beginning of the twenty-first century, although China had come a long way in economic development, the size of its economy was still trivial compared to major states. China had its eyes fixed on joining the WTO. Although any new entrant is required to negotiate with every existing member of the WTO, what it will really need is for major and leading members to agree. The US at that time, with some other reasons of course, was keen on luring developing countries into this system, which was basically its home court, and welcomed China's WTO membership. China was accepted into the major world trade order in 2001.

[15] M Cartland, G Depayre and J Woznowski, 'Is Something Going Wrong in the WTO Dispute Settlement?' (2012) 5 *Journal of World Trade* 979, 984.

[16] The last time the US widely applied Sections 301 and 232 was in the 1990s, when the rapid development of Japan rattled the US, in order to force Japan to open up its markets.

Without a doubt, China took advantage of the WTO system to the fullest to become the second largest economy in the world, and now has a voice and stance that others cannot ignore. Naturally, this development has raised some alarm and concerns among the 'old money' holders of the global society, and has even led to hostility against China. In order to defuse this tension, China presented its development to the world as 'peaceful development', which would benefit not only itself, but also other countries. China now is also promoting the building of a community with 'a shared future for mankind':

> We must keep in mind both our internal and international imperatives, stay on the path of peaceful development, and continue to pursue a mutually beneficial strategy of opening up. We will uphold justice while pursuing shared interests, and will foster new thinking on common, comprehensive, cooperative, and sustainable security. We will pursue open, innovative, and inclusive development that benefits everyone, boost cross-cultural exchanges characterized by harmony within diversity, inclusiveness, and mutual learning; and cultivate ecosystems based on respect for mature and green development. China will continue its efforts to safeguard world peace, contribute to global development, and uphold international order.[17]

Compared to the trade policy of the US (which will be discussed in section III), China's policy has been relatively consistent from its opening up in the late 1970s. China's strategy is to '… support multilateral trade regimes and work to facilitate the establishment of free trade areas and build an open world economy. … China adheres to the fundamental national policy of opening up and pursues development with its doors open wide.'[18] Based on the policy of promoting multilateral trade relationships, China has gone to great lengths to defend the WTO, help multilateral agreements to materialize and push further multilateral negotiations. In China's National Plan of 2014–2015, it was emphasized that:

> We will increase multilateral, bilateral, and regional economic cooperation. … We will put into practice the strategy of developing the Silk Road Economic Belt and the 21st Century Maritime Silk Road, and build the China-Pakistan Economic Corridor and the Bangladesh-China-India-Myanmar Economic Corridor. We will speed up infrastructure connectivity with our neighbours. We will upgrade the China–ASEAN Free Trade Zone, strive to complete the talks on regional comprehensive economic partnership agreements, build the Free Trade Area of the Asia-Pacific, and carry on negotiations of investment agreements with the US and the European Union.[19]

[17] Report of the 19th National Congress of the Communist Party of China (CCP), October 2017.

[18] Report of the 19th National Congress of the CCP, October 2017.

[19] 'Report on the Implementation of the 2014 Plan for National Economic and Social Development and on the 2015 Draft Plan for National Economic and Social Development' submitted by the National Development and Reform Commission (NDRC) and approved by the Third Session of the Twelfth National People's Congress, 5 March 2015.

B. Specific Trade Policies

First, China has put a great deal of efforts into the Belt and Road Initiative (B&R), a regional cooperation platform in order to promote China's economic relationships with countries along the B&R. The Report of the 19th National Congress of the CCP stresses:

> China will actively promote international cooperation through the Belt and Road Initiative. In doing so, we hope to achieve policy, infrastructure, trade, financial, and people-to-people connectivity and thus build a new platform for international cooperation to create new drivers of shared development. We should pursue the Belt and Road Initiative as a priority, give equal emphasis to 'bringing in' and 'going global', follow the principle of achieving shared growth through discussion and collaboration, and increase openness and cooperation in building innovation capacity.[20]

Second, China has paid special attention to free trade agreements (FTAs) and added a FTA provision to the Foreign Trade Law in 2004. In 2007, China strived to 'implement FTA strategy and strengthen bilateral and multilateral trade cooperation'.[21] Later, in 2012, China stressed again 'coordinating bilateral, regional and multilateral market-opening and cooperation, accelerating the FTA strategy, [and] promoting connections with neighbouring countries'.[22] China focused on accelerating FTA strategy from 2013. President Xi pointed out the issue of 'accelerating fulfilment of the free trade area strategy and the building of a new open economic system' at the meeting of the Political Bureau of the CCP Central Committee.[23] Specifically, China

> will keep to the world trading system and rules, persist in bilateral, multilateral, regional and sub-regional openness and cooperation, seek more converging interests with other countries and regions, and carry out the free trade zone strategy at a faster pace with neighboring countries as the basis. [China] will reform the management systems of market access, customs oversight, inspection and quarantine, and others, and accelerate negotiations on environmental protection, investment protection, government procurement, e-commerce and other such new fields, so as to form a global, high-standard network of free trade zone[s].[24]

This policy includes the great effort China put into the Regional Comprehensive Economic Partnership (RCEP). The RCEP was initiated by the Association

[20] Report of the 19th National Congress of the CCP, October 2017. See also J Chaissea and M Matsushita, 'China's "Belt and Road" Initiative – Mapping the World's Normative and Strategic Implications' (2018) 52 *Journal of World Trade* 163.

[21] Report of the 17th National Congress of the CCP, October 2007.

[22] Report of the 18th National Congress of the CCP, November 2007.

[23] Xi's speech at the meeting of the Political Bureau of CCP Central Committee at 6 December 2014.

[24] 'Decision on Some Major Issues Concerning Comprehensively Deepening Reforms' approved by the Third Plenary Session of the 18th CCP Central Committee, 12 November 2013, http://www.china.org.cn/china/third_plenary_session/2014-01/16/content_31212602.htm, last visited 2 November 2018.

of Southeast Asian Nations (ASEAN), and subsequently six other countries, including China and India, were invited to jointly form one FTA to promote the regionalization of Asia. China has been very active during the negotiation of the RCEP and hopes to take a leading role in regional cooperation.

Apart from that, China has taken an active part in the BRICS Forum and the G20 Leaders Summit. As mentioned above, the BRICS Forum contains five large emerging developing economies. China's intention is to build a community of (would be) like-minded countries with a similar level of development. If it succeeds, the forum could be a representative of, and voice for, emerging markets. However, economic ties between the BRICS countries are not as close as hoped for. The BRICS countries' foreign investment totalled $197 billion in 2016, but only 5.6 per cent took place among BRICS members. As for the G20 Leaders Summit, this is a platform for dialogue, established by developed economies in response to the 2008 financial crisis, and it is not able to make substantive progress on the issues that really matter.

Finally, when it comes to domestic measures, in order to carry out its trade policy, China has been working relentlessly to build a new, open economic system. The specific measures include relaxing control over investment access, accelerating the construction of free trade areas, and further opening up inland and border areas.[25]

C. Special Focus on FTAs

Among these measures, special attention should be paid to China's FTA strategy, since it is the only thing mentioned above that has actual international legal binding force. China's perception of FTAs is that they are 'a new platform to further opening up to the outside and speeding up domestic reforms, an effective approach to integrate into global economy and strengthen economic cooperation with other economies, as well as particularly an important supplement to the multilateral trading system'.[26] As to the implementation of this strategy, China started to 'accelerate the setting up of a network of FTAs with a foothold in neighbouring regions, radiating across the area involved in "Belt and Road Initiatives" and embracing the world with high standards.'[27]

Therefore, China has reached out to sign FTAs with the Association of Southeast Asian Nations (ASEAN),[28] and further with Chile, Pakistan, New Zealand,

[25] 'Decision on Major Issues Concerning Comprehensively Deepening Reforms' approved at the Third Plenary Session of the 18th CCP Central Committee, 12 November 2013.

[26] http://fta.mofcom.gov.cn/english/index.shtml, last visited 27 June 2018.

[27] Guideline of State Council to Accelerate the Implementation of Free Trade Zone Strategy, 17 December 2015.

[28] ASEAN includes Malaysia, Indonesia, Thailand, the Philippines, Singapore, Brunei, Viet Nam, Laos, Myanmar and Cambodia.

Singapore, Peru, Costa Rica, Iceland, Switzerland, Korea, Australia and Georgia. All of the FTAs are agreements on trade in goods, services and on investments (with few exceptions). As for the areas covered, the China-Korea FTA has the widest range, while most FTAs only cover trade in goods, services, intellectual property, transparency, investments, movement of natural persons and investor-state dispute settlement (ISDS). Worth noting is that almost all of these FTAs carry a chapter of cooperation. (See Tables 3.1 to 3.3 and Figure 3.1.)

Table 3.1 FTAs Concluded by China

FTA	Concluded	Into force	Supplemented or upgraded
ASEAN	November 2002 (1st)	1 July 2003	Service, Investment, upgraded
Chile	November 2005	1 October 2006	Supplementary Agreement on Service 13 April 2008, upgrading negotiation launched November 2016, concluded Nov. 2017
Pakistan	November 2006	July 2007	Agreement on Trade in Service February 2009 Protocol on Banking Service April 2015 Second Phrase negotiation
New Zealand	April 2008	1 October 2008	upgrading negotiation started November 2016
Singapore	October 2008	1 Jan. 2009	under upgrading negotiation
Peru	April 2009	1 March 2010	Joint study on upgrading launched 23 November 2016
Costa Rica	April 2010	1 August 2011	
Iceland	April 2013	10 July 2014	
Switzerland	July 2013	1 July 2014	Joint study on upgrading launched January 2017
Korea	June 2015	20 December 2015	
Australia	June 2015	20 December 2015	Declaration of Intent on the Deliberation of Related Contents, March 2017
Georgia	October 2016		

Source: Table based on information on China's trade partners from Ministry of Commerce of the People's Republic of China. See http://fta.mofcom.gov.cn (in Chinese), last visited 27 June 2018.

Table 3.2 Subject matters of China's FTAs

FTA	Concluded	Goods	Services	Investment	Update negotiation
ASEAN	November 2002 (Framework) October 2003 October 2010 November 2012	November 2004 October 2010 November 2012 (SPS/ TBT)	January 2007 November 2011	August 2009	September 2014 concluded November 2015 DS November 2004
Chile	November 2005	√	April 2008	September 2012	May 2015
Pakistan	November 2006 October 2008	√	February 2009	√	
New Zealand	April 2008	√	√	√	
Singapore	October 2008	√	√	×	
Peru	April 2009	√	√	√	
Costa Rica	April 2010	√	√	BIT 2007	
Iceland	April 2013	√	√	√	
Switzerland	July 2013	√	√	×	
Korea	June 2015	√	√	√	
Australia	June 2015	√	√	√	

Source: Table based on information on China's trade partners from Ministry of Commerce of the People's Republic of China. See http://fta.mofcom.gov.cn (in Chinese), last visited 27 June 2018.

China's FTAs bear the following features. First, its partners are relatively small economies and also geographically scattered. Second, the FTAs do not have a wide coverage or comprehensive sector-specific chapters or provisions, but focus on cooperation. It seems that what matters is the cooperative attitude rather than specific rules. Third, they all have relatively limited market access, their issues are also scattered, and they lack regulatory coherence and a grand plan. In conclusion, China does not limit itself to starting FTAs with near neighbours, but also starts with easy topics. They usually confirmed a cooperative attitude, agreed on a few easy matters, and then left the rest to future negotiation.

Table 3.3 Chapter-Based Issues Covered by China's FTAs

FTA	Goods	Services	Financial Services	Telecom	Movement of Natural Persons	E-Commerce	Investment	ISDS	IP	Rules of Origin	Competition Policy	Environment	Transparency	Cooperation	Labor
ASEAN	√	√	×	×	×	×	√	√	×	×	×	×	×	√	×
Chile	√	√	×	×	×	×	√	√	×	×	×	×	√	√	×
Pakistan	√	√	×	×	×	×	√	√	×	×	×	×	√	×	×
New Zealand	√	√	×	×	√	×	√	√	√	×	×	×	√	√	×
Singapore	√	√	×	×	√	×	×	×/√	×	×	×	×	×	√	×
Peru	√	√	×	×	√	×	√	√	√	×	×	×	√	√	×
Costa Rica	√	√	×	×	√	×	BIT 2007		√	×	×	×	√	√	×
Iceland	√	√	×	×	x	×	×	×	√	×	√	×	×	√	×
Switzerland	√	√	×	×	x	×	×	×	√	×	√	√	×	√	×
Korea	√	√	√	√	√	√	√	√	√	√/×	√	√	√	√	×
Australia	√	√	×	×	√	√	√	√	√	×	×	×	√	×	×
Georgia	√	√	×	×	×	×	×	√	√	√	√	√	√	√	×

Source: Table based on information on China's trade partners from Ministry of Commerce of the People's Republic of China. See http://fta.mofcom.gov.cn (in Chinese), last visited on 27 June 2018.

Figure 3.1 Geographic distribution of countries that entered into FTAs with China

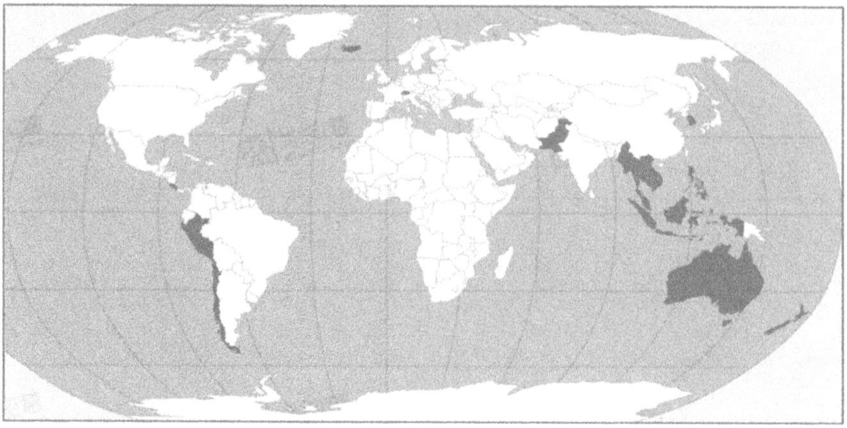

Source: Graph based on information on China's trade partners from Ministry of Commerce of the People's Republic of China. See http://fta.mofcom.gov.cn/ (in Chinese), last visited 27 June 2018.

D. Some Criticisms and Suggestions

There are many challenges to China's FTA pattern. First, trade issues are not independent from each other. Rather, they intersect and overlap with each other, and together they form a comprehensive network. The existing FTAs have narrow coverage and scattered issues, which in itself is not enough to achieve the goal of enhancing free trade and developing future FTAs. In addition, the more fragmented the network, the more difficult domestic coordination between departments will be.

Second, China has difficulties balancing the liberalization and vested interests of a certain sector, between its offensive (going abroad) and defensive (preserving domestic markets) interests, between different regions with developmental disparity, and between trade surplus and foreign currency reserves. China not only fails to take a comprehensive view, but also lacks trans-positional consideration. For example, China made some serious commitments when entering the WTO, some of which exceed the benchmark of the WTO. One example of this is Article 11 Protocol on the Accession of the People's Republic of China (Accession Protocol), which imposes restrictions on export taxes and charges, which are not imposed on other members (WTO-plus provisions).[29] Also, in Article 7 of Accession Protocol,

[29] This issue also led to the cases which determined that 'WTO-plus' obligations stipulated in China's Accession Protocol were not subject to the general exceptions in Article XX of the GATT 1994 if not explicitly stated so. See DS 394 and DS 431 of the DSB.

China virtually renounced its right to impose certain performance requirements on inbound investments, which exceeds the relevant provisions of the Agreement on Trade-Related Investment Measures (TRIMs). The inability to impose certain performance requirements poses a threat and creates uncertainty to China's bilateral investment treaties.[30] It is likely that China has not thought through the relationship between WTO commitments and FTAs.

Finally, China has met great difficulty in regional FTA negotiation. The reasons behind this are relatively similar to those behind the stand-down of WTO negotiations. There are too many conflicting interests between China and its prospective partners, and China tends to be inflexible regarding package deals. Therefore, it is difficult for China to coordinate the process of negotiation or make compromises. In conclusion, this tendency of loosely connected and piecemeal liberalization makes it very difficult for China to form a level surface of trade order, and achieve its goals.

There are a few ways out of this predicament. China should pursue more comprehensive FTAs that cover a greater number of trade issues, and that are of higher quality in drafting and contain deeper commitments in exchange for access to larger foreign markets. In addition, China should pursue more bilateral FTAs, as they are much easier to conclude than regional ones. Also, bilateral FTAs are more flexible and may fit each industry's different needs. Finally, the requirement of approval of FTAs by the People's Congress has greatly hindered their implementation. China should switch from approval to registration of FTAs to accelerate their implementation and the transformation of government functions.

IV. Trade Strategy of the US

A. Rewriting International Trade Rules Based on 'America First' Principle

US trade strategy took a u-turn after Donald Trump was sworn in as President of the US. Until 2015, the US trade policy was 'taking on the status quo'[31] under President Obama, which recognized the fact that '[T]he pace of globalization and technological change is not slowing down. We need to take on that challenge.'[32] In order to do this, the US focused its main efforts on the TPP, 'seeking to put the United States at the center of a trade zone'.[33] At that time, the US considered its

[30] See LY Han, 'Regulation of Performance Requirements in the Context of International Trade and Investment Rules' (in Chinese) (2017) 6 *Jurists Review* 116, 126.

[31] 2015 Trade Policy Agenda, Office of the US Trade Representative (USTR) 6–7.

[32] Ibid. 6–7.

[33] Ibid 6–7.

existing agreements to be a success, and backed the WTO up, as always,[34] reflecting its continuing faith in multilateral trade systems. The 2015 Trade Policy Agenda by the United States Trade Representative (USTR) was unequivocally clear that:

> The World Trade Organization remains the critical forum for strengthening the multilateral rules-based trading system and enforcing global trade rules, while serving as an important bulwark against protectionism. In 2015, the United States will build on recent multilateral trade negotiating successes by continuing to play a leading role in the multilateral trading system. … The United States is once again playing a lead role in resuming a discussion with WTO members to conclude the Doha Round of global trade negotiations. … This year, as these difficult discussions progress, we will continue to push the ultimate goal of the Round, which is to reduce trade barriers in order to expand global economic growth, development, and opportunity.[35]

However, since Trump's presidency, things have been going in a shockingly different direction. The US has renegotiated some of its most important FTAs, claiming they were flawed and not acceptable.[36] The US withdrew from TPP, which it had built almost single-handedly (the US would consider re-joining TPP (or CPTPP) only if it could 'get some wins'[37]), denouncing it as a waste of time, and asserting that the US would be able to strike better deals without it.[38] The US has also aggressively criticized and impeded the WTO's work, and defended its measures against the rulings of DSB as if the WTO were its enemy. The US is relentlessly putting its national security first and aggressively enforcing its domestic laws – giving up playing by the existing international rules.

President Obama tried to develop a new regional trade system without discarding the WTO; President Trump has discarded not only the WTO, but also regional deals, and has been focusing on reaching bilateral deals. In a bilateral relationship, the power game is more important than rule-making, which suits President Trump's 'America first' idea perfectly, as he said at the Asia-Pacific Economic Cooperation (APEC) Summit:

> From this day forward, we will compete on a fair and equal basis. We are not going to let the United States be taken advantage of anymore. I am always going to put America first the same way that I expect all of you in this room to put your countries first. The United States is prepared to work with each of the leaders in this room today to achieve mutually beneficial commerce that is in the interest of both your countries and mine. That is the message I am here to deliver.[39]

[34] Ibid 23, 32–33.

[35] Ibid 33.

[36] 2018 Trade Policy Agenda, Office of the US Trade Representative (USTR), p. 8.

[37] https://insidetrade.com/daily-news/perdue-trump-could-be-persuaded-rejoin-tpp-after-he-gets-some-%E2%80%98wins%E2%80%99, last visited 27 June 2018.

[38] 2018 Trade Policy Agenda (n 36) 12.

[39] https://www.whitehouse.gov/briefings-statements/remarks-president-trump-apec-ceo-summit-da-nang-vietnam, last visited 27 June 2018.

Based on this idea, President Trump proposed the idea of an 'Indo-Pacific dream'[40] and offered 'a renewed partnership with America to work together to strengthen the bonds of friendship and commerce between all of the nations of the Indo-Pacific, and together, to promote our prosperity and security'.[41] However, it was not a regional offer, but a bilateral one. In President Trump's own words:

> I will make bilateral trade agreements with any Indo-Pacific nation that wants to be our partner and that will abide by the principles of fair and reciprocal trade. What we will no longer do is enter into large agreements that tie our hands, surrender our sovereignty, and make meaningful enforcement practically impossible. Instead, we will deal on a basis of mutual respect and mutual benefit. We will respect your independence and your sovereignty.[42]

Some achievements have been made. In May 2018, the 'Joint Statement on the Trilateral Meeting of the Trade Ministers of the United States, Japan, and the European Union (EU)' showed clear signs of bilateral negotiations and compromises, and also pointed out a direction future trade rules would take.[43] Working on bilateral agreements gives the US an effective way to find 'like-minded' states. On a relevant note, the same thing happened to the US attitude not only towards multilateral trade systems, but also towards developing countries. In 2015, the US took a friendly perspective to developing countries and tried to reach mutual development by helping them.

> The Obama Administration's efforts to help developing countries to build capacity to harness the power of trade also helps U.S. producers and exporters by enhancing their opportunities to connect with billions of new customers abroad. Thus, by expanding our trade with the developing world we also support jobs and economic growth here at home.[44]

By contrast, in 2018, the US changed its attitude completely. It complained that 'there are no WTO criteria for what designates a "developing country"', and that a 'country may "self-declare" itself as a developing country, thus entitling itself to all "special and differential" treatment' and flexibilities afforded to developing countries under WTO agreements or negotiations. The US thought it unfair for some advanced countries, such as China, to receive these benefits as developing countries. All in all, the US considered the treatments given to developing countries to be a system that could be easily taken unfair advantage of.

[40] President Trump first proposed the idea of the 'Indo-Pacific dream' at the APEC CEO Summit on November 10, 2017, which offered a renewed partnership with America by trying to make bilateral trade agreements with Indo-Pacific nations.

[41] https://www.whitehouse.gov/briefings-statements/remarks-president-trump-apec-ceo-summit-da-nang-vietnam, last visited 27 June 2018.

[42] Ibid.

[43] https://ustr.gov/about-us/policy-offices/press-office/press-releases/2018/may/joint-statement-trilateral-meeting, last visited 15 July 2018.

[44] 2015 Trade Policy Agenda (n 31) 44.

B. Targeting China's Allegedly Unfair Trade Practices

The US has been targeting many Chinese practices such as intellectual property protection for a long time, but recently its accusations have grown much more comprehensive and thorough. The US (together with some other states) were hoping that by showing the non-market economy status of China, they might pick on other issues that mattered more, such as state-owned enterprises (SOE). The US Department of Commerce's International Trade Administration issued a more-than-200-page memorandum titled 'China's Status as a Non-Market Economy' on 26 October 2017,[45] which questioned China's basic economic system, industrial policy, SOE and the leadership of the CCP:

> At its core, the framework of China's economy is set by the Chinese government and the Chinese Communist Party (CCP), which exercise control directly and indirectly over the allocation of resources through instruments such as government ownership and control of key economic actors and government directives. The stated fundamental objective of the government and the CCP is to uphold the 'socialist market economy' in which the Chinese government and the CCP direct and channel economic actors to meet the targets of state planning. The Chinese government does not seek economic outcomes that reflect predominantly market forces outside of a larger institutional framework of government and CCP control. In China's economic framework, state planning through industrial policies conveys instructions regarding sector specific economic objectives, particularly for those sectors deemed strategic and fundamental.[46]

The accusation was so strong and deep-rooted that aggressive measures were bound to follow. The US even found partners to back it up. In May 2018, the USTR released a 'Joint Statement on Trilateral Meeting of the Trade Ministers of the United States, Japan, and the European Union'. The three major economies in the world joined voices on the issue of industrial subsidies, technology transfer policies and practices, and market-oriented conditions, which are all concerns 'with the non-market-oriented policies of third countries'.[47] The statement reads:

> The Ministers confirmed their shared objective to address non-market-oriented policies and practices that lead to severe overcapacity, create unfair competitive conditions for our workers and businesses, hinder the development and use of innovative technologies, and undermine the proper functioning of international trade, including where existing rules are not effective.[48]

[45] A-570-053, available at https://enforcement.trade.gov/download/prc-nme-status/prc-nme-review-final-103017.pdf, last visited 27 June 2018.

[46] Memorandum on China's Status as a Non-Market Economy, 4.

[47] Joint Statement on Trilateral Meeting of the Trade Ministers of the United States, Japan, and the European Union, Office of the US Trade Representative (USTR), 31 May 2018.

[48] Ibid.

The actions which followed were in line with these statements. In 2018, the US used its domestic laws to the fullest to cope with the situation. As stated in the annual trade policy agenda of the US:

> We will use all tools available – including unilateral action where necessary – to support this effort. … Of course, as a sovereign nation, China is free to pursue whatever trade policy it prefers. But the United States, as a sovereign nation, is free to respond. Under President Trump's leadership, we will use all available tools to discourage China – or any country that emulates its policies – from undermining true market competition.[49]

These are not just words. In January 2018, the US claimed that the import of steel and aluminum constituted a risk to national security and imposed an import tariff that could be exempted upon negotiation. This was a move where the US used the tariff as a 'poker chip', attempting to achieve different gains from different countries, including China, which has not yet been exempted. In February 2018, the US imposed a ban on one of China's largest technology companies, ZTE, due to its violation of a pre-existing settlement agreement with the US government. The ban prohibited any US companies or individuals from exporting to or trading with ZTE for seven years. The period of the ban was extremely suggestive, because it coincides with China's 'Made in China 2025' policy. Also, in March 2018, USTR released its special 301 investigation report specifically on China and pointed out a series of China's failures to protect US intellectual property. Apart from bringing up a case at the WTO, USTR issued a list of products involving 50 billion dollars in trade which would be subject to tariffs. From June to August 2018, the US took successive steps to raise tariffs on products worth of hundreds of billions of dollars imported from China.

V. Trade Relations between the US, China and India

A. The Relations between the US and China

The trade war between China and the US is certainly a hot topic nowadays. In order to see past the surface, one must backtrack and look at major previous encounters between these two countries. Only then may we find that the hostile attitude towards China is not surprising, since there are many hints in the history of the China-US trade relationship that the US has always taken a wary and cautious stance towards China. The US and China had no trade relationships until 1979, when the China-US Agreement on Trade Relations was signed, granting each other the most-favoured-nation treatment. According to the Jackson-Vanik Amendment,[50]

[49] 2018 Trade Policy Agenda (n 36) 2 and 4.

[50] The Jackson-Vanik amendment is contained in Title IV of the Trade Act of 1974, intending to affect US trade relations with countries with non-market economies.

China must pass an annual review every year to keep the most-favoured-nation treatment. Initially, the period 1979–89 was somewhat a honeymoon stage for the US and China. However, after the 1990–91 Foreign Relations Authorization Act, the annual review became increasingly difficult. In 2000, the situation began to improve when Permanent Normal Trade Relations for China was signed. From then on, annual review was not needed and China could enjoy most-favoured-nation treatment according to WTO rules after its accession. Since its accession to the WTO, China has transformed from a poor country into the world's second largest economy, and the attitude of the US has also changed rapidly from worries regarding ideology to real fear of China's power. The US opined that current trade rules had benefited China too much.

The legal trigger for the trade war between the US and China was Article 15 of the Accession Protocol. In December 2016, China had been a member of the WTO for 15 years. According to the Accession Protocol, Article 15(a)(ii) should expire,[51] which creates doubts as to whether an importing member can use an analogue country's price for comparison to determine the dumping margin. Article 15(d) of the Accession Protocol states: 'In any event, the provisions of subparagraph (a)(ii) shall expire 15 years after the date of accession.' This is one of the three ways to stop applying subparagraph (a), which sets out how to determine the price for comparison for China's industries to determine the dumping margin. Article 15(a)(ii) states:

> The importing WTO Member may use a methodology that is not based on a strict comparison with domestic prices or costs in China if the producers under investigation cannot clearly show that market economy conditions prevail in the industry producing the like product with regard to manufacture, production and sale of that product.

This provision led to two cases in the WTO where China claimed that the US and the European Union (EU) had still been using the old methodology after the expiration,[52] and also a heated debate over China's economic status.

The provision, to be fair, left room for different interpretations. China believes that the expiry means that WTO Members are no longer able use a methodology that is not based on a strict comparison with domestic prices or costs in China for purposes of anti-dumping comparisons, and that any methodology that is not based on domestic price has to go. Meanwhile, the US (and the EU) considers that the expiry simply shifts the burden of proof. The 'legal authority to reject prices or costs not determined under market economy conditions flows from GATT 1994 Articles VI:1 and VI:2 and the need to ensure comparability of prices and costs when establishing normal value'.[53] According to the US, before the expiry

[51] Protocol on the Accession of the People's Republic of China, Art 15(d).

[52] See *United States – Standards for Reformulated Conventional Gasoline* (DS 515) and *European Union – Measures Related to Price Comparison Methodologies* (DS 516) of DSB.

[53] 2018 Trade Policy Agenda (n 36) 19.

of 15 years, it was the producers that had to prove market economy conditions; after the expiry, members of the WTO can still reject domestic prices if they can prove the nonexistence of market economy conditions.

The US (and some other states) took up the challenge valiantly, and more accusations followed. The US government publicly said: '[T]here is significant concern that the WTO is unable to manage the rise of countries – notably China – that pay lip service to the values of free trade but intentionally avoid, circumvent, or violate the commitments accompanying those values.'[54] Since then, many steps have been taken to deal with the rapidly growing, out-of-control competition.

President Obama's strategy was to create a new, widespread free trade zone that did not include China and where the US could be leader again, ie TPP, which was also on some level a countermeasure aimed at RCEP. He gave his opinion very decidedly to the Washington Post that '[t]he TPP would let America, not China, lead the way on global trade':

> China is negotiating a trade deal (RCEP) that would carve up some of the fastest-growing markets in the world at our expense, putting American jobs, businesses and goods at risk. … The world has changed. The rules are changing with it. The United States, not countries like China, should write them. Let's seize this opportunity, pass the Trans-Pacific Partnership and make sure America isn't holding the bag, but holding the pen.[55]

Although Trump has taken a more aggressive and direct path, the purpose, or part of the purpose behind all these actions is the same as the reason why Obama jump-started the TPP: to tackle the risk that China could no longer be contained by existing rules. Rather than trying to make new rules, as Obama did, Trump has simply waged trade war against China to attempt force his ways through. The most frequently mentioned words about the proposed bilateral trade concept are 'open, free, fair, reciprocal'.[56] These words mean 'no' to government planners or state-owned enterprises, because they would not be open or fair. What is 'reciprocal' then? From the claim in Commerce Secretary Wilbur Ross' speech at the National Press Club Headliners Luncheon that the deficit was caused by differences in tariffs in 21 of 23 major product categories, with Chinese tariffs far higher than those of the US, a result of protectionism (see Figure 3.2),[57] it can be inferred that 'reciprocal' means other countries should impose tariffs and other trade barriers at the same level as the US. The well-being of private industry or investment should rely completely on themselves. Due to China's special ideology and system, the situation is extra tricky.

[54] Ibid 29.

[55] https://www.washingtonpost.com/opinions/president-obama-the-tpp-would-let-america-not-china-lead-the-way-on-global-trade/2016/05/02/680540e4-0fd0-11e6-93ae-50921721165d_story.html?utm_term=.c1975d4b17d9, last visited 27 June 2018.

[56] https://ustr.gov/about-us/policy-offices/press-office/press-releases/2017/november/ustr-lighthizer-statement, last visited 27 June 2018.

[57] https://www.commerce.gov/news/speeches/2018/05/remarks-secretary-wilbur-l-ross-national-press-club-headliners, last visited 24 May 2019.

Figure 3.2 Average tariffs for the United States and China

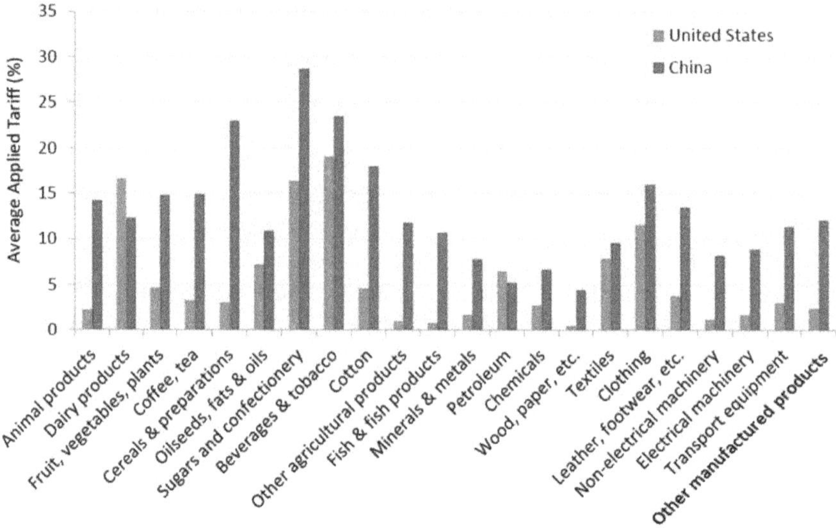

Source: Graph based on tariff profiles from the World Trade Organization, MFN Applied Tariffs, 2016. Prepared by Industry & Analysis, International Trade Administration, U.S. Department of Commerce. See First Chart in Remarks by Secretary Wilbur L. Ross at the National Press Club Headliners Luncheon on 14 May 2018.

But again, the provision of the Accession Protocol was only the trigger. Measures taken by the US had the smell of power play all over them. The US brought up three 'hostages' (raising tariffs, intellectual property protection and ZTE) which it was ready to 'kill' if China did not give it what it wanted. If it were not clear enough:

> A China analyst who has advised the administration on China trade issues told *Inside U.S. Trade* that 'ZTE is the precondition to a deal for the Chinese.' 'The administration apparently told members that ZTE is separate from trade – that's a lie,' the source said. 'ZTE is a precondition for trade talks.'[58]

Recently, the accusation has expanded from trade to politics. US Vice President Pence publicly accused China of using its power 'to interfere in the domestic policies of this country (meaning the US) and to interfere in the politics of the United States.' What's worse,

> China has initiated an unprecedented effort to influence American public opinion, the 2018 elections and the environment leading into the 2020 presidential elections. To put it bluntly, President Trump's leadership is working; and China wants a different American President.[59]

[58] https://insidetrade.com/daily-news/lawmakers-pledge-to-block-ZTE-deal-that-China-sees-as-precondition-for-trade-talks, last visited 27 June 2018.

[59] https://www.whitehouse.gov/briefings-statements/remarks-vice-president-pence-administrations-policy-toward-china, last visited 23 October 2018.

A new regime of China-US trade relations has dawned. At present, there will be no new trade or investment agreement at all between them unless China makes commitments satisfactory to the US, which still considers the trade deficits 'blameful and shameful'.[60] Whatever comes in the future, it is guaranteed that a long list of compromises will be behind it.

B. The Relations between China and India

Due to the size of India's population and its geopolitical power, China and the US are each trying to draw India to its own side. However, India is not taking sides yet.

The relationship between China and India has been extremely complicated and not always peaceful. The border dispute has been a long-standing issue. In 1959 the Dalai Lama fled China and went into exile in India, which granted the Dalai Lama political asylum. This incident has cast a never-ending shadow over the China-India relationship. In the 1960s, '[i]t seems that China wanted to build a strategic railway from Xinjiang to Tibet passing through eastern Kashmir, a plan that was seen by India as a catastrophe, because it would have linked China to Pakistan[61] in a very direct way'[62] which eventually led to the 1962 conflict.

Besides political disaccord, India has long had trade deficits with China (see Table 3.4).

Table 3.4 Figures on China-India trade (unit: US$ billion)

	Goods			
China/total	2014	2015	2016	2017
Export (Ranking)	13.31/319.54 (4)	9.69/266.71 (4)	8.96/264.04 (4)	12.48/296.55 (4)
Import (Ranking)	58.27/460.11 (1)	61.14/391.65 (1)	60.65/359.55 (1)	72.05/446.94 (1)
Deficit	44.96	51.45	51.69	59.57

Source: Table based on information from Ministry of Commerce of the People's Republic of China. See https://countryreport.mofcom.gov.cn/indexType.asp?p_coun=%D3%A1%B6%C8, last visited 27 June 2018.

[60] https://www.commerce.gov/news/speeches/2018/05/remarks-secretary-wilbur-l-ross-national-press-club-headliners, last visited 24 May 2019.

[61] India and Pakistan have always had a tense relationship, and the close ties between China and Pakistan had a negative influence on those of China and India, especially when India and Pakistan were on bad terms.

[62] SF Cioculescu and S Petre, 'China and India: Learning from History, Building the Present and Avoiding Narratives on their "Unescapable Clash"' (2013) 2 *Romanian Political Science Review* 287, 291–92.

Table 3.5 Initiations of Anti-dumping Investigations

Reporting member	**2015**			**2016**			**2017**			**2018 January–June**		
	China	**India**	**US**	**China**	**India**	**US**	**China**	**India**	**US**	**China**	**India**	**US**
China		0	2		0	1		2	4		0	2
India	10			19			15			14		
US	6			11			10			21		

Source: Table based on information on China's trade partners from Ministry of Commerce of the People's Republic of China. See http://cacs.mofcom.gov.cn/ (in Chinese), last visited 15 July 2018.

As one of the ramifications of the trade deficit, India has been much keener to start anti-dumping investigations against China (and so has the US for that matter) (see Table 3.5). As Indian analyst Mohan Malik rightly concludes, Indian-Chinese relations are complicated by layers of rivalry, mistrust and occasional cooperation, not to mention actual geographical disputes.[63]

Regarding FTA, so far India has concluded only a few FTAs (see Table 3.6), and is negotiating with countries such as Thailand, the US, Australia, Indonesia and New Zealand (see Table 3.6).

Table 3.6 Main FTAs Concluded by India

FTA	**Concluded**	**Into force**	**Supplemented or upgrade**
SAFTA	January 2004	January 2006	
Singapore CECA	June 2005	August 2005	Protocol-Goods December 2007
Malaysia CECA			Implementation
ASEAN Agreements			
Africa Trade Agreements			
Chile PTA	March 2006	September 2007	Expansion-Goods May 2017
Japan CEPA	February 2011		Implementation
Korea CEPA			
Sri Lanka FTA			
MERCOSUR PTA	2003		

[63] Ibid 290.

Trade agreements of which India and China are both members include the First Agreement on Trade Negotiations among Developing Member Countries of the Economic and Social Commission for Asia and the Pacific (also known as the Bangkok Agreement) of 2005 and the WTO Agreement. With Asian countries, such as Bangladesh, China, India, the Republic of Korea, Sri Lanka and Laos, the Bangkok Agreement was limited to tariff reduction on an agreed number of tariff lines, and did not cover other areas of trade. In terms of bilateral agreement between India and China, a Five-Year Development Program for Economic and Trade Cooperation between China and India was signed on 18 September 2014. This program has laid down a medium-term road map for promoting balanced and sustainable development of economic and trade relations between the two countries. There is no FTA between India and China. There was an India Regional Trade Arrangement Joint Feasibility Study listed on the Ministry of Commerce (MOFCOM) website in 2015, but this has not been listed since. Another feature worth noting is that neither China nor India took leadership in FTA negotiations. It seems that these two major countries have some power but still refrain from using it.

In an attempt to draw India to side with it, China is resorting to the Belt and Road Initiative and appealling to 'a community with a shared future for mankind', and also putting great effort into the RCEP. However, India is not excited about China's Belt and Road Initiative, and did not participate in the First Belt and Road Forum for International Cooperation. Furthermore, India has always been hesitant to join the RCEP, worrying that opening up markets might put pressure on many Indian industries. Despite that, there is some progress. In May 2018, the Indian Prime Minister Modi visited China, the fifth time since taking office, and held an informal meeting with President Xi.[64] It is uncertain whether this visit will shed some new light on China-India relations.

C. The Relations between the US and India

India was a founding member of the Non-Aligned Movement (NAM) during the Cold War and tried to take a path that was neither capitalism nor communism. But it befriended the Soviet Union to a greater extent than it did the US. Only after the dissolution of the Soviet Union in 1990s did India choose to take on an economic system similar to the market economy of the US. At present, India is the largest democracy in the world, and its importance to the US cannot be overstated.

The US is seeking to use the 'Indo-Pacific dream' to draw India closer. The US has made quite some progress with its 'Indo-Pacific dream'; however, the US and India were not on very good terms in the summer of 2018. On one hand, the trade

[64] https://news.sina.cn/gj/2018-05-02/detail-ifzyqqip9932784.d.html?vt=4&sid=223723, last visited 27 June 2018 (in Chinese).

war that the US waged against other countries has touched a nerve in India, which took several measures to deal with the situation, including declaring retaliatory duties on certain products imported from the US. On the other hand, due to trade conflict, the minister-level meeting between India and the US has been postponed several times. While India and the US may not see eye to eye on certain things, their recognition of each other still means a lot to both of them. Therefore, India restrained itself from using retaliatory duties for a few months, and the minister-level meeting finally took place in New Delhi on 7 September 2018. It seems that the friendship between India and the US is not a lost hope after all.

Nowadays, with the US clashing with many major economies around the world, including China, several questions remain unanswered: Where will the world trade order go? Will the 'Indo-Pacific dream' work? What is the difference between these ideas and how they will affect the world trade order? Will the aggressive measures of the US be effective or will the US start another round of searching for a new world trade order?

VI. Looking Forward

Regarding the WTO, in spite of the many setbacks faced by the WTO, it is undeniable that the WTO is still essential to the order and stability of the world trade system. Therefore, supporting and upholding the multilateral trading system of the WTO would benefit the world, including both India and China.

With regards to the CPTPP, this shows that the world can move along to achieve at least some interim results without having to wait for the capricious US. Neither China nor India was involved in the TPP or CPTPP. It is about time for India and China and the world trading community to reflect on their joining of the CPTTP. Related questions include how will the CPTTP interact with the RCEP and the 'Indo-Pacific dream'?

With regards to the Sino-US relationship, the US has begun a whole new trade relationship with China. At present, no concessions between the two are in sight. One retaliation has been met by yet another. However, as the extraordinary diplomat Henry Kissinger has observed:

> The relationship between China and the United States has become a central element in the quest for world peace and global well-being … It has been a complex journey, for both societies believe they represent unique values. American exceptionalism is missionary. It holds that the United States has an obligation to spread its values to every part of the world. China's exceptionalism is cultural. China does not proselytize; it does not claim that its contemporary institutions are relevant outside China. But it is the heir of the Middle Kingdom tradition, which formally graded all other states as various levels of tributaries based on their approximation to Chinese cultural and political forms; in other words, a kind of cultural universality.[65]

[65] H Kissinger, *On China* (New York, The Penguin Press, 2011) Preface.

This was a rather in-depth and precise analysis of the existing conflict between China and the US, except that now the said exceptionalism has somewhat changed. The US chooses its friends based on their approximation to American cultural and political forms, which is democracy, multi-party system and a strictly defined market economy. Its exceptionalism is still missionary and it criticizes all countries that do not fit its criterion. China takes a more mild and low-key approach, proposing the idea of 'peaceful development'. China does not seek universal recognition, but does not tolerate its institution being used as a punching bag.

Kissinger also pointed out a way out of the conflict of the two exceptionalisms: 'the appropriate label for the Sino-American relationship is less partnership than "co-evolution", proposing effort toward a Pacific Community'.[66] Kissinger seems to suggest that China and the US do not have to be partners, but should give each other space to develop for the Pacific Community to prosper. China does not need to deny everything proposed by the US. The 'Indo-Pacific dream' is a bilateral system that every country can take advantage of, which is acceptable to the US, India and China. The three countries should join efforts in building constructive relations, not confronting blocs, to realize the Indo-Pacific dream.

The Report of the 19th National Congress of the CCP stated that China 'will promote coordination and cooperation with other major countries and work to build a framework for major country relations featuring overall stability and balanced development'.[67] The statement was in line with the 'co-evolution' idea, but how to achieve this idea and to reach a new balance with major countries, especially the US under the current 'trade war' circumstances, remains a great challenge.

[66] Ibid, Epilogue.
[67] Report of the 19th National Congress of the CCP, October 2017.

4

The Future of China's Trade Pact and Intellectual Property Rights

HAN-WEI LIU AND SI-WEI LU*

I. Introduction

This chapter explores the trajectory of China's intellectual property rights (IPRs) regimes over the past decades and its possible implications for the contour of future Asian trade negotiations. The international IPR regime has witnessed a sea change. Although the Agreement on Trade-Related Aspects of Intellectual Property Rights (TRIPs)[1] of the World Trade Organization (WTO) created a baseline for IPR protection, such standards seemed unsatisfactory in the eyes of many.[2] The WTO Members from both developing and least developed worlds had been struggling with full implementation of their TRIPs obligations.[3] By contrast, developed countries with significant stakes in this field have begun to rebalance the landscape by pushing forward more rigorous IP rules – often

* Dr Han-Wei Liu is a Lecturer, Monash University, Australia. Si-Wei Lu is a PhD Student, National Chengchi University, Taiwan.

[1] Agreement on Trade-Related Aspects of Intellectual Property Rights, 15 April 1994, Marrakesh Agreement Establishing the World Trade Organization, Annex 1C, 33 ILM 1197 (1994).

[2] See SK Sell, 'TRIPs Was Never Enough: Vertical Forum Shifting, FTAs, ACTA, and TPP' (2011) 18 *Journal of Intellectual Property Law* 44 (discussing the complicated, competing and inconsistent norm-setting processes of the international IP rule-making arena since the inauguration of TRIPs).

[3] See eg LR Helfer, 'Regime Shifting: The TRIPs Agreement and New Dynamics of International Intellectual Property Lawmaking' (2004) 29 *Yale Journal of International Law* 1, 24 (arguing 'how TRIPs fostered a growing belief, shared by many developing countries, NGOs and commentators, that TRIPs was a coerced agreement that should be resisted rather than embraced'); JH Reichman, 'The TRIPS Agreement Comes of Age: Conflict or Cooperation with the Developing Countries?' (2000) 32 *Case Western Reserve Journal of International Law* 441 (identifying key negative factors causing developing countries behind the schedule in implementing TRIPs, such as unlimited transaction costs, uneven distribution of benefits, and new demands of higher protection); PK Yu, 'The International Enclosure Movement' (2007) 82 *Indiana Law Journal* 827, 888 (indicating TRIPs is biased against less developed countries).

dubbed 'TRIPs-Plus' – through bilateral trade negotiations.[4] More recently, such efforts have gained new momentum in what is known as mega-regionalism – trade blocs with a major share of global trade. Led by the US, the Trans-Pacific Partnership (TPP) Agreement aimed to build up a 'Gold Standard' for the twenty-first century,[5] though such efforts were held back after Trump took over the White House.[6] While the remaining 11 Pacific Rim nations have agreed to proceed by replacing the TPP with the Comprehensive and Progressive Agreement for Trans-Pacific Partnership (CPTPP),[7] a set of IPR clauses from the TPP have been suspended.[8]

[4] For example, in a number of bilateral trade agreements, including the European Free Trade Association's (EFTA) preferential trade agreements, and Switzerland negotiated so-called 'TRIPs-Plus' elements, mainly focusing on enhanced protection in patent and plant variety protection. B Mercurio, 'TRIPs-Plus Provisions in FTAs: Recent Trend' in L Bartels and F Ortino (eds), *Regional Trade Agreements and the WTO Legal System* 215 (Oxford University Press, 2006); Helfer (n 3) 23; P Drahos, 'BITs and BIPs' (2001) 4 *Journal of World Intellectual Property* 791, 792–807.

[5] See eg KG Weatherall, 'Intellectual Property in the TPP: Not the New TRIPs' (2016) 17 *Melbourne Journal of International Law* 257, 276; 'The Trans-Pacific Partnership: TPP, RIP?', *The Economist* (20 June 2015), https://www.economist.com/leaders/2015/06/20/tpp-rip (indicating Hillary Clinton, as Obama's Secretary of State, had underscored the TPP's importance over time and called it the 'gold standard' of trade pacts); I Kullgren, 'Yes, Clinton Did Call TPP the "Gold Standard"', *Politico* (9 October 2016), https://www.politico.com/blogs/2016-presidential-debate-fact-check/2016/10/yes-clinton-did-call-tpp-the-gold-standard-229501 (quoting from Hillary Clinton, 'This TPP sets the gold standard in trade agreements to open free, transparent, fair trade – the kind of environment that has the rule of law and a level playing field'). See also HW Liu, 'Inside the Black Box: Political Economy of the TPP's Encryption Clause' (2017) 51 *Journal of World Trade* 310 (noting how the TPP is reckoned to be a twenty-first century high standard agreement from a regulatory viewpoint).

[6] Office of the Press Secretary, 'Presidential Memorandum Regarding Withdrawal of the United States from the Trans-Pacific Partnership Negotiations and Agreement', the White House (23 January 2017), https://www.whitehouse.gov/the-press-office/2017/01/23/presidential-memorandum-regarding-withdrawal-united-states-trans-pacific.

[7] The CPTPP is a free trade agreement between 11 countries in the Asia-Pacific region, including Australia, Brunei, Canada, Chile, Japan, Malaysia, Mexico, New Zealand, Peru, Singapore and Viet Nam. These members account for 13.5% of world GDP and involve the livelihoods of 500 million people. Modelled on the TPP, the CPTPP includes commitments to liberalize in key areas such as textiles, technical barriers to trade, sanitary and phytosanitary measures, competition, labour and dispute settlement. Though the elements of the CPTPP partially resemble the text of the TPP, they contain some significant differences, as several key items from the TPP are suspended under the CPTPP. On 8 March 2018, the CPTPP has been signed by the member countries in Santiago. 'CPTPP: 11 Countries Sign Pacific Trade Deal in Chile', *The Santiago Times* (9 March 2018) https://santiago-times.cl/2018/03/09/cptpp-11-countries-sign-pacific-trade-deal-in-chile.

[8] According to the full text of the CPTPP, a number of IPR-related articles are suspended, such as patentable subject matter (Arts 18.37.2 and 18.37.4), protection of test data (Art 18.50), biologics (Art 18.51), term of protection for copyright (Art 18.63), and technological protection measures (TPMs) (Art 18.68). As a result of such suspensions, signatories will have more flexibility on patentable subject matters, retain flexibility to extend terms of protection for patent rights, and no longer be required to change data or market protection settings for new medicines. Also, they will not have to extend the term of copyright protection up to 70 years, or expand protection to digital locks for copyright protection, TPMs. As at September 2018, it is unknown whether these suspended provisions will be reinstated later. For the full text of the CPTPP, see Government of Canada, 'Full Text of the Agreement', http://international.gc.ca/trade-commerce/trade-agreements-accords-commerciaux/agr-acc/cptpp-ptpgp/text-texte/cptpp-ptpgp.aspx?lang=eng; see also W New, 'TPP Texts Show Suspended IP Provisions', *Intellectual Property Watch* (16 November 2017), https://www.ip-watch.org/2017/11/16/tpp-texts-show-suspended-ip-provisions; J Smith et al, 'From TPP To CPTPP: Suspensions to IP Provisions', Gowling WLG (7 February 2018), https://gowlingwlg.com/en/insights-resources/articles/2018/from-tpp-to-cptpp-suspensions-to-ip-provisions.

As both sides of the Atlantic have been struggling with the political dynamics in the era of Trump and Brexit, China has emerged as a great economic power. China alone accounted for 19.1 per cent of global gross domestic product (GDP) trade value from 2015 to 2017 and has become one of the largest trading partners for almost every nation.[9] With such economic growth, China is likely to increasingly create high-value goods that call for stronger IPR protection.[10] As one of its strategic plans to move up the global value chain, China in 2008 initiated what is known as the 'National IP Strategy'.[11] Since then, China has rolled out various reforms.[12] Despite such IP reforms, China's laws and practices on IPRs have been, time and again, under attack from its trading partners in the WTO.[13] As over a decade has elapsed since China's WTO accession, it seems prime time to take stock and assess the Chinese IPR regime today. Such a fresh account is crucial not only because of China's changing economic interest in IPRs over time, but its geopolitical power in forming the international economic order,[14] and therefore, the future Asian trade negotiations.

The decline of the WTO has led China to join its global competitors by redirecting its resources into non-WTO contexts. To this date, China has concluded 16 bilateral free trade agreements (FTAs),[15] while negotiating the Regional Comprehensive Economic Partnership (RCEP) – the largest trade bloc, with an estimated 40 per cent of the world's GDP.[16] Together, such a complex web of international

[9] WTO, 'Trade Profile: China' (2018), http://stat.wto.org/CountryProfiles/CN_e.htm; C Picker and L Toohey, 'China in the International Economic Order: New Directions and Changing Paradigms' in L Toohey et al (eds), *China in the International Economic Order: New Directions and Changing Paradigms* (Cambridge University Press, 2015).

[10] B Mercurio, 'China, Intellectual Property Rights, and the WTO: Challenging but Not a Challenge to the Existing Legal Order' in L Toohey et al (eds), *China in the International Economic Order: New Directions and Changing Paradigm* (Cambridge University Press, 2015).

[11] See The State Council of the People's Republic of China, 'Outline of the National Intellectual Property Strategy' (2008) http://www.wipo.int/wipolex/en/text.jsp?file_id=125982.

[12] See eg SIPO, 'National Patent Development Strategy (2011-2020)' (11 November 2010) https://graphics8.nytimes.com/packages/pdf/business/SIPONatPatentDevStrategy.pdf.

[13] See eg Mercurio (n 10) at 302–09; K Thomas, *Assessing Intellectual Property Compliance in Contemporary China: The WTO Trade Organisation TRIPS Agreement* (Palgrave Macmillan, 2017) 93–99.

[14] On China's strategic role of standardization, see HW Liu, 'China Standard Time: The Boundary of Techno-Nationalism' in SY Peng et al (eds), *Mega-Regionals in Governing Science and Technology in the Mega-RTA Era: Regulatory Divergence and Convergence* (Edward Elgar Publishing, 2018) 114, 114–40.

[15] Up to September 2018, China has signed 16 FTAs with trading partners such as Maldives, Georgia, Australia, Korea, Switzerland, Iceland, Costa Rica, Peru, Singapore, New Zealand, Chile, Pakistan, ASEAN, Hong Kong, Macau and Chile. See China's FTA Agreements, http://fta.mofcom.gov.cn/english/index.shtml.

[16] RCEP is a proposed free trade agreement negotiated between 16 nations in East Asia, which comprises 10 members of the Association of Southeast Asian Nations (ASEAN) as a bloc, containing Brunei, Cambodia, Indonesia, Laos, Malaysia, Myanmar, Philippines, Singapore, Thailand and Viet Nam, as well as six ASEAN FTA partners, including Australia, China, India, Japan, South Korea and New Zealand. The economies included in the 16 nations cover 45% of world's population and about 40% GDP of the world. Launched in November 2012, RCEP aims at achieving a modern, comprehensive, high-quality and mutually beneficial economic partnership agreement among its members. Its negotiations focus on trade and non-trade discussions, such as trade in goods and services, investment, economic and technical cooperation, IP, dispute settlement, and small and medium enterprises (SMEs). After over 23 rounds of negotiations, RCEP members hope to wrap up deal by the end of 2018.

trade and investment agreements may help China shape or at least co-shape the international IPR regime in the age of mega-regionalism. China's evolving IPR regime and its interactions with trade agreements, therefore, merit deeper considerations.

Against this backdrop, this chapter focuses on three broader sets of analytical issues. Section II begins by taking stock of and re-examining China's evolving IPR regime in the pre- and post-WTO era. Section III considers China's negotiating strategies by examining the design of IPR provisions in its FTAs. Building upon these observations, section IV summarizes China's recent practices and seeks to map out its possible role in setting future Asian and global IP norms.

II. Taking Stock: China's IP Practices in the WTO Context

This section sets the stage by sketching out the changing face of the Chinese IPR regime in the pre- and post-WTO era. On the latter in particular, we examine the way in which China has addressed IPR issues strategically through three vantage points: the Transitional Review Mechanism (TRM), the Trade Policy Review Mechanism (TPRM), and the Dispute Settlement Mechanism (DSM). This background will allow us to gain a deeper understanding of how China has reshaped its IPR policies while integrating into the global economy over the past few decades.

A. Early Years: China and IPRs

With the establishment of the People's Republic of China (PRC) in 1949, China's IPR regime built by the Nationalist Party was entirely abolished.[17] Although afterwards there were attempts to introduce Western-style ideology by conferring 'property rights' to incentivize inventors, this liberal approach was short-lived, and superseded by a socialist approach penetrating most Chinese IP laws.[18] Instead,

See Regional Comprehensive Economic Partnership (RCEP), http://asean.org/?static_post=rcep-regional-comprehensive-economic-partnership; 'RCEP Negotiations Expected to Be Concluded this Year', VNA (1 September 2018), https://en.vietnamplus.vn/rcep-negotiations-expected-to-be-concluded-this-year/137500.vnp.

[17] Thomas (n 13) 13.

[18] The PRC government abolished all the Nationalist Party laws and decrees and started enacting regulations patterned on the Soviet model, such as the Provisional Regulations on the Guarantee of Invention Rights and Patent Rights, the Provisional Regulations on Awards for Inventions, Technical Improvements and Rationalization Proposals Concerning Production, and the Provisional Regulations Governing Trademark Registration, to fill the legal vacuum before it reintroduced IP laws in the late 1980s. Ibid at 13–15; QJ Kong, *WTO, Internationalization and the Intellectual Property Rights Regime in China* (Marshall Cavendish International, 2005) 6.

Communist China granted inventors monetary payment rather than proprietary rights – with inventions taken as property rights that belonged to the public.[19] China's IPR protection before the 1970s was, in the eyes of many, in a dreadful state, since the concept of 'private property' largely ran counter to the Communist ideology and IPRs were therefore treated as collective property.[20]

In the 1980s, China embarked on its open-door policy, which considered IPR protection to be a strategic tool for re-integrating into the global economy.[21] To this end, China launched various collaborative programs. The IP Cooperation Programme with the EU and dialogues on IPRs with trading partners, including the US, Japan, Korea and France, were among many telling examples. Cooperation with other countries increased in terms of frequency and scope. Among other commitments, the most salient was China's participation in major international IP organizations and treaties, such as the World Intellectual Property Organization (WIPO), the Paris Convention on Industrial Property, the Berne Convention of Protection of Literary and Artistic Works, and the Madrid Agreement Concerning International Registration of Marks.[22] To further open up its agenda, China also committed itself to the Sino-US Memorandum of Understanding (MOU) to establish an IPR regime in line with international regimes. Together, these cooperative efforts played a crucial role in incrementally bringing China's IPR system up to international standards in a constructive manner.[23]

In tandem with its commitments under bilateral or multilateral settings, China began enacting IP laws. Milestone legislation included the Trademark Law in 1982, the Patent Law in 1984, and the Copyright Law in 1990. Meanwhile, IPR-related regulatory agencies came into existence: the State Intellectual Property Office (SIPO) in charge of patent affairs, the National Copyright Administration of China (NCAC) responsible for copyright administration, and the State Administration for Industry and Commerce (SAIC) handling trademark matters.[24] Notwithstanding such IPR frameworks, the Chinese government still received criticisms from key trading partners.[25] Some were concerned that enforcement of copyright and trademark in China were practically non-existent; others mentioned that what right holders received from infringers were nothing more than letters of court decisions; still others argued that corruption had infested the Chinese IPR regime.[26] Bitter and extensive, these criticisms more or less enhanced China's awareness of the need to take IPRs and related interests seriously. To reinforce China's position in

[19] Kong (n 18) 16.
[20] See Mercurio (n 10) 296.
[21] Kong (n 18) 3.
[22] See Mercurio (n 10) 296.
[23] Kong (n 18) 3–4.
[24] See M Li, 'The Process of Intellectual Property Law Reform in China' (2018) 8 *Queen Mary Journal of Intellectual Property* 26, 28.
[25] Thomas (n 13) 17.
[26] See Kong (n 18) 3–4.

the global economy, the Chinese government then took another, more significant, step by joining the WTO, which served as a new catalyst for China's improvement of its IPR policies in the context of the multilateral trading system.

B. Post-WTO Practices

On 10 November 2001, the WTO officially announced China's accession.[27] China in its Accession Protocol committed to implementing the WTO agreements 'through revising its existing domestic laws and enacting new ones in full compliance with the WTO Agreements'.[28] As TRIPs is one of the WTO-covered agreements, China's commitment implied significant transformations of basic IP laws, regulations and judicial interpretations.[29] As noted above, TRIPs created a baseline for IPR protection, which consists of general principles like national treatment, as well as substantive obligations, such as the criteria under which IPRs are conferred, the coverage of those rights, and the exceptions to the rules. Previous studies on China's WTO entry have indicated that China had fulfilled less than half of the TRIPs obligations.[30] The remaining problems in complying with TRIPs included, for instance, removing discrimination in enforcement procedure, granting well-known marks for foreigners, and introducing regulations regarding injunctions.[31]

Given the volume of arguably unmet requirements, China's compliance with the WTO agreements merits close examination. To capture the benefits of the commitments undertaken by WTO Members, the WTO has set up review mechanisms for monitoring Members' status in implementing the WTO agreements. In terms of TRIPs, there are currently three prominent forums: first, TRM, a special system established as an annual review tailored for China's IPR system surveillance; second, TPRM, a peer review mechanism scrutinizing Members' trade policies and practices; and third, DSM, a forum served to recognize and deter non-compliance by the WTO Members. By observing China's interactions vis-à-vis other WTO Members in these three venues, the following discussion assesses the evolving Chinese IPR regime.

[27] When China became a member of the WTO in 2001, the Protocol of Accession was negotiated to a substantial degree of specificity, containing in particular obligations relating to the rule of law. See *Accession of the People's Republic of China* (23 November 2001) WT/L/432.

[28] See Report of the Working Party on the Accession of China (1 October 2001) WT/ACC/CHN49, paras 68, 70.

[29] For an overview of the process to enact or amend China's IP laws, see Li (n 24) 30–34; T Cottier, 'Emerging Doctrines of Good Governance: The Impact of the WTO and China's Accession' in FM Abbott (ed), *China in the World Trading System: Defining the Principles of Engagement* (Springer Publishing, 1998) 119, 119–25.

[30] See KE Maskus, *Intellectual Property Rights in the WTO Accession Package: Assessing China's Reforms* (2002).

[31] Ibid.

i. TRM

Given the concerns of the WTO Members, China's Accession Protocol set up the TRM to ensure China's compliance with the WTO obligations.[32] Annual reviews conducted under the TRIPs Council's procedures document China's IP practices for eight consecutive years, from 2002 to 2009. On top of that, the General Council also undertook a final review of China's compliance with the WTO commitments in 2011.[33] Generally, one can observe China's post-WTO IPR protection by dividing the relevant practices into two phases: for the first five years of China's WTO membership, the reviews centred on the scheduled phase-in of key commitments under the Accession Protocol. From 2007 to 2011, the focus of the reviews then shifted to China's compliance with its full range of WTO obligations.

a. Phase-in Period (2001–2006)

During the phase-in period – the first five years after its WTO accession – China diligently fulfilled the WTO commitments, initiating across-the-board amendment of laws and regulations to protect IPRs. In this context, the amended Patent Law laid down the criteria for granting compulsory licences and introduced judicial review for administrative decisions on patents, utility models and design;[34] the revised Copyright Law extended the coverage of copyrighted works and provided the amount of remuneration;[35] and the Trademark Law was revised to expand the scope of eligible subject matter of trademarks, and spelled out the protection of geographical indications and well-known trademarks.[36] Additionally, judicial interpretations set out rules for judicial injunctions before lawsuits.[37] These active reforms not only deepened China's integration into the multilateral trading system, but strengthened its economic reforms.

Notwithstanding such reforms, China's IP practices were far from mature in the eyes of many. There were various concerns raised by developed countries, notably the US, EU and Japan, during this period, which included China's high level of infringement, ineffective criminal prosecutions, local protectionism, institutional deficiencies and non-transparent administration.[38] China's initial response to

[32] See *Accession of the People's Republic of China* (n 27), art 18.

[33] Ibid art 18.4 ('The review … will take place after accession in each year for eight years. Thereafter there will be a final review in year 10 or at an earlier date decided by the General Council').

[34] TRIPs Council, Minutes of Meeting (8 November 2002) IP/C/M/37/Add.1, para 20 ('IP/C/M/37/Add.1').

[35] Ibid.

[36] Ibid.

[37] TRIPs Council, Transitional Review under Section 18 of the Protocol on the Accession of the People's Republic of China (9 December 2004) IP/C/34, para 69 ('IP/C/34').

[38] See eg TRIPs Council, Transitional Review under Section 18 of the Protocol on the Accession of the People's Republic of China (21 November 2005) IP/C/39, para 55 ('IP/C/39'); Ibid para 83; TRIPs Council, Transitional Review Under Section 18 of the Protocol on the Accession of the People's Republic of China (21 November 2006) IP/C/43, para 63 ('IP/C/43'); IP/C/M/37/Add.1 (n 34) para 38.

these challenges, as shown by the way it addressed the follow-up questions at the TRM, implicitly suggested that excessive burdens on China were unacceptable.[39] Instead of addressing these concerns under the TRM, China revealed its reluctance and limited participation, noting that it would rather answer these problems through channels other than the TRM, such as the WTO enquiry point or bilateral channels.[40]

b. Post-phase-in Period (2007–2011)

At the end of the phase-in period, the WTO Members turned to focus on China's compliance with its full range of WTO obligations. While China's IP laws on the books had undergone sweeping amendments to meet international standards, its lack of skills to enforce laws had led to a series of criticisms. For example, the US, EU and Japan remained troubled by rampant infringement,[41] online piracy,[42] and IP theft[43] owing to the feeble deterrent effect of IP enforcement. For the EU, access to China's enforcement system was complicated and costly due to the legalization requirements for litigation and the high bar for criminal prosecution.[44] Likewise, the US remained concerned about local protectionism and non-transparency of the IP practices.[45] Certain issues raised by Members had not been addressed by China, who maintained that every issue unanswered should be considered out of the TRM, refusing to merit specific extension or offer further information.[46] Such resistance resulted in frictions between China and Members – some of which were elevated into trade disputes before the DSM.[47]

While certain trade disputes on IPR-related matters emerged, other Members also expressed their frustration about China's IP practices. WTO Members and

[39] See IP/C/M/37/Add.1 (n 34) para 94.

[40] Ibid paras 85, 90.

[41] TRIPs Council, Transitional Review Under Section 18 of the Protocol on the Accession of the People's Republic of China (7 December 2007) IP/C/47, paras 13, 19, 205 ('IP/C/47'); TRIPs Council, Transitional Review Under Section 18 of the Protocol on the Accession of the People's Republic of China (18 November 2008) IP/C/50, paras 4, 6, 14 ('IP/C/50'); TRIPs Council, Transitional Review Under Section 18 of the Protocol on the Accession of the People's Republic of China (11 December 2009) IP/C/55, paras 2, 8, 11 ('IP/C/55'); TRIPs Council, Transitional Review Under Section 18 of the Protocol on the Accession of the People's Republic of China (17 November 2011) IP/C/60, para 2 ('IP/C/60').

[42] IP/C/47 (n 41) para 13; IP/C/50 (n 41) para 9; IP/C/60 (n 41) paras 10, 12, 21.

[43] IP/C/60 (n 41) paras 12, 16.

[44] IP/C/47 (n 41) para 20; IP/C/50 (n 41) para 7; IP/C/55 (n 41) para 2; ibid para 22.

[45] IP/C/47 (n 41) para 11; IP/C/50 (n 41) para 3; IP/C/55 (n 41) para 7; IP/C/60 (n 41) para 17.

[46] IP/C/47 (n 41) para 76; IP/C/50 (n 41) para 23.

[47] For example, the IP dispute complaint by the US in 2007 (*China – Measures Affecting the Protection and Enforcement of Intellectual Property Rights*, Panel Report (26 January 2009) WT/DS362/R, the IP dispute between the European Communities and China in 2008, *China – Measures Affecting Financial Information Services and Foreign Financial Information Suppliers*, Panel Report (3 May 2008) WT/DS372/1, the IP complaint filed by the US in 2018 (*China – Certain Measures Concerning the Protection of Intellectual Property Rights*, Panel Report (26 March 2018) WT/DS542/1, and, as of September 2018, the latest dispute filed by the EU (*China – Certain Measures on the Transfer of Technology*, Panel Report (6 June 2018) WT/DS549/1.

China fell out over a range of substantive and procedural matters.[48] For many, major problems embedded in China's IPR protection framework included unacceptable levels of IP infringement, technology transfer requirement of discriminatory nature, and a complicated and expensive IPR regime.[49] In some contexts, over time, China has been criticized for the way in which it managed other Members' questions. In some cases, China denied these criticisms altogether by questioning the statistics relied upon by some of the Members.[50] On other occasions, China argued that certain challenges – such as those on internet piracy – in fact fell outside the scope of the TRM.[51] As part of its defence strategy, China also invited Members from the developed world to reflect upon its IP laws from a historical perspective, appreciate what it had done in meeting WTO obligations, and support its IPR regime.[52] Not until the last TRM meeting in 2011 did China respond to questions in more detail.[53] In short, these reviews revealed that China had been resisting pressure from Members to tackle problems at the TRM. To keep track of China's IP practices around and after TRM reviews, it will be necessary to turn to the reviews under the second forum – the TPRM.

ii. TPRM

The TPRM is a standing mechanism that enables regular collective evaluation of the full range of Members' trade policies and practices.[54] China, as one of the four Members with the greatest market shares, is reviewed every two years at present.[55] From 2006 to 2016, the TPRM has undertaken six reviews of China to assess its performance on IPR issues.

At the time of the first TPRM review, in 2006, five years had elapsed since China's WTO accession. According to the first review report, the Chinese government had taken remarkable steps to update its regime on IPR protection, which included amendments to basic IP laws and establishment of an extensive administrative framework. Key legislative reforms involved judicial review regarding design and utility models under the Patent Law.[56] There were also efforts towards

[48] IP/C/47 (n 41) paras 2–7.

[49] Ibid paras 13, 19, 20; IP/C/50 (n 41) paras 6, 7, 14; IP/C/55 (n 41) paras 8, 11, 44; IP/C/60 (n 41) paras 2, 3, 4, 12, 21, 22, 26, 30.

[50] IP/C/50 (n 41) para 21; IP/C/55 (n 41) paras 12, 14.

[51] IP/C/47 (n 41) paras 21, 72; IP/C/50 (n 41) para 23.

[52] IP/C/50 (n 41) para 41.

[53] See IP/C/60 (n 41) paras 36–54.

[54] See J Chaisse and M Matsushita, 'Maintaining the WTO's Supremacy in the International Trade Order: A Proposal to Refine and Revise the Role of the Trade Policy Review Mechanism' (2013) 16 *Journal of International Economic Law* 9, 9–36; X Zhang, 'Implementation of the WTO Agreements: Framework and Reform' (2003) 23 *Northwestern Journal of International Law and Business* 383, 406.

[55] Zhang (n 54) 407.

[56] TPRB, Trade Policy Review Report by the Secretariat: People's Republic of China (Revision) (26 June 2006) WT/TPR/S/161/Rev.1, p 147 ('WT/TPR/S/161/Rev.1').

combating patent, trademark and copyright infringements.[57] Despite such efforts, however, China's IPR system still received harsh criticism from its trading partners in the first TPRM review, in which they expressed concerns about numerous problems, including local protectionism, endemic corruption, light penalties, insufficient personnel training, and inadequate coordination among agencies.[58] As an illustration, the first review singled out that insufficient fines and penalties pursuant to prosecution measures posed a major problem for China's IPR regime.[59] Another challenge for China's IPR system was the local protection culture.[60] At that time, it was not uncommon for the government authorities to turn a blind eye to infringing activities and to give preference to local dealers, thus allowing the theft of IP in China to flourish.[61]

According to the second TPRM review in 2008, China continually channelled policies into IPR protection. In part driven by the US-Sino IP dispute before the DSM, the Chinese government actively enhanced international cooperation with others. It established working groups and information exchanging mechanisms with trading partners,[62] meanwhile revising parts of its IP laws.[63] The WIPO Copyright Treaty (WCT) and Performances and Phonograms Treaty (WPPT), ratified by China, came into force in 2007.[64] Despite the efforts on IPR protection, China's enforcement in this regard was still considered weak. Just as in the previous review, Members challenged the fines and penalties imposed to deter IP infringement – even though the threshold for criminal prosecution had been lowered.[65] Moreover, Members found it difficult to enforce China's administrative and judicial decisions; inadequate infrastructure and manpower were problematic, too.[66]

In 2008, China issued the National Intellectual Property Strategy, which underscored IP as an essential element for the nation's innovation capacity.[67] Based on this strategy, China embarked on several IPR policies to enhance its IP-intensive industries.[68] According to the third TPRM review in 2010, China turned to emphasize the protection of indigenous IP and increase its share of

[57] TPRB, Trade Policy Review Report by the People's Republic of China (17 March 2006) WT/TPR/G/161, paras 57–59 ('WT/TPR/G/161').

[58] WT/TPR/S/161/Rev.1 (n 56) para 303.

[59] Ibid paras 19, 272.

[60] Ibid paras 25, 303.

[61] Ibid para 313.

[62] TPRB, Trade Policy Review Report by the Secretariat: People's Republic of China (Revision) (12 August 2008) WT/TPR/S/199/Rev.1, para 218 ('WT/TPR/S/199/Rev.1').

[63] Ibid para 20; Trade Policy Review Report by the People's Republic of China (7 May 2008) WT/TPR/G/199, para 48 ('WT/TPR/G/199').

[64] WT/TPR/S/199/Rev.1 (n 62) para 218; WT/TPR/G/199 (n 63) para 53.

[65] WT/TPR/S/199/Rev.1 (n 62) para 20.

[66] Ibid para 242.

[67] TPRB, Trade Policy Review Report by the People's Republic of China (26 April 2010) WT/TPR/G/230, para 37 ('WT/TPR/G/230').

[68] Ibid.

IPR-intensive commodities.[69] Under the monitoring of other Members, China continued its efforts to reform its IPR system. On the Patent Law, for instance, China increased penalties against infringement and allowed compulsory licensing for patented pharmaceutical products.[70] To moderate Members' concerns, efforts were made to promote transparency in its IPR regime.[71] Still, various trading partners voiced concerns about corruption and ineffective enforcement of IPRs, especially at the regional and local levels, urging China to introduce greater transparency, customs control and criminal prosecution.[72]

According to the fourth TPRM review in 2012, it was apparent that China had adopted a myriad of measures to address IP infringement issues in response to pressure from Members. First, it complied with the panel report from the DSM and promulgated the amended Regulations on Customs Protection of Intellectual Property Rights.[73] Second, the SAIC began to build up an e-commerce monitoring system against online sales of infringing commodities.[74] In addition, a national campaign inaugurated in 2010 became a permanent cabinet-level enforcement structure, increasing accountability for IP infringement at the provincial level.[75] China further improved its Patent Law Implementation Regulations to include new provisions relating to national security clearance and genetic resources,[76] and coordinated the administrative enforcement with criminal justice.[77] Still, despite these improvements, China had, in the eyes of some, achieved only modest progress in relation to bringing transparency to its IPR regime.[78]

It bears noting that, while stepping up its IPR protection regime, China had been concerned about certain industries which have significant impact on its economic development. According to the fifth TPRM review, in 2014, it was notable that a number of regulations were amended, partially to shorten examination pendency for green technologies.[79] Likewise, to improve trademark application and examination, the third amendment of the Trademark Law introduced online

[69] Ibid. See also TPRB, Trade Policy Review Report by the Secretariat: People's Republic of China (Revision) (20 July 2012) WT/TPR/S/264/Rev.1, para 275 ('WT/TPR/S/264/Rev.1').

[70] TPRB, Trade Policy Review Report by the Secretariat: People's Republic of China (Revision) (5 July 2010) WT/TPR/S/230/Rev.1, para 158 ('WT/TPR/S/230/Rev.1'); WT/TPR/S/264/Rev.1 (n 69) para 291.

[71] WT/TPR/S/230/Rev.1 (n 70) para 5.

[72] Ibid para 9; WT/TPR/S/264/Rev.1 (n 69) para 321.

[73] WT/TPR/S/264/Rev.1 (n 69) paras 323–24.

[74] Ibid para 305.

[75] Ibid para 279; TPRB, Trade Policy Review Report by the People's Republic of China (8 May 2012) WT/TPR/G/264, paras 31–32 ('WT/TPR/G/264').

[76] WT/TPR/S/264/Rev.1 (n 69) para 282 (noting 'Patent rights … are protected by … its Implementation Regulations …, which in the last amendment adds provisions on national interest clearance (confidentiality examinations), and patents based on genetic resources').

[77] WT/TPR/G/264 (n 75) para 33.

[78] WT/TPR/S/264 (n 69) para 5. Based on the 2001 Corruption Perception Index, China ranked 75th among 183 countries, with a ranking of corruption level nearly equivalent to the one measured in 2009.

[79] TPRB, Trade Policy Review Report by the Secretariat: People's Republic of China (Revision) (7 October 2014) WT/TPR/S/300/Rev.1, para 3.211 ('WT/TPR/S/300/Rev.1').

electronic application;[80] similar fine-tuning amendments could also be found in related patent regulations that sought to optimize the patent filing procedures.[81] Moreover, Chinese citizens increasingly filed patent applications through the Patent Cooperation Treaty (PCT) system.[82] Another salient form of progress was China's forceful combat against infringing activities. For instance, administrative regulations of copyright enhanced fines for infringements,[83] and the Trademark Law raised the amount of compensation for trademark infringement. In addition, enforcement actions demanded the timely reporting of and active intervention against IP infringements, with a focus on copyright online infringement activities.[84] For the sake of transparency, China made its enforcement and judicial actions available to the public for scrutiny.[85]

As the sixth TPRM review, in 2016, stated, China had enhanced its IPR regime, both at the regulatory and administrative levels.[86] China launched several actions to advance its enforcement machinery, for example, China's Customs authorities hunted down thousands of batches of IP infringing products under its QingFeng Action, a program to curb counterfeit exporting activities.[87] The Supreme People's Court decided to establish national appellate courts for IP in the future, after establishing three intermediate IP courts in Beijing, Shanghai and Guangzhou.[88] Criticisms of China's IP practices seemed to dwindle in number, but there were nevertheless concerns about the existence of IP infringement, counterfeiting of commodities, and enforcement issues.[89] The next part will examine those conflicts that were raised and addressed through the formal DSM, which can shed some light on China's IP practices after its WTO accession.

iii. DSM

The DSM addresses the most egregious compliance issues in the WTO.[90] In a more specific sense, the DSM deals with disputes between Members by adjudicating cases under WTO agreements so as to enhance the enforcement of WTO rules.[91]

[80] Ibid para 3.223.

[81] Ibid para 3.211.

[82] Ibid para 3.201.

[83] Ibid para 3.233.

[84] Ibid paras 3.245, 3.251.

[85] TPRB, Trade Policy Review Report by the People's Republic of China (27 May 2014) WT/TPR/G/300, para 2.28 ('WT/TPR/G/300').

[86] TPRB, Trade Policy Review Report by the People's Republic of China (15 June 2016) WT/TPR/G/342, para 2.22 ('WT/TPR/G/342').

[87] Ibid para 2.23; TPRB, Trade Policy Review Report by the Secretariat: People's Republic of China (Revision) (12 October 2016) WT/TPR/S/342/Rev.1, para 3.254 ('WT/TPR/S/342/Rev.1').

[88] WT/TPR/S/342/Rev.1 (n 87) paras 3.250–51.

[89] Ibid para 3.243.

[90] R Bhala, 'Hegelian Reflections on Unilateral Action in the World Trading System' (1997) 15 *Berkeley Journal of International Law* 159, 164–65.

[91] Zhang (n 54) 394.

Since China's WTO accession in 2001, there have been four IP disputes to which China was a primary party. Among the four IP cases, only the first dispute has had a panel report issued by the WTO.[92] Therefore, the following will examine the first IP dispute in greater detail, then briefly outline the latest developments of subsequent disputes.

a. China's Copyright and Trademark Issues

On 10 April 2007, the US lodged its request for consultations regarding China's measures on IPR protection. Shortly thereafter, Japan, Canada, the European Community (EC) and Mexico joined the consultation process, which resolved one of the issues. With three issues remaining in dispute, a Panel was formed on 13 December 2007.[93] Within 14 months of examination, the Panel held that, among the three issues, the US had established inconsistency of China's Copyright Law and Customs measures with TRIPs, while failing to demonstrate that China's criminal thresholds were inconsistent with TRIPs.

(i) Article 4(1) of China's Copyright Law Denied Publication or Distribution of Works, if Such Works Were Prohibited by Laws

The first issue is related to copyright. Article 4(1) of China's Copyright Law denied publication or distribution of works if such works were prohibited by law.[94] According to the US, this Article failed to protect copyright in prohibited works, being inconsistent with Article 5(1) of Berne Convention as incorporated by Article 9.1 of TRIPs.[95] It further maintained that, if works were denied copyright protection under the Copyright Law, the enforcement provisions would not be available either.[96] Therefore, the US argued that China also failed to provide enforcement measures under the Copyright Law and thus contravened Article 41.1 of TRIPs.[97] In response, China countered that the denial of 'the publication of works' did not equal the denial of 'copyright protection';[98] rather, copyright protection was vested upon creation regardless of publication, and the legal portions of a prohibited work still enjoyed protection.[99] The Panel held that

[92] On the discussion of IP disputes between China and the US, see Thomas (n 13) 95–99; G Cheung, *Intellectual Property Rights in China: Politics of Piracy, Trade and Protection* (Routledge, 2009) 24, 24–38.

[93] *China – Measures Affecting the Protection and Enforcement of Intellectual Property Rights*, Panel Report (26 January 2009) WT/DS362/R, para 1.2.

[94] Ibid para 7.18.

[95] Ibid para 7.16.

[96] Ibid para 7.161.

[97] With regard to TRIPs, some jurisprudence exists over whether a WTO member's copyright scheme affords sufficient protection to another member's holders of IPRs on audiovisual content. Cf *US – Section 110(5) Copyright Act*, Panel Report (15 June 2000) WT/DS160/R.

[98] *China – Measures Affecting the Protection and Enforcement of Intellectual Property Rights* (n 93) paras 7.21, 7.32.

[99] Ibid para 7.17.

China's Copyright Law not only denied the protection of works prohibited by law but also caused uncertainty for works prohibited by law,[100] and that while China had the right to prohibit the publication or distribution of works, the denial of copyright protection and the absence of enforcement were not justified, and declared that the provision was inconsistent with Articles 9.1 and 41.1 of TRIPs.[101]

(ii) Measures on the Disposal of Infringing Goods Confiscated by the Customs Authorities

The crux of the second issue touched upon the remedy of copyright and trademark infringement. Here, three measures on the disposal of infringing goods confiscated by the Customs authorities were under attack.[102] These measures created a 'compulsory scheme', requiring the Customs authorities to first attempt to donate, auction or sell the infringing commodities before destroying them.[103] The US alleged that through the first three measures, the authorities were not authorized to order destruction of unlawful goods. The infringing goods would likely (re)enter channels of commerce, or cause harm to the right holder, thus violating TRIPs Article 59.[104] To rebut, China contended that donation and sale of infringing goods also constituted disposal of goods.[105] Such disposal would have the products outside the channels of commerce in order to avoid harm to the right holder.[106] The US responded by arguing that, where these disposal options preclude authority to destroy or dispose of all infringing goods, they are not in accordance with the spirit of Article 46 of TRIPs.[107]

The Panel was of the view that first, the obligation to grant authority to destroy commodities under Article 59 of TRIPs was not applicable to Customs measures to the extent they apply to exports, because this Article did not apply to goods destined for exportation;[108] second, regarding importation, the Panel clarified that even if the Customs measures granted authority to order donation, auction or sale of infringing goods, this did not interfere with the authority to order the destruction or disposal of infringing goods.[109] To this effect, the Chinese

[100] Ibid paras 7.28–192.
[101] Ibid.
[102] Ibid paras 7.193–96.
[103] Ibid para 7.197.
[104] Ibid.
[105] Ibid para 7.198.
[106] Ibid.
[107] Ibid para 7.199; The relevant parts of Art 46 and Art 59 provide as follows: Article 59 '[C]ompetent authorities shall have the authority to order the destruction or disposal of infringing goods in accordance with the principles set out in Article 46'; Article 46 states: 'the judicial authorities shall have the authority to order that goods that they have found to be infringing be … disposed of outside the channels of commerce in such a manner as to avoid any harm caused to the right holder, or … destroyed'. TRIPs Agreement (n 1) Arts 59 and 46.
[108] See *China – Measures Affecting the Protection and Enforcement of Intellectual Property Rights* (n 93) paras 7.212–31.
[109] See ibid paras 7.234–354.

Customs measures were in line with Article 59 of TRIPs, as it incorporated principles set out in the first sentence of Article 46.[110] Nevertheless, with respect to importation, the Panel found that the Customs measures were 'inconsistent with Article 59 of TRIPs, as it incorporates the principles set out in the *fourth* sentence of Article 46'[111] in that the disputed measures allowed infringing goods to be released into market after the simple removal of the trademark unlawfully affixed 'in more than just exceptional cases'.[112]

(iii) Thresholds for Criminal Procedures for IP Infringement

The final issue involved criminal punishment for infringement of copyright and trademark. China's Criminal Law and two Interpretations of the Supreme People's Court set out the thresholds for criminal procedures for IP infringement.[113] These criminal measures excluded certain copyright and trademark infringement from criminal liability, when the infringement fell below the thresholds amounts of revenue, illicit gain or infringing goods.[114] The US argued that China had failed to offer criminal procedures and penalties for cases of wilful trademark and copyright infringement that had met the TRIPs standard of 'commercial scale', and had therefore breached Articles 41.1 and 61 of TRIPs.[115] The core issue was whether the numerical threshold was too high to capture all counterfeiting cases with a commercial scale.[116] To substantiate its argument, the US offered evidence from sources such as press releases, notes and information[117] which were found by the Panel to be casual hearsay, informal remarks and anonymous conjecture, not derived from authoritative sources.[118] The Panel ruled that the US failed to demonstrate the disputed measures were inconsistent with China's obligation under the first sentence of Article 61 of TRIPs.[119] At the end of the battle, China's Copyright Law and the Customs measures were found to be inconsistent with TRIPs.[120]

b. The Cases in the Making: Unfair Technology Transfer Regime?

The second IP dispute against China was initiated by the EC in 2008. This dispute involved China's measures allegedly violating the provision on undisclosed

[110] See ibid para 7.355.
[111] See ibid para 7.394.
[112] See ibid paras 7.356–93.
[113] See ibid paras 7.396–98.
[114] See ibid paras 7.399–479.
[115] See ibid paras 7.480, 7.494.
[116] Ibid paras 7.494–681.
[117] Ibid paras 7.627, 7.628, 7.629, 7.631.
[118] See ibid.
[119] See ibid para 7.681.
[120] The Customs measures include the Regulations on Customs Protection of Intellectual Property Rights, the Measures for the Implementation of the Customs IPR Regulations, and Public Notice No 16/2007. Ibid paras 7.193–96.

information under TRIPs, while it was settled by the parties without forming a Panel.[121] A decade later, on 26 March 2018, the US once more requested WTO consultations with China to address five Chinese measures which the US alleged were an unfair technology transfer regime and constituted discriminatory licensing restrictions, thus violating TRIPs.[122] Within three months, the EU also requested consultations with China concerning measures pertaining to the transfer of foreign technology into China. At the time of writing, consultations are still in progress; if they fail to resolve the matters, a Panel may be established to adjudicate the cases.[123]

C. Summary

It is crucial to point out that, from the reform era to the post-WTO period, China has been gradually improving its IPR regime by considering its external relationships, global norms and, above all, its own need for long-term development. The TRM seems to have limited impact, as China has been reluctant to answer critical questions. Yet, what the Chinese government had done before the TRM triggered subsequent formal dispute resolutions resulted in certain modification

[121] See *China – Measures Affecting Financial Information Services and Foreign Financial Information Suppliers*, Request for Consultations by the European Communities (3 May 2008) WT/DS372/1.

[122] The measures at issue include the Foreign Trade Law of the People's Republic of China, Regulations of the People's Republic of China on the Administration of the Import and Export of Technologies, Law of the People's Republic of China on Chinese-Foreign Equity Joint Ventures, Regulations for the Implementation of the Law of the People's Republic of China on Chinese-Foreign Equity Joint Ventures, and Contract Law of the People's Republic of China. See *China – Certain Measures Concerning the Protection of Intellectual Property Rights*, Request for Consultations by the United States (26 March 2018) WT/DS542/1. For how WTO dispute settlement can respond to challenges presented by the rise of China, see M Wu, 'The 'China, Inc.' Challenge to Global Trade Governance' (2016) 57 *Harvard International Law Journal* 261.

[123] The measures at issue include the Foreign Trade Law of the People's Republic of China, Regulations of the People's Republic of China on the Administration of the Import and Export of Technologies, Measures for the Administration of Registration of Technology Import and Export Contracts of the People's Republic of China, Working Measures for Outbound Transfer of Intellectual Property Rights (For Trial Implementation), Law of the People's Republic of China on Chinese-Foreign Equity Joint Ventures, Regulations for the Implementation of the Law of the People's Republic of China on Chinese-Foreign Equity Joint Ventures, Contract Law of the People's Republic of China, Interpretation of the Supreme People's Court concerning Some Issues on Application of Law for the Trial of Cases on Disputes over Technology Contract, Anti-Unfair-Competition Law of the People's Republic of China, Anti-Monopoly Law, Regulations of 31 December 2010, for the Industry and Commerce Administrations on the Prohibition of Abuse of Dominant Market Position, Regulation on the Prohibition of Conduct Eliminating or Restricting Competition by Abusing Intellectual Property Rights, Notice of the State Council on Printing and Distributing the 'China Manufacturing 2025', Law of the People's Republic of China on Progress of Science and Technology, Opinions on Encouraging Technology Importing and Innovation and Promoting Changes in Pattern of Trade Growth, Several Opinions of 9 October 2014, of the State Council on Promotion of the Development of the Science and Technology Service Industry, Questions and Answers Around Regulations on Administration of Technology Import and Export of People's Republic of China. See *China – Certain Measures on the Transfer of Technology*, Request for Consultations by the European Union (6 June 2018) WT/DS549/1.

of China's IP practices, as the reviews at the TPRM indicated. Thus, it is generally agreed that China's participation in the WTO will benefit China and the rest of the world. For China, the benefits it reaps from accession are extensive, including dispelling the anxiety of trading partners, bringing forth the IPR regime reform, yielding a myriad of economic profits, and most importantly, fostering national innovation.[124] For the world, China's WTO accession means China will follow international standards for IP protection and its commitments to other international agreements in the future.[125] Notwithstanding China's efforts in bringing its IPR regime in line with TRIPs, developed countries have long been dissatisfied with the way in which the Chinese government enforces the IP laws. It remains to be seen, therefore, how the Chinese government will approach the IPR issues amid the trend of mega-regionalism.

III. Looking Forward: China's Approaches to IPR in Mega-Regionalism

A. IPR Clauses of China's Preferential Trade Agreements (PTAS)

With the emergence of the new wave of regional integration, China began to contemplate the possibility of signing FTAs in the mid-1990s. Driven by economic and political considerations, China has taken a cautious approach on its FTA strategy for economic cooperation.[126] China has signed 16 FTAs with trading partners across Asia (ASEAN, Georgia, Hong Kong, Macau, Maldives, Pakistan, Singapore and Korea), Europe (Iceland, Norway and Switzerland), America (Chile, Costa Rica and Peru), and Oceania (New Zealand and Australia).[127] Most of the FTAs in force include IPR provisions, and those FTAs with an IP chapter were concluded after 2008.

Roughly, the Chinese approach to managing IPR issues in the FTAs can be divided into four types. Category I reveals China's reluctance to include IPR

[124] Thomas (n 13) 17.

[125] See W Steinberg, 'Monitor with No Teeth: An Analysis of the WTO China Trade Review Mechanism' (2005) 6 *UC Davis Business Law Journal* 2.

[126] See H Gao, 'China's Strategy for Free Trade Agreements: Political Battle in the Name of Trade' in R Buckley et al (eds), *East Asian Economic Integration: Law, Trade and Finance* (Edward Elgar Publishing, 2011) (discussing China's FTA strategy by analysing its engagement in FTA negotiations). On China's FTA approach to regulatory coherence, see CF Lin and HW Liu, 'Regulatory Rationalisation Clauses in FTAs: A Complete Survey of the US, EU and China' (2018) 19 *Melbourne Journal of International Law* 8, 17–21.

[127] The China-Chile update FTA and the China-Maldives FTA have been respectively signed in November 2017 and December 2017, yet were not in force as of September 2018. China's FTA Agreements (n 15).

protection as part of the FTA package. This category refers to those FTAs without any IPR regulations. The FTAs with Hong Kong (2003) and Macau (2003), and China-Singapore FTA (2008) fall within this camp. China's Closer Economic and Partnership Arrangements (CEPAs) with Hong Kong and Macau in 2008 are basic agreements, each with a supplement to vaguely cover IPR protection and cooperation on branding.[128] Since Singapore is a member of the China-ASEAN FTAs, it is also subject to the China-ASEAN FTAs (2003) – at least recognizing the commitments under the WTO disciplines on IPRs.[129]

Type II refers to FTAs that in some ways address certain IPR issues but have no standalone IP chapter. FTAs of this type include China-ASEAN FTAs, China-Chile FTA (2005) and China-Pakistan FTA (2005).[130] In this category, the IPR clauses are rather vague in scope and depth, mainly reiterating TRIPs commitments or emphasizing the need for mutual cooperation. The China-Chile FTA, for instance, embodies four IPR provisions on geographical indications, border measures and the aims and means of IP cooperation.[131] Also, the China-Pakistan FTA has only two clauses on IPR-related border measures and investment.[132] As for Type III, it consists of FTAs with an IP chapter including general IPR provisions, such as the FTAs with New Zealand (2008), Iceland (2008), Peru (2009) and Costa Rica (2009). There are eight clauses in the IP chapter of the China-New Zealand FTA, covering principles on IP, the framework of cooperation, consultation and references to the protection of genetic resources, traditional knowledge and folklore, without detailed rules.[133] The China-Peru FTA is a more comprehensive version of the China-New Zealand FTA, consisting of five provisions with a special focus on the principles in the Convention on Biological Diversity.[134] The IP chapter of

[128] See eg Supplement III to the Mainland and Hong Kong Closer Economic Partnership Arrangement, Art II(1) (27 June 2006) (noting IPR protection is one of its tasks on cooperation); Supplement V to the Mainland and Macau Closer Economic Partnership Arrangement (29 July 2008) (requiring the protection of IPR and cooperation on brand promotion as additional tasks); PH Chen, 'Cross-Straits Economic Cooperation Framework Agreement, Cross-Strait Agreement on Intellectual Property Right Protection and Cooperation, and Implications of One-China' (2014) 36 *Houston Journal of International Law* 59, 87–88.

[129] See Agreement on Trade in Goods of the Framework Agreement on Comprehensive Economic Co-Operation Between the People's Republic of China and the Association of Southeast Asian Nations, Art 7 (4 November 2002) ('China-ASEAN FTA'); Chen (n 128) 85–86.

[130] But see K Trojanová, 'The Intellectual Property Rights in China's Trade Policy', Association for International Affairs, Research Paper 2/2015, 6 (noting the China-Pakistan FTA contains no IPR regulations).

[131] Free Trade Agreement Between the People's Republic of China and the Government of the Republic of Chile, Arts 10, 11, 106, 111 (18 November 2005) ('China-Chile FTA').

[132] Free Trade Agreement Between the Government of the People's Republic of China and the Government of the Islamic Republic of Pakistan, Arts 10, 46 (21 February 2009) ('China-Pakistan FTA').

[133] Free Trade Agreement Between the Government of the People's Republic of China and the Government of New Zealand, Arts 159–66 (7 April 2008) ('China-New Zealand FTA').

[134] Free Trade Agreement Between the Government of the People's Republic of China and the Government of the Republic of Peru, Arts 144–48 (27 April 2009) ('China-Peru FTA').

the China-Costa Rica FTA has nine provisions, stressing the Doha Declaration regarding public health issues.[135]

Type IV features a complex chapter covering substantive clauses on IPR protection. The trading partners under this approach are Switzerland (2013), Korea (2015), Australia (2015) and Georgia (2017). For instance, the IP chapter of the China-Switzerland FTA has 22 detailed clauses governing the availability, scope, use, acquisition and maintenance of IPRs.[136] The China-Korea FTA includes 31 provisions in its IP chapter, with 11 Articles addressing patent, copyright, trademark and plant variety protection, as well as generic resources, traditional knowledge and folklore.[137] The China-Australia FTA includes 24 clauses in its IP chapter, covering issues like basic public health, collective management of copyright, internet service provider liability, well-known trademarks and plant breeder rights.[138]

More specifically, on the level of IPR protection, Types I, II and III generally exclude TRIPs-plus arrangements. A handful of exceptions exist: some require contracting parties to comply with additional international IP conventions,[139] while others expand subject matters of IPR protection. As an illustration, the China-Pakistan FTA covers the protection of technical processes, trade-names and goodwill.[140] China's FTAs with New Zealand, Peru and Costa Rica even include generic resources, traditional knowledge and folklore.[141] By contrast, Type IV contains stronger IPR clauses that expand protectable subject matters and enhance enforcement mechanisms.[142] A telling example is the eligible subject matters of trademark, the scope of patentability for biotechnological inventions, and the protection of test data regarding pharmaceutical and agricultural chemical products in market approval procedures under the China-Switzerland FTA.[143] Moreover, the China-Switzerland FTA expands IP categories to include plant

[135] Free Trade Agreement Between the Government of the People's Republic of China and the Government of the Republic of Costa Rica, Arts 109–17 (8 April 2010) ('China-Costa Rica FTA').

[136] Free Trade Agreement Between the Government of the People's Republic of China and the Swiss Confederation, Arts 11.1–11.22 (6 July 2013) ('China-Switzerland FTA').

[137] Free Trade Agreement Between the Government of the People's Republic of China and the Republic of Korea, Arts 15.1–15.31 (1 June 2015) ('China-Korea FTA').

[138] Free Trade Agreement Between the Republic of Australia and the Government of the People's Republic of China, Arts 11.1–11.18 (17 June 2015) ('China-Australia FTA').

[139] Eg China-Peru FTA (n 134), Art 145, China-Costa Rica FTA (n 135) Art 111, Free Trade Agreement Between the Government of the People's Republic of China and the Government of Iceland, Art 64 (15 April 2013) ('China-Iceland FTA'); B Lindstrom, 'Scaling Back TRIPs-Plus: An Analysis of Intellectual Property Provisions in Trade Agreements and Implications for Asia and the Pacific' (2010) 42 *New York University Journal of International Law and Politics* 917, 927.

[140] See Chen (n 128); China-Pakistan FTA (n 132) Art 46.

[141] China-New Zealand FTA (n 133) Art 135, China-Peru FTA (n 134) Art 145, China-Costa Rica FTA (n 135) Art 111.

[142] For an overview of TRIPs-plus clauses in other FTAs, see Mercurio (n 4); See also H Wang, 'The Features of China's Recent FTA and Their Implications: An Anatomy of the China-Korea FTA' (2016) 11 *Asian Journal of WTO and International Health Law and Policy* 115.

[143] China-Switzerland FTA (n 136) Arts 11.7, 11.8, 11.11, 11.13.

varieties, genetic resources and traditional knowledge.[144] In terms of enforcement, it contains sophisticated requirements for border measures that cover both imported and exported goods.[145] Figure 4.1 illustrates the typology.

Figure 4.1 The Categorization of China's IPR Clauses in its FTAs

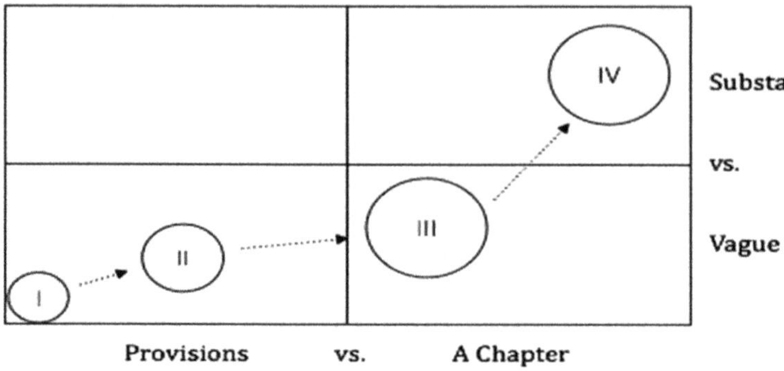

Despite the differences, there is nevertheless a common feature: much of the language of IPR clauses in China's FTAs generally reflects what has been done under TRIPs. Given its formidable economic and political power at both bilateral and regional levels, the way in which China approaches the IPR issues may spill over and have implications for the mega-regional negotiations.

B. New Developments in Mega-Regional Negotiations

i. RCEP

The objective of RCEP is to promote economic integration and cooperation among ASEAN Members and their FTA partners, including China.[146] Launched in November 2012, the RCEP members have undergone 23 rounds of negotiations, addressing issues ranging from services, investment, competition and dispute settlement, to IP. At the time of writing, none of the official negotiating texts has been released. Nevertheless, the latest leaked texts of the IP chapter may shed light on China's position in the RCEP context.[147] According to the leaked draft, the IP chapter may include 13 sections, and much of the language implies a TRIPs-Plus

[144] Ibid Arts 11.9, 11.10.
[145] Ibid Arts 11.16, 11.19, 11.21.
[146] On the examination of the IP norms the RCEP seeks to develop, see PK Yu, 'The RCEP and Trans-Pacific Intellectual Property Norms' (2017) 50 *Vanderbilt Journal of Transnational Law* 673.
[147] Regional Comprehensive Economic Partnership Intellectual Property Chapter (15 October 2015), https://www.keionline.org/wp-content/uploads/RCEP-IP-Chapter-15October2015.docx ('draft RCEP IP Chapter').

spirit. Key IPR provisions that have been opposed and proposed by China are highlighted as follows.

a. What China has Opposed

Generally, China reveals no interest in full-fledged, TRIPs-Plus duties. On the issue of international conventions, China has resisted a provision that would require ratification of IPR-related agreements to which China was not a party, including the Patent Law Treaty, the Rome Convention and the Hague Agreement.[148] Similarly, regarding specific IPRs, China has been against several clauses on TRIPs-Plus patent protection, such as the introduction of data exclusivity and patent term extension.[149] Other provisions opposed by China include the protection of new plant varieties, copyright collective management organizations and stronger protection for broadcast.[150] As for enforcement, China has rejected arrangements on criminal liability for aiding, abetting and importing infringing goods, as well as the provision on transparency of final judicial decisions and administrative rulings, which involve amendments to domestic laws and further burden the Chinese government.[151]

b. What China has Proposed

While a weak IPR regime seemed attractive, China's rapid economic and technological development called upon policymakers to reflect upon the demand for a higher level of protection. Thus, China did propose some that went beyond TRIPs. First, China proposed to include a section on the protection of genetic resources, traditional knowledge and folklore, as it domestically required the disclosure of generic resources.[152] Also, China called for amendments to the scope of the subject matter of trademark and to cover the procedural improvements concerning trademark application and registration, including the maintenance of 'a trademark classification system that is consistent with the Nice Agreement Concerning the International Classification of Goods and Services for the Purposes of the Registration of Marks.'[153] On copyright, the Chinese government urged inclusion

[148] Ibid Art 1.7.6.
[149] Ibid Arts 5.13, 5.16.
[150] Ibid Arts 5.19, 2.2, 2.6.
[151] Ibid Arts 9*quater*.2, 9*quater*.4, 9*quater*.5, 11 Alt 2.
[152] See ibid Art 7.1 (noting that 'The Parties also recognise the importance of providing disclosure of origin or sources of GRTK used in relevant IP applications'). See also Implementing Regulations of the Patent Law of the People's Republic of China (2010) Art 26 (noting 'Where the applicant seeks to apply for patent for such invention-creation completed on genetic resources, he or it shall so state in the request, [and] fill in prescribed forms issued by the Patent Administration Department under the State Council').
[153] On the subject matter of trademark protection, for example, China proposed the inclusion of 'three-dimensional shapes' among 'signs capable of distinguishing the goods and services of one

of a provision prohibiting government use of infringing computer software.[154] As for procedural matters, China joined others by recognizing the 'importance of providing efficient administration of intellectual property system'.[155] In short, although it remains to be seen how the RCEP IP chapter will be inked, the above proposals are somewhat in line with the overall trajectory of China's approach to IPR in FTAs discussed above: China has growing interest in some areas, but not in others. From time to time, however, it rejects those involving adverse effects or high implementation costs. Besides the RCEP, China's One-Belt-One-Road (OBOR) initiative is another forum that may have implications for the global IP norms setting by the Chinese government.

ii. One-belt-one-road (OBOR)

Proposed by the Chinese President Jin-ping Xi in 2013, the OBOR initiative is a development initiative that aims at fostering the economic integration of the continental and maritime regions, which include the continents of Asia, Europe and Africa, covering over 65 countries.[156] So far, the OBOR initiative has not yet launched any official trade agreements in general, and none specifically on IPRs. Presumably, however, since the OBOR policy aims to expand China's technology, industries and outbound investment, IPR protection would play a crucial role in realizing the objective of the OBOR initiative.[157]

In fact, the OBOR initiative has begun to influence China's IP landscape. In the aftermath of the OBOR initiative, China has taken a myriad of measures that emphasize IPR protection for the implementation of the OBOR. To enhance the awareness of IPR protection for technology industries, the SIPO presented a report on IPR protection along the OBOR route at a Conference.[158] In a high level

undertaking from those of other undertakings'. Ibid Art 3.1.3. On the registration and application of trademarks, the Chinese government called for an advanced procedural system to facilitate trademark registration and application. Ibid Art 3.5.

[154] Ibid Art 2.4.

[155] Ibid Art 13.1.

[156] J Chaisse and M Matsushita, 'China's 'Belt and Road' Initiative: Mapping the World's Normative and Strategic Implications' (2018) 52 *Journal of World Trade* 163, 163–85.

[157] The Vision and Actions on Jointly Building the Silk Road Economic Belt and 21st-Century Maritime Silk Road provides the aims of the OBOR policy to foster the development of technologies and industries such as ocean engineering technologies, marine biopharmacy, and environmental protection industries, and to welcome foreign firms to invest in China, as well as to expand mutual investment areas along the Belt and Road (eg expressing 'We should expand mutual investment areas … and promote cooperation in marine-product farming, deep-sea fishing, aquatic product processing, seawater desalination, marine biopharmacy, ocean engineering technology, environmental protection industries, marine tourism and other fields'). National Development and Reform Commission of the People's Republic of China (NDRC) et al, 'Vision and Actions on Jointly Building Silk Road Economic Belt and 21st-Century Maritime Silk Road' (2017) http://en.ndrc.gov.cn/newsrelease/201503/t20150330_669367.html.

[158] Yidai yilu ji lamei youguan guojia huo diqu zhishi chanquan huanjing baogao fabu hui zaijing zhaokai (一带一路暨拉美有关国家或地区知识产权环境报告发布会在京召开) [The Conference

'Belt and Road' Conference, China's IP agencies teamed up with the WIPO to urge closer collaboration in IPR-related services, harmonization of IP rules, interoperability of databases, and joint human resources training.[159] The 2017 Belt and Road Forum further underscored cooperation on innovation by encouraging exchanges on innovation and business start-up models regarding IPRs.[160] All of these may pave the way for regional innovation and development under the OBOR initiative, and push forward the Chinese IP reforms.

Specifically, China's IP reforms have rightfully echoed the OBOR initiative's proposition of interconnectivity and value creation.[161] Notably, China has signed the Hague Convention on Choice of Court Agreements, which provides an international framework for the mutual recognition and enforcement of court judgments, to expand its jurisdictions along the Belt and Road route.[162] China also assures foreign enterprises of a better business environment and stronger IPR protection.[163] According to a WIPO report on China's IPR enforcement, the Chinese government has been actively enhancing collaborative cross-agency, cross-regional and cross-border efforts, taking nationwide actions to combat IP infringement.[164] For instance, the amendment bill to Patent Law has increased penalties for infringement and introduced procedures to standardize nationwide enforcement.[165] On a judicial level, China has continued to establish specialized IP courts or chambers in major cities to reinforce the judiciary's ability to

on the IP Environment Regarding the OBOR Countries and Regions in Latin America Was Held in Beijing], SIPO (15 July 2016) http://www.sipo.gov.cn/jldzz/gsn/gsnzyhd/1040348.htm (English translation available).

[159] WIPO, 'High Level 'Belt and Road' Conference Urges Closer IP Collaboration for Economic Growth' (27 July 2016) http://www.wipo.int/about-wipo/en/offices/china/news/2016/news_0008.html.

[160] Innovation Circle Network, 'Belt and Road Forum 2017' (2017), http://www.innovationcircle.net/belt-and-road-forum-2017.5983496-97612.html.

[161] The Vision and Actions describes China's goals to promote intergovernmental cooperation in science and technology and international technology transfer by countries along the Belt and Road, which involve extensive reforms in IPR protection and enforcement ('We should promote intergovernmental cooperation … and reach new cooperation consensus. We should increase our cooperation in science and technology, establish joint labs (or research centers), international technology transfer centers … and work together to improve sci-tech innovation capability …') NDRC et al (n 157). See also JA Lee, 'The New Silk Road to Global IP Landscape' in L-C Wolff and C Xi (eds), *Legal Dimensions of China's Belt and Road Initiative* (Wolters Kluwer, 2016) 417, 418.

[162] As the time of writing, the Hague Convention on Choice of Court Agreements has been ratified by Singapore, Mexico and most EU Members. China and the US have signed but not yet ratified this Convention. HCCH, '37: Convention of 30 June 2005 on Choice of Court Agreements', https://www.hcch.net/en/instruments/conventions/status-table/?cid=98.

[163] See eg Xinhua, 'China Assures Foreign Firms of More Opening Up, Better IPR Protection', Belt and Road Portal (20 September 2018), https://eng.yidaiyilu.gov.cn/qwyw/rdxw/66851.htm.

[164] See Coordinating the Enforcement of Intellectual Property in China: Experiences from the National and Local Level, Advisory Committee on Enforcement (30 August 2017) WIPO/ACE/12/5 REV.2, 14–17.

[165] See Er ling yiqi nian zhongguo zhishi chanquan baohu zhuangkuang (二〇一七年中国知识产权保护状况) [The IPR Protection Report in China: The Year 2017], SIPO (25 April 2018) 2.

handle IP disputes.[166] Public awareness of IPRs has been increased, evidenced by nearly 226,000 IP litigation cases raised in China in 2017.[167] At present, there is an ongoing overhaul that will restructure the SIPO to improve the IP management regime.[168] Based on the WIPO's online statistics, Chinese citizens were the second largest source of international patent applications filed through the PCT system in 2017.[169] In China, Chinese citizens lodged nearly 1.25 million applications for inventions in 2017, bigger than the sum of applications filed by the combined citizens of the US, Japan and Germany.[170] It remains to be seen how the Chinese government will take advantage of the OBOR initiative in relation to the making of new IP norms in the future.

IV. Conclusion

China remains the globe's leading trader, and unceasingly strives for innovation-oriented growth. While being a latecomer in IP laws, the past few decades have witnessed a sea change in China's IPR regime while this country re-oriented towards the global economy. Since its WTO accession, China has amended its IPR regime to meet international standards. Yet, problems like ineffective enforcement, IP infringements and IP theft have attracted recurring criticism. With its robust economic growth and advancement in technology, China is embarking on new IP strategies towards innovation and a knowledge-based economy. As with the domestic IP reforms, China has also reinvented some of its FTAs in recent years. Based on the analysis of China's approaches to IPRs in FTAs at three levels – bilateral, regional and multilateral – it can be seen that China's policymakers have been increasingly concerned with IPRs to promote its long-term national interests. Currently, China actively enhances IPR protection and cooperation under the framework of OBOR at home and abroad. The OBOR initiative may serve as a vantage point to observe the way that China manages the IPR issues vis-à-vis its trading partners, and therefore, has implications for the future Asian trade negotiations and international IP rules. The recent Sino-US trade war, critiques of China's IPR system, and the complex political economy, of course, may well affect the world's future IP landscape.

[166] Gene Quinn, 'Navigating the Patent Landscape in China', IPWatchdog (23 May 2018), http://www.ipwatchdog.com/2018/05/23/navigating-patent-landscape-china/id=97611/.

[167] The IPR Protection Report in China: The Year 2017 (n 165) 6.

[168] The State Council of PRC, 'China to Restructure State Intellectual Property Office' (13 March 2018), http://english.gov.cn/state_council/ministries/2018/03/13/content_281476076446534.htm.

[169] WIPO, 'Who Led the Most PCT Patent Applications in 2017?' (2017), http://www.wipo.int/export/sites/www/ipstats/en/docs/infographic_pct_2017.pdf.

[170] SIPO, 'The Statistics Data on Patent Applications in China: The Year 2017' (2018) 1–2.

5

The RCEP Negotiations and Asian Intellectual Property Norm Setters

PETER K. YU*

I. Introduction

Since the early 2010s, the parallel negotiations on the Trans-Pacific Partnership (TPP) and the Regional Comprehensive Economic Partnership (RCEP) have garnered considerable attention from policymakers and commentators. While these two sets of mega-regional negotiations have sparked fears about the ratcheting up of Asian intellectual property standards, they have also raised questions about whether the resulting agreements would eventually create tensions, conflicts or rivalry that would complicate the intellectual property norm-setting environment in this fast-growing region.

In January 2017, the United States withdrew from the TPP following the inauguration of the Trump administration. A year later, the 11 remaining partners established a transition pact known as the Comprehensive and Progressive Agreement for Trans-Pacific Partnership (CPTPP). This quick and sudden turn of events not only had a significant impact on the RCEP negotiations, but also had serious ramifications for Asian intellectual property developments. Today, the RCEP remains the first and only mega-regional agreement that Asian countries have negotiated without the participation of either the European Union or the United States.

This chapter closely examines the RCEP negotiations and the Asian countries' recent efforts to set regional intellectual property norms. The chapter begins with a brief discussion of the evolution of the RCEP negotiations, noting the initial

* Professor of Law, Professor of Communication and Director, Center for Law and Intellectual Property, Texas A&M University. This chapter draws on research the author conducted for earlier articles in the *SMU Science and Technology Law Review* and the *Vanderbilt Journal of Transnational Law* and a book chapter published by Routledge.

rivalry between the TPP and the RCEP, the United States' withdrawal from the former, and the adoption of the CPTPP. The chapter then highlights the different intellectual property provisions in the draft RCEP intellectual property chapter, focusing on the four main branches of intellectual property law as well as the areas of intellectual property enforcement and pro-development measures. Although this chapter analyses the only publicly available text of that chapter, which was dated October 2015, it also takes into account the CPTPP partners' suspension of select TPP intellectual property provisions as well as the time elapsed since the preparation of the draft RCEP text. The chapter concludes by outlining the role of each Asian norm setter in the RCEP negotiations – namely, the Association of Southeast Asian Nations (ASEAN),[1] China, India, Japan and South Korea. Except for China, all of these negotiating parties have advanced draft negotiating texts for the development of the RCEP intellectual property chapter.

II. The Evolving RCEP Negotiations

The RCEP negotiations were launched in November 2012, more than two years after the beginning of the TPP negotiations. Although these two sets of mega-regional negotiations are often analysed together, the RCEP negotiations were established not solely as a reactive response or a defensive measure. Instead, the negotiations, which can be traced back to the turn of the millennium, built on prior efforts in various fora to facilitate economic integration and cooperation in the Asia-Pacific region. These fora include ASEAN+3 (ASEAN, China, Japan and South Korea), ASEAN+6 (ASEAN+3, Australia, India and New Zealand) and the Asia-Pacific Economic Cooperation (APEC) Forum.

Within ASEAN+3 and ASEAN+6, countries in the Asia-Pacific region have actively explored ways to facilitate greater regional economic integration and cooperation. In October 2001, the East Asian Vision Group, which was charged with 'develop[ing] a road map to guide future regional cooperation', recommended that the ASEAN+3 leaders should establish the East Asia Free Trade Area.[2] Although China strongly supported this proposal, Japan and other Asian countries had serious reservations about China's potential dominance in this pact.[3]

[1] The 10 current ASEAN members are Brunei Darussalam, Cambodia, Indonesia, Laos, Malaysia, Myanmar, the Philippines, Singapore, Thailand and Vietnam. They negotiate as a bloc in the RCEP negotiations.

[2] Mark Beeson, *Institutions of the Asia-Pacific: ASEAN, APEC and Beyond* (Routledge, 2009) 78; Shujiro Urata, 'Japan's FTA Strategy and a Free Trade Area of the Asia-Pacific' in Charles E Morrison and Eduardo Pedrosa (eds), *An APEC Trade Agenda? The Political Economy of a Free Trade Area of the Asia-Pacific* (Singapore Institute of Southeast Asian Studies, 2007) 106.

[3] Beeson (n 2) 88; Shintaro Hamanaka, 'Trans-Pacific Partnership versus Regional Comprehensive Economic Partnership: Control of Membership and Agenda Setting' (2014) *Asian Development Bank, Working Paper Series on Regional Economic Integration* No 146, 10; Meredith Kolsky Lewis, 'Achieving a Free Trade Area of the Asia-Pacific: Does the TPP Present the Most Attractive Path?' in CL Lim, Deborah Kay Elms and Patrick Low (eds), *The Trans-Pacific Partnership: A Quest for a*

In August 2006, Japan advanced an alternative proposal concerning the Comprehensive Economic Partnership in East Asia.[4] Covering not only the ASEAN+3 members but also the three remaining ASEAN+6 members (Australia, India and New Zealand), this partnership aimed to dilute China's influence in the regional pact while adding to the mix a major source of natural resources – namely, Australia.[5]

Around that time, APEC members also actively explored regional integration and cooperation efforts. In November 2006, APEC began studying the concept of a Free Trade Area of the Asia-Pacific (FTAAP).[6] Three years later, the APEC leaders pledged to create an agreement to realize this conceptual vision. As Fred Bergsten observed at that time, the proposed pact could achieve the following:

- catalyse a substantively successful [Doha Development Round of Trade Negotiations];
- offer an alternative 'Plan B' to restore the momentum of liberalization if Doha does falter badly;
- prevent a further, possibly explosive, proliferation of bilateral and sub-regional [preferential trade agreements] that create substantial new discrimination and discord within the Asia-Pacific region;
- avoid renewed risk of 'drawing a line down the middle of the Pacific' as East Asian, and perhaps Western Hemisphere, regional initiatives produce disintegration of the Asia-Pacific rather than the integration that APEC was created to foster;
- channel the China-U.S. economic conflict into a more constructive and less confrontational context that could defuse at least some of its attendant tension and risk; and
- revitalize APEC itself, which is now of enhanced importance because of the risks of Asia-Pacific and especially China-U.S. fissures.[7]

Since then, the APEC leaders have endorsed various declarations laying down the incremental steps needed to realize the FTAAP. These documents include the *Pathways to FTAAP*, which was adopted in November 2010, and the *Beijing Roadmap for APEC's Contribution to the Realization of the FTAAP*, which was released four years later.

In November 2011, ASEAN, with the support of both China and Japan, proposed merging the initiatives concerning the East Asia Free Trade Area and the Comprehensive Economic Partnership in East Asia to form the RCEP.[8] At the

Twenty-First Century Trade Agreement (CUP, 2012) 227; Meredith Kolsky Lewis, 'The Trans-Pacific Partnership: New Paradigm or Wolf in Sheep's Clothing?' (2011) 34 *Boston College International and Comparative Law Review* 27, 50–51.

[4] Lewis, 'Achieving a Free Trade Area' (n 3) 228; Urata (n 2) 106–07.

[5] Mark Beeson, *Regionalism and Globalization in East Asia: Politics, Security and Economic Development* (Palgrave Macmillan, 2007) 224; Urata (n 2) 111.

[6] Lewis, 'Achieving a Free Trade Area' (n 3) 223.

[7] C Fred Bergsten, 'A Free Trade Area of the Asia-Pacific in the Wake of the Faltering Doha Round: Trade Policy Alternatives for APEC' in Morrison and Pedrosa (n 2) 32–33.

[8] Hamanaka (n 3) 11; Ganeshan Wignaraja, 'The Regional Comprehensive Economic Partnership: An Initial Assessment' in Tang Guoqiang and Peter A Petri (eds), *New Directions in Asia-Pacific Economic Integration* (East-West Center, 2014) 94.

19th ASEAN Summit in Bali, Indonesia, the ASEAN leaders adopted the *Framework for Regional Comprehensive Economic Partnership*. Formal negotiations were finally launched at the 21st ASEAN Summit in Phnom Penh, Cambodia in November 2012. As the ASEAN+6 leaders announced in their *Joint Declaration on the Launch of Negotiations for the Regional Comprehensive Economic Partnership*, the RCEP negotiations were established to

- [a]chieve a modern, comprehensive, high-quality and mutually beneficial economic partnership agreement establishing an open trade and investment environment in the region to facilitate the expansion of regional trade and investment and contribute to global economic growth and development; [and]
- [b]oost economic growth and equitable economic development, advance economic cooperation and broaden and deepen integration in the region through the RCEP, which will build upon our existing economic linkages.

Although this joint declaration did not specifically mention the TPP, which purported to rival the RCEP, there is no denying that the development of this United States-led partnership had greatly accelerated the RCEP negotiations.[9] The establishment of the RCEP was particularly urgent when the TPP intentionally excluded two major ASEAN+6 economies, China and India.[10] Also excluded were other key ASEAN+6 members, such as Indonesia, the Philippines, South Korea and Thailand. While some of these countries had been invited to the TPP negotiations but declined to participate,[11] others had simply been ignored.

Undoubtedly, there were both economic and non-economic reasons for not inviting these countries to the TPP negotiations. Yet, the outcome was the same: while the excluded countries would still be able to join the TPP once it had been established, they would not be able to shape the standards involved and could only accept the final terms as agreed upon by the original negotiating parties. Such an outcome was highly unattractive, if not unacceptable, to large Asian economies such as China and India. It is therefore unsurprising that these countries turned their time, attention and energy towards the RCEP, an alternative regional pact featuring standards that would reflect their own preferences and experiences.[12]

[9] Du Ming, 'Explaining China's Tripartite Strategy toward the Trans-Pacific Partnership Agreement' (2015) 18 *Journal of International Economic Law* 407, 424; Hamanaka (n 3) 13; Michael Wesley, 'Who Calls the Tune? Asia Has to Dance to Duelling Trade Agendas' (*The Conversation*, 19 October 2014), https://theconversation.com/who-calls-the-tune-asia-has-to-dance-to-duelling-trade-agendas-32813, accessed 26 July 2018.

[10] Peter K Yu, 'TPP and Trans-Pacific Perplexities' (2014) 37 *Fordham International Law Journal* 1129, 1132–63.

[11] Alan Raybould, 'Thailand Says to Join Trans-Pacific Partnership Trade Talks' (Reuters, 18 November 2012), http://www.reuters.com/article/2012/11/18/us-asia-obama-trade-idUSBRE8AH06R20121118, accessed 26 July 2018; Yoo Choonsik, 'South Korea Moves Closer to Joining TPP Trade Talks' (Reuters, 29 November 2013), http://www.reuters.com/article/2013/11/29/us-korea-trade-tpp-idUSBRE9AS06M20131129, accessed 26 July 2018.

[12] Hamanaka (n 3) 12–15.

At the time of writing, ASEAN+6 members have already entered into 25 rounds of negotiations. Although no draft negotiating text has been officially released, the leaked texts of a number of chapters have been made available online by Knowledge Ecology International, a nongovernmental organization that has paid close attention to international intellectual property negotiations. Included in these leaked drafts were the 15 October 2015 version of the proposed RCEP intellectual property chapter, the draft negotiating texts from ASEAN, India, Japan and South Korea, as well as the proposed RCEP investment chapter.[13] Even though this investment chapter does not focus specifically on intellectual property issues, it establishes an investor-state dispute settlement mechanism that will have serious ramifications for regional intellectual property developments.[14]

Once the RCEP negotiations conclude, it is anticipated that the final text will cover a wide range of areas. Among those listed in the preamble of the *Guiding Principles and Objectives for Negotiating the Regional Comprehensive Economic Partnership* (*Guiding Principles*) are 'trade in goods, trade in services, investment, economic and technical cooperation, intellectual property, competition [and] dispute settlement'. Beyond these areas, working or sub-working groups have been established to address rules of origin; customs procedures and trade facilitation; legal and institutional issues; sanitary and phytosanitary measures; standards, technical regulations and conformity assessment procedures; electronic commerce; financial services; and telecommunications.

Given this large number of working and sub-working groups, it remains to be seen whether their establishment will result in the creation of standalone chapters in each specific area. Regardless of how the final agreement is structured, however, the RCEP Agreement is likely to be as ambitious as the TPP Agreement, which contains 30 different chapters. In light of this expansive and comprehensive coverage, questions have already emerged about the potential rivalry, compatibility and complementarity between these two mega-regional agreements.

At first glance, there does not seem to be any major rivalry between the TPP and RCEP intellectual property chapters. Although considerable differences

[13] Peter K Yu, 'The RCEP and Trans-Pacific Intellectual Property Norms' (2017) 50 *Vanderbilt Journal of Transnational Law* 673, 683–84, fn 41–46. The draft negotiating texts submitted by ASEAN and India are available at https://www.keionline.org/22781, accessed 28 July 2018. The text submitted by Japan is available at https://www.keionline.org/22695, accessed 28 July 2018. The text submitted by South Korea is available at https://www.keionline.org/22777, accessed 28 July 2018.

[14] For the present author's discussions of investor-state dispute settlement, see Peter K Yu, 'Conceptual and Institutional Improvements to Investor-State Dispute Settlement' in Christophe Geiger (ed), *Research Handbook on Intellectual Property and Investment Law* (Edward Elgar Publishing, 2019); Peter K Yu, 'Crossfertilizing ISDS with TRIPS' (2017) 49 *Loyola University Chicago Law Journal* 321; Peter K Yu, 'The Investment-Related Aspects of Intellectual Property Rights' (2017) 66 *American University Law Review* 829; Peter K Yu, 'Investor-State Dispute Settlement and the Trans-Pacific Partnership' in Christophe Geiger (ed), *Intellectual Property and the Judiciary* (Edward Elgar Publishing, 2018); Peter K Yu, 'The Pathways of Multinational Intellectual Property Dispute Settlement' in Christopher Heath and Anselm Kamperman Sanders (eds), *Intellectual Property and International Dispute Resolution* (Kluwer Law International, 2019).

exist, both agreements have called for higher standards for intellectual property protection and enforcement, going beyond what the TRIPS Agreement currently requires.[15] Moreover, as this chapter will discuss later, the United States' withdrawal from the TPP and the subsequent adoption of the CPTPP have led to the suspension of a significant number of TPP intellectual property provisions.[16] This suspension has greatly minimized the potential rivalry between the CPTPP and the RCEP.

III. The RCEP Intellectual Property Chapter

When the ASEAN leaders adopted the *Framework for Regional Comprehensive Economic Partnership* in November 2011, it was unclear – at least to outsiders – whether the agreement would include an intellectual property chapter.[17] The omission of such a chapter was plausible, considering the wide variation in intellectual property protection and enforcement among ASEAN+6 members.[18] Its inclusion, however, was equally logical, as such inclusion had, by then, become a standard feature of any new bilateral, regional or plurilateral trade agreement.

By the time the ASEAN leaders adopted the *Guiding Principles* in August 2012, it became clear that the RCEP Agreement would contain an intellectual property chapter, or at least some intellectual property provisions. Part V of those principles stated specifically that 'the text on intellectual property in the RCEP will aim to reduce [intellectual property]-related barriers to trade and investment by promoting economic integration and cooperation in the utilization, protection and enforcement of intellectual property rights'. A Working Group on Intellectual Property was eventually established at the third round of the RCEP negotiations in Kuala Lumpur in August 2015. Shortly afterwards, ASEAN, India, Japan and South Korea submitted their negotiating texts for the development of the proposed intellectual property chapter.

At the time of writing, no draft text of the RCEP intellectual property chapter had been officially released. Nevertheless, the October 2015 negotiating text had

[15] Yu (n 13) 685; Peter K Yu, 'TPP, RCEP, and the Crossvergence of Asian Intellectual Property Standards' in Peng Shin-yi, Liu Han-wei and Lin Ching-fu (eds), *Governing Science and Technology under the International Economic Order: Regulatory Divergence and Convergence in the Age of Megaregionals* (Edward Elgar Publishing, 2018) 292; Peter K Yu, 'TPP, RCEP and the Future of Copyright Normsetting in the Asia-Pacific' in Susan Corbett and Jessica C Lai (eds), *Making Copyright Work for the Asian Pacific? Juxtaposing Harmonisation with Flexibility* (ANU Press, 2018).

[16] Peter K Yu, 'Thinking about the Trans-Pacific Partnership (and a Mega-Regional Agreement on Life Support)' (2017) 20 *SMU Science and Technology Law Review* 97, 105.

[17] Yu (n 13) 720–31.

[18] Peter K Yu, 'Clusters and Links in Asian Intellectual Property Law and Policy' in Christoph Antons (ed), *Routledge Handbook of Asian Law* (Routledge, 2017) 148; Peter K Yu, 'Intellectual Property and Asian Values' (2012) 16 *Marquette Intellectual Property Law Review* 329, 339–70.

been leaked to the public via the Internet. Based on this draft text, the intellectual property chapter would likely include 13 sections: (1) general provisions and basic principles; (2) copyright and related rights; (3) trademarks; (4) geographical indications; (5) patents; (6) industrial designs; (7) genetic resources, traditional knowledge and folklore; (8) unfair competition; (9) enforcement of intellectual property rights; (10) cooperation and consultation; (11) transparency; (12) transitional period and transitional arrangements; and (13) procedural matters.

Although this chapter does not explore in detail each of these 13 sections, the following discussion will highlight the key provisions concerning the four main branches of intellectual property law, as well as those on intellectual property enforcement and pro-development measures. When analysing the draft RCEP intellectual property chapter, it is worth recalling that other draft RCEP chapters, such as those on investment and electronic commerce, could include provisions relevant to intellectual property rights. The TPP investment chapter, for example, became highly controversial after Philip Morris and Eli Lilly used the investor-state dispute settlement mechanism to address their intellectual property disputes with host states.[19]

A. Copyright

In the area of copyright and related rights, the draft RCEP intellectual property chapter includes the usual language found in free trade agreements (FTAs) requiring accession to the two Internet treaties administered by the World Intellectual Property Organization (WIPO) – the WIPO Copyright Treaty and the WIPO Performances and Phonograms Treaty (Article 1.7.6(g) and (h)). Going beyond the terms of the TPP Agreement, the draft RCEP chapter also requires accession to the Beijing Treaty on Audiovisual Performances and the International Convention for the Protection of Performers, Producers of Phonograms and Broadcasting Organizations (Rome Convention) (Article 1.7.6(h) and (i)).

In addition, the draft RCEP chapter includes the usual provisions on technological protection measures and electronic rights management information (Article 2.3, 2.3*bis* and 2.3*ter*). These provisions are nonetheless shorter and more flexible than those found in Articles 18.68 and 18.69 of the TPP Agreement. Targeting online streaming and other new means of digital communication, the draft RCEP chapter also includes provisions addressing the unauthorized communication, or the making available, of a copyright work to the public (Article 2.1.1 and 2.1.2).

[19] *Philip Morris Brands Sàrl v Oriental Republic of Uruguay*, ICSID Case No ARB/10/7, Award, 8 July 2016; *Philip Morris Asia Ltd v The Commonwealth of Australia*, PCA Case No 2012-12, Award on Jurisdiction and Admissibility, 17 December 2015; *Eli Lilly and Company v Government of Canada*, ICSID Case No UNCT/14/2, Final Award, 16 March 2017.

The push for such provisions is understandable, considering the increasing volume of copyright infringement litigation concerning works disseminated through streaming or other digital technologies.[20]

Similar to Article 18.80 of the TPP Agreement, the draft RCEP chapter includes a provision prohibiting government use of infringing computer software (Article 2.4). Unlike Article 18.63 of the TPP Agreement, however, the draft RCEP chapter does not extend the copyright term beyond the life of the author plus 50 years – the international minimum standard set by Article 7(1) of the Berne Convention for the Protection of Literary and Artistic Works. The draft RCEP chapter also does not include detailed provisions on Internet service providers, secondary liability for copyright infringement and the notice and takedown mechanism – provisions that can be found in Articles 18.81 and 18.82 of the TPP Agreement. Notwithstanding their omission, Internet-related provisions could easily have been negotiated as part of the yet-to-be-disclosed electronic commerce chapter.

To the disappointment of consumer advocates and civil society organizations, South Korea proposed language that would require countries to 'take effective measures to curtail repetitive infringement of copyright and related rights on the Internet or other digital network' (Article 9*quinquies*.3). In addition, Japan called for the disclosure of information concerning the accounts of allegedly infringing Internet subscribers (Article 9*quinquies*.4). It further advanced a footnote supporting 'a regime providing for limitations on the liability of, or on the remedies available against, online service providers while preserving the legitimate interests of [the] right holder' (Article 9*quinquies*.2, fn 43).

Even more alarming to Asian developing countries, the draft RCEP chapter offers stronger and more expansive protection to broadcasters than the TPP intellectual property chapter, covering such issues as the unauthorized retransmission of television signals over the Internet (Article 2.6). As Jeremy Malcolm commented:

> [B]ased on the current text proposals, [the] RCEP may actually impose more stringent protections for broadcasters than the TPP does. The TPP allows authors, performers and producers to control the broadcast of their work, but it does not bestow any independent powers over those works upon broadcasters. [The] RCEP, in contrast, could create such new powers; potentially providing broadcasters with a 50 year monopoly over the retransmission of broadcast signals, including retransmission of those signals over the Internet.[21]

[20] Among the leading cases in this area are *American Broadcasting Companies v Aereo Inc* (2014) 134 SCt 2498 before the United States Supreme Court; Case C-275/15, *ITV Broadcasting Ltd v TVCatchup Ltd (Main Proceedings)* EU:C:2017:144 before the Court of Justice of the European Union; and *Maneki TV* Saiko Saibansho (18 January 2011) 65 Minshū 121 before the Japanese Supreme Court.

[21] Jeremy Malcolm, 'RCEP: The Other Closed-Door Agreement to Compromise Users' Rights' (Electronic Frontier Foundation, 20 April 2016), https://www.eff.org/deeplinks/2016/04/rcep-other-closed-door-agreement-compromise-users-rights, accessed 27 July 2018.

B. Trademark

In the trademark area, the draft RCEP intellectual property chapter includes the usual FTA language requiring accession to the Protocol Relating to the Madrid Agreement Concerning the International Registration of Marks, the Singapore Treaty on the Law of Trademarks and the Trademark Law Treaty (Article 1.7.6(d) and (e)). The draft RCEP chapter also includes provisions broadening the subject matter of trademark protection, which extend coverage to sound and scent marks and signs in three-dimensional shapes (Article 3.1.2 and 3.1.3).

In addition, the draft RCEP chapter covers the procedural improvements relating to trademark application and registration, including the maintenance of 'a trademark classification system that is consistent with the Nice Agreement Concerning the International Classification of Goods and Services for the Purposes of the Registration of Marks' (Articles 3.3, 3.4, 3.5 and 3.5*bis*). The draft RCEP chapter, however, does not include extensive language on domain names, in particular names in country-code top-level domains – language that can be found in Article 18.28 of the TPP Agreement.

At the time when the leaked text was prepared, the RCEP negotiating parties remained in disagreement over the extent of protection for well-known trademarks, including protection through the recognition of the *WIPO Joint Recommendation Concerning Provisions on the Protection of Well-Known Marks* (Article 3.10.3). The parties also strongly disagreed on ways to address the relationship between trademarks and geographical indications, as well as the latter's eligibility for trademark protection (Articles 3.2, 3.9 and 4.1). Compared with those in Section E of the TPP Agreement, the geographical indications provisions in Section 4 of the draft RCEP chapter are significantly shorter.

C. Patent

In the patent area, the draft RCEP intellectual property chapter includes the usual FTA provisions concerning the 1991 Act of the International Convention for the Protection of New Varieties of Plants (UPOV), the Budapest Treaty on the International Recognition of the Deposit of Microorganisms for the Purposes of Patent Procedure, the Patent Cooperation Treaty (PCT) and the Patent Law Treaty (Article 1.7.6(a), (b), (j) and (k)). The draft RCEP chapter also includes the usual – and usually ineffective – language concerning the Doha Declaration on the TRIPS Agreement and Public Health and the Protocol Amending the TRIPS Agreement (Article 1.7.1, 1.7.2, 1.7.3 and 1.7.4).

Like those in Section F(A) of the TPP Agreement, the draft patent provisions cover both substantive rights and procedural issues, including those concerning patent application and examination and the maintenance of 'a patent classification system that is consistent with the Strasbourg Agreement Concerning the International Patent Classification' (Article 5.18). Although Japan initially called for the protection of new uses for, or new forms of, known substances, directly undercutting Section 3(d) of the Indian Patents (Amendment) Act of 2005, the draft RCEP chapter does not offer such protection. Nevertheless, that chapter reveals the continued disagreement between the negotiating parties over the appropriate standards concerning worldwide novelty for patents (Article 5.12), patent term restoration (or extension) as compensation for the time lost due to unreasonable regulatory delay (Article 5.13), patents for new plant varieties (Article 5.19) and the handling of patent-related information disclosed during the one-year grace period (Article 5.14).

D. Trade Secret

In the area of trade secrets and other undisclosed information, the draft RCEP intellectual property chapter includes the relevant provisions in two sections: Section 5 for patents and Section 8 for unfair competition. The patent section includes a TRIPS-plus provision requiring the introduction of a data exclusivity regime, which prevents the reliance on clinical trial data submitted for the marketing approval of pharmaceuticals (Article 5.16). However, no provision focuses specifically on biologic medicines, a highly contentious and controversial topic during the TPP negotiations.[22]

Compared with those in the patents section, the unfair competition section of the draft RCEP chapter does not seem to go significantly beyond the requirements of Article 39 of the TRIPS Agreement. Nevertheless, some civil society organizations lamented the RCEP negotiators' 'failure to explicitly address the need for exceptions to trade secret protection for whistleblowers, journalists, and other disclosures in the public interest … [a] missed opportunity'.[23]

E. Intellectual Property Enforcement

In the area of intellectual property enforcement, Section 9 of the draft RCEP intellectual property chapter includes the usual provisions concerning civil, criminal and administrative procedures and remedies, as well as provisional and border measures. Although a considerable portion of the draft language in the enforcement section merely reaffirms the existing rights and obligations under the TRIPS Agreement, the proposed language increases the obligations concerning the seizure and destruction of allegedly infringing goods, including the grant of authority

[22] Burcu Kilic and Courtney Pine, 'Decision Time on Biologics Exclusivity: Eight Years Is No Compromise' (*Intellectual Property Watch*, 27 July 2015), http://www.ip-watch.org/2015/07/27/decision-time-on-biologics-exclusivity-eight-years-is-no-compromise, accessed 27 July 2018.

[23] Malcolm (n 21).

to take ex officio action (Article 9*ter*.5) and to seize or destroy the materials or implements used to create infringing goods (Articles 9*bis*.5, 9*bis*.6, 9*bis*.10 and 9*quater*.6). The draft RCEP chapter also seeks to empower judicial authorities to determine damages for intellectual property infringement based on lost profits, the market price or the suggested retail price (Article 9*bis*.2(i)).

Like Article 18.77.4 of the TPP Agreement, the draft RCEP chapter calls for criminal procedures and penalties for unauthorized camcording in cinemas (Article 9*quinquies*.5). Unlike the TPP intellectual property chapter, however, the draft RCEP chapter does not have extensive provisions on criminal procedures and penalties. Nor do these provisions apply to trade secret infringement or the circumvention of technological protection measures. The draft provisions on border measures are also less detailed and less invasive (Article 9*ter*).

At the time of the leaked text, the RCEP negotiating parties strongly disagreed on the appropriate standards concerning criminal liability for aiding and abetting (Article 9*quater*.4), the award of attorneys' fees (Article 9*bis*.4) and obligations relating to intellectual property enforcement in the digital environment (Article 9*quinquies*). Facing strong opposition from its negotiating partners, South Korea remained the lone party calling for the provision of pre-established damages (Article 9*bis*.3).

F. Pro-development Measures

Apart from provisions strengthening the protection and enforcement of intellectual property rights, the draft RCEP intellectual property chapter includes provisions that facilitate the introduction of pro-development measures. In the area of copyright and related rights, the draft chapter includes language requiring accession to the Marrakesh Treaty to Facilitate Access to Published Works for Persons Who Are Blind, Visually Impaired or Otherwise Print Disabled (Article 1.7.6(i*bis*)). Some negotiating parties, most notably Australia, have also pushed for stronger language on copyright limitations and exceptions beyond the mere recitation of the three-step test, as laid out in Article 13 of the TRIPS Agreement and Article 10(1) of the WIPO Copyright Treaty. Article 2.5.3 of the draft RCEP chapter states that '[e]ach party shall endeavour to provide an appropriate balance in its copyright and related rights system by providing limitations and exceptions … for legitimate purposes including education, research, criticism, comment, news reporting, libraries and archives and facilitating access for persons with disability'. The purposes listed in this provision are very similar to those found in the preamble of the US fair use provision.[24]

In addition, the draft RCEP chapter includes a section on genetic resources, traditional knowledge and folklore (Section 7), which is more lengthy and detailed

[24] 17 USC § 107.

than Article 18.16 of the TPP Agreement. The language in the RCEP chapter can be traced back to the ten-paragraph proposal advanced by India in its draft negotiating text. Despite opposition from Australia, India, Japan, New Zealand and South Korea, China also proposed language that would require the disclosure of the source of origin of genetic resources (Article 7.1). The proposed language resembles Article 26 of the Chinese Patent Law, which requires those applying for patents to disclose the traditional knowledge and genetic resources used in their inventions.

At the time of the leaked text, the RCEP negotiators debated whether Section 12 should be about transitional periods and arrangements or about special and differential treatment. The provision of the latter is a key distinction between the RCEP and the TPP.[25] Principle 4 of the *Guiding Principles* specifically declares that '[t]aking into consideration the different levels of development of the participating countries, the RCEP will include appropriate forms of flexibility including provision for special and differential treatment, plus additional flexibility to the least-developed ASEAN Member States, consistent with the existing ASEAN+1 FTAs, as applicable'. The provision of such flexibility is especially attractive to the developing-country members of ASEAN+6, which have consistently benefited from special and differential treatment. Cases in point are the early harvest programs in the ASEAN-China Free Trade Area, which provided for the early opening of markets for select goods and services.[26]

Special and differential treatment is also necessitated by the existence of least developed countries in ASEAN, and by extension the RCEP.[27] Three of the four newest ASEAN members – Cambodia, Laos and Myanmar – fall within the category of least developed countries. In June 2013, a TRIPS Council decision extended the TRIPS transition period for least developed countries to 1 July 2021.[28] With respect to pharmaceuticals, the decision further delayed the introduction of patents and the protection for undisclosed test or other data until

[25] Shujiro Urata, 'A Stages Approach to Regional Economic Integration in Asia Pacific: The RCEP, TPP, and FTAAP' in Tang and Petri (n 8) 127.

[26] Henry Gao, 'The RTA Strategy of China: A Critical Visit' in Ross Buckley, Vai Io Lo and Laurence Boulle (eds), *Challenges to Multilateral Trade: The Impact of Bilateral, Preferential and Regional Agreements* (Kluwer Law International) 63; Wang Jiangyu, 'Association of Southeast Asian Nations–China Free Trade Agreement' in Simon Lester and Bryan Mercurio (eds), *Bilateral and Regional Trade Agreements: Case Studies* (CUP, 1st edn, 2009) 198; Peter K Yu, 'Sinic Trade Agreements' (2011) 44 *UC Davis Law Review* 953, 996–97; Peter K Yu, 'Sinic Trade Agreements and China's Global Intellectual Property Strategy' in Christoph Antons and Reto M Hilty (eds), *Intellectual Property and Free Trade Agreements in the Asia-Pacific Region* (Springer, 2015).

[27] Barry Desker, 'ASEAN Integration Remains an Illusion' (*East Asia Forum*, 2 April 2015), http://www.eastasiaforum.org/2015/04/02/asean-integration-remains-an-illusion, accessed 28 July 2018; Urata (n 25) 127.

[28] Council for Trade-Related Aspects of Intellectual Property, 'Extension of the Transition Period under Article 66.1 for Least Developed Country Members: Decision of the Council for TRIPS of 11 June 2013', IP/C/64, 11 June 2013, para 1.

1 January 2033.[29] Compared with the RCEP, the TPP does not include any least developed country, even though Article 18.83.4 offers transition periods to six of the 12 partners – namely, Brunei Darussalam, Malaysia, Mexico, New Zealand, Peru and Vietnam.

G. Summary

Like any other treaty in mid-negotiations, the draft RCEP intellectual property chapter includes a wide variety of bracketed texts. While some of the draft provisions are stronger than, or similar to, their TPP counterparts, other language is much weaker. The draft RCEP text also includes language that cannot be found in the TPP Agreement or other TRIPS-plus FTAs. Given that 'nothing is agreed until everything is agreed'[30] – a favourite aphorism of treaty negotiators and other government officials – it remains to be seen what the final RCEP intellectual property chapter will look like, or even whether the final agreement will include an intellectual property chapter.

When the RCEP negotiations conclude, it is possible that much of the bracketed language in the draft intellectual property chapter will have been retained or only slightly altered. If so, the finalized chapter will require the poorer ASEAN+6 members to offer higher levels of intellectual property protection and enforcement than what the TRIPS Agreement currently requires. Such higher levels of protection and enforcement explain in large part why the draft RCEP intellectual property chapter has been a major concern among policymakers, commentators, activists, consumer advocates and civil society organizations, especially in regard to issues such as access to essential medicines and digital communication.[31]

IV. The CPTPP and the RCEP Negotiations

Although the draft RCEP intellectual property chapter has provided many important insights into the negotiation process and the positions taken by the divergent negotiating parties, any analysis of that draft will have to take into consideration

[29] Council for Trade-Related Aspects of Intellectual Property, 'Extension of the Transition Period under Article 66.1 of the TRIPS Agreement for Least Developed Country Members for Certain Obligations with Respect to Pharmaceutical Products', IP/C/73, 6 November 2015, para 1.

[30] Henrique C Moraes, 'Dealing with Forum Shopping: Some Lessons from the Negotiation on SECURE at the World Customs Organization' in Li Xuan and Carlos Correa (eds), *Intellectual Property Enforcement: International Perspectives* (Edward Elgar Publishing, 2009) 176.

[31] '2015 Oct 15 Version: RCEP IP Chapter' (Knowledge Ecology International, 19 April 2016), https://www.keionline.org/23060, accessed 27 July 2018; Malcolm (n 21); 'New Threat against Affordable Medicines in Trade Negotiations with India and ASEAN' (Médecins Sans Frontières, 21 April 2016), https://msfindia.in/new-threat-against-affordable-medicines-trade-negotiations-india-and-asean, accessed 27 July 2018.

key developments that have occurred after October 2015. As far as the impact on the RCEP negotiations is concerned, the two most notable developments in the past three years have to be the United States' withdrawal from the TPP and the subsequent adoption of the CPTPP.[32]

In February 2016, the TPP Agreement was signed with great fanfare in Auckland, New Zealand. By the end of that year, Japan had become the first country to ratify the Agreement.[33] New Zealand also passed the requisite bill to provide such ratification.[34] Notwithstanding these supportive developments, the TPP encountered a major setback with the arrival of the US Trump administration. On 23 January 2017, President Donald Trump fulfilled his campaign promise by signing a memorandum directing the US Trade Representative to 'withdraw the United States as a signatory to the [TPP and] … from TPP negotiations'.[35]

Shortly after the United States' withdrawal, Australia, Japan, Singapore and New Zealand explored ways to resuscitate the TPP Agreement.[36] At a May 2017 APEC meeting in Hanoi, Vietnam, the 11 remaining TPP partners reaffirmed their commitment to establishing the mega-regional partnership and agreed to explore the development of a process to move the partnership forward without the United States' participation.[37] A few months later, these countries 'agreed on the core elements' of the CPTPP, opting to retain the majority of the original pact while suspending those provisions that had been pushed by US negotiators but were of no, or very limited, interest to the remaining TPP partners.[38]

On 23 January 2018, exactly a year after President Trump signed his presidential memorandum, the CPTPP negotiations concluded in Tokyo, Japan. With ratifications by Mexico, Japan, Singapore, New Zealand, Canada, Australia and Vietnam – more than the six parties needed to bring the agreement into force – the CPTPP has now entered into force. Notwithstanding these developments, the CPTPP is not the same as the mega-regional agreement negotiated by the 12 original TPP members. While the TPP was designed to cover '40% of global GDP [gross domestic product] and some 30% of worldwide trade in both

[32] Yu (n 16) 101–10.

[33] Kaori Kaneko and Yoshifumi Takemoto, 'Japan Ratifies TPP Trade Pact to Fly the Flag for Free Trade' (Reuters, 9 December 2016), https://www.reuters.com/article/us-japan-tpp-idUSKBN13Y0CU, accessed 27 July 2018.

[34] 'TPP Bill Signed by Parliament as US Signals Its End' (Radio New Zealand, 15 November 2016), http://www.radionz.co.nz/news/political/318141/tpp-bill-signed-by-parliament-as-us-signals-its-end, accessed 27 July 2018.

[35] 'Presidential Memorandum regarding Withdrawal of the United States from the Trans-Pacific Partnership Negotiations and Agreement' (2017) 82 *Federal Register* 8497.

[36] Bhavan Jaipragas, 'Can the Trans-Pacific Partnership Be Salvaged? Forget Trump – Malaysia, Australia, New Zealand Think So' (*South China Morning Post*, 24 January 2017), http://www.scmp.com/week-asia/geopolitics/article/2065021/trans-pacific-partnership-salvageable-forget-trump-malaysia, accessed 27 July 2018.

[37] Associated Press, 'Pacific Ministers Commit to Move Ahead with Pact without US' (*US News and World Report*, 21 May 2017), https://www.usnews.com/news/business/articles/2017-05-21/pacific-ministers-commit-to-move-ahead-with-pact-without-us, accessed 27 July 2018.

[38] 'Trans-Pacific Partnership Ministerial Statement', 11 November 2017, para 3.

goods and services',[39] the loss of the United States and 'nearly 62 percent of TPP GDP'[40] has caused the size of the mega-regional partnership to shrink by more than half.

Article 1 of the CPTPP incorporates by reference all 30 chapters of the TPP Agreement, including the intellectual property chapter. Yet Article 2 suspends the following intellectual property provisions:

(a) Article 18.8 (National Treatment): the last two sentences of footnote 4;
(b) Article 18.37 (Patentable Subject Matter)
 (i) paragraph 2: all of this paragraph;
 (ii) paragraph 4: the last sentence;
(c) Article 18.46 (Patent Term Adjustment for Unreasonable Granting Authority Delays): all of this Article including footnotes 36 through 39;
(d) Article 18.48 (Patent Term Adjustment for Unreasonable Curtailment): all of this Article including footnotes 45 through 48;
(e) Article 18.50 (Protection of Undisclosed Test or Other Data): all of this Article including footnotes 50 through 57;
(f) Article 18.51 (Biologics): all of this Article including footnotes 58 through 60;
(g) Article 18.63 (Term of Protection for Copyright and Related Rights): all of this Article including footnotes 74 through 77;
(h) Article 18.68 (Technological Protection Measures (TPMs)): all of this Article including footnotes 82 through 95;
(i) Article 18.69 (Rights Management Information (RMI)): all of this Article including footnotes 96 through 99;
(j) Article 18.79 (Protection of Encrypted Program-Carrying Satellite and Cable Signals): all of this Article including footnotes 139 through 146;
(k) Article 18.82 (Legal Remedies and Safe Harbours): all of this Article including footnotes 149 through 159;
(l) Annex 18-E (Annex to Section J): all of this Annex;
(m) Annex 18-F (Annex to Section J): all of this Annex

At the time of writing, it is too early to predict how the adoption of the CPTPP will affect the RCEP negotiations, or even whether the CPTPP will ever enter into force. Nevertheless, if the CPTPP partners' suspension of the more controversial TPP intellectual property provisions is any guide, it will not be too far-fetched to assume that the RCEP negotiating parties, by now, may have already removed or modified those provisions that have identical or similar coverage as the suspended TPP provisions.

Although the United States has had no direct influence at the negotiation table, some of its demands at the TPP negotiations managed to enter into the RCEP

[39] David A Gantz, 'The TPP and RCEP: Mega-Trade Agreements for the Pacific Rim' (2016) 33 *Arizona Journal of International and Comparative Law* 57, 59.

[40] Ankit Panda, 'Here's What Needs to Happen in Order for the Trans-Pacific Partnership to Become Binding' (*The Diplomat*, 8 October 2015), http://thediplomat.com/2015/10/heres-what-needs-to-happen-in-order-for-the-trans-pacific-partnership-to-become-binding, accessed 27 July 2018.

negotiations. The inclusion of these demands is unsurprising, considering that the demands had been transformed into TPP standards and seven of the 16 RCEP negotiating parties had signed the TPP Agreement. Because of their overlapping memberships, these parties were understandably eager to negotiate the RCEP in a way that would allow them to join the pact without violating the commitments made under the TPP Agreement.

With the arrival of the CPTPP and the suspension of the more controversial TPP provisions, however, the negotiating positions of these overlapping parties may have changed. Thus, if we are to provide a more accurate prediction of the outcome of the RCEP negotiations, we will have to compare the draft RCEP intellectual property chapter with the portion of the TPP intellectual property chapter that has been incorporated by reference into the CPTPP. This comparison suggests that the RCEP negotiating parties may have already removed or scaled back those provisions covering the extension of copyright and patent terms, the protection for undisclosed test or other data that have been submitted for marketing approval of pharmaceutical products, and the support for technological protection measures and electronic rights management information.

Moreover, three years have already elapsed since the development of the October 2015 negotiating text, which was prepared shortly before the tenth negotiation round in Busan, South Korea. With more than 15 new rounds of negotiations, it is highly possible that the positions of the RCEP negotiating parties on some of the draft provisions have evolved – at times considerably. Even before the adoption of the CPTPP, some of these negotiating positions might have changed due to the negotiating parties' shifting internal preferences, the uncertainty surrounding the future of the TPP Agreement, and the United States' withdrawal from the TPP.

In sum, the negotiation of the TPP Agreement and its subsequent developments have had a considerable impact on the negotiation of the RCEP intellectual property chapter. Because the CPTPP partners have now adopted a much less ambitious – or, for some, much less intrusive – intellectual property chapter, it is likely that the RCEP negotiating parties will push to do the same. Although the standards in the final RCEP intellectual property chapter will still be more stringent than what the TRIPS Agreement currently requires, the impact of that chapter on Asian intellectual property norm-setting will be less far-reaching than it would have been had the TPP Agreement entered into force.

V. Asian Intellectual Property Norm Setters

Most scholarship on the RCEP negotiations has focused on the negotiating history and textual development of the RCEP intellectual property chapter as well as the impact of the United States' withdrawal from the TPP and the subsequent adoption of the CPTPP. What has been underanalysed, however, are the divergent positions taken by the RCEP negotiating parties. Indeed, if we are to better grasp the evolution and future development of the RCEP negotiations, we will have to develop a fuller understanding of the positions taken by these parties. The remainder of this chapter will therefore be devoted to examining the positions taken by the five Asian parties in the RCEP negotiations.[41] Except for China, all of these parties submitted draft negotiating texts for the development of the RCEP intellectual property chapter.

A. ASEAN

Although ASEAN provides an economic community of over 600 million people[42] – larger than that of the European Union – the association is generally not considered a major player in international or regional intellectual property negotiations. Nevertheless, the RCEP negotiations were built around the 10-member-strong ASEAN, and the association has bilateral agreements with all of the six other negotiating partners.[43] As the preamble of the *Guiding Principles* states explicitly, the RCEP negotiations 'will recognize ASEAN Centrality in the emerging regional economic architecture and the interests of ASEAN's FTA Partners in supporting and contributing to economic integration, equitable economic development and strengthening economic cooperation among the participating countries'.[44]

Thus, 'having signed an FTA with ASEAN is the precondition for participation in RCEP negotiations'.[45] Even after the negotiations conclude, accession will be extended only to ASEAN's FTA partners. As Principle 6 of the *Guiding Principles* further stipulates:

> Any ASEAN FTA Partner that did not participate in the RCEP negotiations at the outset would be allowed to join the negotiations, subject to terms and conditions that would be agreed with all other participating countries. The RCEP agreement will also have an open accession clause to enable the participation of any ASEAN FTA partner that did not participate in the RCEP negotiations and any other external economic partners after the completion of the RCEP negotiations.

The recognition of ASEAN centrality is interesting because ASEAN has a unique style of negotiation. Commonly referred to as the 'ASEAN Way', negotiations

[41] The diverse positions taken by Australia and New Zealand are equally important to a full understanding of the RCEP negotiations, but this section does not explore those positions, due in large part to this volume's focus on Asia and the length and scope of this chapter.

[42] 'ASEAN Economic Community', http://asean.org/asean-economic-community, accessed 27 July 2018.

[43] Hamanaka (n 3) 11.

[44] On the role of ASEAN in the RCEP negotiations, see Yoshifumi Fukunaga, 'ASEAN's Leadership in the Regional Comprehensive Economic Partnership' (2015) 2 *Asia and Pacific Policy Studies* 103; Peter A Petri and Michael G Plummer, *ASEAN Centrality and the ASEAN-US Economic Relationship* (East-West Center, 2014).

[45] Hamanaka (n 3) 11.

involving ASEAN members are conducted in 'a process of regional interactions and cooperation based on discreteness, informality, consensus building and non-confrontation styles which are often contrasted with the adversarial posturing, majority vote and other legalistic decision-making procedures in Western multilateral negotiations'.[46] While this harmonious approach to regional cooperation has facilitated diplomacy and enhanced security in Southeast Asia, it has also slowed down the negotiation process, resulting in what Mark Beeson has described as 'accommodating the slowest ship in the convoy'.[47]

Thus far, commentators have been sceptical of the ability of the RCEP negotiating parties to recognize, or maintain, ASEAN centrality. As Shintaro Hamanaka observed, 'ASEAN's centrality would not be assured inside [the] RCEP, where it could possibly be sidelined by larger and more powerful economies such as [China] and Japan'.[48] To be sure, there is always fear that such powerful economies would dominate the negotiating process. Nevertheless, we cannot overlook the important roles played by Singapore and a few highly populous, middle-income ASEAN members, especially in areas in which China and Japan have no, or very limited, interest in asserting their positions.

From the very beginning, Singapore has assumed leadership in the negotiations on the RCEP intellectual property chapter, serving crucially as the first chair of the Working Group on Intellectual Property. Its eagerness to lead in the intellectual property area is unsurprising. Singapore has not only entered into an FTA with the United States, but it is also one of the first Asian countries to have done so – with its agreement adopted eight years before the signing of the Korea–United States Free Trade Agreement (KORUS FTA) in February 2011. Because Singapore is a small, but highly urbanized, city-state that focuses primarily on foreign investment, high-tech exports, a knowledge-based economy and a reliance on service industries,[49] intellectual property rights have played an indispensable role in the country's economic development.

In addition to Singapore, ASEAN includes a few middle-income countries that have strong potential to shape Asian intellectual property developments. In a study on the 'middle intellectual property powers', the present author analysed 10 countries that are outside the Organisation for Economic Co-operation and Development (OECD) and that have a gross national income per capita of less than US$15,000 and some of the world's highest volumes of high-tech exports.[50]

[46] Amitav Acharya, *Constructing a Security Community in Southeast Asia: ASEAN and the Problem of Regional Order* (Routledge, 3rd edn, 2014) 63.

[47] Beeson (n 2) 32.

[48] Hamanaka (n 3) 14.

[49] Beeson (n 5) 165; David Llewellyn, *Invisible Gold in Asia: Creating Wealth through Intellectual Property* (Marshall Cavendish Business, 2010) 157; Ng-Loy Wee Loon, 'Singapore' in Paul Goldstein and Joseph Straus (eds), *Intellectual Property in Asia: Law, Economics, History and Politics* (Springer, 2009) 240.

[50] Peter K Yu, 'The Middle Intellectual Property Powers' in Randall Peerenboom and Tom Ginsburg (eds), *Law and Development in Middle-income Countries: Avoiding the Middle-income Trap* (CUP, 2014).

Among the ASEAN members included in this study were Indonesia, Malaysia, the Philippines and Thailand. The study further noted that another highly populous ASEAN member – Vietnam – could make a strong case for inclusion in this group.

This study resonates with the well-cited studies conducted by Goldman Sachs analysts. Following their pioneering work on the BRIC countries, Jim O'Neill and his associates conducted a study in 2005 on the so-called N-11 ('Next Eleven') countries. This 2005 study sought to determine which countries are likely to follow the trajectory of the BRIC countries (Brazil, Russia, India and China) to pose considerable challenge to major developed economies. Included among the N-11 countries were three ASEAN members: Indonesia, the Philippines and Vietnam.[51]

B. China

During the TPP negotiations, many policymakers and commentators considered China as 'the elephant in the room'.[52] If China could play such an important role despite being excluded from the negotiations, it could certainly play an even bigger role in the RCEP negotiations, in which it actively participated and continues to do so. Indeed, political science literature explained why China was eager to develop an alternative mega-regional partnership. As Hamanaka declared:

> [T]he formation of regional integration and cooperation frameworks can be best understood as a dominant state's attempt to create its own regional framework where it can exercise some exclusive influence .... For an economy that wants to increase its influence, establishing a regional group where it can be the most powerful state – dominating other members in terms of material capacity – is convenient. ... By assuming [such] leadership, an economy can set a favorable agenda and establish convenient rules. In addition, the most powerful state can increase influence through prestige and asymmetric economic interdependence with others.[53]

Interestingly, China did not arrive at the economic and intellectual property scenes until the early 2000s. Since its accession to the World Trade Organization (WTO) in December 2001, it has successfully established itself as a dominant Asian economic power. Today, it is not only the world's largest exporter and trading nation,[54] but also its largest, or second largest, economy, depending on metrics

[51] Jim O'Neill, Dominic Wilson, Roopa Purushothaman and Anna Stupnytska, 'How Solid Are the BRICs?' (2005) *Goldman Sachs Global Economics Paper* No 134, 7–8.

[52] Peter K Yu, 'Intellectual Property Negotiations, the BRICS Factor and the Changing North–South Debate' in Rostam J Neuwirth, Alexandr Svetlicinii and Denis De Castro Halis (eds), *The BRICS-Lawyers' Guide to Global Cooperation* (CUP, 2017) 162.

[53] Hamanaka (n 3) 1–2.

[54] C Fred Bergsten, Charles Freeman, Nicholas R Lardy, Derek J Mitchell, *China's Rise: Challenges and Opportunities* (Peterson Institute for International Economics, 2009) 9; Angela Monaghan, 'China

and methodology.[55] According to the 2018 Global Innovation Index, China currently ranks seventeenth among the world's most innovative countries.[56]

In the past decade, the country has also slowly emerged as one of the world's leading intellectual property powers. Based on the latest WIPO statistics, China stood behind only the United States in the number of PCT applications in 2018.[57] Included among the world's top 10 corporate PCT applicants were Huawei Technologies, ZTE Corporation and BOE Technology Group. For the same year, China ranked third in the number of international trademark applications under the Madrid Agreement Concerning the International Registration of Marks and its related protocol.[58]

Since 1994, the Chinese Patent Office, which later became the State Intellectual Property Office (SIPO) and now the National Intellectual Property Administration of China (CNIPA), has been recognized as an international searching authority for PCT purposes. Beginning in 2007, SIPO has also met with the European Patent Office, the Japan Patent Office, the Korean Intellectual Property Office and the US Patent and Trademark Office to identify ways to streamline and harmonize the patent examination systems. These so-called 'IP5' discussions have consolidated SIPO's status as 'a player in the top tier of patent offices that will dominate the emerging system of global patent administration'.[59]

While piracy and counterfeiting problems remain, China has proactively shifted its economic focus from the imitation model to a new innovation model.[60] In June 2008, the State Council adopted the National Intellectual Property Strategy, which aimed to strengthen the country's indigenous innovative capacities. This strategy strongly indicates the Chinese leaders' growing understanding of the important role that intellectual property protection can play in driving a country's economy.[61]

Surpasses US as World's Largest Trading Nation' (*The Guardian*, 10 January 2014), https://www.theguardian.com/business/2014/jan/10/china-surpasses-us-world-largest-trading-nation, accessed 27 July 2018.

[55] Joseph E Stiglitz, 'The Chinese Century' (*Vanity Fair*, January 2015), https://www.vanityfair.com/news/2015/01/china-worlds-largest-economy, accessed 27 July 2018.

[56] Soumitra Dutta, Bruno Lanvin and Sacha Wunsch-Vincent (eds), *Global Innovation Index 2018: Energizing the World with Innovation* (Cornell University, INSEAD and World Intellectual Property Organization, 2018) xx.

[57] 'Who Filed the Most PCT Patent Applications in 2018?' (World Intellectual Property Organization, 19 March 2019), http://www.wipo.int/export/sites/www/ipstats/en/docs/infographic_pct_2018.pdf, accessed 22 May 2019.

[58] 'Who Filed the Most Madrid Trademark Applications in 2018?' (World Intellectual Property Organization, 19 March 2019) http://www.wipo.int/export/sites/www/ipstats/en/docs/infographic_madrid_2018.pdf, accessed 22 May 2019.

[59] Peter Drahos, *The Global Governance of Knowledge: Patent Offices and Their Clients* (CUP, 2010) 233.

[60] Li Yahong, *Imitation to Innovation in China: The Role of Patents in Biotechnology and Pharmaceutical Industries* (Edward Elgar Publishing, 2010); Peter K Yu, 'The Rise and Decline of the Intellectual Property Powers' (2012) 34 *Campbell Law Review* 525, 529–32.

[61] Peter K Yu, 'A Half-Century of Scholarship on the Chinese Intellectual Property System' (2018) 68 *American University Law Review* 1045, 1079–85; Peter K Yu, 'The TRIPS Enforcement Dispute' (2011) 89 *Nebraska Law Review* 1046, 1123.

Notwithstanding all of these developments in the intellectual property area, China has declined to advance a draft text for the negotiations on the RCEP intellectual property chapter. Out of all the provisions included in the leaked text, China proposed only the language in Article 7.1, which covers the disclosure of the source of origin of genetic resources. This language bears strong resemblance to Article 26 of the Chinese Patent Law. It is also consistent with the proposed Article 29*bis* of the TRIPS Agreement, which aims to create a similar disclosure obligation under the WTO rules.[62] That proposal has been cosponsored by three RCEP negotiating parties – namely, China, India and Thailand.

C. India

Like China, India has had very impressive economic and technological developments. Thus far, India has yet to compete effectively against China, due in large part to its poor infrastructure, bureaucratic red tape and failure to attract a substantial amount of foreign direct investment.[63] Nevertheless, India, which already has the world's second largest population, is catching up fast and possesses strengths that China may not have. These strengths include a younger workforce with a good command of English, higher population growth, superior capital efficiency, strong investment growth potential and a high level of entrepreneurship.[64] Some commentators have even predicted that India will overtake China economically in the second half of this century.[65]

In the intellectual property area, India has also garnered significant attention. The strength of its software industry speaks for itself.[66] Its generic pharmaceutical industry, which features such companies as Ranbaxy and Dr Reddy's Laboratories, is also considered one of the most important and sophisticated in the world.[67] Because India 'makes more than a fifth of the world's generic drugs'[68] and 85 per cent of generic HIV/AIDS antiretrovirals in sub-Saharan Africa,[69] commentators

[62] General Council, 'Doha Work Programme – The Outstanding Implementation Issue on the Relationship between the TRIPS Agreement and the Convention on Biological Diversity: Communication from Brazil, China, Colombia, Cuba, India, Pakistan, Peru, Thailand and Tanzania – Revision', WT/GC/W/564/Rev.2, 5 July 2006.

[63] 'The Rise of India' in Pete Engardio (ed), *CHINDIA: How China and India Are Revolutionizing Global Business* (McGraw-Hill, 2006) 49; 'Why India May Be Destined to Overtake China' in Engardio (ibid) 27.

[64] 'The Rise of India' (n 63); 'Why India May Be Destined to Overtake China' (n 63).

[65] 'The Rise of Chindia' in Engardio (n 63) 14; 'Why India May Be Destined to Overtake China' (n 63).

[66] Suma S Athreye, 'The Indian Software Industry' in Ashish Arora and Alfonso Gambardella (eds), *From Underdogs to Tigers: The Rise and Growth of the Software Industry in Brazil, China, India, Ireland, and Israel* (OUP, 2006).

[67] Sudip Chaudhuri, *The WTO and India's Pharmaceuticals Industry: Patent Protection, TRIPS, and Developing Countries* (OUP, 2005) 180–221.

[68] Kamal Nath, *India's Century* (McGraw-Hill, 2008) 110.

[69] Colleen Chien, 'HIV/AIDS Drugs for Sub-Saharan Africa: How Do Brand and Generic Supply Compare?' (2007) 2 *PLOS ONE* e278.

have noted the significant impact that a reduced supply of Indian generic drugs would have on access to essential medicines in the developing world.[70]

In December 2007, the Indian Patent Office was finally designated as an international searching authority for PCT purposes. Since October 2013, that Office has been operating as such an authority. In the future, India is likely to join China, Japan and South Korea as an Asian leader in PCT applications. Based on WIPO statistics, in 2018 China and India were 'the only two middle-income countries among the top 15 origins of PCT applications'.[71]

As if these accomplishments were not enough, India, along with Brazil, has for decades been the undisputed leader of the developing world in international intellectual property negotiations.[72] Before the arrival of the TRIPS Agreement, India demanded the revision of both the Berne Convention for the Protection of Literary and Artistic Works and the Paris Convention for the Protection of Industrial Property, the two leading international intellectual property conventions.[73] The goodwill and leadership that the country developed during this early period continue even today. Although it remains unclear whether 'India and Brazil are prepared to provide the general leadership on intellectual property issues that they once did',[74] India is likely to continue to feature prominently in regional and international intellectual property debates.[75]

As far as the RCEP negotiations are concerned, India's position is the most predictable. Many of the provisions in its draft negotiating text reaffirmed commitments already made in the TRIPS Agreement. This draft text also emphasized the various flexibilities that developing countries managed to retain through hard-fought battles at the TRIPS negotiations. Nevertheless, its 10-paragraph proposal on genetic resources, traditional knowledge and folklore stood out in the text. This important proposal eventually paved the way for a dedicated section in the draft RCEP intellectual property chapter (Section 7) that is more lengthy and detailed than its counterpart in the TPP Agreement (Article 18.16).

Moreover, both China and India hold special places in any international or regional negotiations involving Asia, including the RCEP negotiations. Indeed, their collective leverage and mutual significance have led Pete Engardio, the former Asia correspondent for *BusinessWeek*, to coin the term 'Chindia'.[76] In the

[70] Kenneth C Shadlen, 'Is AIDS Treatment Sustainable?' in Obijiofor Aginam, John Harrington and Peter K Yu (eds), *The Global Governance of HIV/AIDS: Intellectual Property and Access to Essential Medicines* (Edward Elgar Publishing, 2013) 36; Peter K Yu, 'Access to Medicines, BRICS Alliances, and Collective Action' (2008) 34 *American Journal of Law and Medicine* 345, 388–89.

[71] 'China Drives International Patent Applications to Record Heights; Demand Rising for Trademark and Industrial Design Protection' (World Intellectual Property Organization, 21 March 2018), http://www.wipo.int/pressroom/en/articles/2018/article_0002.html, accessed 27 July 2018.

[72] Yu, 'Access to Medicines' (n 70) 350–51.

[73] Ibid 351.

[74] Peter Drahos, 'Developing Countries and International Intellectual Property Standard-Setting' (2002) 5 *Journal of World Intellectual Property* 765, 765.

[75] Yu, 'Access to Medicines' (n 70) 351.

[76] Pete Engardio, 'Introduction' in Engardio (n 63).

past decade, Asian leaders, especially those in Southeast Asia, have increasingly linked the two countries together when discussing the region's future development. As Singapore's Senior Minister Goh Chok Tong declared:

> I like to think of new Asia as a mega jumbo jet that is being constructed. Northeast Asia, comprising China, Japan and South Korea, forms one wing with a powerful engine. India, the second wing, will also have a powerful engine. The southeast Asian countries form the fuselage. Even if we lack a powerful engine for growth among the 10 countries, we will be lifted by the two wings.[77]

D. Japan

Of all the Asian countries negotiating the RCEP, Japan has the strongest and most sophisticated economy. In Mark Beeson's view, this country is 'especially important as an exemplar of a highly successful *Asian* state'.[78] Although China overtook Japan to become the world's second largest economy on an aggregate basis in 2010, Japan still dominates China dramatically on a per capita basis. With a GDP per capita of US$38,430.29 in 2017, Japan is one of the world's richest countries.[79] By contrast, with a GDP per capita of only US$8,826.99, China is still classified as a middle-income country – and, until recently, only a lower middle-income country. Indeed, China's GDP per capita remains lower than that of Malaysia (US$9,951.54), not to mention Japan, Singapore, South Korea and the resource-rich Brunei Darussalam.

In the area of intellectual property protection, Japan has improved considerably in the past three decades. In the early 1980s, Japan was widely criticized for its limited intellectual property protection, in part to explain away the large US–Japan trade deficit.[80] By the time of the TRIPS negotiations, however, Japan had slowly assumed the role of a key trilateral partner with the United States and the then European Communities – thanks in no small part to the push by local and foreign intellectual property industries.[81]

As far as the RCEP negotiations are concerned, Japan is most comfortable championing the high TPP standards for intellectual property protection and enforcement. Commentators have also noted how Japan played the 'RCEP card' to

[77] 'Singapore is the Global City of Opportunity' (Singapore Ministry of Communications and Information, 15 March 2005), https://www.mci.gov.sg/pressroom/news-and-stories/pressroom/2005/3/singapore-is-the-global-city-of-opportunity?page=206, accessed 27 July 2018.

[78] Beeson (n 5) 106.

[79] 'GDP Per Capita (Current US$)', http://data.worldbank.org/indicator/NY.GDP.PCAP.CD, accessed 26 May 2019.

[80] Michael P Ryan, *Playing by the Rules: American Trade Power and Diplomacy in the Pacific* (Georgetown University Press, 1995) 16–17; Jayashree Watal, *Intellectual Property Rights in the WTO and Developing Countries* (Kluwer Law International, 2001) 24.

[81] Duncan Matthews, *Globalising Intellectual Property Rights: The TRIPS Agreement* (Routledge, 2002); Susan K Sell, *Private Power, Public Law: The Globalization of Intellectual Property Rights* (CUP, 2003) 96–120.

increase its leverage in the TPP negotiations.[82] Given Japan's strategic involvement in both the TPP and the RCEP, it is understandable why Japan and several other TPP partners worked tirelessly to resuscitate the former after the United States' withdrawal.

Indeed, many of the provisions in Japan's draft negotiating text parallel those found in the TPP Agreement and other TRIPS-plus FTAs. For instance, Article XX.C.2 of this text called for the protection of new uses for, or new forms of, known substances – similar to Article 18.37.2 of the TPP Agreement. This position, however, directly challenged India's position, as reflected in Section 3(d) of the Indian Patents (Amendment) Act of 2005. Likewise, Japan called for the disclosure of information concerning the Internet accounts of alleged infringers (Article 9*quinquies*.4) while advancing a footnote to address the limitations on online service provider liability (Article 9*quinquies*.2, fn 43). Both issues were covered more extensively in Section J of the TPP Agreement. Interestingly, the CPTPP partners have since suspended Article 18.82 of that agreement, which covers Internet-related 'legal remedies and safe harbours'.

E. South Korea

Although South Korea does not have the same economic or negotiating power as Japan, nor the size of China or India, South Korea joins Japan in supporting high standards for intellectual property protection and enforcement. South Korea's position is understandable. The country already has a highly successful home electronics industry that produces many innovative products. Today, it also has the world's fifth largest volume of PCT applications.[83] Among corporate applicants, Samsung Electronics and LG Electronics – both household names in the West – had the sixth and eighth largest volumes of PCT applications, respectively.

Moreover, the Korean Intellectual Property Office has been very active in the past decade. As one of the 'Asian trilaterals', this office regularly engages in policy dialogues with its counterparts in China and Japan.[84] As noted earlier, the office is also among the five leading patent offices that have participated in the 'IP5' discussions to identify ways to streamline and harmonize the patent examination systems.

In June 2007, South Korea signed the initial version of the KORUS FTA, which eventually came into effect in March 2012 following the conclusion of several new agreements. Included in this FTA is an extensive intellectual property chapter that seeks to align South Korea's intellectual property standards with those of the United States. The agreement also includes side confirmation letters, focusing on limitations on Internet service provider liability and online piracy prevention.

[82] Hamanaka (n 3) 12.
[83] World Intellectual Property Organization (n 57).
[84] Drahos (n 59) 233.

To a large extent, the KORUS FTA has coloured South Korea's position in the RCEP negotiations. For example, the country proposed language that would require signatories to take effective measures to curtail repetitive online copyright infringement (Article 9*quinquies*.3). This language parallels Article 18.30(b)(iv)(A) of the KORUS FTA, which conditions the eligibility for the limitations and exceptions concerning Internet service providers on the providers' 'adoption and reasonable implement[ation of] a policy that provides for termination in appropriate circumstances of the accounts of repeat infringers'.

At the time when the leaked text was prepared, South Korea was also the lone party calling for the provision of pre-established damages (Article 9*bis*.3), facing strong opposition from its negotiating partners. The proposal parallels Articles 18.10.6 and 18.10.13(b) of the KORUS FTA, which call for the provision of similar damages. Article 18.10.6 states explicitly that '[p]re-established damages shall be in an amount sufficient to constitute a deterrent to future infringements and to compensate fully the right holder for the harm caused by the infringement'.

Taken together, the TRIPS-plus positions taken by South Korea do not align well with the more moderate positions taken by China, India and some ASEAN members. It is therefore small wonder that Jeremy Malcolm lamented:

> [F]ar from setting up a positive alternative to the TPP, South Korea is channeling the [US Trade Representative] at its worst here – what on earth are they thinking? The answer may be that, having been pushed into accepting unfavorably strict copyright, patent, and trademark rules in the process of negotiating its 2012 free trade agreement with the United States, Korea considers that it would be at a disadvantage if other countries were not subject to the same restrictions.[85]

Indeed, by increasing the costs of Korean goods and services and thereby undercutting their global competitiveness, the KORUS FTA has provided South Korea with a strong perverse incentive to level the playing field by introducing similar cost-raising standards to other ASEAN+6 members through the RCEP.

VI. Conclusion

In the 1990s and the 2000s, most Asian countries were struggling with the difficult transition to the new trade and intellectual property standards imposed upon them through the negotiation of the TRIPS Agreement and, for some, through an arduous WTO accession process. Today, however, many of these countries have taken increasingly active roles in setting regional intellectual property norms. Gone are the days when they would accept without question those norms that have been established in the developed world.

[85] Jeremy Malcolm, 'Meet RCEP, a Trade Agreement in Asia That's Even Worse than TPP or ACTA' (Electronic Frontier Foundation, 4 June 2015), https://www.eff.org/deeplinks/2015/06/just-when-you-thought-no-trade-agreement-could-be-worse-tpp-meet-rcep, accessed 28 July 2018.

Interestingly, just as Asian countries have secured greater autonomy to determine for themselves what intellectual property norms to adopt, they have also begun to warm up to those intellectual property norms that have now been enshrined in the TRIPS Agreement. Although the perception of that agreement likely varies, depending on whether it is compared with those new TRIPS-plus bilateral, regional and plurilateral trade agreements, the Asian countries' willingness to accept higher intellectual property standards in the RCEP negotiations, or at least their ambivalence towards those standards, suggests that these countries have now started to recognize the alignment of the TRIPS norms with their self-interests.

As the economic and technological capabilities of Asian countries continue to rise, the intellectual property norm-setting picture will become even more complex. While one could still invoke the North–South divide to account for the difference between the positions taken by Asian countries and those taken by the more developed members of the international community, that divide does not fully explain the positions embraced by the former, especially the fast-growing, middle-income Asian countries. Instead, one needs to develop a deeper and more holistic understanding of the different positions taken by the major Asian intellectual property norm setters as well as the progress each of them has made in building an intellectual property system that is tailored to local needs, interests, conditions and priorities.

PART II

Investor-State Arbitration and Intellectual Property

6

Recalibrating the Balance in International Investment Agreements

TOMOKO ISHIKAWA*

I. Introduction

A. International Investment Agreements and Intellectual Property Rights Protection

International investment agreements (IIAs) and investment arbitration have proliferated in the last three decades. As of the end of 2018, there were over 3,300 IIAs, and the total number of known investor-to-state arbitration cases was 942.[1] Several mega-regional IIAs have been concluded or have been under negotiation in the last few years, in particular in the Asia-Pacific region.

At the same time, the IIA regime[2] faces ever-increasing criticism. The backlash against the IIA regime has led to withdrawal from the Convention on the Settlement of Investment Disputes between States and Nationals of Other States (ICSID Convention)[3] and termination and renegotiation of IIAs by several countries.[4] Equally importantly, many Asian countries, including India, Indonesia and Thailand, have expressed, in various forms, severe criticism of IIAs and

* Nagoya University. All online information last accessed 7 October 2018.

[1] United Nations Conference on Trade and Development (UNCTAD), World Investment Report 2019: Special Economic Zones, UNCTAD/WIR/2019, 99; UNCTAD, IIA Issues Note: Fact Sheet on Investor-State Dispute Settlement Cases in 2018, 1.

[2] Krasner defines the term 'regime' as 'implicit or explicit principles, norms, rules and decision-making procedures around which actor expectations converge in a given issue-area' (Stephen Krasner, 'Structural Causes and Regime Consequences: Regimes as Intervening Variables' in Stephen Krasner (ed), *International Regimes* (NY 1983) 1–22, 1). In accordance with this definition, this chapter defines the IIA regime as a system consisting of principles, norms, rules and decision-making procedures that cover the issues of: (a) substantive rights and obligations concerning the promotion and protection of foreign investment; and (b) the investor-to-state dispute settlement mechanism.

[3] They include Bolivia (denunciation effective November 2007), Ecuador (denunciation effective January 2010) and Venezuela (denunciation effective July 2012).

[4] In October 2018, the Netherlands adopted its new model bilateral investment treaty (BIT), which 'is intended to serve as the basis for the re-negotiation of the 79 BITs that are currently in place between the

investment arbitration.[5] According to the UNCTAD World Investment Report 2018, in 2017 '[i]nvestment treaty making has reached a turning point', because the number of effective treaty terminations outpaced the number of new IIA conclusions for the first time since 1983.[6] Concerns over investment arbitration have prompted a fundamental reform proposal of the investor-to-state dispute settlement mechanism.[7]

Under many IIAs, intellectual property rights (IPRs) qualify as 'investments',[8] and investment arbitration has been increasingly used to challenge the host state's regulatory measures which negatively affect IPRs. At the same time, several IPR-related investment arbitration cases involve the tension between the protection of IPRs and other public interests of the host state, in particular public health. In the *Philip Morris* cases,[9] the governmental restrictions on tobacco packaging were claimed to violate the relevant IIAs on the ground that such restrictions were an unlawful limitation of the right to use a protected trademark and thereby infringed the company's IPRs. In *Eli Lilly v Canada*,[10] a US pharmaceutical company claimed that Canadian Federal Court judgments that invalidated its pharmaceutical patents amounted to a violation of certain investment protection obligations under NAFTA. While none of these high-profile and highly controversial cases succeeded either at the jurisdictional phase or on the merits, they gave rise to concerns over the possible negative implications of the IIA regime for the regulatory power of the host state to protect public health.[11]

The IIA regime deeply interacts with the protection of IPRs, not only because IIAs and investment arbitration have been increasingly relied upon for the protection

Netherlands and States outside the EU' (De Brauw Blackstone Westbroek, 'New model treaty to replace 79 existing Dutch bilateral investment treaties' available at https://www.debrauw.com/newsletter/new-model-treaty-to-replace-79-existing-dutch-bilateral-investment-treaties/?output=pdf).

[5] See Julien Chaisse 'The Shifting Tectonics of International Investment Law – Structure and Dynamics of Rules and Arbitration on Foreign Investment in the Asia-Pacific Region' (2015) 47(3) *George Washington International Law Review* 563.

[6] UNCTAD, 'World Investment Report 2018: Investment and New Industrial Policies' UNCTAD/WIR/2018, 88.

[7] Reform of the investor-to-state dispute settlement mechanism, including the possibility of setting up an international investment court, is currently under discussion at the United Nations Commission on International Trade Law (UNCITRAL) (see http://www.uncitral.org/uncitral/en/commission/working_groups/3Investor_State.html).

[8] In the definition of 'investment', some IIAs make explicit reference to IPRs, while others include IPRs in general expressions such as 'intangible property' and 'every kind of assets'. See Carlos Correa and Jorge E Viñuales, 'Intellectual Property Rights as Protected Investments: How Open are the Gates?' (2016) 19 *Journal of International Economic Law* 91.

[9] *Philip Morris Asia Limited v The Commonwealth of Australia*, UNCITRAL, PCA Case No. 2012-12, Award on Jurisdiction and Admissibility (17 December 2015) and *Philip Morris Brands Sàrl, Philip Morris Products SA and Abal Hermanos SA v Oriental Republic of Uruguay*, ICSID Case No ARB/10/7, Award (8 July 2016).

[10] *Eli Lilly and Company v The Government of Canada*, UNCITRAL, ICSID Case No UNCT/14/2, Award (16 March 2017).

[11] See eg Valentina S Vadi, 'Towards a New Dialectics: Pharmaceutical Patents, Public Health and Foreign Direct Investments' (2015) 5 *NYU Journal of Intellectual Property & Entertainment Law* 113; Daniel J Gervais, 'Intellectual Property: A Beacon for Reform of Investor-state Dispute Settlement' (2019) 40 *Michigan Journal of International Law* 289.

of IPRs, but also because the IPR-related investment arbitration cases highlight the tension between IPRs as protected 'investment' and other social values of the host state. Therefore, the recent developments in the IIA regime towards greater recognition of the public interest of the host state is highly relevant to the future direction of the protection of IPRs.

Against this background, this chapter focuses on the question of how the following two concerns may be addressed: (a) IIAs may lead to a limited scope of regulatory power of the host state; and (b) foreign investments may have negative impacts on the public interest in the host state.

B. Two Major Concerns

First, there is the increasingly voiced concern that investment treaty obligations and the possibility of facing investment arbitration cause 'regulatory chill', ie reduction of the willingness and ability of the host state to adopt regulatory measures that would potentially interfere with foreign investment.[12] The concern over the negative impact of an IIA regime on the host state's legitimate regulatory power has been expressed in the Report of the United Nations Special Representative of the Secretary-General on the issue of human rights and transnational corporations and other business enterprises in the following terms:

> [R]ecent experience suggests that some (investment) treaty guarantees and contract provisions may unduly constrain the host Government's ability to achieve its legitimate policy objectives, including its international human rights obligations. That is because under threat of binding international arbitration, a foreign investor may be able to insulate its business venture from new laws and regulations, or seek compensation from the Government for the cost of compliance.[13]

Second, there is the increasing criticism of the 'one-sided' structure of the IIA regime. With a limited number of exceptions, IIAs impose obligations of

[12] The majority of the Tribunal in *Clayton/Bilcon v Canada* stated that it agreed with the dissenting arbitrator's position that 'in interpreting and applying (Chapter 11) … a NAFTA tribunal must be sensitive to the need to avoid "regulatory chill", including with respect to protection of the environment'. *William Ralph Clayton and others v Government of Canada*, PCA Case No. 2009-04, Award on Jurisdiction and Liability (17 March 2015) para 737.

[13] Report of the Special Representative of the Secretary-General, 'Business and human rights: Towards operationalizing the "protect, respect and remedy" framework' (22 April 2009) A/HRC/11/13 para 30 (referring to *Piero Foresti, Laura de Carli and others v Republic of South Africa* (ICSID Case No ARB (AF)/07/1)). Arguments that point out the possibility of regulatory chill include: Ole Kristian Fauchald, 'International Investment Law and Environmental Protection' (2008) 17 *YbIEL* 3, 8; David A Gantz, 'The Evolution on FTA Investment Provisions: From NAFTA to the US – Chile Free Trade Agreement' (2004) 19 *AUILR* 679, 679; Charles H Brower, 'Investor-State Disputes Under NAFTA: The Empire Strikes Back' (2001) 40 *Columbia JTL* 43, 45 (in which Brower observed that NAFTA Chapter 11 claims have 'horrif[ied] Canadian and US publicists', and raised concern over the chilling effect on the exercise of regulatory authority). See also separate opinion of Bryan Schwartz in *SD Myers v Canada*, First Partial Award (13 November 2000) para 203. By contrast, there are views that question the significance of this effect, see eg Andrew Newcombe, 'Book review, Gus Van Harten,

investment promotion and protection on host states, without providing investors' obligations. Likewise, access to IIA-based investment arbitration is, in practical terms, available only to investors, despite the fact that neither the ICSID Convention nor the UNCITRAL arbitration rules restrict access to investment arbitration by host states.[14] The absence of a mechanism in IIA-based arbitration to hold investors accountable for their conduct has been subject to increasing criticism.[15]

There are two considerations which lie behind these criticisms. First, investor-to-state disputes have evolved from traditional expropriation cases (ie governmental interference with the physical assets of the foreign investors when dispute arises) to conflicts that arise out of regulatory interference with various aspects of the investment. The wide coverage of most IIAs in terms of both the definition of investment and the activities of host states covers 'nearly every aspect of the host state's legal system'.[16] As a result, in the IIA-based investor-to-state dispute settlement – whether investment arbitration or investment court – the host state's regulatory measures are assessed in light of their conformity with obligations under IIAs.[17] Since the beginning of the twenty-first century, this 'judicial review' function of investment arbitration has generated serious concern. In 2010, Spears observed that:

> Over the last decade, concerns about competition between the international investment law regime and other normative orders have become particularly acute, as investors

Investment Treaty Arbitration and Public Law' (2008) 71 *MLR* 147, 150; Gus Van Harten and Dayna Nadine Scott, 'Investment Treaties and the Internal Vetting of Regulatory Proposals: A Case Study from Canada' (2017) 8(3) *Investment Treaty News* 8. One author casts doubt on the existence of this effect, as 'of all concluded ICSID cases up to 2014, 48% related to executive or administrative actions, whereas only 9%, related to legislative acts' (Marina Kofman, 'International Investment Arbitration and the Rule of Law' (2017) available at https://www.ruleoflaw.org.au/international-investment-arbitration/).

[14] The drafters of the ICSID Convention did consider that both investors and the states should have access to arbitration under the Convention. See the report of the World Bank Executive Directors, para 13: '... the Convention permits the institution of proceedings by host States as well as by investors and the Executive Directors have constantly had in mind that the provisions of the Convention should be equally adapted to the requirements of both cases' (available at http://icsidfiles.worldbank.org/icsid/ICSID/StaticFiles/basicdoc/basic-en.htm).

[15] Jose Daniel Amado, Jackson Shaw Kern and Martin Doe Rodriguez, *Arbitrating the Conduct of International Investors* (CUP, 2018) 10; Helene Bubrowski, 'Balancing IIA Arbitration through the Use of Counterclaims' in Armand de Mestral and Celine Levesque (eds), *Improving International Investment Agreements* (Routledge, 2013) 212, 215. See also, Emma Aisbett, Bernali Choudhury, Olivier de Schutter, Frank Garcia, James Harrison, Song Hong, Lise Johnson, Mouhamadou Kane, Santiago Peña, Matthew Porterfield, Susan Sell, Stephen E Shay and Louis T Wells, Rethinking International Investment Governance: Principles for the 21st Century (2018) (available at http://ccsi.columbia.edu/files/2018/09/Rethinking-Investment-Governance-September-2018.pdf) 106.

[16] Rudolf Dolzer, 'The Impact of International Investment Treaties on Domestic Administrative Law' (2005) 37 NYU *Journal of Intellectual Property & Entertainment Law* 953, 956. See also Francisco S Nogales, 'The NAFTA Environmental Framework, Chapter 11 Investment Provisions, and the Environment' (2002) 8 *Annual Survey of International & Comparative Law* 97, 109; Muthucumaraswamy Sornarajah, *The International Law on Foreign Investment* (Cambridge, 3rd edn, 2010) 11; J Ferguson, 'Note, California's MTBE Contaminated Water: An Illustration of the Need for an Environmental Interpretive Note on Article 1110 of NAFTA' (2000) 11 *Colorado Journal of International Environmental Law and Policy* 499, 499 (in the context of NAFTA Chapter 11).

[17] Sornarajah (n 16) 22.

> in a growing number of cases have challenged sensitive legislative and administrative measures that ordinarily would fall within the exclusive purview of sovereign states or that implement the host state's other international obligations.[18]

Second, there is an increasing recognition that there are circumstances where foreign investors' activities have significant implications for the public interest in the host state. Foreign investors are often involved in activities that were once in the public sector,[19] including the provision of essential infrastructure systems (eg electricity and gas, communication systems and water and sewage management). Likewise, well-financed foreign investors often invest in large-scale projects that have grave environmental implications, such as waste management, exploration and exploitation of natural resources, and mining. This has given rise to strongly voiced concerns over the negative impacts of their activities on the public interest in the state in question, with respect to the protection of the environment, human rights and labour rights etc.

Against this background, the following sections examine two developments in the practice of IIA-making which aim to address the following concerns over the system: inclusion of general exception clauses and references to investors' responsibility.

II. General Exceptions

A. Different IIA Practices with Respect to General Exception Clauses

The growing concerns over the limited scope of regulatory power of the host state are reflected in the evolution of IIA provisions. A recent piece of statistical research by Alschner and Skougarevskiy reveals that while early IIAs 'contain several protection clauses, but very few exception or arbitration provisions', more recent IIAs are 'deeper' in the sense that they 'contain considerably more exceptions, provide for more detailed arbitration procedures and also entail more protective provisions'.[20] For example, it has been observed that recent IIAs tend to provide more 'precise' substantive standards of investment protection, with a view

[18] Suzanne A Spears, 'The Quest for Policy Space in a New Generation of International Investment Agreements' 13(4) *JIEL* 1037, 1038. See also Julien Chaisse and Marine Polo 'Globalization of Water Privatization – Ramifications of Investor-State Disputes in the 'Blue Gold' Economy' (2015) 38(1) *Boston College International & Comparative Law Review* 1.

[19] Michael K Addo, 'Human Rights and Transnational Corporations – an Introduction' in MK Addo (ed), *Human Rights Standards and the Responsibility of Transnational Corporations* (1999) 3, 7.

[20] Wolfgang Alschner and Dmitriy Skougarevskiy, 'Convergence and Divergence in the Investment Treaty Universe: Scoping the Potential for Multilateral Consolidation' (2017) 8(2) *Trade, Law, and Development* 153, 163–64. They also observe that recent IIAs are more divergent in content than older IIAs.

to constraining investment tribunals' interpretative discretion.[21] Such precision is typically found in the provisions of fair and equitable standards of treatment[22] and indirect expropriation.[23]

An increasing number of recent IIAs provide exception clauses[24] as a way of addressing the concern over the reduced scope of regulatory power. The expected function of exception clauses is to exempt certain measures that are *prima facie* inconsistent with IIA obligations from liability. Forms of general exception clauses may be categorized into the following types: (1) incorporation of General Agreement on Tariffs and Trade (GATT) Article XX and/or General Agreement on Trade in Services (GATS) Article XIV *mutatis mutandis*, (2) provisions that are modelled on GATT Article XX and GATS Article XIV, and (3) public order exceptions. An example of the last type of exception clauses is Article XI of the Argentina-US BIT,[25] which has produced many (and inconsistent) precedents in investment arbitration cases.[26] It provides the 'necessity' exception in the following terms:

> This Treaty shall not preclude the application by either Party of measures necessary for the maintenance of public order, the fulfillment of its obligations with respect to the maintenance or restoration of international peace or security, or the protection of its own essential security interests.

In comparison with this type of exception clause, exception clauses that incorporate or are modelled on GATT Article XX and GATS Article XIV provide a wider range of public interest as grounds for justification of the measure. GATT/GATS-style general exception clauses are increasingly found in IIAs that cover the phase of pre-establishment of investment, ie the investment liberalization aspect. As an example, Article 28.3(1) of the Canada-EU Comprehensive Economic and Trade Agreement (CETA) incorporates GATT Article XX for the purposes of certain chapters including Sections B (Establishment of investment) and C (Non-discriminatory treatment) of the investment chapter. Article 28.3(2) provides the following exceptions, modelled on GATS

[21] Caroline Henckels, 'Protecting Regulatory Autonomy through Greater Precision in Investment Treaties: The TPP, CETA, and TTIP' (2016) 19(1) *JIEL* 27, 28. She defines the term 'precision' as 'the specificity by which state commitments are articulated in a treaty provision in terms of the conduct that is proscribed or obligated' (ibid at 30).

[22] Eg Article 8.10 of the EU-Canada Comprehensive Economic and Trade Agreement (CETA) (signed 2016, provisionally entered into force 2017 (however, investment protection is outside the scope of the provisional application); Article 9.6 and Annex 9-A of the Comprehensive and Progressive Agreement for Trans-Pacific Partnership (CPTPP) (entered into force 2018).

[23] Eg Art 8.12 and Annex 8-A of the CETA; Art 9.7 and Annex 9-B of the CPTPP.

[24] Exception clauses are distinguished from the provisions on 'non-conforming measures' that carve out regulatory measures specified in Annexes from the scope of certain investment protection obligations.

[25] Argentina-United States of America BIT (signed 1991, entered into force 1994).

[26] See eg August Reinisch, 'Necessity in International Investment Arbitration – An Unnecessary Split of Opinions in Recent ICSID Cases? Comments on *CMS v. Argentina and LG&E v. Argentina*' (2006) 3 TDM 4.

Article XIV, with respect to certain chapters including Sections B and C of the investment chapter:

> … subject to the requirement that such measures are not applied in a manner which would constitute a means of arbitrary or unjustifiable discrimination between the Parties where like conditions prevail, or a disguised restriction on trade in services, nothing in this Agreement shall be construed to prevent the adoption or enforcement by a Party of measures necessary:
>
> (a) to protect public security or public morals or to maintain public order;
> (b) to protect human, animal or plant life or health; or
> (c) to secure compliance with laws or regulations which are not inconsistent with the provisions of this Agreement including those relating to:
>   (i) the prevention of deceptive and fraudulent practices or to deal with the effects of a default on contracts;
>   (ii) the protection of the privacy of individuals in relation to the processing and dissemination of personal data and the protection of confidentiality of individual records and accounts; or
>   (iii) safety.

It should, however, be noted that the CETA applies the general exceptions clause to certain aspects of the investment chapter only, namely 'establishment of investment' and 'non-discriminatory standard', excluding other investment protection obligations from the scope of application of the clause. Moreover, the Comprehensive and Progressive Agreement for Trans-Pacific Partnership (CPTPP), another recent mega-regional IIA, does not apply the general exceptions clause to its investment chapter. Chapter 29 (exceptions and general provisions) of the CPTPP incorporates and applies GATT Article XX and paragraphs (a), (b) and (c) of GATS Article XIV to selected chapters of the agreement, but the investment chapter is not included in the chapters that are subject to these general exception clauses. Instead, its investment chapter provides certain conditions and exceptions with respect to certain obligations such as performance requirements (Article 9.10(3)) and expropriation (Annex 9-B).[27] In addition, Article 9.16 provides that:

> Nothing in this Chapter shall be construed to prevent a Party from adopting, maintaining or enforcing any measure otherwise consistent with this Chapter that it considers appropriate to ensure that investment activity in its territory is undertaken in a manner sensitive to environmental, health or other regulatory objectives.

B. Different Views on the Transplantation of GATT/GATS-style General Exception Clauses into IIAs

There are divergent views on the inclusion of general exception clauses modelled on GATT Article XX and GATS Article XIV in IIAs. Kurtz supports this approach

[27] It should however be noted that CETA, which applies general exception clauses to the investment chapter, provides conditions and exceptions to expropriation similar to those under the CPTPP.

by stating that: 'one possibility for rigorous, future treaty practice would be a mix and match approach of combining parts of GATS Article XIV with GATT Article XX'.[28] He argues that:

> A better and sustainable pathway for the future is a modelling strategy whereby state parties take the best features of WTO law and then tailor resulting flexibilities both in light of contemporary concerns and the distinct institutional context of investment law.[29]

The Appellate Body in the *Thailand – Cigarette* case stated that the analysis of GATT Article XX requires 'a panel to find and apply a "line of equilibrium" between a substantive obligation and an exception'.[30] Given this function of GATT Article XX, its inclusion in IIAs, on its face, appears to provide better balance between investment protection and the public interest of the host state. It is, at least, clear that the intention of the drafting parties behind the incorporation of general exception clauses from the GATT and GATS, is to secure the regulatory leeway of the contracting parties. Indeed, there is a possibility that an '*effet utile* interpretation might suggest that the parties intended to provide the host State greater regulatory flexibility … than that provided by other IIAs without general exceptions'.[31]

Nevertheless, the textual transplant of GATT Article XX and GATS Article XIV may also produce a counterproductive effect, ie guiding the arbitral tribunal to allow less regulatory space to the host state in light of IIA obligations. This is because the textual transplant which disregards the differences between trade and investment may well result in a less flexible consideration of the host state's public policy objectives in investment arbitration, as discussed below.

In contrast to the GATT and GATS, ie state to state exchange of liberalization of market access for foreign goods and services,[32] the IIA regime offers a mechanism to protect foreign investment which operates in the domestic legal framework of the host state.[33] Every stage of foreign investment, ie not only establishment and admission but also management, operation, expansion, maintenance, use, enjoyment and disposal, is subject to domestic laws, regulations and administrative orders. Foreign direct investment (FDI), which brings not only products but also production processes to the host state, interacts deeply with the society of the host state. In many cases, FDI brings certain benefits to the country

[28] Jürgen Kurtz, *The WTO and International Investment Law: Converging Systems* (CUP, 2016) 197.

[29] Ibid 227.

[30] *Thailand – Customs and Fiscal Measures on Cigarettes from the Philippines*, WT/DS371/AB/R, Report of the Appellate Body, para 173.

[31] Andrew Newcombe, 'The Use of General Exceptions in IIAs: Increasing Legitimacy or Uncertainty' in Armand De Mestral and Céline Lévesque (eds) *Improving International Investment Agreements* (Routledge, 2012) 267, 277–28.

[32] Nicholas DiMascio and Joost Pauwelyn, 'Nondiscrimination in Trade and Investment Treaties: Worlds Apart or Two Sides of The Same Coin?' (2008) 102 *American Journal of International Law* 48, 54.

[33] For the relationship between host state sovereignty and the rules of foreign investment, see Rudolf Dolzer and Christoph Schreuer, *Principles of International Investment Law* (OUP, 2008) 7.

in which the investors operate, including greater tax revenue, creation of employment opportunities and skills development, scientific development, and transfer of new technologies and sound management practices through linkages with local firms.[34] However, as noted (see section I), there are circumstances where the activities associated with FDI have a range of negative impacts on the public interest in the host state. The deep interaction of FDI with the society of the host state, and the public interest issues associated with FDI, necessitate extensive regulation by the host state with respect to FDI.[35]

This strongly suggests that, in the IIA regime, the elements for consideration that are included in GATT Article XX and GATS Article XIV – in particular legitimate policy objectives to protect public interest, the nexus between the objective and the measure, and the manner by which the measure is implemented – should be considered in the assessment of whether or not the regulatory measure in question constitutes a violation of IIA obligations. The determination of a breach of IIA obligations requires a holistic analysis based on consideration of these factors and all other circumstances of the case. This requires a balancing exercise between the protection of foreign investment and 'any legitimate policy objective' (in contrast to the closed list of exceptions in GATT Article XX)[36] of the host state. This is indeed the approach adopted by many arbitral tribunals. In the context of national treatment obligations, DiMascio and Pauwelyn observe that:

> In the investment context, the broad reference to investors 'in like circumstances' has consistently enabled tribunals to balance investor interests with an unlimited list of legitimate government concerns – a list far broader than the exceptions in GATT Article XX.[37]

Thus, Lévesque argues that:

> There is no need for recourse to the exception clause if legitimate objectives are fully considered as part of the interpretation of the primary obligation. Such an interpretation would go against the principle of effectiveness in treaty interpretation.[38]

This is contrasted with the approach adopted in World Trade Organization (WTO) jurisprudence on the GATT and the GATS, according to which this balancing exercise in light of policy objectives is conducted in the examination of general exception clauses.

[34] Peter Kusek and Andrea Silva, 'What Matters to Investors in Developing Countries: Findings from the Global Investment Competitiveness Survey' (2017) *Global Investment Competitiveness Report 2017/2018: Foreign Investor Perspectives and Policy Implications* 19, 31–33; Marcel Kordos and Sergej Vojtovic, 'Transnational Corporations in the Global World Economic Environment' (2016) 230 *Procedia – Social and Behavioral Sciences* 150, 153.

[35] DiMascio and Pauwelyn (n 32) 58: 'with respect to investment the importing country has … more rights to regulate foreign investment, as FDI generally leaves a bigger footprint than trade'.

[36] Ibid 76.

[37] Ibid 82–83.

[38] Céline Lévesque, 'The Inclusion of GATT Article XX Exceptions in IIAs: A Potentially Risky Policy' in Roberto Echandi and Pierre Sauve (eds), *Prospects in International Investment Law and Policy: World Trade Forum* (CUP, 2013) 363, 367.

In the *US – Gambling* case, the Appellate Body observed that:

> Both of these provisions (Article XIV of the GATS and Article XX of the GATT 1994) affirm the right of Members to pursue objectives identified in the paragraphs of these provisions even if, in doing so, Members act inconsistently with obligations set out in other provisions of the respective agreements, provided that all of the conditions set out therein are satisfied.[39]

In the *EC – Seal Products* case, the Appellate Body stated that:

> In our view, the fact that, under the GATT 1994, a Member's right to regulate is accommodated under Article XX, weighs heavily against an interpretation of Articles I:1 and III:4 that requires an examination of whether the detrimental impact of a measure on competitive opportunities for like imported products stems exclusively from a legitimate regulatory distinction.[40]

Then, a measure that constitutes a *prima facie* violation of a non-discrimination standard is excused by reference to the following considerations in the framework of general exception clauses: whether or not the measure falls within the exhaustive list of public interests; if it is 'necessary', 'relating' or 'designed and applied' to the specified public interest; and whether it meets the conditions that are set out in the *chapeau*, ie it is not applied in a manner that would constitute arbitrary or unjustifiable discrimination and is not a disguised restriction on trade.

If incorporation of GATT Article XX and GATS Article XIV in IIAs directs the tribunal to conduct such a balancing exercise, under the same constraint of general exception clauses as under the GATT and GATS,[41] it means that the host state needs to prove that the concerned measure: (a) falls within the closed categories of public interests;[42] (b) passes the necessity and other connection test; and (c) meets the *chapeau* requirements. This may well result in less flexible consideration being given to the host state's public policy objectives,[43] a consequence that is contrary to the intention behind the incorporation of general

[39] *United States – Measures Affecting the Cross-Border Supply of Gambling and Betting Services*, Report of the Appellate Body, WT/DS285/AB/R (20 April 2005) para 291.

[40] *European Communities – Measures Prohibiting the Importation and Marketing of Seal Products*, WT/DS400/AB/R, WT/DS401/AB/R, Report of the Appellate Body (22 May 2014) para 5.125. While in Chile-Tax Measures on Alcoholic Beverages, the Appellate Body recognized the relevance of 'the purpose or objectives of a Member's legislature and government' in examining the existence or absence of a breach under Art III:2 of the GATT, it relied on the object and purpose of the measure not to balance competing interests, but to conclude that the application of dissimilar taxation of directly competitive or substitutable products will 'afford protection to domestic production'. *Chile-Tax Measures on Alcoholic Beverages*, WT/DS87/AB/RWT/DS87/AB/R, Report of the Appellate Body (13 December 1999) paras 62–66.

[41] Spears (n 18) 1059–60.

[42] Newcombe points out that 'since they provide a closed list of legitimate policy objectives, their inclusion might have the unintended consequence of limiting the range of legitimate objectives available to the state'. Newcombe (n 31) 279.

[43] Ibid 280; Spears (n 18) 1063; Howard Mann, 'Investment Agreements and the Regulatory State: Can Exceptions Clauses Create a Safe Haven for Governments?' (2007) IISD Background Papers for the Developing Country Investment Negotiators' Forum, 11-2.

exception clauses to accord greater regulatory flexibility for the protection of the public interest of the host state.

As of the date of writing, there has been no case in which an investment arbitration tribunal interpreted and applied general exception clauses that incorporate or are modelled on GATT Article XX and GATS Article XIV, and therefore it remains to be seen whether the concerns discussed above are substantiated. Meanwhile, the approach adopted by the CPTPP might well signal a shift from the textual transplantation of GATT/GATS-style general exception clauses to clarification, or greater precision, in the scope of individual IIA obligations and the inclusion of conditions and exceptions tailored to each obligation. It should be noted that, according to the leaked text of the investment chapter of the RCEP,[44] it appears to adopt the same approach as the CPTPP on this issue.

III. Investors' Obligations and Corporate Social Responsibility

A. References to Investors' Obligations in IIAs

Another interesting element found in the CPTPP is the reference to the notion of corporate social responsibility (CSR). As discussed below, there are an increasing number of IIAs that make references to investor responsibility in various forms.

There is as yet no general international law on obligations of corporations as binding rules. In the 1970s, the United Nations established the Commission on Transnational Corporations.[45] It issued drafts of codes of conduct for transnational corporations which were binding on corporations in 1978, 1983, 1988 and 1990,[46] but these attempts failed, 'with parties citing irreconcilable differences and north-south divisions'.[47] The UN's renewed attempt to develop Norms on Business and Human Rights as rules that directly bind corporations and to create

[44] Leaked text available at http://www.bilaterals.org/?rcep-draft-investment-chapter&lang=en. For a detailed analysis of the text, see Amokura Kawharu and Luke Nottage, 'Models for Investment Treaties in the Asian Region: An Underview' (2016) *Sydney Law School Legal Studies Research Paper No* 16/87, available at http://ssrn.com/abstract=2845088 (accessed 20 January 2017) 38–41. See also Julien Chaisse and Richard Pomfret 'The RCEP and the Changing Landscape of World Trade – Assessing Asia-Pacific Investment Regionalism Next Stage' (2018) 11(4) *Law and Development Review* 1.

[45] Economic and Social Council Resolution 1913 (LVII), 5 December 1974.

[46] United Nations Centre on Transnational Corporations, Codes of conduct, formulations by the Chairman, UN Doc E/C 102/8 (1978); Draft code of conduct on Transnational Corporations, UN Doc E/1983/17/rev 1 (1983); Draft Code of Conduct on Transnational Corporations, UN Doc E/1988/39/add. 1 (1988); Development and International Economic Cooperation: Transnational Corporations, UN Doc E/1990/94.

[47] Daniel Aguirre, *The Human Right to Development in a Globalized World* (Routledge 2008) 212. See also Tagi Sagafi-nejad and John H Dunning, *The UN and Transnational Corporations: From Code of Conduct to Global Compact* (Indiana University Press, 2008) 122; Theodore H Moran, 'The United Nations and transnational corporations: a review and a perspective' (2009) 18(2) *Transnational Corporations* 91, 93.

'a global network of human rights obligations enforceable against multinational corporations', also failed due to opposition from certain, mostly developed, states.[48] Instead, the then UN Commission on Human Rights (now the Human Rights Council) decided to develop a set of norms as non-binding principles – the UN Guiding Principles on Business and Human Rights – which set out states' duties and CSRs.[49] Work to draft an 'international legally binding instrument on transnational corporations and other business enterprises with respect to human rights' has been in process[50] since the UN Human Rights Council adopted the resolution on its elaboration.[51] However, this attempt has lacked support from developed countries[52] as well as the international business community.[53] At the 2002 Johannesburg World Sustainable Development Summit, an NGO proposed launching negotiations on binding instruments on corporate accountability,[54] but the Plan of Implementation of the World Summit on Sustainable Development[55] did not pursue this path. Instead, it called for the promotion of voluntary initiatives to '[e]nhance corporate environmental and social responsibility and accountability'.[56]

This does not mean, however, that states lack the competence to conclude an international treaty that provides directly binding obligations on corporations.[57]

[48] Larry Catá Backer, 'On the Evolution of the United Nations "Protect-Respect-Remedy Project": The State, the Corporation and Human Rights in a Global Governance Context' (2011) 9 *Santa Clara Journal of International Law* 37, 45–46.

[49] UN Guiding Principles on Business and Human Rights (endorsed by the Human Rights Council in June 2011), available at http://www.ohchr.org/Documents/Publications/GuidingPrinciplesBusinessHR_EN.pdf.

[50] 'Zero draft' was published by the UN Human Rights Council's open-ended intergovernmental working group on transnational corporations and other business enterprises with respect to human rights in July 2018. See also Peter Muchlinski, 'The Impact of a Business and Human Rights Treaty on Investment Law and Arbitration', in Surya Deva and David Bilchitz (eds), Building a Treaty on Business and Human Rights: Context and Contours (CUP 2017) 346–374.

[51] Human Rights Council, 'Elaboration of an International Legally Binding Instrument on Transnational Corporations and Other Business Enterprises with Respect to Human Rights', A/HRC Res. 26/9 (14 July 2014).

[52] Fourteen members of the Human Rights Council, including the United States, Japan and the member states of the European Union opposed the adoption of the resolution.

[53] International Chamber of Commerce et al, 'Response of the international business community to the "elements" for a draft legally binding instrument on transnational corporations and other business enterprises with respect to human rights' (20 October 2017), available at https://www.ohchr.org/Documents/HRBodies/HRCouncil/WGTransCorp/Session3/BIAC-FTA-BSCI-ICC-IOE.pdf.

[54] Friends of the Earth International, 'FoEI position paper for the WSSD' (January 2002) available at https://friendsoftheearth.uk/sites/default/files/downloads/corporate_accountability.pdf.

[55] UN, Report of the World Summit on Sustainable Development, Annex: Plan of Implementation of the World Summit on Sustainable Development (4 September 2002) ('WSSD Plan of Implementation') UN Doc A/CONF.199/20.

[56] Ibid para 18. See also paras 49 and 140. See also Jennifer Clapp, 'Transnational Corporations and Global Environmental Governance' in Peter Dauvergne (ed), *Handbook of Global Environmental Politics* (Edward Elgar 2005) 284, 294–95; Angelica Bonfanti, 'Applying Corporate Social Responsibility to Foreign Investment: Failures and Prospects' in Tullio Treves, Francesco Seatzu and Seline Trevisanut (eds), *Foreign Investment, International Law and Common Concerns* (Routledge 2014) 230, 234–36.

[57] Patrick Dumberry, 'L'entreprise, sujet de droit international? Retour sur la question à la lumière des développements récents du droit international des investissements' (2004) 108(1) *Revue generale de droit international public* 103, 116: 'Il ne fait pas de doute, et cela n'est d'ailleurs guère contesté, que les Etats ont la compétence et le pouvoir de créer de "nouveaux" sujets de droit par le biais de leurs relations avec d'autres sujets de droit'. See also, OHCHR, 'Interim report of the Special Representative of the Secretary-General on the issue of human rights and transnational corporations and other

For example, there are international environmental agreements (IEAs) that provide obligations on juridical persons concerning activities that are extremely hazardous, such as the peaceful use of nuclear energy, transport of oil and transport of hazardous substances.[58]

There are IIAs and model IIAs that include provisions on investors' responsibilities in the form of binding obligations. Article 9 of the Agreement on Promotion, Protection and Guarantee of Investments among Member States of the Organization of the Islamic Conference (OIC Agreement)[59] provides that:

> The investor shall be bound by the laws and regulations in force in the host state and shall refrain from all acts that may disturb public order or morals or that may be prejudicial to the public interest. He is also to refrain from exercising restrictive practices and from trying to achieve gains through unlawful means.

Likewise, Article 13 of the Investment Agreement for the Common Market for Eastern and Southern Africa (COMESA) Common Investment Area[60] provides that:

> COMESA investors and their investments shall comply with all applicable domestic measures of the Member State in which their investment is made.

Part 3 of the Model Bilateral Investment Treaty of the Southern African Development Community (SADC),[61] entitled 'Rights and Obligations of Investors and State', includes several provisions on investors' obligations. In particular, Article 11 provides that:

> Investors and Investments shall comply with all laws, regulations, administrative guidelines and policies of the Host State concerning the establishment, acquisition, management, operation and disposition of investments.

Article 9 of the OIC Agreement was discussed in the case of *Al-Warraq v Indonesia*.[62] In this case, the claimant investor was the owner of an Indonesian bank called Bank Century, and the dispute arose out of criminal proceedings concerning the

business enterprises' E/CN.4/2006/97 (2006) para 65: 'there are no inherent conceptual barriers to states deciding to hold corporations directly responsible [under international law] … by establishing some form of international jurisdiction (by John Ruggie, the Special Representative of the Secretary-General on human rights and transnational corporations and other business enterprises)'.

[58] Eg Paris Convention on Third Party Liability in the Field of Nuclear Energy of 29th July 1960 (entered into force 1 April 1968), as amended by the Additional Protocol of 28th January 1964 and by the Protocol of 16th November 1982, July 29, 1960, Art 3(a), 956 UNTS 251; International Convention on Civil Liability for Oil Pollution Damage, Nov 29, 1969 (entered into force 19 June 1975) 26 UST 765, 973 UNTS 3 (replaced by 1992 Protocol, entered into force 30 May 1996. The 2000 amendment entered into force 1 November 2003); Vienna Convention on Civil Liability for Nuclear Damage, May 21, 1963, 1063 UNTS 265. There are also agreements that provide the obligations of contracting states to establish the liability of legal persons under their domestic legal framework (eg Art 4 of the Basel Convention on the Control of Transboundary Movements of Hazardous Wastes and Their Disposal).

[59] OIC Agreement (signed 1981, entered into force 1988).

[60] Investment Agreement for the COMESA Common Investment Area (signed 2007, not yet in force).

[61] SADC Model Bilateral Investment Treaty of the Southern African Development Community (2010), available at http://www.iisd.org/itn/wp-content/uploads/2012/10/sadc-model-bit-template-final.pdf.

[62] *Hesham Talaat M Al-Warraq v Republic of Indonesia* (*Al-Warraq v Indonesia*), UNCITRAL, Final Award (15 December 2014).

bailout of the bank. In the criminal proceedings based on the complaints lodged by the central bank of the Republic of Indonesia about banking irregularities with regard to the bailout, including the allegation that bailout funds had been used to fund the 2009 presidential election campaign, the claimant was convicted of theft, corruption and money laundering.[63] His assets in Indonesia were confiscated.[64]

The tribunal did find a breach of fair and equitable treatment on the part of Indonesia with respect to the criminal proceedings,[65] based on the finding that Indonesia had failed to properly notify the claimant of the criminal charges against him and that several elements of the trial *in absentia* violated both the International Covenant on Civil and Political Rights (ICCPR) and the Indonesian Code of Criminal Procedure.[66] The tribunal, however, proceeded to examine 'Application of Article 9 of the OIC Agreement', and determined that, as a result of the investor's various breaches of Indonesian laws and actions that were prejudicial to the public interest, he had 'deprived himself of the protection afforded by the OIC Agreement',[67] and that 'the doctrine of "clean hands" renders the Claimant's claim inadmissible'.[68] It therefore concluded that:

> [T]he Claimant has breached Article 9 of the OIC Agreement by failing to uphold the Indonesian laws and regulations and in acting in a manner prejudicial to the public interest. The Claimant's actions were also prejudicial to the public interest. The Tribunal finds that the Claimant's conduct falls within the scope of application of the 'clean hands' doctrine, and therefore cannot benefit from the protection afforded by the OIC Agreement.[69]

It also concluded that the doctrine of 'clean hands' precluded the awarding of damages to the claimant.[70] Also, the tribunal mentioned Article 9 in examining the question of whether the tribunal has jurisdiction over counterclaims raised by Indonesia against the claimant investor. In answering this question in the affirmative, the tribunal referred to Article 9 as an element that supports this conclusion:

> An investor of course has a general obligation to obey the law of the host state, but Article 9 raises this obligation from the plane of domestic law (and jurisdiction of

[63] Ibid paras 108–25 and 141.

[64] Ibid para 161.

[65] Although the OIC Agreement does not provide fair and equitable treatment guarantee, the tribunal concluded that this standard was incorporated from other IIAs to which Indonesia is a party, by the application of its most-favoured-nation clause (Art 8). Ibid paras 540–55.

[66] Ibid paras 556–621.

[67] Ibid para 645.

[68] Ibid para 646.

[69] Ibid para 647.

[70] Ibid para 654. In *Blusun v Italy*, the Court of Criminal Cassation of Italy confirmed a criminal conviction for fraud against the claimants on the ground that the claimants misrepresented the actual size and nominal power of the plants in obtaining a necessary authorization. However, as the claim that the claimants' company was guilty of fraud was not proven in the arbitration proceedings, the Tribunal concluded that 'in the absence of any such evidence, the "clean hands" doctrine has nothing to operate on'. *Blusun SA, Jean-Pierre Lecorcier and Michael Stein v Italian Republic*, ICSID Case No ARB/14/3, Award (27 December 2016) para 273.

> domestic tribunals) to a treaty obligation binding on the investor in an investor state arbitration. … The fact that the Contracting Parties imposed treaty obligations on investors (which the Claimant assented to by accepting the open offer of investment arbitration made by the Respondent in the OIC Agreement) confirms the interpretation of Article 17 that permits counterclaims by the respondent state.[71]

Certainly, in this particular case, the investor's claims would have been precluded by the application of the 'clean hands' doctrine even without Article 9. Also, Indonesia's counterclaims in this case did not succeed on their merits.[72] Nevertheless, the tribunal 'applied' the investor's obligations set out in Article 9 as conditions for protection under the OIC Agreement. Newcombe and Marcoux argue that 'this (the *Al-Warraq* tribunal's approach) is where the future development of the investment treaty regime lies – a symmetrical regime in which foreign investors have international rights as well as obligations'.[73] Likewise, the High Commissioner for Human Rights' Report on human rights, trade and investment suggests that: 'States could consider the issue of legal responsibility of investors within discussions concerning continuing investment liberalization and consider acknowledging these responsibilities in investment agreements'.[74] However, the number of IIAs that have adopted this approach is still limited.

B. Reference to Corporate Social Responsibility in IIAs

Instead of providing binding obligations on investors, a number of recent IIAs include references to the concept of CSR. As noted, there is no general international law that binds corporations. Likewise, there is no general international law that imposes responsibility on private persons to pay compensation as a consequence of their international wrongdoings – in particular, Part II of the Articles on State Responsibility[75] is not applicable to private persons. In *Urbaser v Argentina*,

[71] Ibid para 663.

[72] The tribunal dismissed the counterclaims on the grounds that: the counterclaim did not distinguish the actions of the claimant from the actions of various other entities, which was against the principle that 'the necessary parties to the counterclaim must be the same as the parties to the primary claim' (citing *Saluka Investments BV v The Czech Republic*, UNCITRAL (Decision on Jurisdiction over the Czech Republic's Counterclaim of 7 May 2004) para 49); and whereas the counterclaim was based on frauds committed against Bank Century, the legal basis of the Respondent's rights to recover these losses was demonstrated. *Al-Warraq v Indonesia* (n62) paras 669–70.

[73] Andrew Newcombe and Jean-Michel Marcoux, 'Case Comment, *Hesham Talaat M Al-Warraq v Republic of Indonesia*: Imposing International Obligations on Foreign Investors' (2015) 30(3) *ICSID Review* 525, 532.

[74] UN Economic and Social Council, 'Human Rights, Trade and Investment: Report of the High Commissioner for Human Rights' (2 July 2003) E/CN.4/Sub.2/2003/9 para 59.

[75] International Law Commission, Draft Articles on the Responsibility of States for Internationally Wrongful Acts, 53 UN GAOR Supp (No 10) at 43, UN Doc A/56/10 (2001).

the tribunal aptly pointed out the absence of secondary rules governing the respondent's counterclaims:

> The Tribunal also notes that Respondent does not state any legal ground for any individual's right to claim damages as a consequence of an alleged violation of the human right to water. Respondent does not demonstrate either that the alleged violation of such human right entails a duty of reparation equally based on international law, with the effect that the individuals concerned by such an alleged harm obtain an appropriate compensation.[76]

Instead, in the international law sphere, various 'soft law' instruments have been adopted to advance the concept of corporate responsibility, including: the OECD Guidelines for Multinational Enterprises,[77] the International Labor Organization (ILO)'s Tripartite declaration of principles concerning multinational enterprises and social policy (the MNE Declaration),[78] the Ten Principles of the UN Global Compact,[79] and the International Financial Corporation (IFC)'s Performance Standards on Social and Environmental Sustainability.[80] The ISO 26000 Guidance Standard on Social Responsibility[81] is an important example of private CSR initiatives. These instruments provide non-binding standards and guidelines for business entities' conduct with respect to issues concerning human rights, labour, the environment and anti-corruption, or provide obligations on governments to promote and encourage business practices that are in compliance with international standards of CSR in their territories.

Article 9.17 (Corporate Social Responsibility) of the CPTPP provides that:

> The Parties reaffirm the importance of each Party encouraging enterprises operating within its territory or subject to its jurisdiction to voluntarily incorporate into their internal policies those internationally recognised standards, guidelines and principles of corporate social responsibility that have been endorsed or are supported by that Party.

Likewise, Article 7 (Corporate Social Responsibility) of the Netherlands' draft model BIT, issued in May 2018, provides that:

> The Contracting Parties reaffirm the importance of each Contracting Party to encourage investors operating within its territory or subject to its jurisdiction to voluntarily incorporate into their internal policies those internationally recognized standards,

[76] *Urbaser SA and Consorcio de Aguas Bilbao Bizkaia, Bilbao Biskaia Ur Partzuergoa v The Argentine Republic* (*Urbaser v Argentina*), ICSID Case No ARB/07/26, Award (8 December 2016) para 1220.

[77] OECD Guidelines for Multinational Enterprises (1976) available at http://mneguidelines.oecd.org/guidelines/.

[78] Tripartite declaration of principles concerning multinational enterprises and social policy (MNE Declaration) (5th ed, 2017) available at http://www.ilo.org/empent/Publications/WCMS_094386/lang--en/index.htm.

[79] Ten Principles of the UN Global Compact (1999) available at https://www.unglobalcompact.org/what-is-gc/mission/principles.

[80] Performance Standards on Social and Environmental Sustainability (2006 and 2012 versions) available at https://www.ifc.org/wps/wcm/connect/Topics_Ext_Content/IFC_External_Corporate_Site/Sustainability-At-IFC/Policies-Standards/Performance-Standards.

[81] See http://www.iso.org/iso/home/standards/iso26000.htm.

> guidelines and principles of corporate social responsibility that have been endorsed or are supported by that Party, such as the OECD Guidelines for Multinational Enterprises, the United Nations Guiding Principles on Business and Human Rights, and the Recommendation CM/REC(2016) of the Committee of Ministers to Member States on human rights and business.

Although outside the specific context of investment, the CETA also makes references to CSR in Preamble, Chapter 22 (Trade and Sustainable Development), Chapter 24 (Trade and Environment) and Chapter 25 (Bilateral Dialogues and Cooperation).[82] In particular, Article 24.12(1) provides that:

> The Parties recognise that enhanced cooperation is an important element to advance the objectives of this Chapter, and commit to cooperate on trade-related environmental issues of common interest, in areas such as:
>
> ...
>
> (c) the environmental dimension of corporate social responsibility and accountability, including the implementation and follow-up of internationally recognised guidelines;
>
> ...

From the text of these provisions, it is clear that they concern the incorporation of international CSR standards in the domestic framework of states. This suggests that the primary focus of these provisions is on the elements of CSR that are compatible with regulations. As such elements, most fundamental responsibilities of a company are identified in the Ten Principles of the UN Global Compact: the protection of human rights, the environment, labour rights and abstention from corrupt practices. They are distinguished from positive corporate contribution to societal development,[83] which is of a fundamentally voluntary nature and has been developed as part of their strategic business activities by many corporations, especially in the form of 'counter-efforts to evade, oppose, de-legitimize and co-opt such "unwarranted" pressures' (to regulate their conduct).[84] The OECD, in its 2008 annual report on Guidelines for Multinational Enterprises, explains the distinction between the corporate obligations, which are subject to laws and regulations, and voluntary elements of CSR:

> The first obligation of business is obeying laws and regulations. Responsible business conduct also entails responding to societal expectations that may be communicated through channels other than law (e.g. governmental organisations, within the workplace, by local communities and trade unions, in dialogue with other civil society organisations, via the press and so forth).[85]

[82] Likewise, the Colombia-Ecuador-EU-Peru Trade Agreement (signed 2012, entered into force 2013), in Title IX (Trade and Sustainable Development), provides that: 'The Parties agree to promote best business practices related to corporate social responsibility' (Art 271(3)).

[83] Bonfanti (n 56) 232.

[84] Ronen Shamir, 'Between Self-Regulation and the Alien Tort Claims Act: On the Contested Concept of Corporate Social Responsibility' (2004) 38(4) *Law & Society Review* 635, 644.

[85] OECD, 'Annual Report on the OECD Guidelines for Multinational Enterprises' (2008) available at http://www.oecd.org/daf/inv/mne/employmentandindustrialrelations-2008annualreportontheoecdguidelinesformultinationalenterprises.htm, at 237. For this distinction, see also European Commission,

When the host state has enacted domestic laws and regulations incorporating international CSR standards, a violation of such domestic laws on the part of the investor may be considered either at the jurisdictional phase (as a matter of jurisdiction or admissibility) or at the merits phase,[86] either through the so-called 'legality requirement' in the relevant IIA[87] or the principle that investments must be made in good faith.[88]

Even in the absence of such domestic laws and regulations on CSR, investors' conduct that falls below the internationally accepted CSR standards may be considered in the assessment of substantive investment protection obligations. Although detailed analysis of the potential role of CSR in an investor state arbitration is outside the scope of this chapter, there have been suggestions on how the concept may inform the tribunal's assessment of the existence and scope of the host state's liability under the IIA. Bonfanti argues that:

> As a breach of CSR could delegitimize the investors' expectations … as a result of the former's lack of compliance with the 'clean hands requirement', it would therefore provide arbitrators with an authoritative ground for striking a balance between states' sovereignty and investors' legitimate expectations.[89]

Likewise, Muchlinski suggests the role of CSR in balancing the host states' IIA obligations and corporate responsibilities through interpretation of these obligations:

> That such an interpretation may be increasingly called for cannot be doubted. Indeed, it may be an integral issue in many investor-state disputes. Where the investor claims the breach of an IIA protective standard by the respondent state, the latter may respond by referring to the investors' corporate conduct as a justification for its regulatory reaction which leads to the investor's claim.[90]

Also, Sauvant and Ünüvar observe that the contracting states' reaffirmation of the importance of promoting internationally accepted CSR standards in an IIA

'Promoting a European Framework for Corporate Social Responsibility' (DOC/01/9, 18 July 2001), Section II.

[86] See eg *Inceysa Vallisoletana SL v Republic of El Salvador*, ICSID Case No ARB/03/26, Award (2 August 2006) paras 186–88; *Gustav Hamester GmbH & Co KG v Republic of Ghana*, ICSID Case No ARB/07/24, Award (18 June 2010) para 127; *ECE Projektmanagement v Czech Republic*, UNCITRAL, PCA Case No 2010-5, Award (19 September 2013) para 3.168.

[87] Provisions on the compliance with domestic law take various forms in IIAs. For example, the legality requirement may be incorporated in the definition of 'investment', or in the provisions on the scope of protection of the treaty, or in the provisions requiring host States to admit or accept foreign investments; or whether the illegality concerns the initiation of the investment or the performance of the investment (depending on the language of the legality requirement).

[88] See eg *Phoenix Action, Ltd v Czech Republic*, ICSID Case No ARB/06/5, Award (15 April 2009) para 113; *Hamester v Ghana* (n87) paras 123–24; *Metal-Tech Ltd v Republic of Uzbekistan*, ICSID Case No ARB/10/3, Award (4 October 2013).

[89] Bonfanti (n 56) 246.

[90] Peter Muchlinski, 'Corporate Social Responsibility' in Peter Muchlinski et al (eds), *The Oxford Handbook of International Investment Law* (OUP, 2008) 637, 682. See also Leyla Davarnejad, 'Strengthening the Social Dimension of International Investment Agreements by Integrating Codes of Conduct for Multinational Enterprises' (2008) *OECD Global Forum on International Investment* available at http://www.oecd.org/investment/globalforum/40352144.pdf (accessed 7 October 2018) at 11.

indicates their expectations that foreign investors' activities in their territories be compatible with these standards.[91]

As noted, an increasing number of recent IIAs provide references to CSR[92] and, to a lesser extent, investors' obligations concerning their conduct.[93] In light of the increasing criticisms of the one-sided structure of the IIA regime (see section I) and concerns over the negative impact of investors' activities on the public interest of the host state, recognition of investors' responsibilities in IIAs may indeed be the direction that should be taken by the future IIA negotiations.

IV. Conclusion

While IIAs and investment arbitration have been increasingly recognised as a useful tool to enforce the protection of IPRs, several high-profile cases involving the tension between IPRs and the public interest of the host state have produced growing public concerns over the IIA regime. The recent developments in the IIA regime incorporating a response to these concerns and recent investment arbitration case law are, therefore, highly relevant to the IPR protection.

This chapter examined two types of changes in recent IIA-making which demonstrate greater sensitivity regarding the public interest, as well as including a wider variety of provisions for balancing competing interests. The first change discussed was the inclusion of general exception clauses modelled on GATT Article XX and GATS Article XIV, and the second was the provisions on investor responsibility and CSR. With respect to the former, this chapter has demonstrated the risk that the textual transplant of general exception clauses from GATT Article XX and GATS Article XIV might result in less regulatory flexibility. It should be noted that neither the CPTPP nor the leaked text of the RCEP applies these GATT/GATS-style general exception clauses to the investment chapter.

This chapter has also discussed the potential effects of including provisions on investor responsibilities in IIAs. While this question requires further extensive research including a case-by-case analysis, it is undeniable that there is an imbalance between the lack of an effective mechanism to hold transnational

[91] Karl P Sauvant and Güneş Ünüvar, 'Can host countries have legitimate expectations?' (2016) 183 *Columbia FDI Perspectives* 1.

[92] Eg EU-Columbia/Peru FTA (2013) (Art 271(3): 'The Parties agree to promote best business practices related to corporate social responsibility'); Nigeria-Singapore BIT (2016) Art 11. It is observed that 'since 2010 Canada has included a voluntary corporate social responsibility ("CSR") provision in the BITs it signs' (Rainbow Willard and Sarah Morreau, 'The Canadian Model BIT – A Step in the Right Direction for Canadian Investment in Africa?' *Kluwer Arbitration Blog* (18 July 2015) available at http://kluwerarbitrationblog.com/2015/07/18/the-canadian-model-bit-a-step-in-the-right-direction-for-canadian-investment-in-africa/. See eg Canada-Benin FIPA (signed 2013, entered into force 2014) (Art 16); Canada-Serbia FIPA (signed 2014, entered into force 2015) (Art 16).

[93] Eg Argentina-Qatar BIT (2016) (Art 12: 'Investors operating in the territory of the host Contracting Party should make efforts to voluntarily incorporate internationally recognized standards of corporate social responsibility into their business policies and practices'); Ghana Model BIT (2008) Art 12.1.

corporations accountable for their conduct and the heavy protection of foreign investment in the IIA regime, and that in certain cases investors' activities do have a grave impact on the public interest of the host state. Including an explicit recognition of internationally accepted standards of corporate responsibility in IIAs may indeed be a step towards redressing this imbalance.

7

Issuance of Compulsory Patent Licences and Expropriation in Asian BITs and FTA Investment Chapters

A Study of India, China, Malaysia and Thailand

PRABHASH RANJAN*

I. Introduction

A very important feature of bilateral investment treaties (BITs) is that these treaties allow foreign investors to bring claims directly against host states before an international arbitral forum for alleged treaty breaches. This is known as investor-state dispute settlement (ISDS) system. From a negligible number in early 1990s, the total number of known treaty-based ISDS cases rose to 942 as of 1 January 2019.[1] In recent times, many foreign investors have started using ISDS to challenge a host state's regulatory measures pertaining to intellectual property rights (IPR).[2] To

* Assistant Professor, Faculty of Legal Studies, South Asian University. All online materials last accessed 20 March 2018. Some parts of this chapter draw from author's following work: Prabhash Ranjan, 'Pharmaceutical Patents and Expropriation in Indian Bilateral Investment Treaties' in Mahdev Mohan and Chester Brown (eds), *Regulation and Investment Disputes: Asian Perspectives* (Cambridge University Press, forthcoming).

[1] UNCTAD, 'Fact Sheet on Investor–State Dispute Settlement Cases in 2018, https://investmentpolicy.unctad.org/publications/1202/fact-sheet-on-investor-state-dispute-settlement-cases-in-2018?utm_source=World+Investment+Network+%28WIN%29&utm_campaign=e418d9704c-EMAIL_CAMPAIGN_2017_05_18_COPY_01&utm_medium=email&utm_term=0_646aa30cd0-e418d9704c-70031781. See also Julien Chaisse, 'The Shifting Tectonics of International Investment Law – Structure and Dynamics of Rules and Arbitration on Foreign Investment in the Asia-Pacific Region' (2015) 47(3) *George Washington International Law Review* 563 (reviewing the increase of ISDS cases in the Asia-Pacific region).

[2] *Eli Lilly and Company v Government of Canada*, ICSID Case No UNCT/14/2, Notice of Intent to Submit a Claim to Arbitration under NAFTA Chapter Eleven (7 November 2012), www.italaw.com/sites/default/files/case-documents/italaw1172.pdf; *Philip Morris Asia Limited v The Commonwealth of Australia*, PCA Case No 2012-12, Award on Jurisdiction and Admissibility (17 December 2015),

give some examples, foreign investors have used ISDS to challenge the following regulatory measures: invalidation of a pharmaceutical patent by a domestic court on the ground of 'inutility';[3] adoption of legislation mandating plain packaging of tobacco products;[4] and adoption of regulations that prohibit tobacco companies from selling different variants for each family brand combined with the regulation that images of the health warning on cigarette packets should increase from 50 per cent to 80 per cent of the cigarette packets.[5] Recently, a question before an ISDS tribunal was whether a trademark could qualify as an investment under the Panama-United States Trade Promotion Agreement.[6]

Although analysing the interface between IPR and international investment law began before investors started using ISDS to challenge IPR-related host state regulatory measures,[7] the topic started to attract much more attention after these

www.italaw.com/sites/default/files/case-documents/italaw7303_0.pdf; *Philip Morris Brands Sàrl, Philip Morris Products SA and Abal Hermanos SA v Oriental Republic of Uruguay*, ICSID Case No ARB/10/7, Award (8 July 2016), www.italaw.com/sites/default/files/case-documents/italaw7417.pdf.

[3] Eli Lilly, a US pharma company, has challenged the invalidation of its patent by a Canadian federal court – *Eli Lilly v Government of Canada,* ICSID Case No UNCT/14/2, Notice of Intent to Submit a Claim to Arbitration under NAFTA Chapter Eleven (7 November 2012) www.italaw.com/sites/default/files/case-documents/italaw1172.pdf; also see Valentia Vadi, 'Towards a New Dialectics: Pharmaceutical Patents, Public Health and Foreign Direct Investments' (2015) 5 *New York University Journal of Intellectual Property and Entertainment Law* 113, 117; Henning Grosse Ruse-Khan, 'Challenging Compliance with International Intellectual Property Norms in Investor-state Dispute Settlement' (2016) 19 *Journal of International Economic Law* 246, 241; Kathleen Liddell and Michael Waibel, 'Fair and Equitable Treatment and Judicial Patent Decisions' (2016) 19 *Journal of International Economic Law* 145, 155–56.

[4] Philip Morris challenged Australia's legislation requiring tobacco products to be sold in plain packets of a specified colour without graphic logos and with health warnings on the front and back side of the pack covering 75% and 90% of the space – see Tania Voon and others, 'Intellectual Property Rights in International Investment Agreements: Striving for Coherence in National and International Law' in CL Lim and Bryan Mercurio (eds), *International Economic Law After the Crisis: A Tale of Fragmented Disciplines* (Cambridge University Press 2015) 380. See also Julien Chaisse, 'Exploring the Confines of International Investment and Domestic Health Protections – Is a General Exceptions Clause a Forced Perspective' (2013) 39(2/3) *American Journal of Law & Medicine* 332.

[5] *Philip Morris Brands Sàrl, Philip Morris Products SA and Abal Hermanos SA v Oriental Republic of Uruguay*, ICSID Case No ARB/10/7, Award (8 July 2016), www.italaw.com/sites/default/files/case-documents/italaw7417.pdf.

[6] *Bridgestone Licensing Services Inc and Bridgestone Americas Inc v Republic of Panama*, ICSID Case No ARB/16/34, Decision on Expedited Objections (13 December 2017) para 164.

[7] Carlos Correa, 'Bilateral Investment Agreements: Agents of New Global Standards for the Protection of Intellectual Property Rights' (*GRAIN*, 3 August 2004), www.grain.org/article/entries/125-bilateral-investment-agreements-agents-of-new-global-standards-for-the-protection-of-intellectual-property-rights; Carlos M Correa, 'Investment Protection in Bilateral and Free Trade Agreements: Implications for the Granting of Compulsory Licenses' (2004) 26 *Michigan Journal of International Law* 331; Lahra Liberti, 'Intellectual Property Rights in International Investment Agreements: An Overview' (2010) OECD Working Paper on International Investment 2010/01, www.oecd.org/daf/inv/investment-policy/WP-2010_1.pdf; Rachel A Lavery, 'Coverage of Intellectual Property Rights in International Investment Agreements: An Empirical Analysis of Definitions in a Sample of Bilateral Investment Agreements and Free Trade Agreements' (2009) 6 *Transnational Dispute Management Journal* 1; Prabhash Ranjan, 'Medical Patents and Expropriation in International Investment Law' (2008) 5(3) *Manchester Journal of International Economic Law* 72; Christopher Gibson, 'A Look at the Compulsory License in Investment Arbitration: The Case of Indirect Expropriation' (2010) 25(3) *American University International Law Review* 368.

arbitral notices were issued.[8] Notwithstanding the growing literature, there is a dearth of country or region-specific studies examining the interface between IPR and international investment law. This chapter is a modest attempt to partially fill this gap by focusing on the question of whether issuance of compulsory patent licences (CPL) on pharmaceutical patents, amount to indirect expropriation[9] under the BITs and FTA investment chapters of India,[10] China,[11] Thailand[12] and Malaysia.[13] This is a pertinent question to ask because in most BITs and FTA investment chapters of these countries, IPRs (which includes patents) are part of

[8] Bryan Mercurio, 'Awakening the Sleeping Giant: Intellectual Property Rights in International Investment Agreements' (2012) 15 *Journal of International Economic Law* 871; Lukas Vanhonnaeker, *Intellectual Property Rights as Foreign Direct Investments: From Collision to Collaboration* (Edward Elgar: Cheltenham, 2015) 9–27.

[9] It is important to bear in mind that regulatory measures related to pharmaceutical patents such as the invalidation of patents or the issuance of CPL could also be challenged under other substantive BIT provisions such as fair and equitable treatment (FET) – Liddell and Waibel discuss the tensions between the interpretation of national patent laws by domestic courts and how FET obligations under BITs could be challenged – see Liddell and Waibel (n 3); also see Mercurio who discusses the various substantive BIT grounds such as national treatment, most favoured nation and FET under which foreign investors can challenge regulatory measures pertaining to IPRs – Mercurio (n 8) 882–901. However, given the constraints of space, this chapter only focuses on expropriation.

[10] India has signed 83 BITs: see UNCTAD, 'India: BITs' (Investment Policy Hub), http://investmentpolicyhub.unctad.org/IIA/CountryBits/96#iiaInnerMenu. India has terminated a large number of these BITs. The list of terminated treaties is available at the website of the Ministry of Finance, Government of India (https://dea.gov.in/bipa). Generally most BITs continue to remain effective for a period of 10 to 15 years (depending on treaty language) for the investments made before the termination of the BIT. For example, Art 15(3) of India-Indonesia BIT states, 'Notwithstanding termination of this Agreement … the Agreement shall continue to be effective for a further period of fifteen years from the date of its termination in respect of investments made or acquired before the date of termination of this Agreement'. For the evolution of India's BITs, see Prabhash Ranjan, 'India and Bilateral Investment Treaties – A Changing Landscape' (2014) 29 *ICSID Review-FILJ* 419. Also see Prabhash Ranjan, *India and Bilateral Investment Treaties: Refusal, Acceptance, Backlash* (Delhi, OUP, 2019) India has signed five free trade agreements (FTAs) containing investment chapters: UNCTAD, 'India: Treaties with Investment Provisions' (Investment Policy Hub), http://investmentpolicyhub.unctad.org/IIA/CountryOtherIias/96#iiaInnerMenu.

[11] China has signed around 150 BITs and FTAs with investment chapters, out of which some have been terminated and some have not been enforced – see UNCTAD, 'China: Bilateral Investment Treaties' (Investment Policy Hub) http://investmentpolicyhub.unctad.org/IIA/CountryBits/42. For a general commentary on Chinese BITs, see Wenhua Shan and Norah Gallagher, *Chinese Investment Treaties: Policies and Practice* (OUP, 2009); Wang Guiguo, *International Investment Law: A Chinese Perspective* (Routledge, 2014); Tyler Cohen and David Schneiderman, 'The Political Economy of Chinese Bilateral Investment Treaty Policy' (2017) 5(1) *Chinese Journal of Comparative Law* 110.

[12] Thailand has signed around 50 BITs and FTA investment chapters see UNCTAD, 'Thailand: Bilateral Investment Treaties' (Investment Policy Hub), http://investmentpolicyhub.unctad.org/IIA/CountryBits/207.

[13] Malaysia has signed more than 70 BITs, out of which some have not been enforced and some have been terminated: UNCTAD, 'Malaysia: Bilateral Investment Treaties' (Investment Policy Hub), http://investmentpolicyhub.unctad.org/IIA/CountryBits/127#iiaInnerMenu. Malaysia has also signed several FTAs with investment chapters – UNCTAD, 'Malaysia: Treaties with Investment Provisions' (Investment Policy Hub), http://investmentpolicyhub.unctad.org/IIA/CountryOtherIias/127#iiaInnerMenu. For more on Malaysian BITs see Sufian Joseph, Muhammad Faliq Abd Razak and Mohammad Azim Mazlan, 'Malaysia and Investor-State Dispute Settlement: Learning from Experience' in Julien Chaisse and Luke Nottage (eds), *International Investment Treaties and Arbitration Across Asia* (Brill, 2018) 216.

the definition of investment. This arguably extends the jurisdiction of an ISDS tribunal to measures such as CPL that may have an impact on a foreign investor's patent right and thus the investor's investment. In recent times, a number of ISDS claims have been brought against countries like India,[14] China[15] and Thailand,[16] making their regulatory measures including CPLs vulnerable to such claims by foreign investors.

CPL is defined generally as the granting of a licence by a government to a third party to use the patent without the consent of the patent holder.[17] CPL is recognized as an important regulatory tool in the hands of countries to be used for purposes such as making available patented medicines that are not accessible to large number of people.[18] The Doha Declaration on TRIPS and Public Health recognizes the importance of CPLs for public health purposes.[19] It also recognizes the right of countries to issue CPLs on any ground they deem fit. These grounds may include: high price of medicines, non-working of patents etc.

[14] *White Industries Australia Ltd v The Republic of India*, Final Award (30 November 2011), www.italaw.com/sites/default/files/case-documents/ita0906.pdf; *CC/Devas (Mauritius) Ltd, Devas Employees Mauritius Private Limited and Telcom Devas Mauritius Limited v Republic of India*, PCA Case No 2013-09, Award on Jurisdiction and Merits (25 July 2016), www.italaw.com/sites/default/files/case-documents/italaw9750.pdf; *Deutsche Telekom v India*, Notice of Arbitration (not public) (2 September 2013), www.italaw.com/cases/2275; *Vodafone International Holdings BV v Government of India [I]*, PCA Case No 2016-35, Notice of Arbitration (not public) (17 April 2014), www.italaw.com/cases/2544; *Vodafone Group Plc and Vodafone Consolidated Holdings Limited v Government of India [II]*, UNCITRAL (UK BIT Claim), www.italaw.com/cases/5713; *Cairn Energy PLC and Cairn UK Holdings Limited (CUHL) v Government of India*, PCA Case No 2016-7, www.italaw.com/cases/5709.

[15] *Ekran Berhad v People's Republic of China*, ICSID Case No ARB/11/15 investmentpolicyhub.unctad.org/ISDS/Details/427; *Ansung Housing Co Ltd v People's Republic of China*, ICSID Case No ARB/14/25, Award (9 March 2017), www.italaw.com/sites/default/files/case-documents/italaw8538.pdf; *Hela Schwarz GmbH v People's Republic of China*, ICSID Case No ARB/17/19, Procedural Order No 2 (10 August 2018), www.italaw.com/sites/default/files/case-documents/italaw9908.pdf, accessed 28 October 2018.

[16] *Werner Schneider, acting in his capacity as insolvency administrator of Walter Bau Ag (In Liquidation) v The Kingdom of Thailand* (formerly *Walter Bau AG v The Kingdom of Thailand*), Award (1 July 2009), www.italaw.com/sites/default/files/case-documents/ita0067.pdf; *Kingsgate Consolidated Ltd v The Kingdom of Thailand*, http://investmentpolicyhub.unctad.org/ISDS/Details/825.

[17] 'Compulsory Licensing of Pharmaceuticals and TRIPS' (WTO, March 2018), www.wto.org/english/tratop_e/trips_e/public_health_faq_e.htm; also see Sara M Ford, 'Compulsory Licensing Provisions under TRIPS Agreement: Balancing Pills and Patents' (2000) 15 *American University Law Review* 941; Theresa Beeby Lewis, 'Patent Protection for the Pharmaceutical Industry: A Survey of Patent Laws of Various Countries' (1996) 30 *International Lawyer* 835, 845.

[18] V Kuek, K Phillips and JC Kohler, 'Access to Medicines and Domestic Compulsory Licensing: Learning from Canada and Thailand' (2011) 6(2) *Global Public Health* 111.

[19] As explained by Chaisse and Guennif, 'the Doha declaration does highlight the right to healthcare and access to medicines, but the international rules as they exist today are still markedly in favour of manufacturing in developed countries to the detriment of poor countries. This is the entire point of the developing countries', and in particular India's, position, who are currently engaged in fresh international negotiations in search of a better balance between the urgent necessity to guarantee the most under-privileged populations as satisfying as possible access to medicines, especially to fight epidemics, and the consideration of the drug industry's financial compulsions. In any event, this problem has transcended from the national level into the international level.' See Julien Chaisse and Samira Guennif, 'Present Stakes around Patent Political Economy' (2007) 2(1) *Asian Journal of WTO Law and Policy* 65, 92.

In order to study this, the chapter first discusses briefly the concept of expropriation in international investment law (section II). In order to examine whether issuance of CPLs will be expropriation, the chapter will discuss those FTA investment chapters and BITs that exempt issuance of CPLs from the ambit of expropriation (section III). Next, the chapter will discuss those BITs that are silent as regards issuance of CLs (section IV). The chapter concludes by observing that in those BITs that do not exempt issuance of CPLs from the ambit of expropriation, whether issuance of CPL is expropriation or not will be subject to ISDS arbitral discretion (section V).

II. Expropriation under International Investment Law

A very important substantive provision in investment treaties is the rule on expropriation whereby a state is prohibited from 'taking' foreign investment except when expropriation is for public purpose, following due process and against due compensation.[20] If a state expropriates foreign investment satisfying the above stated requirements, it will be a case of lawful expropriation and will not be a breach of the BIT. If the host state expropriates foreign investment without satisfying all these conditions, then the expropriation would be unlawful and thus a breach of the BIT. Expropriation, in its classical sense, refers to direct or formal expropriation, which means that the host state takes away the legal title of the investment.[21] This can be achieved either by nationalization, which is referred to as expropriation of an entire industry or sector,[22] confiscation, requisition or acquisition.

Direct expropriations, which are easily identifiable, have become rare.[23] As modern states increasingly regulate various spheres of life, instances of indirect interference with investor's property rights have become more prominent. However, the difficulty is in determining when such indirect interference constitutes expropriation.[24] Indirect expropriation refers to the deprivation of the substantial benefits flowing from the investment without any formal 'taking' of the property.[25] Whether host country's regulatory measures result in indirect

[20] For more on expropriation in international investment law see Jeswald Salacuse, *The Law of Investment Treaties* (OUP, 2015) 317–28.

[21] Jeswald Salacuse, *The Law of Investment Treaties* (OUP, 2015) 322–25; Andrew Newcombe and Lluís Paradell, *Law and Practice of Investment Treaties: Standards of Treatment* (Wolters Kluwer Law and Business, 2009) 323.

[22] Newcombe and Paradell (n 21) 323.

[23] *Marvin Roy Feldman Karpa v United Mexican States,* ICSID Case No ARB(AF)/99/1, Award (16 December 2002), https://www.italaw.com/sites/default/files/case-documents/ita0319.pdf, para 100.

[24] The *Feldman* tribunal recognized the difficulty by saying that direct expropriation was relatively easy whereas 'it is much less clear when the governmental action that interferes with broadly-defined property rights … crosses the line from valid regulation to compensable taking', para 100.

[25] Rudolf Dolzer and Christoph Schreuer, *Principles of International Investment Law* (OUP, 2nd edn, 2012) 92; Jeswald Salacuse, *The Law of Investment Treaties* (OUP, 2015) 297; *Starrett Housing*

expropriation is a question that has acquired prominence due to a range of sovereign regulatory functions being challenged as acts of expropriation by different foreign investors under BITs in the last decade or so. This includes expropriation cases against Argentina for adopting regulatory measures to save itself from an extremely severe economic and financial crisis; claims of expropriation for environment-related regulatory measures;[26] regulatory measures aimed at addressing the supply of drinking water;[27] and regulatory measures involving sovereign functions like taxation.[28] ISDS tribunals have developed three tests to determine whether indirect or regulatory expropriation has occurred – the 'sole effects' test, the 'police powers' test and the 'proportionality' test. These tests are discussed briefly below.

A. The '*Sole Effects*' Test

The '*sole effects*' test, whereby the crucial factor in determining whether an indirect expropriation has occurred, is solely the effect of the governmental measure on the property, purpose of the regulatory measure being irrelevant.[29] Focus on 'effect' of the regulatory measure to determine indirect expropriation raises the question of how severe the 'effect' must be to come to the conclusion that indirect expropriation has taken place. Tribunals have answered this question by saying that 'under international law, expropriation requires a 'substantial deprivation'.[30] In other words, tribunals have said that the effect should be such that it substantially deprives the investment and hence the test is of 'substantial deprivation' to determine indirect expropriation.[31] The effect can certainly be more than substantial such as in cases

Corporation v Islamic Republic of Iran, 4 Iran-US CTR 122, 154 (1983). See also *Tippetts, Abbett, McCarthy, Stratton and TAMS-AFFA Consulting Engineers of Iran v Islamic Republic of Iran* 6 Iran-US CTR 219, 225 (1984).

[26] See *Metalclad Corporation v United Mexican States*, ICSID Case No ARB(AF)/97/1, Award (30 August 2000), www.italaw.com/sites/default/files/case-documents/ita0510.pdf; *Methanex Corporation v United States of America, NAFTA-UNCITRAL*, Final Award on Jurisdiction and Merits (3 August 2005), www.italaw.com/sites/default/files/case-documents/ita0529.pdf.

[27] See *Biwater Gauff (Tanzania) Ltd v United Republic of Tanzania*, ICSID Case No ARB/05/22, Award (24 July 2008), www.italaw.com/sites/default/files/case-documents/ita0095.pdf.

[28] See *Occidental Exploration & Production Co v Republic of Ecuador*, LCIA Case No UN3467, Final Award (1 July 2004), www.italaw.com/sites/default/files/case-documents/ita0571.pdf; *EnCana Corporation v Republic of Ecuador*, LCIA Case No UN3481, Award (3 February 2006), www.italaw.com/sites/default/files/case-documents/ita0285_0.pdf.

[29] Rudolf Dolzer and Felix Bloch, 'Indirect Expropriation: Conceptual Realignments?' (2003) 5 *International Law Forum du droit international* 155; *AWG Group Ltd v The Argentine Republic*, ICSID Case No ARB/03/19, (30 July 2010), www.italaw.com/sites/default/files/case-documents/ita0055.pdf para 133.

[30] *Pope and Talbot Inc v The Government of Canada*, Ad hoc Tribunal (UNCITRAL), Interim Award (26 June 2000), www.italaw.com/sites/default/files/case-documents/ita0674.pdf, para 96.

[31] PSEG Global Inc, *The North American Coal Corporation and Konya Ingin Electrik Üretim ve Ticaret Limited Sirketi v Republic of Turkey*, ICSID Case No ARB/02/5, Award (19 January 2007), www.italaw.com/sites/default/files/case-documents/ita0695.pdf, paras 278–80; *CMS Gas Transmission Company v The Republic of Argentina*, ICSID Case No ARB/01/8, Decision on Liability (12 May 2005),

where the deprivation is complete or total. For example, the tribunal in *Total SA v Argentina*[32] held that under international law, those measures that do not constitute direct expropriation may nevertheless result in indirect expropriation 'if an effective deprivation of the investment is thereby caused'.[33]

B. The 'Police Powers' Test

Many ISDS tribunals have adopted the 'police powers' test whereby the purpose and context of the regulatory measure assumes significance in determination of expropriation.[34] This doctrine basically means that if a state adopts a measure in the exercise of that state's police powers, there is no liability for any claim of expropriation due to that measure.[35] The best illustration of the police powers doctrine in international investment law is in *Methanex v United States*[36] where the tribunal stated:

> As a matter of general international law, a non-discriminatory regulation for a public purpose, which is enacted in accordance with due process and, which affects, inter alios, a foreign investor or investment is not deemed expropriatory and compensable unless specific commitments had been given by the regulating government to the then putative foreign investor contemplating investment that the government would refrain from such regulation.[37]

Likewise, an ISDS tribunal in *Philip Morris v Uruguay* stated that 'the State's reasonable bona fide exercise of police powers in such matters as the maintenance of public order, health or morality, excludes compensation even when it causes

www.italaw.com/sites/default/files/case-documents/ita0184.pdf, para 262; *Mamidoil Jetoil Greek Petroleum Products Societe Anonyme SA v Republic of Albania*, ICSID Case No ARB/11/24, Award (30 March 2015), www.italaw.com/sites/default/files/case-documents/italaw4228.pdf, paras 566, 570; *Philip Morris Brands Sàrl, Philip Morris Products SA and Abal Hermanos SA v Oriental Republic of Uruguay*, ICSID Case No ARB/10/7, Awards (8 July 2016), www.italaw.com/sites/default/files/case-documents/italaw7417.pdf, paras 191–92.

[32] *Total SA v The Argentine Republic*, ICSID Case No ARB/04/01, Decision on Liability (27 December 2010), www.italaw.com/sites/default/files/case-documents/ita0868.pdf.

[33] *Total SA v The Argentine Republic*, ICSID Case No ARB/04/01, Decision on Liability (27 December 2010), www.italaw.com/sites/default/files/case-documents/ita0868.pdf, para 195.

[34] Maurizio Brunetti, 'Indirect Expropriation in International Law' (2003) 5(3) *International Law Forum du droit international* 150, 151.

[35] Ben Mostafa, 'The Sole Effects Doctrine, Police Powers and Indirect Expropriation under International Law' (2008) 15 *Australian International Law Journal* 267, 272–73.

[36] *Methanex Corporation v United States of America*, NAFTA UNCITRAL, Final Award on Jurisdiction and Merits (3 August 2005), www.italaw.com/sites/default/files/case-documents/ita0529.pdf.

[37] *Methanex Corporation v United States of America*, NAFTA UNCITRAL, Final Award on Jurisdiction and Merits (3 August 2005), www.italaw.com/sites/default/files/case-documents/ita0529.pdf, Part IV Ch D 4 para 7; *Saluka Investments BV v The Czech Republic*, UNCITRAL, Partial Award (17 March 2006), www.italaw.com/sites/default/files/case-documents/ita0740.pdf; *El Paso Energy International Company v The Argentine Republic*, ICSID Case No ARB/03/15, Award (31 October 2011), www.italaw.com/sites/default/files/case-documents/ita0270.pdf, para 240.

economic damage to an investor and that the measures taken for that purpose should not be considered as expropriatory ….'[38]

C. The Proportionality Test

A third approach that some ISDS tribunals have followed to determine indirect expropriation is the proportionality test, which is defined by Kingsbury and Schill as 'a method of legal interpretation and decision making in situations of collisions or conflict of different principles and legitimate public policy objectives'.[39] The proportionality test has three steps,[40] which must be assessed cumulatively.[41] First, whether the measure is suitable for the legitimate public purpose – this will require a causal link between the measure and its object.[42] If the measure satisfies the first step, then the second step would be to find out whether the measure is necessary, ie whether there is a less restrictive alternative measure that would achieve the same objective.[43] If the measure is 'necessary', the third step (also known as proportionality *stricto sensu*) will involve balancing the effects of the measure on the right that has been affected with the public benefit sought to be achieved by the measure.[44]

One of the first ISDS disputes which made a somewhat elaborate reference to the principle of proportionality is *Tecmed v Mexico*.[45] The tribunal cited the European Court of Human Rights (ECtHR) jurisprudence[46] to support the

[38] *Philip Morris Brands Sàrl, Philip Morris Products SA and Abal Hermanos SA v Oriental Republic of Uruguay*, ICSID Case No ARB/10/7, Awards (8 July 2016), www.italaw.com/sites/default/files/case-documents/italaw7417.pdf, para 295. For a critical discussion on how the tribunal dealt with the police powers rule in this case see Prabhash Ranjan, 'Police Powers, Indirect Expropriation in International Investment Law, and Article 31(3)(c) of the VCLT: A Critique of Philip Morris v. Uruguay' (2018) *Asian Journal of International Law*, https://doi.org/10.1017/S2044251318000139, accessed 28 October 2018. Also see *WNC Factoring Ltd (WNC) v The Czech Republic*, PCA Case No 2014-34, Award (22 February 2017), www.italaw.com/sites/default/files/case-documents/italaw8533.pdf – one of the recent cases where police powers rule was used in interpreting the expropriation provision.

[39] Benedict Kingsbury and Stephan Schill, 'Public Law Concepts to Balance Investors' Rights with State Regulatory Actions in the Public Interest – The Concept of Proportionality' in Stephan W Schill (ed), *International Investment Law and Comparative Public Law* (OUP, 2010) 79.

[40] Kingsbury and Schill (n 39) 85–88; Andreas Kulick, *Global Public Interest in International Investment Law* (CUP, 2012) 186–89.

[41] Erlend M Leonhardsen, 'Looking for Legitimacy: Exploring Proportionality Analysis in Investment Treaty Arbitration' (2011) 3(1) *Journal of International Dispute Settlement* 95; Jan H Jans, 'Proportionality Revisited' (2000) 27(3) *Legal Issues of Economic Integration* 239, 240–41.

[42] See also Jans (n 41) 240.

[43] Jans (n 41) 240; Kingsbury and Schill (n 39) 86–87.

[44] Jans (n 41) 241; Kingsbury and Schill (n 39) 87–88.

[45] *Técnicas Medioambientales Tecmed SA v The United Mexican States*, ICSID Case No ARB(AF)/00/2, Award (29 May 2003), www.italaw.com/sites/default/files/case-documents/ita0854.pdf. Also see *Philip Morris Brands Sàrl, Philip Morris Products SA and Abal Hermanos SA v Oriental Republic of Uruguay*, ICSID Case No ARB/10/7, Awards (8 July 2016), www.italaw.com/sites/default/files/case-documents/italaw7417.pdf.

[46] *Mellacher and Others v Austria* (1989) 12 EHRR 391 24; *Pressos Compañía Naviera and Others v Belgium* (1995) 21 EHHR 301, 19; *James and Others v The United Kingdom* (1986) 8 EHRR 123, 19–20.

proportionality test in its determination of indirect expropriation.[47] The tribunal held that 'there must be a reasonable relationship of proportionality between the charge or weight imposed to the foreign investor and the aim sought to be realized by any expropriatory measure'.[48] Often ISDS tribunals have not been consistent in articulating the proportionality principle especially if one keeps the three-step test mentioned above in mind.[49] However, a recent ISDS tribunal in a case known as *PL Holdings v Poland*[50] articulated the three-step proportionality test. The tribunal held that 'to satisfy the [proportionality] principle, a measure must (a) be one that is suitable by nature for achieving a legitimate public purpose, (b) be necessary for achieving that purpose in that no less burdensome measure would suffice, and (c) not be excessive in that its advantages are outweighed by its disadvantages'.[51]

In view of the discussion above, the question is whether the issuance of CPLs amounts to indirect expropriation by interfering with the exclusivity rights that a patent bestows on the patentee. The following section will answer this question for those Indian, Chinese, Malaysian and Thai FTA investment chapters and BITs that exempt issuance of CPLs from the ambit of expropriation.

III. FTA Investment Chapters and Bits Exempting Issuance of CPLs from the Ambit of Expropriation

A. Scope of Exemption for CPL

In order to discuss the scope of exemption for issuance of CPLs, the discussion has been divided into two parts: exempting issuance of CPLs from the ambit of expropriation only; and exempting issuance of CPL from the entire BIT.

[47] *Técnicas Medioambientes Tecmed SA v United Mexican States*, ICSID Case No ARB(AF)/00/2, Award (29 May 2013) para 115.

[48] *Técnicas Medioambientales Tecmed SA v The United Mexican States*, ICSID Case No ARB(AF)/00/2, Award (29 May 2003), www.italaw.com/sites/default/files/case-documents/ita0854.pdf, para 122. Also see *LG&E Energy Corp, LG&E Capital Corp and LG&E International Inc v Argentine Republic*, ICSID Case No ARB/02/1, Decision on Liability (3 October 2006), www.italaw.com/sites/default/files/case-documents/ita0460.pdf para 195; *Azurix Corp v The Argentine Republic*, ICSID Case No ARB/01/12, Award (14 July 2006), www.italaw.com/sites/default/files/case-documents/ita0061.pdf para 312. See also *Electrabel SA v The Republic of Hungary*, ICSID Case No ARB/07/19), Award (25 November 2015), www.italaw.com/sites/default/files/case-documents/italaw4495.pdf, para 179.

[49] Prabhash Ranjan, 'Using the Public Law Concept of Proportionality to Balance Investment Protection with Regulation in International Investment Law: A Critical Reappraisal' (2014) 3(3) *Cambridge Journal of International and Comparative Law* 853.

[50] *PL Holdings Sarl v Republic of Poland*, SCC Case No 2014/163, Partial Award (28 June 2017) www.italaw.com/sites/default/files/case-documents/italaw9378.pdf.

[51] *PL Holdings Sarl v Republic of Poland*, SCC Case No 2014/163, Partial Award (28 June 2017) www.italaw.com/sites/default/files/case-documents/italaw9378.pdf para 355, 391.

i. Exempting Issuance of CPLs from the Ambit of Expropriation Only

Many FTA investment chapters and some BITs of India, China, Malaysia and Thailand, provide that the expropriation provisions shall not apply to the issuance of CPLs. For instance, Article 10.7.6 of the India-Malaysia FTA states that the expropriation provision does not apply to the issuance of compulsory licences granted in relation to intellectual property rights in accordance with the WTO Agreement on Trade Related Aspects of Intellectual Property Rights (TRIPS).[52] Similarly, Article 8(7) of the India-ASEAN investment agreement (Malaysia and Thailand are parties to this agreement) provides that 'this article does not apply to the issuance of compulsory licenses granted in relation to intellectual property rights, in accordance with the TRIPS agreement'.[53] Article 8(6) of the China-ASEAN investment agreement also provides that the expropriation provision shall not apply to issuance of CPL on IPRs that is granted in accordance with the TRIPS agreement.[54] One of the few Chinese BITs that exempts issuance of CPLs from the ambit of expropriation is the China-Colombia BIT signed in 2013. Article 4.6 of the China-Colombia BIT states that CPLs issued in accordance with Articles 30 and 31 of the TRIPS agreement 'may not be challenged' under the expropriation provision. Another Chinese BIT that provides for such provision is China-Canada BIT. Article 10(2) of the BIT provides that the provision on expropriation 'does not apply to the issuance of compulsory licenses granted in relation to intellectual property rights, or to other measures in respect of intellectual property rights, to the extent that such measures are consistent with international agreements regarding intellectual property rights to which both Contracting Parties are parties'.

Likewise, in case of Malaysia, Article 12.8.5 of the Malaysia-Australia FTA exempts CPLs issued in accordance with the TRIPS agreement from the ambit of expropriation.[55] Article 14.5 of the ASEAN Comprehensive Investment agreement

[52] Also see Comprehensive Economic Partnership Agreement between the Republic of India and Japan (signed 16 February 2011, entered into force 1 August 2011) (India-Japan FTA) Art 92.5.

[53] Also see Comprehensive Economic Cooperation Agreement between the Government of Malaysia and the Government of the Republic of India (signed 24 September 2010, entered into force 1 July 2011) (India-Malasia FTA) Art 10.7(6), which provides: 'This Article does not apply to the issuance of compulsory licenses granted in relation to intellectual property rights in accordance with the WTO Agreement on Trade Related Aspects of Intellectual Property Rights.'

[54] Also see Free Trade Agreement Between the Government of New Zealand and the Government of the People's Republic of China (signed 7 April 2008, entered into force 1 October 2008) (China-New Zealand FTA) Art 145(5); Investment Agreement of the Mainland and Hong Kong Closer Economic Partnership Arrangement (signed 28 June 2017, entered into force 28 June 2017) (China-Hong Kong CEPA Investment Agreement) Art 11(3).

[55] Also see Free Trade Agreement between Australia and Malaysia (signed 22 May 2012, entered into force 1 January 2013) (Australia-Malaysia FTA) Art 12.8.5; Free Trade Agreement between the Government of New Zealand and the Government of Malaysia (signed 26 October 2009, entered into force 1 August 2010) (Malaysia-New Zealand FTA) Art 10.8.5; Agreement between the Government of the Islamic Republic of Pakistan and the Government of Malaysia for a Closer Economic Partnership (signed 8 November 2007, entered into force 1 January 2008) (Malaysia-Pakistan CEPA) Art 94.4.

(Malaysia and Thailand are party to this agreement) also exempts CPLs issued in accordance with the TRIPS Agreement from the ambit of expropriation.[56]

Given the fact that issuance of CPLs is exempt from expropriation in some of the FTA investment chapters as discussed above, it implies that issuance of CPLs cannot be challenged as expropriation of foreign investment. However, there is one catch to this proposition. The assertion that issuance of CPLs, in these treaties, are exempt from expropriation is subject to these CPLs being issued in accordance with the TRIPS Agreement.[57] Article 31 of the TRIPS Agreement provides detailed requirements for issuance of compulsory licences.[58] These requirements are in the form of conditions that need to be satisfied while issuing CPLs, such as the scope and duration of the patent shall be limited to the purpose for which it was authorized;[59] such use shall be non-exclusive;[60] the right holder shall be paid adequate remuneration in the circumstances of each case taking into account the economic value of such authorization;[61] and other conditions.[62]

TRIPS Agreement does not restrict the grounds on which CPLs may be issued.[63] In fact, the Doha Declaration on the TRIPS Agreement and Public health makes it quite clear that 'each member [country of the WTO] has the right to grant compulsory licenses and freedom to determine the grounds upon which such licenses are granted'.[64]

In other words, this means that if a CPL is issued in accordance with Article 31 of the TRIPS Agreement, then it would be outside the ambit of expropriation provision of the BIT. Conversely, if issuance of a CPL is not in accordance with the

[56] Also see Agreement Establishing the ASEAN-Australia-New Zealand Free Trade Area (signed 27 February 2009, entered into force 10 January 2010) ASEAN-Australia-New Zealand FTA) Art 9.5; The ASEAN-Republic of Korea Investment Agreement (signed 2 June 2009, entered into force 1 September 2009) (ASEAN-Korea FTA) Art 12.5; Agreement between the Government of the Islamic Republic of Pakistan and the Government of Malaysia for a Closer Economic Partnership (signed 8 November 2007, entered into force 1 January 2008) (Malaysia-Pakistan CEPA) Art 94.4.

[57] See Christopher S Gibson, 'Latent Grounds in Investor-State Arbitration: Do International Investment Agreements Provide New Means to Enforce Intellectual Property Rights?' in Karl P Sauvant (ed), *Yearbook on International Investment Law and Policy 2009–2010* (Columbia University Vale Center and OUP, 2010) 421; Mercurio (n 8) 905–06.

[58] Peter Van den Bossche and Werner Zdouc, *The Law and Policy of the World Trade Organization* (CUP, 4th edn, 2017) 1038.

[59] General Agreement on Trade-Related Aspects of Intellectual Property (signed 15 April 1994, entered into force 1 January 1995) Art 31(c).

[60] General Agreement on Trade-Related Aspects of Intellectual Property (signed 15 April 1994, entered into force 1 January 1995) Art 31(d).

[61] General Agreement on Trade-Related Aspects of Intellectual Property (signed 15 April 1994, entered into force 1 January 1995) Art 31(h).

[62] For other conditions see General Agreement on Trade-Related Aspects of Intellectual Property (signed 15 April 1994, entered into force 1 January 1995) Art 31.

[63] Peter Van den Bossche and Zdouc, *The Law and Policy of the World Trade Organization* (CUP, 4th edn, 2017) 1038. One exception to this is the case of semiconductor technology – See General Agreement on Trade-Related Aspects of Intellectual Property (signed 15 April 1994, entered into force 1 January 1995) Art 31(c).

[64] 'Doha Declaration on the TRIPS agreement and public health', Doha WTO Ministerial Conference (Doha 9 November–13 November 2001) (adopted 14 November 2001) WT/MIN(01)/DEC/2 para 5(b).

TRIPS Agreement, the CPL can be challenged as a potential violation of the expropriation provision of the BIT or the FTA investment chapter as the case may be.

The critical question is, in a situation like this, who will have the jurisdiction to determine whether a CPL has been issued in accordance with the TRIPS Agreement? Let us answer this through a hypothetical example. Assume that a country issues a CPL on a patented drug of a foreign pharma company. This can be challenged before the WTO's dispute settlement body (DSB) by the home state of the foreign pharma company. Additionally, the foreign investor may challenge the issuance of a CPL as a violation of the expropriation provision of the BIT between the investor's home state and the state issuing the CPL before an ISDS tribunal. If indeed such a challenge is brought, the ISDS tribunal, which may not have expertise in WTO law,[65] would have to make a substantive determination as to whether the issuance of CPL is consistent with the TRIPS Agreement. Whether such a challenge has been made or not before the WTO's DSB will not matter to the ISDS tribunal.

If the issuance of CPL is consistent with the TRIPS Agreement, then the tribunal will not go into the question of expropriation. However, if the issuance of CPL is not in accordance with the TRIPS Agreement, then the expropriation provision would continue to apply.[66] This also means that for all practical purposes wherever exemption of CPLs from expropriation is made contingent on the consistency of CPLs with the TRIPS Agreement, it does not exclude the jurisdiction of an ISDS tribunal from examining issuance of CPLs as violations of the BIT. On the one hand, an ISDS tribunal having jurisdiction on issuance of CPL could be seen as interference on the sovereign right of countries to issue such licences. This is more so because it is not possible to be sure of the extent to which an ISDS tribunal will be deferential to the state issuing the CPL. On the other hand, it can also be argued that an ISDS tribunal having jurisdiction to determine whether a CPL has been issued in accordance with the TRIPS Agreement or not will enable a balancing of investors' rights with host state's right to regulate. Such arbitral oversight will ensure that regulatory abuses by host states in issuing CPLs do not go unaddressed.

ii. Exempting Issuance of CPLs from the Ambit of the Entire BIT

Another interesting point is that since these FTA investment chapters exempt issuance of CPLs only from the ambit of expropriation, these measures could still be challenged for violating other substantive obligations such as fair and equitable treatment (FET). In other words, there is restricted immunity given to issuance of CPLs from the ambit of BIT protection. A contemporary example of giving greater immunity to issuance of CPLs from the scope of BIT protection is Article 2.4(iii) of

[65] Mercurio (n 9) 905.
[66] Ibid.

the 2016 Indian Model BIT.[67] Article 2.4 (iii) of the 2016 Model BIT provides that that the treaty shall not apply to 'issuance of compulsory licenses granted in relation to intellectual property rights … to the extent that such issuance, revocation, limitation or creation is consistent with the international obligations of Parties under the WTO Agreement'. This formulation makes the entire treaty inapplicable to issuance of CPLs and is not restricted merely to expropriation. In other words, issuance of CPL cannot be challenged either under the expropriation provision or any other BIT provision as long as the CPL has been issued in accordance with the WTO agreement.[68] The Indian Model BIT, to this extent, is different from the formulations in other treaties of India, China, Indonesia and Malaysia, discussed above. However, Article 2.4(iii) of the Indian Model BIT is similar to the kind of provisions discussed above in the sense that it also gives jurisdiction to an ISDS tribunal to decide whether a CPL has been issued in accordance with the WTO agreement.

It is important to recall the different formulation given in the draft 2015 Indian Model BIT.[69] Article 2.6(v) of the draft Model provided that the treaty shall not apply to 'the issuance of compulsory licenses granted in relation to intellectual property rights, or to the revocation, limitation or creation of intellectual property rights, to the extent that such issuance, revocation, limitation or creation is consistent with the Law of the Host State'. The draft, unlike the final version, did not make any reference to the WTO agreement, but made reference instead to domestic laws, which would better serve the host country's regulatory power. This can be illustrated by a practical example. Assume that the Indian government issues a CPL on a patented drug, which is upheld by the Indian Supreme Court. If the foreign investor challenges this before an ISDS tribunal, under the 2016 Model, the investor would have to show that the issuance of CPL is inconsistent with the WTO agreement. On the other hand, under the draft 2015 Model, the foreign investor would have to show that the CPL has been issued inconsistently with Indian law. It is expected that the arbitral tribunal will be deferential to the Indian court's assessment as to whether CPL has been issued in accordance with Indian law, whereas it will be less deferential when it comes to consistency with the WTO agreement, because here compliance with international law and not India's domestic law will be in question.

[67] Model text for the Indian Bilateral Investment Treaty https://dea.gov.in/sites/default/files/ModelBIT_Annex_0.pdf. It is important to keep in mind that the Indian Model BIT contains two dates – 28 December 2015 given in the letter accompanying the text; and 14 January 2016 on the website of the Ministry of Finance, Government of India as the date of publication of the BIT – www.finmin.nic.in/office-memorandum accessed 20 July 2018. In this chapter the 14 January 2016 date is used, and thus the Model BIT is described as the 2016 Indian Model BIT and *not* the 2015 Indian Model BIT. Also see Prabhash Ranjan and Pushkar Anand, 'The 2016 Model Indian Bilateral Investment Treaty: A Critical Deconstruction' (2017) 38(1) *Northwestern Journal of International Law and Business* 1.

[68] Also see Ranjan and Anand (n 67) 45.

[69] Model Text for the Indian Bilateral Investment Treaty www.mygov.in/sites/default/files/master_image/Model%20Text%20for%20the%20Indian%20Bilateral%20Investment%20Treaty.pdf.

Indian and Chinese approaches on the issue of scope of exemption for CPL differ in RCEP negotiations. RCEP, as is well known, is a proposed FTA between the Association of Southeast Asian Nations (ASEAN) countries (Brunei, Cambodia, Indonesia, Laos, Malaysia, Myanmar, the Philippines, Singapore, Thailand, Vietnam) and six countries of the Asia-Pacific states with which ASEAN has existing FTAs.[70] These countries are Australia, China, India, Japan, South Korea and New Zealand. From the unofficial text of RCEP's investment chapter, it appears that India's position on how issuance of CPLs and limitation or revocation of IPRs should be treated in the investment chapter is the same as India's 2016 Model BIT. In other words, India's position is that issuance of CPLs and revocation of IPRs should be outside the ambit of the investment chapter, provided that the regulatory measure is consistent with the WTO Agreement.[71]

China's approach is different from that of India on the issue of CPLs. Like the FTA investment chapters and some of the recently signed BITs, China's formulation is that issuance of CPLs that are consistent with the TRIPS Agreement shall be exempt from the expropriation provision of the treaty.[72] In other words, issuance of CPL can be challenged as a violation of any other provision of the investment chapter such as the FET provision. These two positions look irreconcilable. Out of the two formulations, the position that the RCEP adopts will clearly be the winning view.

B. Is Revocation or Limitation of Patent Rights Exempted?

Another major point emerging from the previous discussion is what if instead of issuing a CPL, the host state revokes or limits the patent right of a foreign company or a foreign investor? For instance, Section 66 of the Indian Patent Act, 1970 states that 'where the Central Government is of opinion that a patent or the mode in which it is exercised is mischievous to the State or generally prejudicial to the public, it may, after giving the patentee an opportunity to be heard, make a declaration to that effect in the Official Gazette and thereupon the patent shall be deemed to be revoked'. Such revocations of patents are different from issuance of CPLs and thus, the question is whether such revocations are also exempt from challenge under expropriation? These investment treaties do not explicitly cover these situations. This would allow a foreign investor to challenge the revocation or limitation of patents as indirect expropriation under these investment chapters.

Some FTA investment chapters of India, China, Malaysia and Thailand address this problem by excluding not just issuance of CPLs but also revocation

[70] See Julien Chaisse and Richard Pomfret, 'The RCEP and the Changing Landscape of World Trade: Assessing Asia-Pacific Investment Regionalism Next Stage' (2018) 11(3) *Law and Development Review*, https://doi.org/10.1515/ldr-2018-0058, accessed 29 October 2018.

[71] RCEP Draft Investment Text, www.bilaterals.org/IMG/pdf/rcep-draft-investment-text-india.pdf.

[72] RCEP Draft Investment Text, www.bilaterals.org/IMG/pdf/rcep-draft-investment-text-china.pdf.

and limitation of IPRs from the ambit of expropriation provision. For instance, Article 6.5(6) of the India-Singapore FTA provides that

> this Article does not apply to the issuance of compulsory licenses granted in relation to intellectual property rights, or to the revocation, limitation or creation of intellectual property rights to the extent that such issuance, revocation, limitation or creation is consistent with the WTO Agreement on Trade Related Aspects of Intellectual Property Rights.[73]

Likewise, Article 10.5 of the Hong Kong-ASEAN investment agreement provides that

> for greater certainty, [Article 10 on expropriation and compensation] does not apply to the issuance of compulsory licences granted in relation to intellectual property rights, or to the revocation, limitation, or creation of intellectual property rights, to the extent that such issuance, revocation, limitation, or creation is consistent with TRIPS Agreement.

Furthermore, the treaty provides that 'revocation' of intellectual property rights 'includes the cancellation or nullification of such rights' and 'limitation' of intellectual property rights 'includes exceptions to such rights'.

However, even revocation or limitation of a foreign investor's patent right has to be consistent with the TRIPS obligations of these countries. In other words, an ISDS tribunal, as in the previous instances of checking the compliance of issuance of CPL with the TRIPS agreement, will be the arbiter to decide whether the patent right has been revoked or limited in accordance with the TRIPS agreement. If not, then the ISDS tribunal will have the jurisdiction to decide whether any such revocation or limitation violates the BIT or the FTA investment chapter or not as the case may be.

IV. BITs with No Reference to Issuance of CPLs

This section will discuss the different possibilities of foreign investors bringing ISDS claims against the state under those BITs, which unlike the ones discussed before, do not make any reference to issuance of CPLs. Here, the discussion is divided between those BITs where the scope of ISDS is restricted to a narrow issue of 'dispute concerning the amount of expropriation', followed by those BITs where an ISDS tribunal can have jurisdiction over 'any dispute' concerning the investment made by the foreign investor.

[73] Art 10.12(6) of the India-Korea FTA contains language exactly similar to Art 6.5(6) of the India-Singapore FTA: 'This Article does not apply to the issuance of compulsory licences granted in relation to intellectual property rights, or to the revocation, limitation or creation of intellectual property rights, to the extent that such issuance, revocation, limitation or creation is consistent with the TRIPS Agreement.'

A. Not to Challenge CPL Per Se, but its Remuneration

Some Chinese BITs, especially those signed in the 1980s, contain a restricted ISDS clause.[74]

For example, Article 9(1) of the China-Bulgaria BIT states that 'any dispute between contracting state and the investor of the other contracting state concerning the amount for expropriation may be submitted to an ad hoc arbitral tribunal'. Likewise, Article 12(3) of the New Zealand-China BIT provides 'if a dispute involving the amount of compensation resulting from expropriation referred to in Article 6 not be settled within six months after resort to negotiation … it may be submitted to an international arbitral tribunal established by both parties'. All other disputes between the investor and the state shall be settled by the competent domestic courts.[75]

Provisions such as these mean that a foreign investor can bring an ISDS claim against the state only when the dispute is on the question of compensation for expropriation and not for expropriation *per se* or for any other matter. In other words, if a treaty contains a provision such as this, then issuance of a CPL can be challenged only if there is a dispute on the issue of compensation for expropriation and not for the issue whether issuance of a CPL amounts to indirect expropriation or not. A dispute on the issue of compensation for expropriation cannot take place till there is recognition that foreign investment (say patent rights) has been expropriated. It is quite possible that the state may not even accept that issuance of a CPL amounts to expropriation of foreign investment. If this claim of the state is contested by the foreign investor, then the competent domestic court will decide whether issuance of CPL amounts to indirect expropriation or not.

B. To Challenge CPL as a Dispute Including Indirect Expropriation

BITs of India, Malaysia, Thailand and more recent Chinese BITs contain broader ISDS provisions. For instance, Article 10(2) of the Malaysia-Denmark BIT provides for international arbitration to address 'an alleged breach of any right conferred or created by this Agreement with respect to an investment by such

[74] See Nils Eliason, 'Chinese Investment Treaties: A Procedural Perspective' in Luke Nottage and Vivienne Bath (eds), *Foreign Investment and Dispute Resolution Law and Practice in Asia* (New York/ Abingdon, Routledge, 2011) 90.

[75] Similar provisions are available in Agreement between the Government of the Democratic Socialist Republic of Sri Lanka and the Government of People's Republic of China for the Reciprocal Promotion and Protection of Investments (signed 13 March 1986, entered into force 25 March 1987) (China-Sri Lanka BIT) Art 13(3); China and Singapore Agreement on the Promotion and Protection of Investments (with exchanges of letters) (signed 21 November 1985, entered into force 7 February 1986) (China-Singapore BIT) Art 13(3).

national or company'.[76] Likewise, Article 9(1) of the China-Barbados BIT provides that 'any dispute concerning an investment between an investor of one Contracting Party and the other Contracting Party shall, as far as possible, be settled amicably through negotiations between the investor and the other Contracting Party'. Further Article 9(2) provides that 'if any dispute referred to in paragraph 1 of this Article cannot be settled within six months following the date on which the written notification of the dispute has been received by one party from the other party to the dispute, the investor shall have the right to choose to submit the dispute for resolution by international arbitration'.

Since the focus here is on 'any dispute' it has a wide scope to cover disputes alleging that issuance of CPL amounts to indirect expropriation.

Large numbers of BITs of India, China, Malaysia and Thailand do not specify the non-applicability of the expropriation to issuance of CPLs. In other words, these treaties, unlike the treaties discussed in the previous section, do not specifically exempt issuance of CPLs from the ambit of the expropriation provision or from the scope of the treaty. These treaties contain a typical expropriation provision that is broad enough to cover both direct and indirect expropriation. Furthermore, they also subject expropriation to conditions such as public purpose, due process and due compensation.[77]

Consequently, in all these BITs, foreign investors can challenge issuance of CPL as indirect expropriation. Moreover, even if CPL has been issued in a manner consistent with the TRIPS Agreement, the ISDS tribunal shall still have jurisdiction to adjudicate upon such challenges since the treaty does not create any such exception. Since issuance of CPLs would not involve any formal transfer of the title, foreign investors would challenge it as indirect expropriation. Determination of indirect expropriation, also known as regulatory expropriation, is difficult. If a foreign investor were to challenge the issuance of CPL as an indirect expropriation, the outcome will depend on a number of factors, including the question of which of the three tests discussed earlier will an ISDS tribunal adopt to determine indirect expropriation, and the language of the treaty. In order to understand this, the discussion will be divided into two parts: first, those BITs that do not provide guidance on how to determine indirect expropriation and also do not refer to any kind of carve-out provision for general regulatory measures; second, those BITs that contain limited guidance on how to determine indirect expropriation by

[76] Malaysia-China BIT is a slight exception to this rule. See Agreement between the Government of the People's Republic of China and the Government of Malaysia Concerning the Reciprocal Encouragement and Protection of Investments (signed 21 November 1988, entered into force 31 March 1990) (Malaysia-China BIT) Art 7.

[77] For example, see Agreement between the Government of the People's Republic of Bulgaria and the Government of the People's Republic of China Concerning the Reciprocal Encouragement and Protection of Investments (signed 27 June 1989, entered into force 21 August 1994) (China-Bulgaria BIT) Art 4; India and Denmark: Agreement Concerning the Promotion and Reciprocal Protection of Investments (signed 6 September 1995, entered into force 28 August 1996) (India-Denmark BIT) Art 5(1).

making reference to carve-out provisions to safeguard certain kinds of regulatory measures. Another point which will also be discussed is, since issuance of CPL shall require payment of adequate remuneration to the patent holder, whether the foreign investor will challenge issuance of CPLs as expropriation.

i. BITs that do not Provide Guidance to Determine Expropriation and Make No Reference to Carve-out Provisions

Many Indian, Chinese, Thai and Malaysian BITs provide that 'investments shall not be nationalised, expropriated or subject to measures having effect equivalent to nationalisation or expropriation'. Thus, under these BITs, the host state is prohibited not only from nationalizing and expropriating foreign investment, but also from adopting a regulatory measure that has an effect equivalent to nationalization or expropriation.[78] The only criteria mentioned in these BITs to determine indirect expropriation is the 'effect' of the regulatory measure on foreign investment. Arguably, this refers to the 'sole effect test', where indirect expropriation would occur if the regulatory measure results in substantial deprivation of foreign investment. The purpose behind the regulatory measure does not matter in this analysis. Thus, if issuance of CPLs results in substantial deprivation (depending on the degree of interference)[79] either because the CPL is issued for a long duration or because the remuneration provided to the patent holder is inadequate, then it could potentially amount to indirect expropriation.[80]

[78] See Agreement between the Republic of India and the Kingdom of the Netherlands for the promotion and protection of investments (signed 6 November 1995, entered into force 1 December 1996) (India-Netherlands BIT) Art 5(1); India and Denmark: Agreement Concerning the Promotion and Reciprocal Protection of Investments (signed 6 September 1995, entered into force 28 August 1996) (India-Denmark BIT) Art 5(1); Agreement between the Federal Republic of Germany and the Republic of India for the Promotion and Protection of Investments (signed 10 July 1995, entered into force 13 July 1998) (India-Germany BIT) Art 5(1); Agreement between the Government of the United Kingdom of Great Britain and Northern Ireland and the Government of the Republic of India for the Promotion and Protection of Investments (signed 14 March 1994, entered into force 6 January 1995) (India-UK BIT) Art 5(1); Agreement between the Government of the Democratic Socialist Republic of Sri Lanka and the Government of the Republic of India for the Promotion and Protection of Investments (signed 22 January 1997, entered into force 13 February 1998) (India-Sri Lanka BIT) Art 5(1); Agreement between the Government of the Republic of India and the Government of the Socialist Republic of Vietnam for the Promotion and Protection of Investments (signed 8 March 1997, entered into force 1 December 1999) (India-Vietnam BIT) Art 5(1); Agreement between the Government of the Sultanate of Oman and the Government of the Republic of India for the Promotion and Protection of Investments (signed 2 April 1997, entered into force 13 October 2000) (India-Oman BIT) Art 5(1); Agreement between the Government of the Republic of Indonesia and the Government of the Republic of India for the Promotion and Protection of Investments (signed 10 February 1999, entered into force 22 January 2004) (India-Indonesia BIT) Art 5(1); and Agreement between the Government of the Republic of India and the Government of the Union of Myanmar for the Reciprocol Promotion and Protection of Investments (signed 24 June 2008, entered into force 8 February 2009) (India-Myanmar BIT) Art 5(1).

[79] Christopher S Gibson, 'Latent Grounds in Investor-State Arbitration: Do International Investment Agreements Provide New Means to Enforce Intellectual Property Rights?' in Karl P Sauvant (ed), *Yearbook on International Investment Law and Policy 2009–2010* (Columbia University Vale Center and OUP, 2010) 456.

[80] Mercurio (n 8) 914–15.

One critical factor here could be the role that Article 31 of the TRIPS agreement and the Doha declaration on TRIPS and public health, that allows countries to issue CPLs on any ground they deem fit, could play in determination of indirect expropriation. The interpretation of the expropriation provision in the BITs has to be guided by the rules of treaty interpretation contained in the Vienna Convention on the Law of Treaties (VCLT). Article 31(3)(c) of the VCLT[81] requires the treaty interpreted to do the following.[82] First, to determine whether there is a 'rule of international law'.[83] Second, whether such a rule is 'applicable in the relations between the parties'.[84] Third, to determine whether such a rule is 'relevant'.[85] Fourth, if a rule satisfies the three conditions mentioned above, it is admissible in the process of interpretation, ie the rule shall be 'taken into account' in accordance with the chapeaus of Article 31(3).[86] However, it will still be necessary to determine the weight that should be accorded to this admissible rule in the interpretation of the treaty norm.[87]

The TRIPS Agreement and the Doha Declaration on TRIPS and public health are 'an applicable rule in the relation between the parties' under Article 31(3)(c) of the VCLT. Consequently, the TRIPS Agreement and the Doha Declaration will be admissible as an interpretative material in the interpretation of the expropriation provision in the BIT. However, the interpretative weight that will be attached to Article 31 of the TRIPS Agreement and the Doha declaration will depend on how the ISDS arbitral tribunal will take these rules into account keeping the context of the BIT in mind.

On the other hand, it is quite possible that an arbitral tribunal may adopt the 'police powers' test in determining expropriation.[88] If such an approach is adopted, then even if issuance of CPLs amounts to a severe degree of interference with the rights of the investor, it will not amount to expropriation if the CPL has been issued

[81] Article 31(3)(c) of the VCLT provides: 'There shall be taken into account, together with the context' 'any relevant rules of international law applicable in the relations between the parties'.

[82] See Martins Paparinskis, 'Investment Treaty Interpretation and Customary Investment Law: Preliminary Remarks' in Chester Brown and Kate Miles (eds), *Evolution in Investment Treaty Law and Arbitration* (Cambridge University Press, 2011) 65, 73; Bruno Simma, 'Foreign Investment Arbitration: A Place for Human Rights' (2011) 60(3) *International and Comparative Law Quarterly* 573, 584–85; Bruno Simma and Theodore Kill, 'Harmonising Investment Protection and International Human Rights: First Steps towards a Methodology' in Christina Binder and others (eds), *International Investment Law for the 21st Century: Essays in Honour of Christoph Schreuer* (New York, OUP, 2009) 678, 695–99; Richard K Gardiner, *Treaty Interpretation* (New York, OUP, 2008) 259–65.

[83] Simma and Kill (n 82) 679.

[84] Simma and Kill (n 82) 679.

[85] Simma and Kill (n 82) 679; Paparinskis (n 82) 70–71.

[86] Paparinskis (n 82) 65.

[87] Paparinskis (n 83) 65. Also see Prabhash Ranjan, 'Police Powers, Indirect Expropriation in International Investment Law, and Article 31(3)(c) of the VCLT: A Critique of Philip Morris v. Uruguay' 9(1) *Asian Journal of International Law* 98.

[88] For example, in *Saluka v Czech Republic*, the tribunal adopted the police powers approach in determining expropriation, though Art 5 of the Czech-Netherlands BIT, that provided for expropriation, does not contain any specific language (of the kind given in some of the Indian BITs discussed above), concerning the police powers approach in determining expropriation.

for public health purposes following due process and on a non-discriminatory basis.[89]

If a tribunal were to use the test of proportionality, then whether issuance of the CPL would amount to expropriation would depend on: whether issuance of the CPL is suitable to the public health purpose; whether the CPL is necessary to achieve the public health purpose, ie there is no other less restrictive regulatory measure that would achieve the same objective; whether the benefits of issuing the CPL outweigh the costs imposed on the foreign investor.

Given the fact that ISDS tribunals may use any of the three tests mentioned above, whether the issuance of CPL would amount to indirect expropriation or not will, to a considerable extent, depend on the test applied. It would also depend on the discretion of the ISDS tribunal in terms of how it applies the test.

ii. BITs that Provide Limited Guidance to Determine Expropriation by Making Reference to Carve-out Provisions

Some BITs provide limited guidance as to how to determine indirect expropriation. For instance, the India-Jordan BIT states that 'except in rare circumstances, non-discriminatory regulatory actions by a Party that are designed and applied to protect legitimate public welfare objectives including health, safety and the environment concerns do not constitute expropriation or nationalisation'.[90] Likewise, the India-China BIT provides that 'except in rare circumstances, non-discriminatory regulatory measures adopted by a Contracting Party in pursuit of public interest,

[89] Christopher S Gibson, 'Latent Grounds in Investor-State Arbitration: Do International Investment Agreements Provide New Means to Enforce Intellectual Property Rights?' in Karl P Sauvant (ed), *Yearbook on International Investment Law and Policy 2009–2010* (Columbia University Vale Center and OUP, 2010) 458–59.

[90] Agreement between the Government of the Republic of India and the Hashemite Kingdom of Jordan for the Promotion and Protection of Investments (signed 30 November 2006, entered into force 22 January 2009) (India-Jordan BIT) Annex A, Art 3. Similar provisions exist in Agreement between the Government of the Republic of India and the Government of the Republic of Ireland for the Promotion and Protection of Investments (signed 29 June 2007, entered into force 16 December 2008) (India-Iceland BIT) Annex, Art 3; Agreement between the Government of the Republic of India and the Government of the Syrian Arab Republic for the Mutual Promotion and Protection of Investments (signed 18 June 2008, entered into force 22 January 2009) (India-Syria BIT) Annex, Art 3; Agreement between the Government of the Republic of India and the Government of the Republic of Senegal for the Promotion and Protection of Investments (signed 3 July 2008, entered into force 17 October 2009) (India-Senegal BIT) Annex 5.1, Art 3; Agreement between the Government of the Republic of India and the Government of the Republic of Latvia for the Promotion and Protection of Investments (signed 18 February 2010, entered into force 27 November 2010) (India-Latvia BIT) Protocol, Art 5(4)(c); Comprehensive Economic Cooperation Agreement between the Republic of India and the Republic of Singapore (signed 29 June 2005, entered into force 1 August 2005) (India-Singapore CECA) Art 6.11; Comprehensive Economic Partnership Agreement between India and the Republic of Korea (signed 7 August 2009, entered into force 1 January 2010) (India-Korea CEPA) Art 10.18; Agreement between the Government of the Republic of India and the Government of His Majesty the Sultan and Yang Di-Pertuan of Brunei Darussalam on the Reciprocal Promotion and Protection of Investments (signed 22 May 2008, entered into force 18 January 2009) (India-Brunei BIT) Protocol II(d).

including measures pursuant to awards of general application rendered by judicial bodies do not constitute indirect expropriation or nationalization'.[91]

In other words, barring certain rare circumstances, non-discriminatory regulatory measures such as issuance of CPLs will not amount to indirect expropriation if such CPLs have been issued in public interest notwithstanding the effect on foreign investment. It is important to bear in mind that these BITs do not define the meaning of 'except in rare circumstances'.

Some BITs, such as the India-Brunei BIT, also state that 'except in rare circumstances' non-discriminatory measures of a country designed and applied for legitimate public welfare objectives such as health, safety and the environment, do not constitute measures having effect equivalent to nationalization or expropriation. However, the India-Brunei BIT, unlike the India-China BIT, defines 'except in rare circumstances' as a situation where 'a measure or series of measures are so severe in light of their purpose that they cannot be reasonably viewed as having been adopted and applied in good faith'. Given this BIT language, if a CPL is challenged as expropriation provision, the ISDS tribunal will have to assess whether the benefits of the measure on public health outweigh the adverse effects on foreign investment. If yes, then the issuance of a CPL might be tantamount to indirect expropriation.

Similarly, Annex 10 A 3 (b) of the India-Korea FTA investment chapter states that 'except in rare circumstances' refers to 'when measures are extremely severe or disproportionate in light of its purpose and effect'. Thus, whether issuance of CPLs amounts to expropriation or not will depend on whether the public health benefits of the measure are severely disproportionate with the effect of the measure on foreign investment (such as determining how severe is the curtailment of the exclusivity right of the patent holder).

There are some BITs that simply exempt all kinds of non-discriminatory regulatory measures adopted for public benefit such as health, safety and environment, from the purview of expropriation without the phrase 'except in rare circumstances' prefacing the provision.[92] As a result, in these BITs, there is no situation where non-discriminatory issuance of a CPL for public health purpose amount to expropriation. No examination of the benefits of the issuance of CPL will be assessed against the costs imposed on foreign investment.

iii. The Role of Remuneration in the Determination of Expropriation

The final argument that needs to be dealt with is: what is the role of remuneration to the patent holder in a CPL in the determination of expropriation? For

[91] Protocol to the Agreement between the Republic of India and the People's Republic of China on Promotion and Protection of Investments (signed 21 November 2006, entered into force 1 August 2007) (China-India BIT).

[92] Comprehensive Economic Cooperation Agreement between the Government of Malaysia and the Government of the Republic of India (signed 18 February 2011, entered into force 1 July 2011) (India-Malaysia FTA) Art 10.7.

example, section 90 of the Indian Patent Act requires payment of remuneration to the patent holder. Precisely, section 90(1) of the Indian Patent Act provides that 'in settling the terms and conditions of a [compulsory] licence under section 84, the Controller shall endeavour to secure – that the royalty and other remuneration, if any, reserved to the patentee or other person beneficially entitled to the patent, is reasonable, having regard to the nature of the invention, the expenditure incurred by the patentee in making the invention or in developing it and obtaining a patent and keeping it in force and other relevant factors'. In other words, since every case of issuance of CPL shall involve payment of remuneration to the patent holder, why would the patent holder (ie the pharmaceutical company) bring an ISDS claim challenging issuance of CPL as indirect expropriation?

The answer to this question is that since the remuneration requirement in issuance of CPL is quite low when compared to the compensation requirement for expropriation contained in BITs, the foreign investor might prefer to challenge the issuance of CPL as expropriation. For instance, Article 5(1) of the India-Germany BIT states that compensation to be paid for expropriating foreign investment has to

> be equivalent to the value of the expropriated or nationalised investment immediately before the date on which such expropriation or nationalisation became publicly known. Such compensation shall be effectively realisable without undue delay and shall be freely convertible and transferable. Interest shall be paid in a fair and equitable manner for the period between the date of expropriation or nationalisation and the date of actual payment of compensation.[93]

In other words, BIT imposes a more onerous obligation on the state in terms of paying compensation that has to be equal to the value of investment, which is often not the case with remuneration paid for issuance of a CPL. For instance, in case involving issuance of a CPL in India, *Natco v Bayer*,[94] Bayer was awarded a royalty of 7 per cent of total sales,[95] which is not the same as the compensation requirement given in the India-Germany BIT. In Thailand, where CPLs were issued, the patent holders were given royalty rates that ranged from 0.5 per cent to 5 per cent of the

[93] Likewise, Art 4(2) of the China-Germany BIT provides: 'such compensation shall be equivalent to the value of the investment immediately before the expropriation is taken or the threatening expropriation has become publicly known, whichever is earlier. The compensation shall be paid without delay and shall carry interest at the prevailing commercial rate until the time of payment; it shall be effectively realizable and freely transferable. Precautions shall have been made in an appropriate manner at or prior to the time of expropriation for the determination and payment of such compensation'. Similar provisions exist in BITs of Thailand. For instance, Art 6(1) of the India-Thailand BIT states that compensation for expropriation 'shall amount to the genuine market value of the investment expropriated, immediately before the expropriation or before the impending expropriation becomes public knowledge, whichever is earlier, shall include interest at a fair and equitable rate until the date of payment, shall be made without unreasonable delay, be effectively realizable and be freely transferable'.

[94] Also see Thailand Patent Act BE 2522 (1979).

[95] Mansi Sood, 'Natco Pharma Limited v Bayer Corporation and the Compulsory Licensing Regime in India' (2013) 6(1) *NUJS Law Review* 99, 110.

sales revenue of the generic drugs.[96] Some questioned these royalty rates as being quite low.[97]

In other words, the fact that the issuance of a CPL is accompanied by remuneration does not mean that it satisfies an important requirement of expropriation in BITs, ie paying due compensation. The remuneration offered for issuance of CPL under domestic laws is quite low in comparison to the compensation that needs to be paid for expropriation of foreign investment. Consequently, the issuance of CPLs on medicines with remuneration that is too low could still be challenged as expropriation under many BITs.

Moreover, it is also important to bear in mind that when a state issues a CPL, the state might not call it an expropriation but only a regulation, notwithstanding the fact that some remuneration may have been paid to the patent holder. Thus, the question of whether issuance of CPL amounts to expropriation or not may still be relevant when raised before an ISDS tribunal.

V. Conclusion

The discussion in this chapter shows that issuance of CPLs on foreign investors can be challenged as indirect expropriation by foreign investors relying on ISDS. The outcome of such a challenge will depend on two factors. First, the language of the treaty, such as whether it exempts issuance of CPLs from the ambit of what is considered to be expropriation (in which case the governments are free to issue CPLs, as long as these are consistent with the TRIPS Agreement) or whether the expropriation provision in the treaty provides some guidance to determination of indirect expropriation by containing some general carve-out provision. Second, in treaties that do not contain any such language, the outcome of such a challenge will depend on the approach of the arbitral tribunal, such as whether the tribunal uses the 'sole effect' test, the 'police powers' test, or the proportionality test to determine indirect expropriation. This is more so given the inconsistency in the reasoning of ISDS tribunals.

In order to curb arbitral discretion and provide regulatory space to host countries to adopt CPLs without worrying about an ISDS challenge, countries like India, China, Malaysia and Thailand need to draft their treaties carefully. This trend is visible in some of the newer generation BITs such as the 2016 Indian Model BIT and in China-Canada BIT. The focus on treaty language is also evident in the FTA investment chapters that these countries have signed. The formulation that countries can issue CPLs provided they are consistent with the TRIPS Agreement is the correct formulation, as it explicitly recognizes the regulatory right of these countries to adopt a measure for public health purposes, and also ensures that this right is reconciled with the interests of the foreign investors.

[96] Thailand issued seven compulsory licences between 2006–2008, and none were challenged by the patentees.

[97] Eric Bondy and Kamal Saggi, 'Compulsory licensing, price controls, and access to patented foreign products' (2014) (109) *Journal of Development Economics* 217.

PART III

Improving the IP Provisions of CPTPP/RCEP and Redefining Global IP Norms

8

Will RCEP Redefine Norms Related to Pre-grant Opposition and Experimental Use Exceptions in International Patent Law?

PRASHANT REDDY THIKKAVARAPU*

I. Introduction

Since the signing of the Agreement on Trade Related Intellectual Property (TRIPS) in 1994 as a part of the WTO Agreement, patent law has become increasingly international. For most part, TRIPS was perceived as leaning heavily in favour of the rights of the patentees although there are many who argue that TRIPS represents a fair bargain between developed and developing countries.[1] In contrast, the limitations and exceptions to the patentee's rights tend to be couched in language that is more general than specific and is always permissive rather than mandatory. As a result, it took the Doha Declaration in 2001 to clarify that TRIPS, which came into effect in 1995, allowed for compulsory licences.[2] The likely reason for this imbalance between rights and exceptions in the international patent law context is because it is the powerful IP-owners lobby in the United States (US) and the European Union (EU) that set the international patent law agenda.[3]

* Assistant Professor at the National Academy of Legal Studies & Research & External Fellow, Applied Research Centre for Intellectual Assets & the Law in Asia, School of Law, Singapore Management University.

[1] See generally Jayashree Watal, 'The Trips Agreement and Developing Countries' (1997) 1 *The Journal of World Intellectual Property* 281.

[2] The Doha Declaration on the TRIPS Agreement and Public Health, 14 November 2001, WT/MIN(01)/DEC/2.

[3] See eg Frederick M Abbott, Protecting First World Assets in the Third World: Intellectual Property Negotiations in the GATT Multilateral Framework, (1989) 22 *Vanderbilt Journal of Transnational Law* 689, 918; Thomas Cottier, 'The TRIPs Agreement' in Patrick FJ Macrory, Arthur E Appleton and Michael G Plummer (eds), *The World Trade Organization: Legal, Economic and Political Analysis* (Springer Verlag AG, forthcoming 2005) 938; Julien Chaisse and Luan Xinjie, 'Revisiting the Intellectual Property Dilemma – How Did We Get to Strong WTO IPR Regime?' (2018) 34(2) *Santa Clara High Technology Law Journal* 153–78.

For most part, developing countries are reacting, rather than proactively setting the agenda.[4]

Over time as multilateral trade deals failed to make headway, developed countries began pushing bilateral trade deals with a TRIPS-plus agenda.[5] In the last decade, the focus has moved away from bilateral deals to regional deals.[6] The most prominent amongst the new trade deals, are the Comprehensive and Progressive Agreement for Trans-Pacific Partnership (CPTPP) and the Regional Comprehensive Economic Partnership (RCEP). The key difference in terms of membership in both trade deals, is the US. The US was the main mover behind the precursor to the CTPP, the Trans-Pacific Partnership (TPP) (until it pulled out after President Donald Trump took office in 2017), but is not a part of RCEP negotiations. The two major developing economies in RCEP are India and China, neither of whom share the maximalist patent law stance of the US, and there have been predictions for some time that these countries will reframe the international intellectual property (IP) debate.[7] RCEP also includes developed countries such as Japan, Australia and New Zealand.[8]

Given that RCEP is one of the first big trade deals to be negotiated without the participation of either the US or the EU, it will be interesting to observe the direction of this new treaty. From the leaked texts of treaty negotiations, there is evidence to suggest that RCEP will deviate significantly from existing international patent law norms on limitations, exceptions and safeguards.[9]

Two such issues, which form the basis of this chapter, are pre-grant oppositions and the experimental use exception. Both provisions were on the negotiating table during CPTPP but did not make it to the final text of that treaty. Not only does the leaked text of RCEP contain provisions on both pre-grant oppositions and experimental use exception, but the language used in the leaked text suggests that

[4] See generally Peter Drahos, 'Developing Countries and International Intellectual Property Standard Setting' (2002) 5 *The Journal of World Intellectual Property* 765.

[5] See generally Graham Dutfield, '"To Copy is to Steal": TRIPS, (Un)Free Trade Agreements and the New Intellectual Property Fundamentalism' (2006) *The Journal of Information and Technology Law* 1; See also Jean-Frederic Morin, 'Multilateralizing TRIPs-Plus Agreements: Is the US Strategy a Failure?' (2009) 12 *The Journal of World Intellectual Property* 175.

[6] See generally Bryan Mercurio, 'TRIPS-Plus Provisions in FTAs: Recent Trends' in L Bartels and F Ortino (eds), *Regional Trade Agreements and the WTO Legal System* (Oxford University Press, 2006).

[7] See generally Jerome Reichman, 'Intellectual Property in the Twenty First Century: Will the Developing Countries Lead or Follow?' (2009) 46 *Houston Law Review* 1115; Rochelle Cooper Dreyfuss, 'The Role of India, China, Brazil and Other Emerging Economies in Establishing Access Norms for Intellectual Property and Intellectual Property Lawmaking' (30 July 2009). Institute for International Law and Justice Working Paper 2009/5; *NYU School of Law, Public Law Research Paper No 09-53.*

[8] Amiti Sen, 'India in talks with China, Australia, New Zealand to crack mega trade deal', *The Hindu Business Line*, 20 June 2018 available at www.thehindubusinessline.com/economy/india-in-talks-with-china-australia-new-zealand-to-crack-mega-trade-deal/article24212820.ece. On the RCEP negotiations, see also Julien Chaisse and Richard Pomfret 'The RCEP and the Changing Landscape of World Trade Assessing Asia-Pacific Investment Regionalism Next Stage' (2018) 11(4) *Law and Development Review* 1–32.

[9] Single Working Document on the Intellectual Property Chapter, Regional Comprehensive Economic Partnership (RCEP), Free Trade Agreement as made available on Knowledge Ecology International (KEI), 19 April 2015.

both provisions will be mandatory for all RCEP members. This would be a first for an international patent law treaty for two reasons. First, prior attempts during TRIPS negotiation to clearly articulate a list of exceptions failed, which is why the limitations and exceptions in that treaty are so open-ended.[10] Second, even the limitations, exceptions and safeguards found in agreements like TRIPS are usually optional and not mandatory as the leaked draft of RCEP.

This chapter explains the significance of both pre-grant patent opposition and experimental use exceptions from a patent law perspective, and how Americans either oppose, or interpret, these provisions in very narrow terms. Understanding the American stance is important in order to grasp the significance of these provisions being included in RCEP as well as their rejection from CPTPP.

II. Pre-grant Oppositions as a Filter to Improve Patent Quality

One of the key challenges faced by patent offices across the world is ensuring that patent applications are examined properly, so that only high-quality patents are issued.[11] Sometimes even advanced patent offices like the United States Patent & Trademark Office (USPTO), despite all the resources at their disposal end up granting some truly frivolous patents like the infamous patent for 'method of swinging on a swing'[12] or the patent for the method 'to induce cats to exercise by directing a beam of invisible light by a hand-held apparatus onto the floor'.[13]

While patents for methods of swinging on a swing do not have significant implications for the economy, the more troublesome patents are those dealing with cutting edge technology, which can impact the economy and influence competition. Examining these patent applications, is no easy task since most patent applications that are dealing with cutting edge technology require substantial time and expertise to understand. Patent examiners, being part of a permanent bureaucracy, are usually behind the curve when it comes to cutting edge technology.[14] Further complicating the issue is the fact that very often patent agents will draft applications in a particular manner, avoiding certain words and phrases, so as to make it more difficult for patent examiners to conduct prior art searches.[15] On the

[10] Watal (n 1) 314.

[11] See generally JH Barton, 'Reforming the Patent System' (2000) 287 *Science* 1933.

[12] Jeff Hecht, 'Boy takes swing at US patents', *New Scientist*, 17 April 2002, available at www.newscientist.com/article/dn2178-boy-takes-swing-at-us-patents.

[13] K Amiss (1993) *Method of exercising a cat* US5443036A.

[14] Christopher Wong, 'Community Service: Adapting Peer Review to the Patenting Process' (2008) 4 *Journal of Law & Policy* 1, 9–10; Some patent offices are becoming more specialized. See generally Ryan Whelan, 'Complex Innovation' (2018) 17 *Chicago-Kent Journal of Intellectual Property* 226.

[15] Jason Rantanen, 'Peripheral Disclosure' (2012) 74 *University of Pittsburgh Law Review* 1, 14; Kenneth D. Sibley, 'Courts Want Less Drafting, More Crafting in Patent Apps', *Law360*, 5 March 2014, available at www.myersbigel.com/wp-content/uploads/2014/04/Less-Drafting-More-Crafting.pdf.

top of these challenges, most patent offices are usually short of staff despite the increasing number of patent applications being filed every year. It was estimated that even in relatively well-resourced patent offices like USPTO, patent examiners spend on average only 18 hours per patent application.[16]

Once granted, a patent has a relatively long term and vests in the patentee significant monopolistic powers. In most countries, the only way a patent can be revoked once granted is by way of litigation in a court of law. More often than not, judicial proceedings are extremely expensive and time-consuming. As an alternative to waiting for post-grant revocations through expensive judicial proceedings, there have been recommendations in the US to increase the level of scrutiny of patent applications through an administrative proceeding 'peer review system',[17] which is usually less expensive and cumbersome compared to judicial proceedings.

One route adopted by several non-US jurisdictions to improve the scrutiny of patent applications, prior to grant, is to open up the examination process to third parties from the private sector, especially competitors who have the technological expertise to provide valuable inputs to the patent office and the incentive to block such patent applications from translating into granted patents.[18] Such interventions can significantly make up for the resource deficit at most patent offices since industry competitors will usually have employees working in the same area who are better placed to identify the relevant prior art.[19] In order to facilitate such interventions by competitors, it is first necessary for the law to mandate the publication of patent applications prior to them being granted and, second, and more importantly, to provide for a mechanism wherein a competitor can intervene and oppose the grant of the patent application before the patent office.

A. Pre-grant Oppositions as a Signalling Mechanism

A secondary outcome of a pre-grant opposition mechanism is that it serves as a mechanism of signalling to the patent office those patent applications that are commercially valuable or of public interest.[20] This is an important function because a vast majority of granted patents are never commercialized. It is estimated that the percentage of patent applications actually commercialized in advanced knowledge

[16] Brenda Sandburg, 'Speed Over Substance?', *Intellectual Property Magazine* (March 1999) (cf Lemley (n 21) below).

[17] Christopher Wong, 'Community Service: Adapting Peer Review to the Patenting Process' (2008) 4 *Journal of Law & Policy* 1, 9–10.

[18] India is one such jurisdiction. See Feroz Ali Khader, *The Touchstone Effect: The Impact of Pre-Grant Opposition* (Lexis Nexis, 2008).

[19] See Khader (n 18) 39–52 and 123–32.

[20] Mark Lemley, Doug Litchman and Bhaven Sampat, 'What to do about Bad Patents?' (2005) 28(4) *Regulation* 10 (on the importance of identifying patent of commercial significance and harnessing the knowledge of private parties in order to ensure high quality patents).

economies like the US is only 5 per cent.[21] Most patent offices are not in a position to identify the patent applications that are commercially valuable and thus are unable to dedicate more resources and time towards those patent applications that may merit a closer scrutiny in order to protect public interest. However, when a pre-grant opposition mechanism exists in the law, industry competitors will be tracking patent applications, by using the pre-grant opposition mechanism to object to those patent applications that have the potential to interfere with their future businesses.[22] When such pre-grant opposition applications are filed, it is a signal to the patent office that the opposed patent applications are valuable and have the potential to affect the market and consumers in the future. Depending on the public policy outlook of the national patent offices, these patent applications can be the subject of more detailed scrutiny and those applications could be expedited over other patent applications that may not be so valuable to society.

B. The Three Types of Pre-Grant Intervention

A study of national patent laws will reveal that pre-grant oppositions or interventions can be of three types.

The first type of pre-grant interventions, allows third parties merely to submit evidences in the form of a written representation to the patent office raising objections to the invention claimed in the published patent application. They do not become 'party' to the proceedings and usually do not have a right to an oral hearing in such cases. The patent office may or may not consider such written representations when making its final decision on the patent application. In other words, the discretion to consider the arguments and evidence of the opponent lies entirely with the patent office. This form of pre-grant intervention, found in the US and the EU, is considered to be weaker than systems of pre-grant opposition where the opponent becomes party to the proceedings.[23]

A second type of pre-grant intervention is an opposition system that allows for any person, regardless of whether they have commercial interests in the invention sought to be patented, to file a pre-grant opposition after publication of the patent application. Such persons are then made party to the proceedings and their opposition will mandatorily have to be considered by the patent office while making a final decision on whether the patent can be granted. Any final decision of the patent office in such cases will have to be reasoned after considering all the prior art and evidence provided by the third party, thereby ensuring more transparency in the patent examination process. The only example of a country which follows

[21] Mark Lemley, 'Rational Ignorance at the Patent Office' (2001) 95(4) *Northwestern University Law Review* 1, 12.

[22] Khader (n 18) 123–32.

[23] Article 115 of the European Patent Convention (EPC), 35 United States Code (USC) 122(e).

such a pre-grant opposition mechanism is India.[24] While the Indian system is praised for allowing wide-ranging participation, including by access-to-medicine NGOs, there have been complaints that the Indian system is prone to abuse since it is open-ended and ends up creating delays in the grant of patent applications due to the staggered filing of oppositions by the same opponents through various proxies.[25] Although there have been cases where the Indian pre-grant opposition mechanism has been abused, there has been no study to examine the extent of the problem.[26] Even without abuse of the pre-grant system, it is likely that the mere operation of the mechanism does in fact cause delays because once a pre-grant opposition is filed, the patent office has to follow a more rigorous procedure that includes hearing oral argument. Scheduling such a hearing and writing a reasoned decision can take time, leading to delays in the grant of these patents, a fact that is lamented by IP owners.[27]

A third type of pre-grant intervention is an opposition system where the national law gives interested third parties a timeframe of a few months to oppose a patent application after the patent office has finished examining the application and found it in order for grant. The examined patent applications are advertised in the official publications and oppositions are invited within a fixed period of time from 'interested persons', which is usually interpreted as meaning persons from the same industry with competing interests. The opposing parties become party to the proceedings which are then conducted in an adversarial manner and the patent office is expected to render a reasoned decision based on the arguments made during the opposition. Such reasoned decisions, unlike the ordinary grant of patent applications, will explain the reasons behind the decision to grant the patent.

Historically, the opposition system was specified by the Patents Act, 1911 enacted by the British Parliament in the early twentieth century for the British Empire.[28] Many former British colonies retained this mechanism even after independence. This includes developed countries like Australia[29] and New Zealand,[30] albeit with some modifications. This pre-grant opposition mechanism reduces the scope of abuse seen in the Indian system because it allows only 'interested persons'

[24] Section 25(1) of the Indian Patents Act, 1970.

[25] *Dr (Miss) Snehlata Gupte vs Union of India & Ors* WP (C) No 3516 of 2007 before Delhi High Court decided on 15 July 2010 (the court makes an observation that the practice of filing serial pre-grant patent oppositions was an abuse of the process of law and noted the need to discourage such filing).

[26] Item no 17 in 'Issues raised and suggestions received from stakeholders' by the Indian Patent Office during a meeting with IP stakeholders on steps taken for improvement in processes in IPO and their impact, 14 December 2016, available at www.ipindia.nic.in/writereaddata/Portal/News/292_1_ISSUES_Raised_in_Meeting_with_IP_Stakeholders.pdf.

[27] Special 301 Report of the United States Trade Representative (2018) 49 ('Further, patent applicants face costly and time-consuming patent opposition hurdles, long timelines for receiving patents, and excessive reporting requirements').

[28] Section 9 of the Patents and Designs Act, 1911.

[29] Section 59 of the Australian Patents Act, 1990.

[30] Section 92 of the New Zealand Patents Act, 2013.

to file oppositions within a fixed window of four months. The downside, however, of this system is that the opposition process is opened to the public only after the patent office has already finished its examination process. This is not the most efficient process for patent offices, who can otherwise save significant time if they receive industry inputs during their own examination process.

C. The Opposition to Pre-Grant Oppositions in India and Other Countries

Pre-grant opposition mechanisms, especially those that afford a right to a hearing, have been opposed by the pro-patents lobby. The lobbying in India against pre-grant opposition, from the 1950s to 2005, serves as an interesting illustration of the debate on the importance of pre-grant opposition mechanisms.

The Indian system of pre-grant opposition had existed since 1911. In the early days after Independence, when India was studying the need for patent law reform, one of the expert committees, the Tek Chand committee, had recommended the abolition of pre-grant opposition on various grounds including that such a system 'delays the grant of patents by reason of the necessary extension of time caused by such proceedings … entailing a delay of at least nine months after the acceptance of the application'.[31] This fear of delay in grant of patents is one of the most frequently cited reasons by those who oppose pre-grant oppositions.

A second expert committee headed by Justice Ayyangar, constituted by the government of India, criticized the proposal by Tek Chand committee to abolish the pre-grant opposition mechanism, calling it 'retrograde'.[32] In his report, submitted to the Government of India in 1959, Ayyangar cautioned the government that abolition of the pre-grant opposition was 'neither in the interests of the patentees themselves nor calculated to further the progress of research or industry in India'.[33] Examining the nature and number of pre-grant oppositions filed between 1950 and 1957, the Ayyangar report demonstrated that for the 20,222 patents granted in India in this period there were only 140 oppositions filed of which 55 were successful and 47 were unsuccessful, with the remaining being withdrawn or abandoned or dismissed.[34] Of those that were decided, 42 were decided within a year.[35] On the basis of these figures and a study of the nature of opponents, the Ayyangar report concluded that there was no evidence to suggest that pre-grant oppositions are '… entered mala fide with a view to blackmail'.[36] Explaining the monopoly effects of

[31] *Ministry of Industry & Supply, Government of India – Report of the Patent Enquiry Committee* (1948–1950) 146–55.

[32] Justice N Rajagopala Ayyangar, Report on the Revision of the Patent Law (1959) 79.

[33] Ibid 79.

[34] Ibid 83.

[35] Ibid 83.

[36] Ibid 83.

a granted patent on competitors, the Ayyangar report concluded that it was in the public interest to retain a robust system of pre-grant opposition.[37]

Commenting on jurisdictions like the US which lacked any pre-grant opposition mechanism, the Ayyangar report points out how there had been calls within the US to implement such a mechanism to improve the quality of patents. The report concludes by recommending to the government that India to expand the grounds of oppositions to those found in the UK Patents Act 1949.[38]

The new Indian patent law enacted in 1972 reflected the recommendations of the Ayyangar committee report and created a broader pre-grant opposition mechanism that allowed for an opposition to be filed within four months of a patent application being examined and advertised by the Patent Office.[39]

The opposition against India's pre-grant opposition was renewed in the years leading up to the historic Patents (Amendment) Act 2005, which amended Indian law to restore pharmaceutical product patents and hence guarantee compliance with the TRIPS Agreement.[40] The original draft of this law, introduced in Parliament in 2003, proposed doing away the system of pre-grant opposition.[41] The new mechanism proposed by this draft bill replaced the existing pre-grant opposition mechanism with a token pre-grant representation system. Under this system, any person could make a representation to the patent office by submitting written objections to the patent office after a patent application was published but before the patent had actually been granted. After the patent was granted, 'interested persons' were afforded an opportunity to file a post-grant opposition after the patent had been granted.[42]

It is speculated that pressure from American lobbies had led to this severe dilution of an otherwise robust pre-grant opposition mechanism.[43] It was only after criticism from the press and the political opposition that the draft legislation was amended to include a right to be heard at even the stage of pre-grant opposition.[44] As finally enacted, the Patents (Amendment) Act 2005 contained both a pre-grant and post-grant opposition mechanism, with the opponent having a right to be heard in both forms of opposition.[45] Although the Indian Patent Office was initially reluctant to provide oral hearings to opponents at the pre-grant stage (the reason

[37] Ibid 84.

[38] Ibid 84.

[39] Section 25 of the Patents Act, 1970 as originally enacted.

[40] See Julien Chaisse and Samira Guennif, 'Present Stakes around Patent Political Economy: Legal and Economic Lessons from the Pharmaceutical Patent Rights in India' (2007) 2(1) *Asian Journal of WTO Law and Policy (AJWH)* 65.

[41] Prashant Reddy T and Sumathi Chandrashekharan, *Create, Copy, Disrupt: India's Intellectual Property Dilemmas* (Oxford University Press, 2017) 65–66.

[42] Ibid.

[43] Ibid.

[44] Ibid 72.

[45] Section 23 of the Patents (Amendment) Act, 2005 amended the existing section 25 of the principal Patents Act, 1970.

likely being that an oral hearing has to be followed by a reasoned order which is time-consuming), a judgment of the Madras High Court held that it was mandatory for the Patent Office to provide hearings at the stage of pre-grant opposition.[46]

While India was successful in resisting pressure to drop its robust pre-grant opposition mechanism, other countries like Japan have not been as lucky. Japan had a pre-grant opposition mechanism until 1996.[47] The Americans apparently opposed this policy on the grounds that many frivolous oppositions were being filed by opponents through their proxies. The American pressure worked on the Japanese and in 1996 the pre-grant opposition mechanism was scrapped and replaced by a post-grant opposition system.[48]

The Indian history on pre-grant opposition illustrates the importance of pre-grant opposition mechanisms to ensuring the grant of quality patents in developing countries and the resistance to American pressure.

D. International Treaties and Pre-grant Opposition: Can RCEP Set a New International Norm?

Over the decades, international IP treaties have been getting more expansive in their coverage, with each successive treaty widening the scope of the patentee's rights. For most part, the focus has been on patentability standards. Administrative procedures like pre-grant oppositions have received little attention during international IP negotiations, primarily because most of these efforts are pushed by the IP-owners lobby who are interested in the swift grant of patents. This is, however changing with the next generation of regional trade agreements like the CPTPP and RCEP, perhaps because developing countries now have more awareness of, and expertise in, patent law.

The only provisions in TRIPS which have implications for pre-grant oppositions are Articles 41 and 62.[49] These provisions lay down the manner in which member states may provide for the acquisition and maintenance of intellectual property rights covered by TRIPS but do not provide much detail. Article 62 only requires all members to ensure that IP rights are granted 'within a reasonable period of time so as to avoid unwarranted curtailment of the period of protection'.

The story with CPTPP and RCEP, at least during negotiations, is, however, different.

[46] *Indian Network for People Living with HIV/AIDS & Anr vs Union of India* (WP No 24904 of 2008) before the High Court of Madras decided on 2 December 2008.

[47] Feroz Ali Khader, *The Access Regime: Patent Law Reforms for Affordable Medicine* (Oxford University Press, 2015).

[48] Ibid.

[49] Daniel Gervais, *The TRIPS Agreement: Drafting History and Analysis* (Sweet & Maxwell, 1998) 238–39 (explaining that TRIPS went ahead of existing conventions by formulating general rules for the acquisition of IP rights).

According to the leaked text of the CPTPP, published by Wikileaks in 2013, there was a proposal made by New Zealand, Canada, Singapore, Chile and Malaysia to include a mandatory requirement for every signatory to the CPTPP to provide a mechanism to oppose a patent either before or after it has been granted.[50] The provision was as follows:

> [NZ/CA/SG/CL/MY propose: Each Party shall provide a procedure for third persons to oppose the grant of a patent, either before or after the grant of a patent, or both.]

This recommendation by these five countries was reportedly opposed by the US which also released a paper explaining its position and which was leaked.[51] In this paper, the US gives two reasons for opposing pre-grant oppositions. It explains:

> A lengthy or onerous pre-grant patent opposition system can place undue burdens on patent applicants and create additional costs to patent offices, thereby causing uncertainty and deterring innovators and enterprises that would otherwise bring innovative products and services to CPTPP partners. Third parties may exploit pre-grant opposition processes to harass the examiner and/or applicant and seek to delay or confuse the examination process. Moreover, third parties can overburden already strapped patent offices, decrease the efficiency of examination, and delay the granting of pending rights.

In contrast to the pre-grant opposition, the US in its leaked paper recommended two pre-grant procedures, available in its law, which allow third parties to submit prior art documents or a protest petition against a pending application but without a right to be heard.[52] The leaked document reveals that the Americans preferred the existing mechanisms in their national law on the grounds that it protected against third party misuse and is less disruptive to the patent examination system, but does not unnecessarily add to the patent backlog. Neither procedure is as rigorous as the pre-grant opposition mechanism found in old British law or contemporary Indian law.

It appears that American opposition won the day, because the final version of the CPTPP does not contain provisions on pre-grant opposition for patents.

RCEP, however, may end up being a different story because unlike the CPTPP, it does not include the US. According to the leaked text of RCEP the proposed provision on pre-grant oppositions is as follows:[53]

> [JP/KR/IN/NZ/CN propose; ASN oppose: Article 5.14: Ensuring any Person may Provide Information that could Deny Novelty or Inventive step

[50] Wikileaks Release of Secret Trans-Pacific Partnership Agreement: Advanced Intellectual Property Chapter for All 12 Nations with Negotiating Positions (30 August 2013 consolidated bracketed negotiating text).

[51] Briefing Memo: Analysis of the Leaked U.S. Paper on Eliminating Patent Pre-Grant Opposition, *Third World Network*, 7 July 2011 available at www.citizen.org/sites/default/files/analysis-of-leaked-us-paper-on-eliminating-pregrant-opposition.pdf. Full text of the paper available at www.citizen.org/sites/default/files/leaked-us-tppa-paper-on-eliminating-pre-grant-opposition.pdf.

[52] Ibid.

[53] Knowledge Ecology International – 2015 Oct 15 version: RCEP IP Chapter available at www.keionline.org/23060.

> Each Party shall establish or maintain a system which provides, before granting a patent, [NZ/CN/IN/KR propose: at least] one of the following:
> (a) an opportunity for any person to provide the competent authority with information that could deny novelty or inventive step of an invention claimed in the patent application; or
> (b) an opportunity for any person to file an opposition against the patent application.]

The first provision is a relatively non-controversial mechanism to allow any person to provide information that could deny novelty or inventive step. Such mechanisms are found even in US law. The second provision, proposed by New Zealand, China, India and Korea, is a pre-grant opposition system. While the leaked provisions do not provide much detail, it would appear that this provision is meant to allow pre-grant opposition mechanism on the lines followed in India and other countries of the British commonwealth. As explained earlier, the Americans are specifically opposed to such a pre-grant opposition mechanism because in their view, it is open to abuse and delays the grant of patents.

There are two interesting aspects of this proposal made during the RCEP negotiations vis-à-vis the CPTPP negotiations.

The first is that New Zealand was one of the countries that pushed for pre-grant oppositions mechanisms in both CPTPP and RCEP. It is interesting to see how even developed countries are trying to push for safeguards in both negotiations, hoping to succeed at least in one set of negotiations.

The second interesting aspect is how in both the RCEP and the CPTPP, the proposals were worded as mandatory, rather than optional, requirements (although there is an option in the RCEP to choose between a pre-grant intervention and a pre-grant opposition). This appears to be a first for international IP law because so far mandatory language has been used only in the context of increasing standards of IP protection. This is not surprising since international IP treaties are pushed primarily by strong IP lobbies who are seeking to widen the envelope of their IP rights. When it comes to safeguards, the general trend has been to maintain silence or allow individual countries the discretion to set their own standards. For example, TRIPS mandatorily requires all countries to comply with the standards of patentability laid down under Article 27. This provision prohibits countries from enacting national patent laws discriminating between technologies and impacts developing countries who do not want to recognize certain classes of inventions such as pharmaceutical drugs due to their development concerns.[54] However, when it comes to exceptions, limitations and safeguards, TRIPS does not lay down mandatory requirements. The provisions dealings with these issues invariably use the word 'may' and not 'shall'.[55]

In contrast to the above trends in international IP law, it is quite rare to witness proposals such as the one pertaining to mandatory pre-grant opposition in RCEP

[54] Reddy and Chandrashekharan (n 41) 36–78; Also see Watal (n 1) 86–127.
[55] See Arts 30 and 31 in the TRIPS Agreement, 1994.

and CPTPP. While the proposal at the CPTPP failed to pass, it is possible that the final text of RCEP, due by 2019, may adopt mandatory language with regard to either pre-grant intervention or opposition.[56]

III. The Experimental Use Exceptions and its Policy Justification

A. Four Reasons to Support an Experimental Use Exception

The experimental use exception is one of the very important limitations on the rights of the patentees. In simple terms, this limitation allows researchers and scientists to conduct experiments or research on, or with, a patented invention without first requiring the permission of the patentee. In many ways this right to experiment with a patented invention goes to the heart of the policy objectives of patent law.

Traditional theories of patent law have seen patents as a form of a social contract between the inventor and the state wherein the state bestows a monopoly upon the invention for a limited period of time in exchange for disclosing to the public the invention, and the underlying knowledge, that may have otherwise been protected as a trade secret by the inventor.[57] By protecting the information as a trade secret, the underlying information is not disclosed to society as a whole thereby depriving society of information that may otherwise lead to the progress of science and technology. The disclosure function of patent law is complete only when the patentee describes the invention in a manner that allows other to reconstruct and perform the invention. Thus, not only does society benefit from the new invention itself, it also gains from the knowledge spillovers effected by the disclosure function of patents.[58] This addition of new knowledge to the public domain helps society expand the corpus of knowledge and helps the peers of the inventor to gain new knowledge that was not previously known and to innovate further.[59]

The experimental use exception can be seen as furthering the above objectives of patent law in multiple ways. This is because the essence of the monopoly rights bestowed under the patent law includes the right to exclude any person from making or using a patented invention in any manner not sanctioned by the patentee. Briefly put, there are at least four reasons to support an experimental use exception in the law.

[56] Bernama, 'Possibility of substantively concluding RCEP negotiations finally in sight', *New Straits Times*, 29 August 2018.

[57] See generally Lisa Larrimore Ouellette, 'Do Patents Disclose Useful Information?' (2012) 25 *Harvard Journal of Law & Technology* 531.

[58] See generally Sean B Seymore, 'The Teaching Function of Patents' (2010) 85 *Notre Dame Law Review* 621.

[59] There is scholarship questioning whether such disclosure actually helps in dissemination of information. See generally Alan Devlin, 'The Misunderstood Function of Disclosure in Patent Law' (2010) 23 *Harvard Journal of Law & Technology* 401.

The first reason for advocating for an experimental use exception in patent law is that it creates the required space under patent law for curious minds in society to conduct experiments of a purely philosophical nature on the patented invention without seeking permission from the inventor. From the perspective of science and technology, such philosophical inquiries into how inventions actually work are crucial in order to allow scientists to expand the horizons of their scientific knowledge. If such exceptions did not exist in law, scientists could not conduct any inquiries into the working of a patented invention until the patent term of 20 years expired or until a licence for the same was procured from the patentee. In the latter case, this would mean experimenting on patented inventions would get more expensive in the absence of an experimental use exception. It is also possible that many patentees would simply refuse to grant a licence for experimental use.[60]

The second important reason for retaining the experimental use exception in patent law is the fact that it helps competitors to actually test whether the patentee has fulfilled the enabling disclosure requirement of patent law. The requirement of an enabling disclosure goes to the heart of patent law since the grant of a patent monopoly is premised on the inventor's disclosing to society the manner of working the invention. The failure of the patentee to actually make an enabling disclosure in the patent application can be grounds for revocation of the patent in most jurisdictions. In order to establish whether the patentee has made such an enabling disclosure or not, competitors will necessarily have to experiment on the basis of the disclosures made in the patent specification. Without an experimental use exception in the law, competitors may not be able to construct the invention and experiment with it on the basis of the disclosures made in the patent specification. Therefore, the lack of the experimental use exception would likely lead to poorer quality patents. Such insufficient disclosure would allow the patentees to enjoy an unfair monopoly and lead to a net loss in social welfare.[61]

A third important reason for the experimental use exception is that it helps competitors to 'invent around' a patented invention. The patentee has the right to exclude or block any other person from building or using the patented invention. This blocking function of patent law can serve as an incentive for others to try and invent around the patented invention, ie make a new invention that serves the same purpose as the original but without infringing any patents. In order to do this, it is very often necessary for the competitors to experiment with the invention in question before coming up with a competing invention. The only way competitors can conduct such experiments is if the law has an experimental use exception. The introduction of this competing invention would have the result of introducing

[60] See generally Rebecca S Eisenberg, 'Patents and the Progress of Science: Exclusive Rights and Experimental Use' (1989) *University of Chicago Law Review* 1017. See also Jordan P Karp, 'Experimental Use as Patent Infringement: The Impropriety of a Broad Exception' (1991) 100 *Yale Law Journal* 2169.

[61] See generally Katherine J Strandburg, 'What Does the Public Get? Experimental Use and the Patent Bargain' (2004) *Wisconsin Law Review* 81.

competition in the market and encouraging a reduction in price that would benefit the consumer.[62]

A fourth important reason for the experimental use exception is that it allows competitors to meet specialized regulatory requirements in order to enter the market soon as the patent expires. For example, in the case of pharmaceutical drugs that are patented, competitors have to generate clinical data in order to procure regulatory approvals for the generic drugs that they seek to sell once the patent expires. In order to generate such clinical data, the drugs in question have to be tested through clinical studies and such testing would qualify as infringement unless there is an experimental use exception in the law. Without such an exception in the law, competitors could conduct the required testing only after the patents expired. Since such testing and subsequent regulatory approvals can take a few months at the very least, the patentee would get an additional monopoly over and above the patent term. This could result in consumers paying more for the drug in question.[63]

The four reasons listed above demonstrate the importance of the experimental use exception in patent law.

B. The Experimental Use Exception in the US

The experimental use exception has been around in various national patent laws for some time now, although the scope of the exception differs significantly in different countries. While in most countries such an exception has been inserted into the law by the legislature itself, in some other countries like the US it is the judiciary which has carved out such an exception as far back as the nineteenth century. In the case of *Whittemore v Cutter*,[64] Justice Story had remarked that it could '… never have been the intention of the legislature to punish a man, who constructed such a machine merely for philosophical experiments, or for the purpose of ascertaining the sufficiency of the machine to produce its described effects'.

Justice Story expanded on this reasoning in the subsequent case of *Sawin v Guild*[65] where he held that the experimental use exception could be invoked only when there is no profit motive. In pertinent part, Justice Story held that the making of the invention could qualify as patent infringement only if it was made 'with an intent to use for profit, and not for the mere purpose of philosophical experiment, or to ascertain the verity and exactness of the specification. In other words, that the making must be with an intent to infringe the patent-right, and deprive the owner of the lawful rewards of his discovery'.[66]

[62] See generally Andrew S Baluch, 'Relating the Two Experimental Uses in Patent Law: Inventor's Negation & Infringer's Defense' (2007) 87 *Boston University Law Review* 213.

[63] Anthony Tridico et al, 'Facilitating generic drug manufacturing: Bolar exemptions worldwide' (2014) *WIPO Magazine*, available at www.wipo.int/wipo_magazine/en/2014/03/article_0004.html.

[64] 29 F Cas 1120 (CCD Mass 1813) (No 17,600).

[65] 21 F Cas 554 (CCD Mass 1813) (No 12,391).

[66] Ibid.

The experimental use exception has had an interesting journey in American jurisprudence since those early decisions, first expanding its scope before narrowing down in the recent part.

In the early twentieth century case of *Ruth v Stearns-Roger Manufacturing Co*[67] an American district court gave a wide reading to the experimental use exception in the context of academic research. In this case, the defendant was found liable for selling parts of a patented invention to an academic institution, which was using those parts for academic research. The academic institution itself, in this case the Colorado School of Mines, was not found liable for patent infringement on the grounds that it was covered under the experimental use exception. The court's decision was not very detailed. The court simply concluded:

> The use of the patented machine for experiments for the sole purpose of gratifying a philosophical taste or curiosity or for instruction and amusement does not constitute an infringing use … The making or using of a patented invention merely for experimental purposes, without any intent to derive profits or practical advantage therefrom, is not infringement.

Notwithstanding its sparse reasoning, this judgment was presumed to provide a broad defence to academic institutions accused of patent infringement.[68]

The above position has, however, been reversed, to a great extent, in the case of *Madey v Duke*,[69] decided in 2002 by a federal appellate court. The patentee in this case sued Duke University for using a patented invention without a prior licence. By 2002 the nature of university research in the US had changed dramatically. Due to the Bayh-Dole Act, which allowed American universities to commercialize federally funded inventions, American universities had become powerhouses of innovation and patenting. This meant that American universities began to make hundreds of millions of dollars through commercialization deals with industry. It also meant that the American universities began to sue anybody who infringed their patents. This has resulted in multi-million dollars payouts in favour of these universities.[70] The rise in fortunes of American universities due to their culture of patenting has changed the perception of these academic institutions.[71]

In *Madey*, the patentee sued Duke University for infringing his patents by using them in the course of conducting experiments in the university's labs. While the district court held the use to be covered by the experimental use exception, the appellate court reversed the finding on the ground that the university's use was commercial and hence not exempted from the experimental use exception. The appellate court ruled that the experimental use exception was 'very narrow and

[67] 13 F Supp 697 (D Colo 1935).

[68] Elizabeth A Rowe, 'The Experimental Use Exception to Patent Infringement: Do Universities Deserve Special Treatment?' (2006) 57 *Hastings Law Journal* 921, 928.

[69] 307 F 3d 1351 (Fed Cir 2002).

[70] Maureen Farrell, 'Universities That Turn Research into Revenue', *Forbes*, 12 September 2008.

[71] Mark Lemley, 'Are Universities Patent Trolls?' (2008) 18 *Fordham Intellectual Property, Media & Entertainment Law Journal* 611.

strictly limited' to non-commercial uses. Citing its own precedents, the appellate court held that the experimental use defence was limited to actions performed 'for amusement, to satisfy idle curiosity, or for strictly philosophical inquiry'.

According to the appellate court, this exception would not apply when an entity was using the patented invention to further its legitimate business interests regardless of the academic implications. In the case of the academic institutions, the appellate court reasoned that

> major research universities, such as Duke, often sanction and fund research projects with arguably no commercial application whatsoever. However, these projects unmistakably further the institution's legitimate business objectives, including educating and enlightening students and faculty participating in these projects. These projects also serve, for example, to increase the status of the institution and lure lucrative research grants, students and faculty.

Thus, although the experimentation in Duke's case did not have immediate commercial implications, it would lead to further the university's legitimate businesses and was thus held to not be for strictly philosophical inquiry. The court went further to conclude that the 'profit or non-profit status of the user is not determinative' of whether the entity qualified for the experimental use exception.

The decision in *Madey* severely curtailed the experimental use exception under American patent law and the American legislature is yet to respond to overrule the precedent in *Madey*. It has been speculated that the decision would have serious consequences for American universities.[72]

The American legislature did however provide a limited experimental use exception for regulatory purposes. This exception often referred to as the 'Bolar exception' was enacted to specifically overrule the decision of an American judicial decision in the case of *Roche Products v Bolar Pharmaceuticals*.[73] In this case, the defendant was a generic pharmaceutical company, which had used the patented compound to establish the bioequivalence of its generic product with the intention of launching its generic drug soon as the patent expired. The patentee sued Bolar, which then tried arguing the experimental use defence. American courts did not accept this defence and found Bolar liable for patent infringement. The American legislature responded to this decision by carving out a specific experimental use exception for the purpose of generating data that is required by regulatory authorities.[74] The Bolar exemption has been replicated in national patent laws around the world.

Asian countries like Japan and India have experimental use exceptions, albeit to a different extent.

[72] Janice M Mueller, 'The Evanescent Experimental Use Exemption from United States Patent Infringement Liability: Implications for University and Non-profit Research and Development' (2004) 56 *Baylor Law Review* 917.

[73] 733 F 2d 858 (Fed Cir 1984).

[74] 35 US Code § 271.

C. The Experimental Use Exception under Japanese law

Article 69(1) of Japanese Patent Law states: 'A patent right shall not be effective against the working of the patented invention for experimental or research purposes.' This provision has existed in Japanese patent law since 1909 and is reflective of a time when Japan was a net importer of intellectual property.[75] According to one commentator, this experimental use exception was meant to aid Japan's policy of encouraging reverse engineering as a means of boosting industrial growth.[76] According to another commentator, it is likely that this provision would allow the experimental use defence as long as it is not aimed at commercial profit, is contributing to technological progress and is not hurting the interests of the patentee.[77]

This provision was increasingly invoked as a defence by generic pharmaceutical companies, which were being sued by innovator pharmaceutical companies every time that they used a patented invention to generate regulatory data. As per the available scholarship in the English language, Japanese courts have not been consistent in their interpretation of this provision. One set of judicial decisions has apparently rejected the use of this defence by generic pharmaceutical or agro-chemical companies which used the patented invention for the purposes of generating regulatory data that was to be submitted to regulators, and required the experimentation be done with a purpose of advancing technology. A separate line of cases has concluded that the experimental or research requirement contained in Article 69(1) is not subject to any requirement that the experiment actually advances technology and even mere experimentation for the purpose of generating regulatory data would qualify as experimental or research use.[78]

It was only in 1999 that a unanimous decision of the Japanese Supreme Court in the case of *Ono Pharmaceuticals Co Ltd v Kyoto Pharmaceutical Industries Ltd* confirmed that Article 69(1) could be interpreted to permit the testing of a patenting invention for the purpose of generating regulatory data that is to be submitted to the pharmaceutical regulator.[79]

The Japanese example of the experimental use exception provides an interesting contrast to the virtual nullification of the experimental use exception under American law post *Madey*. The fact that a technologically advanced and innovative country like Japan has retained the technology experimental use exception in its law for more than a hundred years is indication enough that the experimental use exception is an important policy issue.

[75] See John A Tessensohn, 'Reversal of Fortune – Pharmaceutical Experimental Use and Patent Infringement in Japan' (1998) *International Legal Studies* 50; Jennifer Johnson, 'The Experimental Use Exception in Japan: A Model for U.S. Patent Law?' (2003) 12 *Pacific Rim Law & Policy Journal* 499, 510.

[76] Ibid.

[77] Kevin Iles, 'A Comparative Analysis of the Impact of Experimental Use Exemptions in Patent Law on Incentives to Innovate' (2005) 4 *Northwest Journal of Technology and Intellectual Property* 61, 76.

[78] Johnson (n 75) 511–18.

[79] Ibid.

D. The Experimental Use Exception in India

The experimental and research use exemption in Indian law is perhaps one of the broadest 'experimental use' provisions in the world. Rather than being worded as an exception or a defence to patent infringement, the provision is worded as one of the conditions on the basis of which a patent is granted. It has been part of Indian law since 1970 when a new law was enacted to replace the previous colonial era patent legislation.

The provision reads as follows:

> 47 Grant of patents to be subject to certain conditions.
>
> The grant of a patent shall be subject to the condition that: … (3) any machine, apparatus or other article in respect of which the patent is granted or any article made by the use of the process in respect of which the patent is granted, may be made or used, and any process in respect of which the patent is granted may be used, by any person, for the purpose merely of experiment or research including the imparting of instructions to pupils …

The Indian legislation is broader than most countries since it uses the phrase 'research' in addition to the phrase 'experiment'. Since the provision is expressly clear that the phrase 'research' includes 'the imparting of instructions to pupils' it would be possible for Indian universities to avoid any liability of the kind imposed on Duke University in the *Madey* case. Theoretically, this would allow universities to save on licensing fees, thereby having an effect of effectively subsidizing scientific research in educational institutions. Such exemptions are by no means alien to Indian intellectual property law and can be found even in Indian copyright law.[80] Such exemptions are not surprising in developing countries like India where financial budgets for predominantly public universities are constantly under stress.

There is no case law on this issue in India but there have been academic discussions on how the provision most likely extends to all kinds of use and not merely non-commercial use.[81] This has been the preferred interpretation because the first draft of the legislation had recommended confining the provision to non-commercial use, before it was redrafted into its present form.[82]

An academic argument has also been made as to how India should leverage its broad experimental use exception to attract foreign investors to set up more R&D centers in India as a strategy to circumvent the potentially high costs of patent licensing for American researchers post the *Madey* decision.[83] This line of

[80] Reddy and Chandrashekharan (n 41) 115–52;

[81] Mehboob Jeelani, 'Shackled by budget cuts for education sector', *The Hindu*, 21 January 2016, available at www.thehindu.com/news/national/Shackled-by-budget-cuts-for-education-sector/article14018122.ece.

[82] Shamnad Basheer and Prashant Reddy T, 'The "Experimental Use" Exception through a Development Lens' (2010) 50(4) *IDEA – The Intellectual Property Review* 831, 856.

[83] Ibid 844.

argument is illustrative of the advantages of retaining a wide experimental use exception in developing countries.

Notwithstanding the existence of this general experimental use exception, India enacted a separate *Bolar*-style exemption in 2002 when it was amending its law to become TRIPS compliant.[84] This provision was a high priority for Indian policy makers because India was on the verge of reinstating a pharmaceutical product patent regime, leading to concerns that Indian generic manufacturers would be severely impacted.[85] The enactment of a *Bolar*-style exemption was meant to facilitate early entry of generics by allowing for the testing of patented compounds for the purpose of generating regulatory data before expiry of the patent term. Unlike the general experimental use exception, this provision is phrased as a defence to patent infringement. The provision is reproduced as follows:

> Section 107A: (a) any act of making, constructing, using, selling or importing a patented invention solely for uses reasonably related to the development and submission of information required under any law for the time being in force, in India, or in a country other than India, that regulates the manufacture, construction, use, sale or import of any product … shall not be considered as an infringement of patent rights

Unlike Section 47, this provision has seen considerable litigation in India because generic pharmaceutical companies in India have argued that the provision applies even when export clients require Indian manufactured pharmaceuticals for the purpose of securing regulatory approvals in such foreign jurisdictions.[86] Given that valid patents subsist in India in the disputed cases, the pharmaceutical patentees have initiated infringement proceedings against the Indian generic manufacturers. These proceedings are yet to achieve finality as the appeals remain pending.[87]

E. The Effort to Introduce an Experimental Use Exception into International Treaties

The 'experimental use' exception has rarely figured in the debate on international patent law during treaty negotiations. This is of little surprise because limitations and exceptions have received very little attention since most treaties dealing with patents have been driven by an IP-maximalist agenda. That said, an experimental use exception will likely be compliant with TRIPS because Article 30 allows for exception to patent rights provided that the exception in question does not unreasonably conflict with the normal exploitation of the patent and does not

[84] Rajya Sabha Secretariat, Report of the Joint Committee on Patents (Second) Amendment Bill, 1999 (2001).

[85] Also see Shamnad Basheer, 'India's Tryst with TRIPS: The Patents (Amendment) Act, 2005' (2005) 1 *Indian Journal of Law & Technology* 26, 29.

[86] *Bayer Corporation v Union of India* WP(C) 1971 of 2014 before the High Court of Delhi.

[87] See generally Sandeep Rathod, 'The Curious Case of India's Bolar Provision' (2018) 14(1) *Journal of Generic Medicines*.

unreasonably prejudice the legitimate interests of the patentee while taking into account all the legitimate interests of third parties.[88] There is at least one decision of the WTO Dispute Settlement Body (DSB) where a *Bolar*-style exception in Canadian patent law was found to be compliant with Article 30 of TRIPS.[89] There has however been no litigation before the WTO-DSB on a general experimental use exception. The experimental use exception remains of interest in international patent law negotiations, however, as is obvious from the CPTPP and RCEP negotiations.

From the leaked version of the initial text of the CPTPP in 2013, it appears that New Zealand, Canada, Singapore, Chile and Malaysia had proposed a wide-ranging exception for experimental use of a patented invention.[90] The text of the provision is as follows:

> Article QQ.E.5ter: {Experimental Use of a Patent}
>
> [NZ/CA/SG/CL/MY propose:
>
> 1. Consistent with [Article QQ.E.5 (Exceptions)], each Party may provide that a third person may do an act that would otherwise infringe a patent if the act is done for experimental purposes relating to the subject matter of a patented invention.
>
> 2. For the purposes of this Article, experimental purposes may include, but need not be limited to, determining how the invention works, determining the scope of the invention, determining the validity of the claims, or seeking an improvement of the invention (for example, determining new properties, or new uses, of the invention).

The above proposal for an experimental use exception never made it to the final text of CPTPP for reasons that have not been disclosed in the public domain. At the time when the text was leaked, there was speculation that the US would strongly object to such an exception, and it is possible that the provision had to be dropped because of American opposition.[91]

The leaked text is however still interesting for two reasons. The first reason is that of the five countries identified as being behind the proposal, three are developed countries rather than developing countries. This is an example of how limitations and exceptions are not important for just developing countries but also for developed countries.

The second reason why the proposed provision is interesting is because of its attempt to articulate the scope of the experimental use exception more sharply.

88 See generally Christopher Garrison, 'Exception to Patent Rights in Developing Countries' (17) (2006) *UNCTAD-ICSTD Project on IPRs and Sustainable Development*, 13–15 International Centre for Trade and Sustainable Development.

89 See Canada-Patent Protection of Pharmaceutical Products (hereafter EC-Canada), WT/DS114/R, 17 March 2000 before the WTO Dispute Settlement Body (DSB).

90 Wikileaks Release of Secret Trans-Pacific Partnership Agreement: Advanced Intellectual Property Chapter for All 12 Nations with Negotiating Positions (30 August 2013 consolidated bracketed negotiating text).

91 Ofer Tur-Sinai, 'The Trans-Pacific Partnership: Experimental Use of Patents on the International Agenda' (2014) 16 *North Carolina Journal of Law & Technology* 63, 86.

Traditionally, international agreements like TRIPS or the Berne Convention on Protection of Literary & Artistic Works have only enunciated the general principles that govern limitations and exceptions without getting into the specifics of the nature of the exception.[92] The language of the proposed CPTPP provision indicates that the movers of this provision wanted to ensure legal cover for persons wanting to test whether the patentee has adequately discharged the disclosure function under patent law, as well as allowing persons apart from the patentee the scope to experiment with the patented invention with a view to determine new properties or new uses of an invention. The latter could be of special significance in the context of pharmaceutical innovation where existing compounds demonstrate the capability to cure multiple diseases.

The final point that should be noted is the permissive nature of the provision, ie countries have the discretion to decide the nature of the exception in their national legislation. This is not remarkable in itself because most international IP treaties impose mandatory obligations only with respect to the rights of IP owners, while maintaining permissive language on the issue of limitations and exceptions.[93] This permissive language is in contrast to the mandatory language used in a similar proposal made during the negotiations regarding RCEP.

The text of the RCEP proposal, as leaked during negotiations, is as follows:

> Without limiting Article 5.2, each Party shall provide that [IN/CN oppose: a third person] [IN/CN propose: any person] may do an act that would otherwise infringe a patent if the act is done [CN/IN propose: solely] for experimental [CN propose; AU oppose: and/] [IN/CN propose; AU oppose: or research] purposes [IN propose; AU/KR oppose: including the imparting of instruction to pupils] relating to the subject matter of a patented invention.][94]

The most remarkable aspect of this proposal is that it is mandatory and requires all member countries to necessarily provide for an experimental use provision. As mentioned earlier, it is rare to find such mandatory language in context of limitations and exceptions for patents rights. One reason for such language could be the fact that most countries negotiating RCEP are developing countries who are net importers of IP and it is only logical for them to advocate for wider experimental use exceptions. But what is perhaps more interesting is that RCEP also includes developed countries like Australia, South Korea and Japan who have strong IP-based industries. From the leaked text, it appears that Australia and South Korea are opposing some of the proposed language but are not objecting to the experimental use provision in its entirety. Interestingly, the mandatory nature of this obligation also does not appear to be an issue of contention. Thus, unlike

[92] Andrew F Christie and Robin Wright, 'A Comparative Analysis of the Three-Step Tests in International Treaties' (2014) 45(4) *International Review of Intellectual Property and Competition Law* 409.

[93] Article 27 of the Agreement on TRIPS is a good example of a mandatory requirement in the international patent law context.

[94] Knowledge Ecology International – 2015 Oct 15 version: RCEP IP Chapter, available at www.keionline.org/23060.

the CPTPP, where the proposed experimental use exception was not to be found at all in the final text, the final text of RCEP will likely see some version of the 'experimental use' exception.

With regard to the scope of the provision, the RCEP proposal contains a fair amount of bracketed text that reveals the contentious issues between the different negotiating parties. It appears that India is trying to ensure that the text of its domestic law is reproduced in the RCEP. The experimental use exception in Indian law uses the phrase 'research', which is defined as including the imparting of instruction to pupils.[95] In the context of the RCEP negotiations, while India and China propose to expand the provision to include both experiment and research, Australia is opposing the addition of 'research' and is seeking to limit the provision to only 'experimental use'. Similarly, both Australia and South Korea, are opposing the Indian proposal to define 'research' as including the imparting of instruction to pupils. While the reason for their opposition is not disclosed, it is again most likely because of the ambiguity associated with the phrase 'instruction' and 'pupil'.

It is also interesting to note how none of the negotiating parties in RCEP have tried to clarify whether experiments conducted in a commercial context will be covered within the scope of the provision. This is interesting because silence on the issue will lead to the presumption that experimentation can take place in the commercial context. As explained earlier, in the *Madey* case the experimental use exception in the US was significantly narrowed down because American universities had become quite commercial.

Thus, the two features of the RCEP proposal that stand out are, first, the apparent consensus, at the time of the leak, on the issue of a mandatory experimental use provision and, second, the silence on whether the defence applies in the commercial context, leading to the presumption that it can be used in the commercial context. While the final text of RCEP is yet to be decided it is highly likely that the experimental use exception will be retained in the final text although the extent of the provision may vary depending on the negotiations. This would be a significant new breakthrough for international patent law because there is no international treaty which contains such a mandatory exception.

IV. Conclusion: Will Asia Lead the Conversation on a More Balanced International Patent Law?

In the last two decades international patent law has expanded to impose more obligations on all countries to protect the rights of the patentees. The conversation to guarantee stronger safeguards like pre-grant patent oppositions as well as limitations and exceptions has been rather limited. Most of the conversation on measures to balance the growing scope of patent law rights has centered around

[95] Section 47(3) of the Patents Act, 1970.

compulsory licences, and even that discussion has been rather limited post the Doha Declaration.[96] Most international instruments on patent law continue to have vaguely worded language on the issue of safeguards or limitations and exceptions which are optional for all member countries, such as Article 30 of TRIPS with a three-step test. This is unlike the mandatory language used in context of patentee rights in Article 27 of TRIPS, where member countries do not have the right to deviate from the minimum requirements imposed by the treaty. There has been little opportunity to balance these obligations in the international patent law context, most likely because of the overwhelming influence of American negotiating power.

If history is any indicator, language related to strong safeguards or limitations and exceptions will be introduced only if there is pressure from developing countries. The history of the Berne Convention is a good example of how it took the threat of a walkout by India and African countries before the developed world agreed to introduce compulsory licensing and the three-step test for limitations and exceptions to copyright law. With the rising A2K movement (The Access to Knowledge Movement) there has been a demand for an international instrument on limitations and exceptions.[97] There has been some progress in this regard with the adoption of international instruments like the Marrakesh Treaty to Facilitate Access to Published Works for Persons Who Are Blind, Visually Impaired or Otherwise Print Disabled. Efforts like this represent the ideal outcome when it comes to balancing rights of all stakeholders because they provide well-articulated limitations and exceptions, rather than vague tests.

In the patent law context, the conversation on safeguards or limitations and exceptions has been comparatively muted. There was an attempt by WIPO's Standing Committee on Patent Law (SCP) to get a conversation started when it commissioned a series of studies on limitations and exceptions under various national patent laws.[98] That conversation never translated into concrete measures.

In this backdrop, it is significant that provisions regarding pre-grant opposition and experimental use exceptions were on the negotiating table at both the CPTPP and the RCEP. While it is now clear that neither provision will be part of the CPTPP, there is still hope for the RCEP because of the presence of giants

[96] Reto Hilty and Kung-Chung Liu, *Compulsory Licensing Practical Experiences and Ways Forward* (Springer Berlin 2014).

[97] The A2K Movement is a coalition of various academics, civil society organizations and activists who are challenging the prevalent understanding of intellectual property rights. They aim to link intellectual property rights to the issues of development, justice and freedom. A Kapczynski, 'The Access to Knowledge Mobilization and the New Politics of Intellectual Property' (2008) 117 *Yale Law Journal* 804.

[98] The WIPO SCP had decided at its 13th session held in March 2009 that the Secretariat would commission external experts a study on exclusions, exceptions and limitations focusing on issues related to public health, education, research and experimentation and patentability of life forms, including from a public policy, socio-economic development perspective, bearing in mind the level of economic development. SCP/13/7 Standing Committee on the Law of Patents, 13th Session, Geneva, March 2009.

like India and China and the absence of the US and the EU. This new negotiating dynamic has not been witnessed before in trade negotiations of this magnitude. If the language found in the leaked text of RCEP, especially the mandatory language on pre-grant oppositions and experimental use, it will mark a new milestone for international patent law norms. Mandatory language on experimental use exceptions and pre-grant opposition are important for developing countries as they trade and invest to a great extent in developed countries. If the RCEP opens the door to mandatory provisions on pre-grant oppositions and experimental use exceptions, this will set a new norm that will influence other patent law related treaties.

9

Patent Term Extension in the Pharmaceutical Sector

An Asian Comparative Perspective

YAOJIN PENG*

I. Introduction

There is no doubt that pharmaceutical products closely relate to the public health and society at large. The pharmaceutical industry is one of the most innovative, competitive and research-intensive industries. Moreover, research and development (R&D) of a new pharmaceutical product is not only complex but also costly and time-consuming.[1] However, this type of product is prone to imitation, often with radically lower costs and much less uncertainty, once its composition is known. Without any legal protection, investors and inventors would not have sufficient incentive to invest in making, developing, and marketing new drugs, and the pharmaceutical industry might come to a standstill.[2] In this regard, patent protection is of great importance for this industry,[3] since a patent grants the patentee a monopoly right to exclude others from making, using, offering for sale, selling or importing the invention in a period of time.[4]

However, before being marketed, pharmaceutical products normally are required to undergo a series of lengthy safety and efficacy approval process

* Associate Professor, Institute of Zoology, Chinese Academy of Sciences, Beijing; University of the Chinese Academy of Sciences, Beijing. All online materials accessed on or before 25 February 2019.

[1] See Dan L Burk and Mark A Lemley, 'Policy Levers in Patent Law' (2003) 89 *Virginia Law Review* 1575, 1616. See also Clawomir Dorocki, 'Contemporary Trends in the Development of the Pharmaceutical Industry in the World' (2014) 25 *Prace Komisji Geografii Przemysłu Polskiego Towarzystwa Geograficznego* 108, 128.

[2] See Burk and Lemley (n 1) 1615–17.

[3] See generally Edwin Mansfield, 'Patents and Innovation: An Empirical Study' (1986) 32 *Management Science* 173.

[4] Article 33 of the Agreement on Trade-Related Aspects of Intellectual Property Rights (TRIPS) provides that 'the term of protection available shall not end before the expiration of a period of twenty years counted from the filing date'.

under governmental administration. As a result, the effective patent term (EPT) of pharmaceutical products has fallen considerably,[5] as even if these products obtain patents, they still cannot be manufactured or placed on the market until the regulatory approval or market authorization (MA) is granted. It is worried that the erosion of EPT of pharmaceutical products due to MA requirement would discourage the investment in the industry. The patent term extension (PTE) system, therefore, has been established, which permits patent holders to enjoy an additional period of exclusivity on the expiry of patents to make up, at least in part, for the insufficient EPT in the pharmaceutical sector, so as to provide incentives to innovation in this field.

In fact, the PTE system originated from the United States (US),[6] and subsequently expanded to other jurisdictions in Europe (eg France, Italy and Germany) and Asia (eg Japan and Korea).[7] Careful research into the literature reveals that most studies were focusing on the PTE system in the US.[8] Recently, the European Commission has conducted a research and assessment on the Supplementary Protection Certificate (SPC) system in the European Union (EU).[9] However, there is a dearth of material focusing on the PTE systems in Asia, in particular from a comparative perspective. This chapter takes an Asian comparative perspective, by analysing the situations under the laws in the US, EU and in three Asian jurisdictions, ie Japan, Korea, and the Republic of China (commonly known as Taiwan). The exploration of laws and policies concerning the PTE in Japan, Korea and Taiwan is promising, since these three jurisdictions represent the economies which were earliest to introduce the PTE system in Asia. In addition, legal practices of these three jurisdictions are often referenced by other Asian jurisdictions, particularly with regard to intellectual property protection.[10] In this regard, the analysis of the PTE systems in the US and these three Asian jurisdictions, as well as the SPC system in the EU, may provide insights to the Comprehensive and Progressive Agreement for

[5] See Alan D Lourie, 'Patent Term Restoration' (1984) 66 *Journal of the Patent Office Society* 526, 527.

[6] See generally ibid (discussing the history of the PTE system in the US).

[7] See Max Planck Institute for Innovation and Competition, 'Annex I: National Reports EU – Study on the Legal Aspects of Supplementary Protection Certificates in the EU' (EU Publications, 31 May 2018), https://publications.europa.eu/en/publication-detail/-/publication/004c1a50-654b-11e8-ab9c-01aa75ed71a1/language-en.

[8] See eg Lourie (n 5); Margo A Bagley, 'Patent Term Restoration and Non-patent Exclusivity in the US' in Josef Drexl and Nari Lee (eds), *Pharmaceutical Innovation, Competition and Patent Law: A Trilateral Perspective* (Edward Elgar, 2013); Jaime F Cárdenas-Navia, 'Thirty Years of Flawed Incentives: An Empirical and Economic Analysis of Hatch-Waxman Patent-Term Restoration' (2014) 29 *Berkeley Technology Law Journal* 1301.

[9] See Max Planck Institute for Innovation and Competition, 'Study on the Legal Aspects of Supplementary Protection Certificates in the EU' (European Commission, 28 May 2018), https://ec.europa.eu/docsroom/documents/29524.

[10] For instance, the first Patent Law of the People's Republic of China was drafted primarily based on referring to patent laws from jurisdictions, including the US, EPO, Japan and Taiwan. See Yuanguo Zhao, *The Drafting History of the Patent Law of China* 47 (Beijing, Intellectual Property Publishing House, 2003).

Trans-Pacific Partnership (CPTPP)[11] as well as to the approach of China, which is currently considering the introduction of the PTE system into its patent law.

This chapter consists of seven sections. After the introduction in section I, section II briefly revisits the origination of the PTE system in the US and attempts to analyse the fundamental basis of this system. Subsequently, section III examines the current PTE system in the US and SPC system in the EU. Importantly, section IV explores in detail the PTE systems in Japan, Korea and Taiwan, and highlights the convergences and divergences to identify the pros and cons of different approaches taken by these three jurisdictions. Section V discusses the PTE system in the context of the CPTPP and Trans-Pacific Partnership Agreement (TPP) and provides several recommendations. Building on the recommendations in section V, section VI discusses and offers advice on the planned incorporation of the PTE system into China's patent law. Section VII draws a conclusion.

II. Initiation and Rationale of PTE

Not surprisingly, the R&D and manufacture of pharmaceutical products are considerably time-consuming, costly, and suffer from a high risk of not covering the investors and inventors' investments. Normally, starting from R&D, to thereafter preclinical and clinical trials, and to being marketed, a new drug would span over 10 years.[12] Moreover, the average cost of innovating and marketing a new drug, nowadays, reaches over one billion US dollars.[13] Due to the high costs and risks of obtaining original pharmaceutical products, manufacturing, launching and maintaining the products in the market, it is fair for innovators and investors to be concerned with the recovery of their investments. Since patents play an important role in the recuperation of investments in the pharmaceutical sector, it is not difficult to imagine that the duration of the monopoly granted by patents, ie the term of the patents, is closely related to the benefit of these innovators and investors.

Moreover, nowadays, in almost all jurisdictions pharmaceutical products, as special products, are required to undergo not only extremely rigorous clinical trials but also MA, in order to ensure their safety, efficiency and quality before

[11] The CPTPP is a revision of a multilateral free trade agreement formerly known as the Trans-Pacific Partnership (TPP), due to the withdrawal of the US from the TPP, see https://www.mfat.govt.nz/assets/CPTPP/Comprehensive-and-Progressive-Agreement-for-Trans-Pacific-Partnership-CPTPP-English.pdf.

[12] See Elina Petrova, 'Innovation in the Pharmaceutical Industry: The Process of Drug Discovery and Development' in M Ding, J Eliashberg and S Stremersch (eds), *International Series in Quantitative Marketing* 29 (Springer, 2014).

[13] See Ros Viorel, 'Protection of Inventions in the Pharmaceutical Sector through Supplementary Protection Certificate' (2015) 22 *Lex ET Scientia International Journal* 7, 10. See also Petrova (n 12) 25 (pointing out that 'in 2005, the average cost of a new drug successfully introduced in the USA was estimated to be $1.3 billion – a hefty 62% increase over the last known estimate of $803 million in 2000').

being marketed. For example, in the US, as early as 1930s, Congress passed the Food, Drug, and Cosmetic Act (FDCA) to address safety issues concerning consumer goods, including drugs and medical devices.[14] Then, the Food and Drug Administration (FDA) of the US required pharmaceutical companies to prove the safety of any new drug prior to sale.[15] Besides, in 1962, the amendments of the FDCA added another requirement: that companies must also prove the efficacy of a drug, before the drug could be marketed.[16] Since then, drugs in the US have been required to be proven to be both safe and effective prior to being marketed. Thus, it can be observed that even though pharmaceutical products have been invented or innovated, the process of bringing these new special products to market is costly and time-consuming.[17]

As mentioned previously, patent protection plays an important role in the pharmaceutical sector. However, the safety and efficacy requirements significantly increase the MA period, and correspondingly result in a *de facto* loss of patent term for patents covering new drugs.[18] In other words, in order to obtain an MA before being able to enter the market, pharmaceutical companies may often lose a long period of monopoly of marketing the products, and thus the EPT is greatly eroded.[19] Even worse, it is possible that before a new drug is marketed or accepted by the market, the period of patent term could have expired. In that case, there were concerns that the reduced EPT, due to necessary lengthy procedures of MA in the pharmaceutical sector, might not provide investors sufficient incentives to develop and market pharmaceutical products.[20] Thus, in order to cope with the reduction of EPT and to promote the innovation of new drugs, the PTE system was established by the 1984 Drug Price Competition and Patent Term Restoration Act (also known as the Hatch-Waxman Act) in the US.[21] In short, this system permits patent holders to enjoy an additional period of exclusivity on the expiry of patents to

[14] See Food, Drug, and Cosmetic Act, Pub L No 75-717, 52 Stat 1040 [1938].

[15] Ibid. See also 'Part II: 1938, Food, Drug, Cosmetic Act' (US Food & Drug Administration, 27 November 2018), https://www.fda.gov/about-fda/fdas-evolving-regulatory-powers/part-ii-1938-food-drug-cosmetic-act; Bagley (n 8) 112–13.

[16] See 'Part III: Drugs and Foods Under the 1938 Act and Its Amendments' (US Food & Drug Administration, 1 February 2018), https://www.fda.gov/about-fda/fdas-evolving-regulatory-powers/part-iii-drugs-and-foods-under-1938-act-and-its-amendments.

[17] Another example is that Directive 2001/83/EC of the European Parliament and of the Council of 6 November 2001 on the Community code relating to medicinal products for human use (OJ L 311/67) has set out the obligation to obtain an MA prior to marketing in all Member States of the EU.

[18] See Cárdenas-Navia (n 8) 1306–07.

[19] See Lourie (n 5) 527 (noting that, from 1966 to 1979, EPT fell from 13.6 years to 9.5 years).

[20] See Cárdenas-Navia (n 8) 1307.

[21] Drug Price Competition and Patent Term Restoration Act of 1984, Pub L No 98-417, 98 Stat 1585 (codified at 21 USC §§ 355, 360 (2012); 35 USC §§ 156, 271 (2012)), amended by Medicare Prescription Drug, Improvement, and Modernization Act of 2003, Pub L No 108-173, 117 Stat 2066. More information about the history of the PTE legislation in the US, see generally Lourie (n 5). The amendments of the FDCA did not relieve the burden of generic companies, which suffered a sharp decline. Thus, the Hatch-Waxman Act was also set out to accelerate approval for generics. See Cárdenas-Navia (n 8) 1307–08. See also Bagley (n 8) 114 (stating that the Hatch-Waxman Act attempted to strike a balance between the needs of pioneer drug companies to recover patent terms lost during the MA and the needs of the public to have reduced cost drugs by enabling generic producers to enter the market quickly after the expiration of the original patent).

compensate, at least in part, for the insufficient EPT in the pharmaceutical sector, so as to provide incentives to innovation in this field.

III. PTE in the US and SPC in the EU

Indeed, the PTE system originated from the US, and was subsequently followed by other jurisdictions in Europe, such as France, Italy and Germany, at the end of the 1980s.[22] In the US, the Hatch-Waxman Act provides for PTE.[23] It has been estimated that under the PTE system the EPT of patented pharmaceuticals has been increased on average by over three and a half years, and drugs with PTEs could account for about 20 per cent of total pharmaceutical sales in the US 12 years ago.[24] In the Member States of the EU, the SPC system, similar to the PTE system, is available in order to overcome the obstacles impeding the circulation of products within the EU market created by heterogeneous PTE laws and systems.[25] Before an in-depth investigation and comparison of Asian PTE systems, this section briefly explores the PTE system in the US and the SPC system in the EU, which will contribute to the understanding of the PTE systems in Asian jurisdictions.

A. PTE in the US

Under the Hatch-Waxman Act, a PTE is not a *sui generis* right but an accessory to the original patent. That is to say, if the patent on which the PTE is based is revoked, the extension would also be invalid. The PTE is not granted ex officio, but upon the patentee's submission of an application to the US Patent and Trademark Office (USPTO).[26] When calculating the period of a PTE, the USPTO may consult with the FDA about the period of regulatory delay.

Patents on both products and methods of using or manufacturing such products, are eligible for PTEs in the US.[27] Not only drugs but also medical devices are eligible for PTEs.[28] Importantly, under the Hatch-Waxman Act, there are several conditions for granting a PTE. The term of the patent should not have expired

[22] See generally Max Planck Institute for Innovation and Competition (n 7).

[23] 35 USC § 156.

[24] See generally Charles Clift, 'The Value of Patent Term Extensions to the Pharmaceutical Industry in the USA' (2008) 5 *Journal of Generic Medicines* 201.

[25] The SPC system in the EU was instituted by the Council Regulation (EEC) No 1768/92 of 18 June 1992 concerning the creation of a supplementary protection certificate for medicinal products (OJ L 182/1). Subsequently, this Regulation was revoked and replaced by Regulation (EC) No 469/2009 of the European Parliament and of the Council of 6 May 2009 concerning the supplementary protection certificate for medicinal products (OJ L 152/1) (the SPC Regulation). In fact, the SPC Regulation has not significantly modified the previous text, and primarily codified the prior regulation and its successive amendments.

[26] See 35 USC § 156(d)(1).

[27] See 35 USC § 156(a).

[28] See 35 USC § 156(f).

before the PTE application is submitted.[29] Moreover, the patented product must have been 'subject to a regulatory review period before its commercial marketing or use'.[30] The patent which is to be extended should never have been previously extended.[31] In other words, a patent can receive extension only once. In addition, in order to obtain a PTE, the drug is required to be 'new',[32] and the MA of the drug should be 'the first permitted commercial marketing or use'.[33] It implies that the 'new' drug should never have been approved for marketing or use previously by a relevant federal agency, such as the FDA. In the situation where more than one patent covers the approved product, the patentee has to choose one to apply for a PTE.[34] The US has established the principle of 'one approved product, one PTE; one patent, one PTE'.

The duration of a PTE is primarily based on the 'regulatory review period' after the patent issue date,[35] contains one-half of the 'testing phase' of the product, plus the entire 'approval phase'.[36] In addition, the Hatch-Waxman Act foresees that the period of extension may not exceed five years,[37] and that the maximum period of EPT with extension is limited to 14 years.[38] The scope of protection during the period of a PTE, on the one hand, is based on the claims of the patent. Rules concerning patent claims, such as the 'broadest reasonable construction' of the claims and the doctrine of equivalents, may be applied to interpret the term-extended patent before US courts.[39] On the other hand, it is essentially limited to the specific product or use approved by the FDA.[40] For instance, in the case *Pfizer, Inc v Dr Reddy's Laboratories, Ltd*,[41] the Federal Circuit explicitly pointed out that 'other, e.g., non-pharmaceutical uses, are not subject to the extension'.[42]

B. SPC in the EU

The SPC system in the EU, established by the SPC Regulation[43] is an essential tool for compensating patent holders for the time lost caused by lengthy MA delay.[44]

[29] See 35 USC § 156(a)(1).
[30] 35 USC § 156(a)(4).
[31] See 35 USC § 156(a)(2).
[32] 35 USC § 156(f)(2)(A).
[33] 35 USC § 156(a)(5)(A).
[34] See Chapter 37 Code of Federal Regulations (CFR) of the US (37 CFR) 1.785(a)–(b) [2017].
[35] 35 USC § 156(c).
[36] 35 USC § 156(c)(2).
[37] See 35 USC § 156(g)(6).
[38] See 35 USC § 156(c)(3).
[39] John R Thomas, 'The USA' in Max Planck Institute for Innovation and Competition (ed), *Annex II: International Reports – Study on the Legal Aspects of Supplementary Protection Certificates in the EU* 90 (European Commission, 2018).
[40] See 35 USC § 156(b).
[41] See *Pfizer Inc, Plaintiff-appellant, v Dr Reddy's Laboratories, Ltd and Dr Reddy's Laboratories, Inc, Defendants-appellees*, 359 F 3d 1361 (Fed Cir 2004).
[42] Ibid 1366.
[43] See n 25.
[44] See Frantzeska Papadopoulou, 'Supplementary Protection Certificates: Still a Grey Area?' (2016) 11 *Journal of Intellectual Property Law & Practice* 372, 372.

Unlike the accessary attribute of the PTE, an SPC provides a *sui generis* exclusive right to a pharmaceutical product.[45] The fundamental objective of the SPC system is to ensure that investors have proper patent term to recuperate their investment and further invest in R&D in the pharmaceutical sector.[46] It is worth mentioning that there is no EU-wide SPC. Instead, any SPC application must be filed before the specific national patent office where the SPC is expected.[47] An SPC in the EU therefore in essence is a national right based on a national basic patent.

i. Concept of 'Product' and 'Active Ingredient'

The subject matter of an SPC is, in principle, the 'product', which is one fundamental issue concerning the SPC system. The SPC Regulation defines the term 'product' as the active ingredient or combination of active ingredients of a medicinal product.[48] The 'active ingredient' and 'combination of active ingredients' have become the crux of interpreting the term 'product'. In the *Massachusetts Institute of Technology* (*MIT*) case, the Court of Justice of the European Union (CJEU) adopted a narrow approach to interpret the 'active ingredient' and 'a combination of active ingredients'.[49] The CJEU asserted that based on the position of the Explanatory Memorandum,[50] the 'active ingredient' should be construed in a strict sense,[51] and held that a substance without any independent therapeutic effect should not treated as an active ingredient.[52] Therefore, the CJEU did not consider a combination of two substances, where only one substance had therapeutic effects of its own for a specific indication and the other substance did not but was necessary for the therapeutic efficacy of the first substance,[53] as a 'combination of active ingredients'.[54]

The CJEU reconfirmed its position in a later case *GlaxoSmithKline Biologicals SA, GlaxoSmithKline Biologicals, Niederlassung der Smithkline Beecham Pharma GmbH & Co KG v Comptroller-General of Patents, Designs and Trade Marks*

[45] The 'product' is specifically defined in the SPC Regulation, which will be discussed later in this subsection.

[46] The purpose is highlighted by the Court of Justice of the European Union (CJEU) in several decisions, see eg Case C-130/11 *Neurim Pharmaceuticals (1991) Ltd v Comptroller-General of Patents* EU:C:2012:489, paras 22–23; Case C-322/10 *Medeva BV v Comptroller General of Patents, Designs and Trade Marks* EU:C:2011:773, [2011] ECR I-12051, paras 30–31; Case C-577/13 *Actavis Group PTC EHF, Actavis UK Ltd v Boehringer Ingelheim Pharma GmbH & Co KG* EU:C:2015:165, para 34.

[47] See Verna Vesanen, 'Has the Court of Justice of the EU Clarified for Once and for All the Law on Supplementary Protection Certificates?' (2017) 39 *European Intellectual Property Review* 42.

[48] See Article 1(b) of the SPC Regulation.

[49] See Case C-431/04 *Massachusetts Institute of Technology* EU:C:2006:291, [2006] ECR I-4089.

[50] See Commission of the European Communities, Proposal for a Council Regulation (EEC) concerning the creation of a supplementary protection certificate for medicinal products (the 'Explanatory Memorandum'), COM(90) 101 final (11 April 1990), para 11.

[51] See Case C-431/04 (n 49), paras 21–22.

[52] Ibid para 25.

[53] Ibid para 13.

[54] Ibid paras 26, 31.

(*GlaxoSmithKline Biologicals*) in 2013,[55] holding that an adjuvant did not fall within the definition of the 'active ingredient', and that a combination of two substances, 'namely an active ingredient having therapeutic effects on its own, and an adjuvant which, while enhancing those therapeutic effects, has no therapeutic effect on its own', did not fall within the definition of 'combination of active ingredients'.[56] Moreover, it is worth noting that following the restrictive approach in *MIT*, the CJEU in another case, *Yissum Research and Development Company of the Hebrew University of Jerusalem v Comptroller-General of Patents* (*Yissum*), pointed out that the therapeutic use of an active ingredient, protected by a basic patent, did not fall within the concept of 'product'.[57]

ii. Conditions for the Grant of an SPC

Article 3 of the SPC Regulation sets forth the conditions for obtaining an SPC. To be specific, an SPC is to be conferred if, in the Member State in which the SPC application is made and at the time of that application, the product is protected by a basic patent in force,[58] a valid MA of the medical product has been granted,[59] the product has not already been the subject of an SPC,[60] and the specified MA must be the first one for the product in the Member State concerned.[61]

a. A Basic Patent in Force

The product must be protected by a basic patent that is in force at the time when the SPC application is made.[62] In fact, 'a basic patent in force' has become one of the most controversial conditions for the grant of an SPC in the EU, with the discussion centring particularly on how to determine if the product is protected by a basic patent. In practice, there have been primarily two different approaches: the infringement test and the disclosure test. The infringement test looks into whether the product infringes the rights deriving from the basic patent, and the disclosure test assesses whether the product is disclosed in the wording of the claims of the basic patent.[63] Based on the flexibility recognized by the CJEU's *Farmitalia Carlo Erba Srl* (*Farmitalia*) decision,[64] which allows national courts to decide

[55] See Case C-210/13 *GlaxoSmithKline Biologicals SA, GlaxoSmithKline Biologicals, Niederlassung der Smithkline Beecham Pharma GmbH & Co. KG v Comptroller-General of Patents, Designs and Trade Marks* EU:C:2013:762.

[56] Ibid para 45.

[57] See Case C-202/05 *Yissum Research and Development Company of the Hebrew University of Jerusalem v Comptroller-General of Patents* EU:C:2007:214, [2007] ECR I-2839, paras 17–18.

[58] See Article 3(a) of the SPC Regulation.

[59] See Article 3(b) of the SPC Regulation.

[60] See Article 3(c) of the SPC Regulation.

[61] See Article 3(d) of the SPC Regulation.

[62] See Article 3(a) of the SPC Regulation.

[63] See Papadopoulou (n 44) 377.

[64] See Case C-392/97 *Farmitalia Carlo Erba Srl* EU:C:1999:416, [1999] ECR I-5553.

how to interpret Article 3(a) of the SPC Regulation, some jurisdictions, such as the United Kingdom (UK), France and Spain, have applied the disclosure test, whereas other jurisdictions, such as Germany and Switzerland, seemed to follow the infringement test.[65]

In *Medeva BV v Comptroller General of Patents, Designs and Trade Marks* (*Medeva*), the CJEU pointed out that in order to be protected by a basic patent, the active ingredients must be 'specified' in the wording of the patent claims.[66] However, the meaning of the term 'specified' remained unclear. Moreover, in *University of Queensland and CSL Ltd v Comptroller General of Patents, Designs and Trade Marks* (*University of Queensland*), the CJEU used another word 'identified', and held that the active ingredients should be 'identified' in the wording of the claims of the basic patent.[67] Another question arose as to whether a product had to be precisely specified or identified by name or by a specific formula, or if it would be sufficient for the product to be described by function,[68] which to some extent, has been settled by the CJEU in 2013 in *Eli Lilly and Company Ltd v Human Genome Sciences Inc* (*Eli Lilly*).[69]

In *Eli Lilly*, the basic patent claimed a protein, but at the same time it was evident from the patent claims that the patent also related to antibodies, including Tabalumab, that were bound specifically to that protein.[70] Given this, although the active ingredient, Tabalumab, was not explicitly 'stated' in the claims of the patent, the claims of the patent would still be infringed.[71] However, the SPC was challenged on the basis that Tabalumab was not 'specified' in the patent claims.[72] Then, three questions were referred to the CJEU, namely

> Whether Article 3(a) of Regulation No 469/2009 must be interpreted as meaning that, in order for an active ingredient to be regarded as being 'protected by a basic patent in force' within the meaning of that provision, the active ingredient must be identified in the claims of the patent by a structural formula, or whether the active ingredient may also be considered to be protected where it is covered by a functional formula in the patent claims.[73]

The CJEU pointed out that the identification of an active ingredient in the basic patent could be by means of either a structural or a functional formula.[74] The CJEU held that the active ingredient would be considered to be covered by the

[65] See Kristof Roox and Christiaen Dekoninck, 'First Belgian Decision on SPC's Coverage of Combination Products' (Kluwer Patent Blog, 17 June 2011), http://kluwerpatentblog.com/2011/06/17/first-belgian-decision-on-spcs-coverage-of-combination-products/?print=pdf.

[66] See Case C-322/10 (n 46) paras 28 and 42.

[67] See Case C-630/10 *University of Queensland and CSL Ltd v Comptroller General of Patents, Designs and Trade Marks* EU:C:2011:780, [2011] ECR I-12231, [2011] OJ C 73/10.

[68] See Papadopoulou (n 44) 377.

[69] See Case C-493/12 *Eli Lilly and Company Ltd v Human Genome Sciences Inc* EU:C:2013:835.

[70] Ibid paras 12–14.

[71] Ibid paras 14–15.

[72] Ibid para 16.

[73] Ibid para 24.

[74] Ibid paras 39–44.

basic patent, as long as the claims of the patent related 'implicitly but necessarily and specifically' to the active ingredient at issue.[75] The CJEU has chosen and adopted the infringement test to determine whether a product is protected by the basic patent. However, in a later case, *Actavis v Boehringer*,[76] the CJEU muddied the water again, pointing out that in order for an active ingredient to be protected by a basic patent, that active ingredient must constitute the 'subject-matter' of the invention covered by the basic patent.[77] Unfortunately, the CJEU has not provided any further explanation of the 'subject-matter' of the invention.

b. A Valid Authorization Obtained and the First MA Requirement

Article 3(b) of the SPC Regulation requires that the product must obtain a valid MA, which allows the patentee to place the product on the market as a medicinal product.[78] It is not necessary for the patentee to obtain an MA, which implies that the holder of the basic patent and the holder of the MA can be different. Moreover, even without the consent of the holder of the MA, an SPC still may be conferred, which was confirmed in the case *Biogen Inc v SmithKline Beecham Biologicals SA* (*Biogen*) by the CJEU.[79] Meanwhile, Article 3(d) of the SPC Regulation provides that the specified MA must be the first one for the product in the country concerned.[80] The first MA is important in terms of being used as reference to calculate the duration of each SPC within Member States.[81]

It is worth noting that in the EU, besides medicinal products for human use, veterinary medicinal products also are subject matter of an SPC.[82] Given this, concerning the 'first MA requirement' under Article 3(d) of the SPC Regulation, a question arises as to whether the existence of an earlier MA, for a veterinary medicinal product, precludes the granting of an SPC for a different application (eg as a medicinal product for human use) which obtained another MA. The CJEU in *Neurim Pharmaceuticals (1991) Ltd v Comptroller-General of Patents* (*Neurim*) provided a negative answer.[83] To be specific, instead of using a purely literal interpretation,[84] the CJEU considered the objectives pursued by the SPC

[75] Ibid, para 44 (the CJEU also pointed out that concerning the determination of whether the claims related, 'implicitly but necessarily and specifically', to the active ingredient, it would be a matter to be determined by national courts).

[76] See Case C-577/13 (n 46).

[77] Ibid, paras 35–38.

[78] Article 3(b) of the SPC Regulation (the MA is granted in accordance with the Directive 2001/83/EC or Directive 2001/82/EC, depending on whether the product is for human or veterinary use).

[79] See Case C-181/95 *Biogen Inc v SmithKline Beecham Biologicals SA* EU:C:1997:32, [1997] ECR I-357.

[80] Article 3(d) of the SPC Regulation.

[81] See Explanatory Memorandum (n 50) 19.

[82] Article 2 of the SPC Regulation.

[83] See Case C-130/11 (n 46).

[84] See Opinion of Advocate General Trstenjak on Case C-130/11 *Neurim Pharmaceuticals (1991) Ltd v Comptroller-General of Patents* EU:C:2012:268, para 23. (Trstenjak pointed out that if following a purely literal interpretation of Article 3(d) of the SPC Regulation, it would conclude that 'any further

Regulation as well as the overall scheme,[85] and held that a patent protecting a new use or a different therapeutic application of a known product might enable an SPC to be granted.[86] But the scope of the SPC, in any event, could only cover the new use of that product, rather than the active ingredient.[87] Based on the *Neurim* decision, it is clear that a patent for a new therapeutic use of an existing active ingredient may generate an SPC, even though the relevant active ingredient has been approved by an MA for a different therapeutic indication. This decision has been welcome, since it is considered to be in line with the fact that a considerable part of modern pharmaceutical research is finding new uses for old products.[88]

c. The Product has not Already been the Subject of an SPC

In accordance with Article 3(c) of the SPC Regulation, in order to obtain an SPC, the product must not have already been the subject of an SPC.[89] This condition has also become one of the most controversial provisions in the SPC Regulation. In reality, a pharmaceutical product may be covered by several basic patents in force, and each basic patent may be held by one or more holders. In such a situation, the CJEU has established the 'one patent, one SPC' rule in *Biogen*,[90] by holding that each of these patents might be designated as a basis for the granting of an SPC, but only one SPC could be granted for each basic patent.[91] Moreover, in *Medeva*, the CJEU appears to consolidate the 'one patent, one SPC' rule, holding that 'where a patent protects a product, in accordance with Article 3(c) of the [SPC] Regulation, only one certificate may be granted for that basic patent'.[92]

In the same situation where a product may be covered by one or more basic patents, and each basic patent may be held by one or more patentees, another ambiguity may arise as to whether the scope of application of Article 3(c) of the SPC Regulation should be restricted to cases where the same applicant had already received an SPC or to cases where all the patent holders had already received an SPC, in particular considering Article 3(2) of Regulation No 1610/96.[93] The CJEU

authorisation to place that active ingredient or that combination of active ingredients on the market as a medicinal product is to be regarded as a later authorisation, on the basis of which – according to the wording of Article 3(d) – an application for a new supplementary protection certificate cannot be made'.)

[85] See Case C-130/11 (n 46) paras 22–24.

[86] Ibid paras 24–25 and 27.

[87] Ibid para 25.

[88] See Papadopoulou (n 44) 378.

[89] See Article 3(c) of the SPC Regulation.

[90] See Case C-181/95 (n 79).

[91] Ibid para 28.

[92] Case C-322/10 (n 46) para 41.

[93] Article 3(2) of the Regulation (EC) No 1610/96 of the European Parliament and of the Council of 23 July 1996 concerning the creation of a supplementary protection certificate for plant protection products (OJ L 198/30) provides that 'the holder of more than one patent for the same product shall not be granted more than one certificate for that product. However, where two or more applications concerning the same product and emanating from two or more holders of different patents are

has clarified this issue in *AHP Manufacturing BV v Bureau voor de Industriële Eigendom* (*AHP Manufacturing*),[94] holding that an applicant might be granted an SPC, even if at the time of the SPC application, a third patent holder had already obtained an SPC or had applied for an SPC for the same product.[95] In this regard, the CJEU has set out the 'one product, one or more SPC' rule in the *AHP Manufacturing* case.

The 'one patent, one SPC' rule only targets cases in which one product is covered by several basic patents, but not the situation where a basic patent covers more than one product. In 2015, *Actavis Group PTC EHF, Actavis UK Ltd v Boehringer Ingelheim Pharma GmbH & Co. KG* (*Actavis v Boehringer*) decided by the CJEU, concerned in particular a situation 'where a basic patent includes a claim to a product comprising an active ingredient for which the holder of that patent has already obtained an SPC, as well as a subsequent claim to a product comprising a combination of that active ingredient and another substance'.[96] To be specific, in this case, Boehringer initially obtained an SPC for the single active ingredient Telmisartan, which was used in the management of high blood pressure. Subsequently, based on the same patent and a subsequent MA, Boehringer got another SPC for a combination of the active ingredients Telmisartan and hydrochlorothiazide (a diuretic). After the granting of this SPC, Boehringer amended the basic patent so as to recite both ingredients. Against this background, the validity of this SPC was challenged in front of the High Court of England and Wales, which referred several questions to the CJEU for preliminary rulings, including whether the SPC Regulation precluded the holder from obtaining a second SPC for that combination.[97] The CJEU emphasized that in the situation where a patent protected several different 'products', then it was possible to obtain more than one SPC associated with each of those different products, provided that each of those products was 'protected' as such by that basic patent,[98] or provided that the added active ingredient in the new combination is covered by the basic patent.[99]

C. Period of an SPC

In the EU, the duration of an SPC is equal to the time that elapsed between the filing date of the basic patent application and the date of the first MA in the EU,

pending, one certificate for this product may be issued to each of these holders.' The second sentence of this provision provides for the possibility of conferring more than one SPC to two or more holders of different basic patents for the same product. See also Case C-482/07 *AHP Manufacturing BV v Bureau voor de Industriële Eigendom* [2009] ECR I-7295, EU:C:2009:501, paras 23 and 25.

[94] Ibid.

[95] Ibid para 43.

[96] Case C-577/13 (n 46) para 25.

[97] Ibid para 25.

[98] Ibid para 33.

[99] See Papadopoulou (n 44) 375.

minus five years.[100] Moreover, similar to the PTE provision in the US, the SPC Regulation also provides a five-year cap, which means that the maximum duration of an SPC is five years.[101] However, the SPC Regulation contains a 15-year limit, which means that the period of the exclusive right granted by a patent and an SPC together may not exceed 15 years.[102] Moreover, the period of the SPC may be extended for a further six months at most,[103] under the Paediatric Regulation 1901/2006, when the clinical trials of certain products have taken place based on a paediatric investigation plan.[104] This primarily aims at providing further incentives for the pharmaceutical sector to engage in clinical trials dealing with paediatric uses of a drug.[105] The CJEU has recently clarified in *Merck Sharp and Dohme Corp v Deutsches Patent- und Markenamt* (*Merck*) that an SPC can be granted with a zero or negative term.[106] The negative or zero duration of an SPC could be useful, since a paediatric extension might be obtained based on the SPC.

IV. Laws and Practice Concerning PTE in Japan, Korea and Taiwan

In Asia, Japan, Korea and Taiwan have already introduced the PTE system, and adopted provisions similar to Hatch-Waxman of the US, though based on various reasons. In general, the purposes of the PTE systems are to promote drug innovation by compensating the lost period due to the lengthy MA. In Japan, the PTE system was introduced by the 1987 revision of the Japanese Patent Act (JPA)[107] to promote the progress of pharmaceutical innovation, by extending the duration of the patent right in cases 'where there is a period during which the patented invention is unable to be worked because pending approvals prescribed by relevant Acts … or any other disposition designated by Cabinet Order'.[108] In Korea, the PTE

[100] See Article 13(1) of the SPC Regulation.

[101] See Article 13(2) of the SPC Regulation.

[102] See Recital 9 of the SPC Regulation.

[103] See Article 13(3) of the SPC Regulation.

[104] Regulation (EC) No 1901/2006 of the European Parliament and of the Council of 12 December 2006 on medicinal products for paediatric use and amending Regulation (EEC) No 1768/92, Directive 2001/20/EC, Directive 2001/83/EC and Regulation (EC) No 726/2004, OJ L 378/1.

[105] See Case C-125/10 *Merck Sharp and Dohme Corp v Deutsches Patent- und Markenamt* EU:C:2011:812, [2011] ECR I-12987, para 34.

[106] Ibid.

[107] Toshiaki Imura, 'Patent Term Extension in Japan: Focusing on the *Pacif Capsule* Decision' in Josef Drexl and Nari Lee (eds), *Pharmaceutical Innovation, Competition and Patent Law: A Trilateral Perspective* (Edward Elgar, 2013).

[108] Article 72(2) of the Japanese Patent Act (JPA). Ryoko Iseki, 'Patent Term Extension in Japan: An Academic and Comparative' in Josef Drexl and Nari Lee (eds), *Pharmaceutical Innovation, Competition and Patent Law: A Trilateral Perspective* (Edward Elgar, 2013) (holding that the legislative intent of the Japanese PTE system is to make up for the disadvantage of patent holders who are not able to work the patented invention for a considerable period until they are able to obtain MAs under the Pharmaceutical Affairs Act).

system was introduced in 1986 due to strong political pressure from the US.[109] Similarly, in Taiwan, the introduction of the PTE system was due to political pressure from the US.[110] At least, based on the legislative reasoning, the aim of the PTE system in Taiwan is to encourage research and development on new drugs,[111] by means of compensating the period of time in which the patent holders of pharmaceuticals and the manufacturing processes cannot implement those patents due to the required MA.[112] However, although based on similar objectives and following the same model as in the US, these three jurisdictions have tailor-made different provisions and interpretations concerning the PTE system.

A. Applicants and Subject Matter for PTE

It is important to first establish a set of rules concerning the eligible applicants of a PTE, ie who has the right to apply for a PTE. These Asian jurisdictions have adopted more stringent requirements, particularly compared with the US, which allows a patentee or its agent to apply for a PTE.[113] To be specific, Japan and Korea are the most stringent, since both jurisdictions only allow patentees to file for a PTE, and if the patent right is held jointly by more than one person, it is necessary for all joint patent owners to file the application.[114] In Taiwan, not only the patentee but also the exclusive patent licensee, if registered with the Taiwan Intellectual Property Office (TIPO), may apply for an extension of the patents.[115] Moreover, it is not necessary for all joint patent owners to apply for a PTE, but each of the owners may file an application.[116] Thus, Taiwan and the US have a relatively liberal requirement concerning the PTE applicants, which is beneficial for patentees who wish to obtain PTEs.

Concerning the PTE-eligible categories of patents, the PTE systems in these jurisdictions do not impose any restrictions, and as in the US and EU, almost all types of patents are eligible for PTE. Meanwhile, the eligible subject matters

[109] See Jun-seok Park, 'Korea' in Max Planck Institute for Innovation and Competition (ed), *Annex II: International Reports – Study on the Legal Aspects of Supplementary Protection Certificates in the EU* (European Commission, 2018).

[110] See Clarice TH Chen, 'Study on Taiwan Pharmaceutical Patent Term Extension System' (in Chinese) (2008) 114 *Intellectual Property Right Journal* 63, 64.

[111] See the Patent Examination Guidelines of Taiwan Intellectual Property Office (hereafter TIPO Patent Examination Guidelines) 2-11-1.

[112] Moreover, according to Article 66 of the Patent Act of Taiwan (TPA), a patentee of an invention unable to practice that patent due to war between Taiwan and foreign countries may extend the patent term once for a period of between 5 to 10 years. Patentees from the foreign country that is at war with Taiwan are not eligible for PTE. Nevertheless, in patent practice, the PTE regime is rarely used in Taiwan.

[113] See 35 USC § 156(d)(1).

[114] See Article 67-3(1)(iv) and Article 67-2(4) of the JPA; Article 90(3), Article 91(4) and Article 91(5) of the Korean Patent Act (KPA).

[115] See Article 57(1)(4) of the TPA. See also the TIPO Patent Examination Guidelines, 2-11-2.

[116] Ibid.

for PTEs in these jurisdictions are quite similar but prescribed in different ways. Japan and Korea put the issue of the subject matter of PTEs in the hands of other regulatory laws or agents, rather than patent laws. In Japan, eligibility for extension is based on whether the subject matter needs MA prior to the sale.[117] In this regard, patents on pharmaceuticals are eligible for PTE in principle, but medical devices, quasi-drugs and cosmetics are not.[118] Similar to Japan, in Korea, the subject matter eligible for PTEs depends on other regulatory laws or regulations, such as other Acts, subordinate statutes and Presidential Decrees.[119] In this regard, patents upon medicinal products may obtain PTEs in Korea according to Article 7 of the Enforcement Decree of the Korean Patent Act (the Enforcement Decree of the KPA).[120] Unlike in Japan and Korea, in Taiwan, the subject matter of PTEs is set out in its Patent Act. Specifically, in Taiwan, patented inventions of pharmaceuticals, manufacturing processes and uses of these pharmaceutical are all eligible for PTEs,[121] but patents on veterinary drugs and medical devices are not.[122] However, in order to obtain a PTE in Taiwan, the PTE applicant is required to have obtained an MA.[123] From this perspective, there seems to be no difference between Taiwan and the other jurisdictions.

B. Concept of the Product and Active Ingredient

In Japan, the JPA has only one provision in connection with the PTE which mentions 'product', that is, 'where the duration of a patent right is extended …, such patent right shall not be effective against any act other than the working of the patented invention for the product which was the subject of the disposition designated by Cabinet Order'.[124] However, the JPA does not give any definition to

[117] According to Article 67(2) of the JPA, a PTE may be granted in cases where regulatory approval requirements are necessary in order to work a patented invention.

[118] See Yoshiyuki Tamura et al, 'Japan' in Max Planck Institute for Innovation and Competition (ed), *Annex II: International Reports – Study on the Legal Aspects of Supplementary Protection Certificates in the EU* 36 (European Commission, 2018) (pointing out that in Japan, based on the Agricultural Chemicals Regulation Act, agricultural chemicals should obtain such approval before marketing. Moreover, in accordance with the Act on Securing Quality, Efficacy and Safety of Products Including Pharmaceuticals and Medical Devices, Regenerative and Cellular Therapy Products, Gene Therapy Products, and Cosmetics, pharmaceuticals also need such approval.)

[119] See Article 89 of the KPA.

[120] Article 7 of the Enforcement Decree of KPA provides that '"invention prescribed by Presidential Decree" in Article 89 (1) of the Act means any of the following inventions: (1) invention of a medicine for which an item license has been granted pursuant to Article 31 (2) or (3) or 42 (1) of the Pharmaceutical Affairs Act to practice a patented invention (limited to a medicine for which an item license has been granted first, among medicines manufactured with a new substance as an effective ingredient (referring to a substance with a new chemical structure in the activated part having medicinal effect; the same shall apply hereafter in this Article)'.

[121] See Article 53 of the TPA.

[122] Ibid; TIPO Patent Examination Guidelines, 2-11-2.

[123] See Article 53 of the TPA.

[124] See Article 68-2 of the JPA.

the term the 'product'. In addition, there is no mention of 'active ingredient' in the JPA. The Japanese Patent Office (JPO) used to interpret the term 'product' broadly, taking the view that 'product' referred to 'active ingredients' and 'usage' implied 'efficacy and effectiveness' of the pharmaceutical product.[125] However, in practice, through a number of judicial decisions, Japan has gradually changed its position concerning the interpretation of the terms 'product' and 'usage' from a broad approach to a narrow approach, which currently considers the PTE eligibility of patents in connection with new formulations or new dosages of ingredients. To be specific, in the 2015 *Bevacizumab* case, the Supreme Court of Japan (SCJ) explicitly pointed out that the 'product' should be understood as being determined by 'the ingredients, quantity, dosage, administration, effectiveness, and effect'.[126] The Intellectual Property High Court of Japan (IPHCJ) applied this narrow interpretation approach in the 2017 *Pharmaceutically Stable Preparation of Oxaliplatinum* case, pointing out that the 'product' prescribed in an MA referred to 'ingredients, quantity, dosage, administration, efficacy, and effects' as a whole.[127] Based on the narrow interpretation, nowadays the PTE system in Japan does not focus only on 'active ingredients' and 'efficacy and effectiveness', but pays more attention to the quantity, dosage and administration of drugs.

In Korea, the Enforcement Decree of the KPA precisely describes 'medicinal products' as products 'manufactured with a new substance as an effective ingredient'.[128] More importantly, 'a new substance' here is further defined to be 'a substance whose chemical structure in the activated part having medicinal effects is new'.[129] The PTE system in Korea primarily focuses on the chemical structure when defining a medicinal product. As a result, in Korean practice concerning the PTE, as long as the chemical structure of the substance is not changed, any product or use that is developed based on the existing drug may not be considered new and, thus, would not be considered PTE-eligible subject matter, such as a new use of a known pharmaceutical product, and a combination of two or more existing active ingredients. However, this general exclusion of second and further medical indications from PTE protection has been criticized by commentators for being incompatible with the intention of the PTE system – ie to foster innovation in the pharmaceutical sector.[130]

Similar to the Japanese approach, in Taiwan, the Patent Act of Taiwan (TPA) does not precisely define the term 'product', nor does it provide any link between

[125] See Imura (n 107) 223–25; Nick Reeve, 'Patent Term Extensions in Japan: A Question of Identity' (Reddie & Grose, 29 February 2016), https://www.reddie.co.uk/2016/02/29/patent-term-extensions-in-japan-a-question-of-identity.

[126] See *Bevacizumab*, Supreme Court of Japan, 2014 (Gyo-Hi) 356, 17 November 2015.

[127] See *Pharmaceutically Stable Preparation of Oxaliplatinum*, Intellectual Property High Court of Japan, Case No 2016(Ne) 10046, 20 January 2017.

[128] Article 7 of the Enforcement Decree of KPA.

[129] Ibid.

[130] See Ulrich M Gassner, 'Recent Developments in the Area of Supplementary Protection Certificates' (2014) 16 *Pharmaceuticals Policy and Law* 45, 53.

the terms 'product' and 'active ingredient'. However, when stipulating the scope of protection concerning the PTE, the TPA refers to 'active ingredient'.[131] Article 56 of the TPA provides that 'the scope of a patent, of which a term extension has been granted, shall be limited to only the active ingredients and use stated in the regulatory approval concerned'.[132] As a result, the product under the TPA refers to 'the active ingredients and use' as a whole.[133] Given this, a combination of two active substances is considered a new product, irrespective of whether each of the active ingredients has been approved by an MA or not.[134] In addition, the TIPO Patent Examination Guidelines further explain 'active ingredients' as ingredients of pharmaceutical formula that have pharmaceutical action.[135] An adjuvant, therefore, is not included in the scope of 'active ingredient' under the TPA, since an adjuvant is only able to modify the effect of one or more other substances, but does not have pharmaceutical action by itself. It seems that Taiwan has followed the former practice of Japan concerning the approach towards interpreting the concept of 'product' in the PTE system. However, Japan has changed its position through judicial decisions, and adopted a narrow interpretation. In contrast, Korea still maintains an extremely broad approach, focusing on the chemical structure of active ingredients.

It is worth noting that the modern pharmaceutical industry is evolving and developing, and nowadays it is mostly based on biological products, second medical indications of already known substances, or combination products.[136] Technologies, such as drug delivery systems (DDS), have emerged and receive increasing attention, and thus elements such as dosage form have become also of great significance when identifying the drugs.[137] In this regard, it appears that the approaches that Korea and Taiwan have taken with regard to the interpretation of the term 'product' do not correspond to the progress of the current pharmaceutical industry.[138]

[131] Article 56 of the TPA provides that 'the scope of a patent, of which a term extension has been granted, shall be limited to only the active ingredients and use stated in the regulatory approval concerned'.

[132] Ibid.

[133] See also TIPO Patent Examination Guidelines, 2-11-2.

[134] Article 7 of the Pharmaceutical Affairs Act of Taiwan stipulates that 'the term "new drugs" as used in this Act shall refer to drugs which are of the preparations having new compositions, new therapeutic compounds or new method of administration as verified and recognized by the central competent health authority'. Moreover, Article 2 of the Pharmaceutical Affairs Act Enforcement Rules of Taiwan prescribes that 'terms used in Article 7 of the [Pharmaceutical Affairs] Act are defined as follows: (1) New composition: a newly invented composition that can be used for pharmaceutical purposes. (2) New therapeutic compound: an already approved drug with new medical efficacy in terms of new indications, reduced side effects, improved therapeutic strength, improved therapeutic period, or altered dosage, or a compound prepared from two or more already approved compositions whose medical efficacy is superior to either of the individual drug compositions. (3) New method of administration: An altered method of administration for an already approved drug.'

[135] See TIPO Patent Examination Guidelines, 2-11-3.

[136] See Papadopoulou (n 44) 373.

[137] See Imura (n 107) 224.

[138] See Imura (n 107) 229–30.

C. Conditions for Granting a PTE

Similar to the PTE system of the US and the SPC system in the EU, each PTE system in these Asian jurisdictions, ie Japan, Korea and Taiwan, also has provided specific conditions for the granting of a PTE. That is to say, if an application for a PTE is submitted to the patent office, an examiner, upon examination, may reject the application only if the examiner finds that one of the conditions is not met.[139] In general, conditions for granting a PTE in these jurisdictions are as follows: (i) the basic patent should be in force; (ii) a valid MA should be obtained; (iii) the MA should be the first authorization; (iv) there is no previous PTE on the product or patent. Although the conditions for the granting of PTEs in these three Asian jurisdictions can be roughly grouped into the above-listed categories, each PTE system still has its own specific prescriptions and interpretations. This subsection continues to analyse these conditions from a comparative perspective.

i. A Basic Patent in Force

In Japan, Article 67(2) of the JPA provides that 'where there is a period during which the patented invention is unable to be worked …, the duration of the patent right may be extended'.[140] Article 67-2(3) of the JPA stipulates that the PTE application should not be filed after the expiration of the duration of a patent right.[141] Based on these two provisions, it is evident that one premise for the granting of a PTE in Japan is that the product should be protected by a valid patent. In the context of Article 67(2) of the JPA, the term that the legislator has chosen is 'patented invention', rather than 'product protected by a patent'. It seems that under the JPA, a PTE may be granted only if the product is the subject matter of the basic patent. Put another way, it is required that an authorized pharmaceutical product should fall within the scope of claims of the patent. Indeed, as the SCJ pointed out in the *Controlled Release Composition* case, the pharmaceutical product should fall within the technical scope of the patent.[142] Based on this statement, in Japan it is not necessary for the product to be recited or specified in the patent claims. As a result, it appears that Japan adopts the 'infringement test' to determine the connection between the MA and the basic patent.

In Korea, Article 90(2) of the KPA[143] also requires the necessity of an effective patent. When dealing with the connection between the patent and the MA, the

[139] See Imura (n 107) 222.

[140] Article 67(2) of the JPA.

[141] Article 67-2(3) of the JPA.

[142] See SCJ Con*trolled Release Composition* 2009 (Gyo-Hi) 326, 28 April 2011.

[143] Article 90(2) of the KPA stipulates that 'an application to register an extension of the term of a patent right … shall be filed within three months from the date on which permission … is obtained. … such application shall not be filed if less than six months are left before the expiration of the term of patent right …'.

Korean Intellectual Property Office (KIPO) regulation requires that the specific active ingredient approved by the MA be stated in the claims of the patent.[144] Moreover, the KIPO Patent Examination Guidelines point out that the authorized matter should have the same composition as the matter disclosed in the claims, or as the matter manufactured by the method described in claims of the patent.[145] It appears that the KIPO has adopted the restrictive approach – the disclosure test – to determine the connection between the MA and the basic patent.

In Taiwan, Article 53(4) of the TPA prescribes that no PTE application may be filed within six months prior to the expiry of the original patent term. Thus, in Taiwan the product must also be protected by a basic patent. In terms of determining the connection between the MA and the basic patent, the TIPO Patent Examination Guidelines point out that the applicant should explain in its PTE application the correlation between the patent claims and the active ingredients and uses (ie the product specified in the MA).[146] The TIPO Patent Examination Guidelines provide a list of examples to further illustrate how to show the 'corresponding relationship'.[147] Based on this list, the product authorized by the MA does not have to be precisely stated in the claims of the basic patent. It is evident that Taiwan has adopted the 'infringement test' to determine the connection between the MA and the basic patent, which is quite similar to the Japanese approach.

ii. A Valid Authorization Obtained

In terms of the condition 'a valid MA obtained', all these three Asian jurisdictions have set forth the rules from both positive and negative aspects. On the one hand,

[144] See Park (n 109) 49, 52.

[145] See KIPO Patent Examination Guidelines, 546.

[146] See TIPO Patent Examination Guidelines, 2-11-5.

[147] TIPO Patent Examination Guidelines provide: '(i) In the case where the patent covers compounds, at least one of the patent claims must correspond to the active ingredients stated in the MA.' (2-11-5) '(ii) In the case where the patent covers a combination, if the combination consists of more than two active ingredients, then the active ingredients stated in the MA must also contain more than two effective ingredients. For instance, if the product described in the MA is a combination of two active ingredients (e.g., a+b), then the corresponding patent claims must be a combination of a+b or A+B (a and b are included within A and B, respectively); if the corresponding patent claims only contain a (or A), or b (or B), or A+B+C (C is the third active ingredient), etc., then there is no "corresponding relationship"; if the corresponding patent claims are a combination of A and B, but the active ingredient stated in the MA is merely a or b, then there is no "corresponding relationship" either. (iii) In the case where the patent concerns the use, at least one claim of the patent must correspond to the use of the active ingredient stated in the MA; if the patent claims are described by pharmaceutical mechanism, and the indication stated in the MA is the name of a specific symptom, then it is necessary to explain the connection between the pharmaceutical mechanism and the specific symptom; if the patent specification has stated the connection between the pharmaceutical mechanism and the specific symptom, then it is necessary to demonstrate the statement.' (2-11-7) '(iv) In the case where the patent involves a manufacturing process, at least one patent claim which involves the process must correspond to the active ingredient stated in the MA (the MA does not describe the manufacturing process); if the patent specification has described the two items, then it is necessary to demonstrate the statement.' (2-11-7 and 2-11-8).

it is required that the PTE application be filed within a time limit after the MA is obtained and, on the other hand, when the MA is not deemed necessary for practising the product or the MA has not been obtained, then the PTE application should be rejected. To be specific, in Japan, the JPA requires that an MA must be obtained as a premise for the granting of a PTE. Article 67-2(3) of the JPA provides that the PTE application should be filed within a time limit after the MA is obtained.[148] In addition, Article 67-3(1)(i) of the JPA stipulates that a PTE application shall be rejected if the MA is not deemed to have been necessary for the practicing of the patented invention.[149] Similarly, in Korea, Article 90(2) of the KPA stipulates that 'a [PTE] application … shall be filed within three months from the date on which permission … is obtained …'.[150] Moreover, Article 91 of the KPA requires an examiner to reject a PTE application in cases where it is deemed that the MA is unnecessary for manufacturing the patented invention, and where the applicants have not obtained an MA.[151] In Taiwan, Article 53(4) of the TPA stipulates that '[w]hen requesting for a [PTE] …, a request form and document(s) of proof must be submitted to the Specific Patent Agency, within three months from the date on which the first permission is obtained'. Furthermore, Article 57(2) of the TPA provides that a PTE application shall be rejected if the patentees or licensees have not obtained the permission. Based on this, in Taiwan, it is also required that a valid MA has been granted.

iii. The First Marketing Authorization

In Japan, there was previously no express provision requiring the MA which a PTE application is based on, to be the first one. As mentioned earlier, the SCJ in the 2015 *Bevacizumab* case changed the practice and established a 'substantial identity' test to determine whether another PTE should be granted in cases where there are already MAs.[152] The SCJ pointed out that the key was to examine the identity of the relevant products specified in the prior and the latter MAs, and the identity should be understood here as to be determined by 'the ingredients, quantity, dosage, administration, effectiveness, and effect'.[153] By a comparison of the products specified in the prior and the latter MAs, if the product specified in the latter MA is 'substantially identical' with the product specified in the prior MA, then a PTE based on the latter MA should be rejected.[154] In this regard, it seems that Japan also requires the MA to be the 'first' one, but what differs from

[148] See Article 67-2(3) of the JPA.
[149] See Article 67-3(1)(i) of the JPA.
[150] Article 90(2) of the KPA.
[151] See Article 91(1), (2) of the KPA.
[152] See *Bevacizumab* case (n 126).
[153] See *Bevacizumab* case (n 126).
[154] Ibid.

the EU is this focus on a narrow interpretation of 'product'. Moreover, Japan attempts to compensate for the delay to the marketing of applicants' invention in all its possible forms, which is in sharp contrast with the viewpoint of the CJEU.[155]

In Korea, Article 7 of the Enforcement Decree of the KPA requires the MA of the patented medicine to be the first one.[156] Considering the definition of the term 'product' analysed before, under the current PTE system in Korea only the first MA for 'a new chemical entity' can be granted a PTE. In Taiwan, according to Article 53 of the TPA, the MA which is used as support for a PTE should be the first authorization concerning the product. Moreover, this first MA can only receive one PTE, and is allowed to be used only once for seeking the PTE.[157] The first MA is to be judged on the combination of active ingredients and usage as a whole, rather than by active ingredients alone, specified in the MA.[158] In this regard, different uses of the same active ingredients may obtain multiple MAs, and in this case each MA may be considered the first one to be used to apply for a PTE.[159] However, it is important to mention that although a new formula or dosage form of drugs may obtain a new MA in Taiwan, it cannot be considered to be the 'first' MA to apply for PTE, since the combination of active ingredients and uses is not changed.[160] If active substances of the two MAs are substantially identical (eg two different types of salts of the same active ingredient), and the uses stated in the MAs are also the same, then the subsequent MA should not be considered the 'first' MA to apply for an extension.[161]

It seems that PTE systems in these three jurisdictions require the MA for the product to be the first one, which is quite similar to the SPC system in the EU. Concerning the determination of the 'first' MA, these jurisdictions have adopted almost the same approach, by comparing the products specified in the prior and the latter MAs, and assessing whether the two products are identical; if the product stated in the latter MA is not identical with the product stated in the prior MA, then the latter MA can be considered the 'first' MA and be used as a support to apply for another PTE. However, the main difference is their different interpretations of the term 'product', ranging from broad (Korea) to middle (Taiwan), and to narrow (Japan), which is the ground for determining the 'first' MA.

[155] See https://www.reddie.co.uk/2016/02/29/patent-term-extensions-in-japan-a-question-of-identity. Case C-443/12 *Actavis Group PTC EHF, Actavis UK Ltd, v Sanofi* EU:C:2013:833, para 40 (the CJEU pointed out that 'the objective of [the SPC Regulation] is not to compensate the holder fully for the delay to the marketing of his inventions or to compensate for such delay in connection with the marketing of those inventions in all its possible forms …').

[156] See Article 7(1) of the Enforcement Decree of the KPA.

[157] See Article 53 of the TPA.

[158] See TIPO Patent Examination Guidelines, 2-11-2.

[159] Ibid.

[160] See TIPO Patent Examination Guidelines, 2-11-3.

[161] Ibid.

iv. No Previous PTE on the Product or Patent

In the US a patent can only be extended once. In contrast, in the EU, the SPC Regulation requires that the 'product' have never been the subject of an SPC. As analysed before, in the EU there are divergent interpretations of the concept 'product'. In the US, since it focuses on 'patent', there has not been any debate, and it is quite clear that one patent can only get one PTE, even though one patent may cover more than one product.

Although the JPA requires an MA to have been obtained, it does not set out a rule like 'the term of the patent has never been extended', which exists in the US Hatch-Waxman Act.[162] In fact, the legislative proposal considered this condition, but ultimately the JPA has still been silent on the issue of whether a patent can be extended only once or more.[163] As mentioned previously, the SCJ, in the 2015 *Bevacizumab* case, has narrowed the interpretation of the 'product' to be understood by 'the ingredients, quantity, dosage, administration, effectiveness, and effect',[164] and has established that a single patent may obtain more than one PTE in Japan. Moreover, in Japan if a product is covered by multiple patents, then each patent may also be extended.

In Korea, one patent can only receive one PTE.[165] The principle of 'one patent, one PTE' has, therefore, been set up in Korea, as in the US Hatch-Waxman Act. Given this, if a single patent contains more than one product, and each product has obtained its own MA, then the applicants must choose just one MA as the support to apply for a PTE. However, unlike in the US, Korea does not have a 'one product, one PTE' rule.[166] In this regard, in Korea, in the case where a product is covered by multiple patents, it is not necessary for the applicants to choose one as a basic patent, but each patent can be extended once.

In Taiwan, based on Article 53 of the TPA, a single patent can only receive one PTE.[167] Put differently, if the term of the patent has been extended once, it cannot obtain another PTE anymore. This is the same as the US and Korea. For instance, in the case where an invention patent covers an active ingredient and its two usages (eg germicide and pesticide), and this patent has already been extended by a term based on the MA for germicide use, then it cannot be extended again based on the other MA for pesticide use. In this situation, the applicant has to choose just one of the MAs to apply for a PTE.[168] As mentioned before, in Taiwan, the MA used as

[162] See 35 USC § 156(a)(2).

[163] See Iseki (n 108) 190.

[164] See *Bevacizumab* case (n 126).

[165] See Park (n 109) 53.

[166] As been demonstrated previously, in the US, when a product is covered by more than one patent, the patent owner must choose only one to apply for a PTE.

[167] See Article 53(1) of the TPA. See also TIPO Patent Examination Guidelines, 2-11-4.

[168] See TIPO, 'Explanation of the TPA' 174 (TIPO, 16 May 2018) https://www.tipo.gov.tw/ct.asp?xItem=532218&ctNode=6952&mp=1 (in Chinese, English translation available). See also TIPO Patent Examination Guidelines, 2-11-4.

support for a PTE should be the first authorization. This first MA can only receive one PTE, and is allowed to be used only once for seeking the PTE.[169] Therefore, after the patent holder(s) has obtained the first MA, then only one patent can be used to apply for a PTE if this MA corresponds to multiple patents.[170] Taiwan in effect has established the 'one product, one PTE' principle. However, this principle may cause a problem in Taiwan when the first MA corresponds to multiple patents, and these patents may be possessed by various holders. In this instance, only one patent may be extended once, but the other patents cannot obtain PTEs, which may be unfair to the holders of the other patents, as their patented inventions also cannot be marketed until the MA has been obtained.

D. Period of a PTE

In general, the PTE system would set forth that the period of extension may not exceed the period during which the relevant patented invention could not be worked or implemented due to clinical trials and the MA. In Japan, the duration of a PTE is equal to 'the period in which the patented invention could not be worked' due to the necessity of obtaining an MA.[171] The 'period' here has been defined by the SCJ in the 1999 *Polypeptides* case as 'the period between the date of the beginning of the test which is required for the approval, or the date of patent registration, whichever is later, and the day before the date when the above approval took effect by reaching the applicant'.[172] Similar to Japan, in Korea only the period elapsed after the date of patent registration could be considered for calculation,[173] and the total duration of a PTE contains the clinical trials phase and the approval phase.[174] In Taiwan, the TPA provides that the period of the extended term may not exceed the period of time during which the patentee is not allowed to practice invention after the issue of the patent due to MA requirements.[175] The calculation of the period of extended term in Taiwan is similar to that in the US and Korea, which contains two phases: the clinical trials (including domestic and/or foreign clinical trials) phase or testing phase, and the domestic approval phase.[176]

Moreover, Korea and Taiwan deduct from the extended term any period which has lapsed due to the fault of patentees. In Korea, the elapsed period attributable

[169] See Article 53 of the TPA.

[170] See TIPO Patent Examination Guidelines, 2-11-4.

[171] See Article 67-3(1)(iii) of the JPA.

[172] See *Polypeptides*, Supreme Court of Japan, 1998 (Gyo-Hi) 43, 22 October 1999.

[173] See KIPO Patent Examination Guidelines, 532.

[174] See KIPO Patent Examination Guidelines, 533.

[175] See Article 53(2) of the TPA.

[176] See Article 4 of the Regulations for Ratifying PTE of Taiwan. The clinical trials phase must be recognized by the TIPO and the Taiwan Minister of Health and Wealth (TMHW) as necessary for issuing the MA.

to the patentee or an applicant during the period of reviewing relevant documents of the application for MA shall be excluded from the calculation of the period.[177] Similarly, in Taiwan, the time period of any delay due to the applicants' negligence, any overlapping time period between domestic and foreign clinical trials, and any overlapping period between the testing phase and the approval phase is deducted from the extended term.[178]

However, the Korean Patent Court has pointed out that non-substantive delay caused by the MA applicants should not be excluded from the extended term.[179] For instance, some products might require regulatory review by more than one government agency, and even if the patentee is responsible for a delay in one agency, this delayed period should not be excluded from the extended term if the review period of another agency was much longer.[180]

To date, none of these three Asian jurisdictions have introduced a fixed-year limit, such as the 14-year limit in the Hatch-Waxman Act and the 15-year limit in the EU SPC Regulation, into their respective PTE system. However, all of them have followed the Hatch-Waxman Act of the US and incorporated a five-year cap into their PTE systems.[181] The underlying assumption is that the five years of PTE will fully compensate most patentees for their loss of patent term.[182] As shown previously, although calculation methods may vary between jurisdictions, the duration of the extended term, in principle, is based on the testing phase and the approval phase. However, it is noteworthy that the term of the two phases is, in effect, not controlled by the PTE applicant, but primarily depends on the nature of the regulated product and the specific practices of the relevant government agency. In this regard, a problem may arise because a period of lost patent term exceeding five years cannot be compensated, even if this lost time is not attributable to the applicants' negligence. Admittedly, as the CJEU has pointed out several times in its judgments, the aim of the PTE system is not to compensate the patent holder fully for the delay to the marketing of the invention.[183] Nevertheless, in the case where most patents on pharmaceutical products cannot obtain sufficient compensation for the lost term, the five-year cap would run counter to the objective of the PTE system and thus be problematic.[184]

[177] See Article 89(2) of the KPA; KIPO Patent Examination Guidelines, 532–33.

[178] See Article 4 of the Regulations for Ratifying PTE of Taiwan.

[179] See 2016Huh21, Korean Patent Court, 16 March 2017; 2016Huh4498, Korean Patent Court, 16 March 2017. See also 'Korean Patent Court Dismisses Generics' Challenges to PTE Terms' (KIM & CHANG Intellectual Property), http://www.kimchang.com/newsletter/2017newsletter/ip/eng/newsletter_ip_en_spring_summer2017_article01.html.

[180] See Park (n 109) 54.

[181] See eg Article 67(2) of the JPA; Article 89(1) of the KPA; Article 53(2) of the TPA.

[182] See Cárdenas-Navia (n 8) 1349.

[183] See eg Case C-443/12 (n 155) para 40; Case C-577/13 (n 46) para 35.

[184] See Cárdenas-Navia (n 8) 1349 (conducting empirical research based on patents that have been extended during the period between 1984 and 2013 under the Hatch Waxman Act in the US, and observing that the five-year cap in the Hatch-Waxman Act would hardly restore most of the patent term for most relevant patents).

E. Scope of the PTE Protection

A PTE in all these Asian jurisdictions merely extends the effective term of a patent and, thus, the right of a PTE is just a patent right per se. However, the scope of protection of a PTE is not as wide as the original patent right (ie patent before expiration), but much more restricted, as it is based on the scope of the MA. In this regard, the scope of PTE protection, in general, exhibits its double nature.

In Japan, according to Article 68-2 of the JPA, the right of a PTE is limited only to the approved product or the specific usage of the product prescribed by the MA, and the product used for that usage.[185] In practice, in PTE infringement cases, Japanese courts generally would investigate the issue of whether the allegedly infringing product falls within the technical scope of the original patent, and then focus on the scope of protection limited to the product of the MA. Through analysing the 'ingredients, quantity, dosage, administration, efficacy, and effects' of the allegedly infringing pharmaceutical product and the said product, the court may determine whether they are 'substantially identical'.[186] By doing so, the court is able to determine whether the allegedly infringing product falls within the scope of PTE protection.

In Korea, the scope of protection by the PTE is limited to the patent, and especially confined to the products or any specific use of the product stated within the MA.[187] In cases where the claims of the original patent include more than one invention, the PTE only covers the invention relating to the approved product. Moreover, a judicial decision by the Korean Intellectual Property Tribunal (KIPT) has pointed out that the doctrine of equivalents cannot be used in infringement cases concerning a PTE.[188] Therefore, Korea has adopted an extremely restrictive interpretation of the scope of PTE protection. In Taiwan, the scope of a PTE is limited to merely the product, which is defined as the active ingredients and uses, described in the MA concerned.[189] Put differently, any ingredients, processes or uses that are identified in the claims of patents but not stated in the MA will not be covered by a PTE in Taiwan.[190] This is similar to the Korean approach. However, it is still unclear whether the doctrine of equivalents can be applied to PTE infringement cases in Taiwan.[191] Importantly, the absence of the doctrine of equivalents in PTE infringement cases in the pharmaceutical sector might go against the interests

[185] See Article 68-2 of the JPA.
[186] See *Pharmaceutically Stable Preparation of Oxaliplatinum* (n 127).
[187] See Article 95 of the KPA.
[188] See 2015Dang3931, Korean Intellectual Property Tribunal, 13 September 2016.
[189] See Article 56 of the TPA.
[190] See TIPO Patent Examination Guidelines, 2-11-21.
[191] See Kung-Chung Liu, 'Taiwan' in Max Planck Institute for Innovation and Competition (ed) *Annex II: International Reports – Study on the Legal Aspects of Supplementary Protection Certificates in the EU* 103 (European Commission, 2018).

of patentees, since competitors can easily produce chemicals with the same active ingredient by simply substituting salts.[192]

V. PTE in the Context of CPTPP and TPP

Article 18.48 of the TPP obliges signatories to provide PTEs or similar *sui generis* protection to compensate for unreasonable delays due to MA requirements of pharmaceutical products. However, Article 18.48 is among the 22 suspended IP provisions of the TPP,[193] because these provisions were priorities for the US in the TPP negotiations, but not for other negotiating members.[194] Although CPTPP members do not have an obligation to establish a PTE system, Japan, New Zealand, Australia, Singapore, Canada and Brunei have already established such a system.[195] Importantly, there still is a possibility that the suspended provisions will be reinstated at a later date when all CPTPP members reach an agreement.[196] Moreover, the CPTPP welcomes the US and other countries that are interested in joining. If the US decides to rejoin the CPTPP, then the suspended IP provisions could be renegotiated and reinstated.[197]

It should be borne in mind that pharmaceutical innovators would benefit more from the granting of PTEs than public and generic companies, which may cause a negative impact on drug costs and availability.[198] Therefore, the PTE to be renegotiated should always be based on the level of development of the pharmaceutical industry in a specific jurisdiction and take into account the public interest. The change of SCJ's PTE practice, as mentioned above, is a good example of how the SCJ aligned the PTE policy with Japan's advanced pharmaceutical industry, whereas the cautious stance of Korea and Taiwan concerning this issue is reasonable and understandable, as it is in line with those jurisdictions' relatively backward pharmaceutical industries.

Introduction of a fixed-year cap and X-year limit into the future PTE provision of the CPTPP or TPP is further recommended, so as to achieve the goal of harmonization and to ensure that the extended patent term would balance the interests of both pharmaceutical innovators and the public.

[192] See Park (n 109) 53.

[193] See CPTPP (n 11).

[194] See Matthew P Goodman, 'From TPP to CPTPP' (CSIS, 8 March 2018), https://www.csis.org/analysis/tpp-cptpp.

[195] See Jeremiah B Frueauf, 'Trans-Pacific Partnership Lost Important IP Provisions' (Sterne Kessler, April 2018), https://www.sternekessler.com/news-insights/publications/trans-pacific-partnership-lost-important-ip-provisions.

[196] New Zealand Ministry of Foreign Affairs & Trade, 'CPTPP vs TPP', https://www.mfat.govt.nz/en/trade/free-trade-agreements/free-trade-agreements-in-force/cptpp/understanding-cptpp/tpp-and-cptpp-the-differences-explained#extension.

[197] See Ernesto Londoño and Motoko Rich, 'U.S. Allies Sign Sweeping Trade Deal in Challenge to Trump' (*New York Times*, 8 March 2018), https://www.nytimes.com/2018/03/08/world/asia/us-trump-tpp-signed.html.

[198] See Albert Gore Jr, 'Patent Term Extension: An Expensive and Unnecessary Giveaway' (1982) 1 *Health Affairs* 25, 33.

VI. Recommendations for China's PTE

China has recently been considering the introduction of the PTE system,[199] as it is believed that the protection measures for innovative drugs need to be improved.[200] Given that China is one of the largest pharmaceutical markets in the world, this section will leverage the preceding discussions, and provide suggestions to the planned incorporation of the PTE system into China's patent law. On 4 January 2019, the Draft Amendment to the Patent Law of the People's Republic of China (CPL) was published for public comments,[201] which provides that in order to compensate for the approval time of innovative drugs, the State Council may decide to extend the period of patents over innovative drugs.[202] The period of extension may not exceed five years, and the maximum period of EPT with extension is 14 years.[203] China has been cautious about extending the patent term for pharmaceutical products. With the CPL Draft Amendment, China seems to believe that the PTE system will not only benefit foreign pharmaceutical companies, but also foster innovation awareness of its domestic companies, and ultimately transform its pharmaceutical sector. The introduction of the PTE system is very likely to happen, as it follows the trend of Japan, Korea and Taiwan and helps to alleviate the trade friction between the US and China.

It is recommended that in the beginning, the relatively conservative approach that Korea and Taiwan have taken for the PTE system might be appropriate for China to follow, since the domestic pharmaceutical industry in China remains backward, particularly compared with the US, EU and Japan.[204] Regarding the interpretation of the term 'product' in the PTE system, it is recommended that China initially focus on 'the active ingredients and use' as a whole, which is the current approach of Taiwan. When its domestic pharmaceutical industry elevates to a certain higher level, China may change its interpretation of the term 'product' from broad to narrow, just as Japan is currently construing the term by 'the ingredients, quantity, dosage, administration, effectiveness, and effect'.[205]

It is further recommended that China choose the disclosure test rather than the infringement test when determining the connection between the MA and the patent. Concerning the scope of PTE protection, China may choose to expressly

[199] On 8 October 2017, the General Office of the Central Committee of the Communist Party of China and the General Office of the State Council of China jointly issued a document to implement a pilot PTE program in the pharmaceutical sector: Opinions on Deepening the Reform of the Evaluation and Approval Systems and Encouraging Innovation on Drugs and Medical Devices.

[200] See generally Yahong Li, *Imitation to Innovation in China: The Role of Patents in Biotechnology and Pharmaceutical Industries* (Edward Elgar, 2010).

[201] Available at www.npc.gov.cn, http://www.npc.gov.cn/npc/flcazqyj/node_8176.htm (in Chinese, English translation available). The CPL was adopted at the 4th Meeting of the Standing Committee of the 6th National People's Congress on 12 March 1984. The current version is the 3rd amendment and was adopted on 27 December 2008.

[202] See Article 43 of the CPL Draft Amendment.

[203] Ibid.

[204] See Dorocki (n 1) 118–19.

[205] See *Bevacizumab* case (n 126).

refuse the doctrine of equivalents, which is the current approach of Korea. It is recommended that the method for calculating the extended term follow the US approach, namely one-half of the 'testing phase' of the product, plus the entire 'approval phase', and deduct the period which has lapsed due to the patentees. Moreover, even though Japan, Korea and Taiwan have not introduced a fixed-year limit of the total EPT with extension, the 14-year limit foreseen in the CPL Draft Amendment should be enacted, as it would function as a ceiling to prevent the additionally compensated patent term from harming China's relatively undeveloped domestic pharmaceutical industry and the public interest, and at the same time benefit pharmaceutical innovators. In addition, excluding the period of foreign clinical trials from the duration of a PTE would also be strongly recommended for the first version of the PTE system in China, since most clinical trials of brand-name pharmaceutical products are conducted abroad. After establishing the PTE system, China's approach may evolve dynamically from conservative to aggressive, so as to better adapt to the development of its domestic pharmaceutical industry.

VII. Conclusion

The PTE system, which compensates pharmaceutical innovators by granting an additional period of patent term for marketing drugs exclusively, is receiving more attention than before, not only in the US and EU, but also in a number of Asian jurisdictions, such as Japan, Korea and Taiwan. However, this chapter has shown that in these jurisdictions, the conditions for granting a PTE are highly controversial, the PTE systems and case law are still evolving, and there remain plenty of uncertainties waiting to be clarified. Indeed, when introducing and tailoring the specific PTE rules and policies, a jurisdiction should consider the development level of its domestic pharmaceutical industry, especially the advantages and disadvantages for the industry. In the event that the PTE system has been reinstated in the context of CPTPP to reach other Asian countries, the latter are advised to learn from the relatively conservative approaches taken by Korea and Taiwan, rather than Japan's aggressive approach.

10

Mitigating the Impacts of Patent Linkage on Access to Medicine

Some Asian Experiences and Suggestions

SU-HUA LEE*

I. Introduction

The United States (US) established complex patent linkage (PL) via the Drug Price Competition and Patent Term Restoration Act of 1984, commonly known as the 'Hatch-Waxman Act'.[1] PL is a mechanism to link the drug approval process for generic drugs with patent clearance, in order to, on the hand, prevent the marketing of generic drugs from infringing patents of the reference patented drugs or original drugs ('original drugs'), and on the other to enhance the generic drugs' market entry. The US has tried to sell PL to its trading partners through bilateral free trade agreements (FTAs), such as the US-Singapore FTA, or multilateral FTAs, such as the Trans-Pacific Partnership (TPP). When negotiating the TPP, the US government, on the one hand, reaffirmed its commitment to the Doha Declaration on the TRIPS Agreement and Public Health[2] and emphasized the importance of public health,[3] and, on the other hand, forced the parties to accept the PL provision

* College of Law, National Taiwan University, Taipei, Taiwan. The author led a research team to help the Taiwanese government draft the amendment bill to introduce patent linkage between 2015 and 2018. All online materials last visited 20 January 2019.

[1] Pub L No 98-417, 98 Stat. 1585 (1984). In 2003 some regulations were amended by the Medicare Prescription Drug Improvement and Modernization Act, Pub L No 108-173, 117 Stat. 2066 (2003). The Hatch-Waxman Act introduced important mechanisms related to pharmaceutical innovation and intellectual property protection, which provide incentives to originator and generics companies, and enhance competition in the pharmaceutical industry. On one hand, originator companies conducting innovation and filing new drug applications (NDA) benefit from the mechanisms of patent term extension and data exclusivity. On the other hand, generics companies take advantage of the Abbreviated New Drug Application (ANDA) process and the experimental use exemption (the 'Bolar exemptions'), which accelerate the introduction of generic drugs to the market.

[2] WT/MIN(01)/DEC/2, 20 November 2001.

[3] Office of the United States Trade Representative (USTR), Trans-Pacific Partnership Trade Goals to Enhance Access to Medicines, available at https://ustr.gov/about-us/policy-offices/press-office/press-releases/2011/september/trade-enhancing-access-medicines.

in Article 18.53, which is entitled 'Measures relating to the Marketing of Certain Pharmaceutical Products'. The TPP has been incorporated into the Comprehensive and Progressive Agreement for Trans-Pacific Partnership (CPTPP), with some provisions suspended (Articles 1 and 2 of the CPTPP).[4] The CPTPP came into force on 30 December 2018. The CPTPP is one of the largest FTAs in the world; its signatories include 11 Asia-Pacific economies.[5] The PL provisions of the TPP have not been suspended by the CPTPP. The Regional Comprehensive Economic Partnership (RCEP), which is currently under negotiation, does not contain provisions on PL, although it introduces some TRIPS-plus provisions.[6]

The establishment of the pharmaceutical PL system seems to be an unavoidable challenge for countries intending to enter bilateral FTAs with the US[7] or join the CPTPP.[8] However, it is generally believed that PL is a 'TRIPS-plus' mechanism which strengthens the protection and enforcement of pharmaceutical patent rights, and which could delay the market entry of generic drugs and cause negative impacts on public health systems, if mechanisms in favour of the generics industry

[4] Government of Canada, 'What does the CPTPP mean for intellectual property?', available at https://international.gc.ca/trade-commerce/trade-agreements-accords-commerciaux/agr-acc/cptpp-ptpgp/sectors-secteurs/ip-pi.aspx?lang=eng.

[5] CPTPP's members include Australia, Brunei, Canada, Chile, Japan, Malaysia, Mexico, New Zealand, Peru, Singapore and Vietnam. The CPTPP keeps its door open to new members. Presently, Thailand, South Korea and Taiwan are seeking to join the CPTPP.

[6] The RCEP was launched in November 2012, which also integrates the IP Chapter. According to the working draft leaked on websites, it includes some TRIPS-plus provisions related to public health issues. For example, it broadens the scope of patentability and provides protection for new forms and new uses of known substances. Furthermore, the mechanism of patent term extension is incorporated, even though neither the Paris Convention for the Protection of Industrial Property nor the TRIPS Agreement imposes an obligation on states to adopt this mechanism for prolonging the protection of pharmaceutical patent. The IP Chapter also imposes an obligation on RCEP's members to adopt a five-year protection of data exclusivity. Opponents believe these provisions might affect access to medicine in developing countries in Asia. See Joint Leaders' Statement on the Negotiations for the Regional Comprehensive Economic Partnership (RCEP), 14 November 2017, https://asean.org/storage/2017/11/RCEP-Summit_Leaders-Joint-Statement-FINAL1.pdf; https://www.keionline.org/23060; Eva Novi Karina, Indonesia and RCEP: Beware the Public Health Risks, November 23, 2018, https://thediplomat.com/2018/11/indonesia-and-rcep-beware-the-public-health-risks.

[7] For instance, Canada introduced PL under the influence of North American Free Trade Agreement (NAFTA), which took effect in January 1994 and was replaced by the United States–Mexico–Canada Agreement (USMCA) in October 2018. In March 1993 the Patents Medicines (Notice of Compliance) Regulations (SOR/93-133) were enacted to establish PL. For more details, see Minister of Health, Guidance Document: Patented Medicines (Notice of Compliance) Regulations, available at https://www.canada.ca/en/health-canada/services/drugs-health-products/drug-products/applications-submissions/guidance-documents/patented-medicines/notice-compliance-regulations.html. Also, the Australia-United States FTA entered into force in January 2005. Article 17.10 covers the drug approval and PL issue. This provision is implemented by Schedule 7 of the US Free Trade Agreement Implementation Act 2004. For more details see https://dfat.gov.au/trade/agreements/in-force/ausfta/official-documents/Pages/official-documents.aspx, http://www.comlaw.gov.au/Details/C2004A01355/Html/Text#param99. For more details about PL in Canada, Singapore, Australia and other countries, see Ravikant Bhardwaj, KD Raju and M Padmavati, 'The Impact of Patent Linkage on Marketing of Generic Drugs' (2013) 18 *Journal of Intellectual Property Rights* 318.

[8] Taiwan is an example. See Yu-Tzu Chiu, 'Taiwan to Create Patent Linkage System for Drug in Quest for TPP Membership', Bloomberg, Daily Report for Executives, 15 August 2014; 'Taiwan Works to Build "Patent Linkage" for Drugs as Part of TPP Bid Prep', *World Trade Online*, 12 August 2014.

are not incorporated. Given different domestic circumstances, there are variations in the implementation of PL. Admittedly, each country has different priorities for protection and enforcement of pharmaceutical patent rights and assurance of the availability and accessibility of medicine.[9]

The purpose of this chapter is to analyse the PL mechanism in the US and under the CPTPP, as well as the implementation of PL in three Asian countries, namely Singapore, South Korea and Taiwan, and provide some suggestions for countries when introducing and implementing PL. Section II discusses the PL mechanism in the US and under the CPTPP. Section III reviews the different challenges under different domestic circumstances in Asia in general and especially in Singapore, South Korea and Taiwan.[10] Section IV examines and compares the implementation of PL in Singapore, Korea and Taiwan against the US. Section V provides some suggestions for countries when introducing and implementing PL.

II. PL Mechanism

A. In the United States

PL, introduced by the Hatch-Waxman Act in the US, tries to strike a balance between the originals and generics industries. The generics industry would benefit from the disclosure of patent information, which is a transparent and effective procedure to identify patents covering original drugs. The mechanism of market exclusivity encourages the generics companies to step forward to challenge the pharmaceutical patents. PL is a legal framework designed to prevent infringing drugs from being launched onto the market while an original drug is still protected by a valid patent. To achieve this goal, a number of steps must be followed by the originator and generics companies, including:

- disclosure of patent information by the originator company, namely the holder of an approved NDA;
- declaration of the patent status by the generics company, namely the company which files the ANDA;

[9] To emphasize the differentiation and different desires for the protection and enforcement of pharmaceutical patent right in Asia, the VIPP (Visionary Intellectual Property Professors for the Betterment of IP Study and Regimes in Asia), an initiative by the Applied Research Center for Intellectual Assets and the Law in Asia (ARCIALA), School of Law, Singapore Management University, published the 'Statement on Intellectual Property Protection for Pharmaceuticals and the Market Approval Mechanisms in Asia', which is available at https://arciala.smu.edu.sg/vipp-project.

[10] In 2017, the VIPP initiated a survey on national healthcare, pharmaceutical industry and IP protection in Asia. Information was provided by Professors GUO He (China), Feroz Ali (India), Masabumi Suzuki, Inchiro Nakayama and Yoshiyuki Tamura (Japan), Heng Gee Lim (Malaysia), Weeloon Loy (Singapore), Hao-Yun Chen and Su-Hua Lee (Taiwan).

- notification to the originator company of filing for market approval by the ANDA filer;
- stay of market approval of the generic drug by the drug authority in order to allow for settlement of the patent dispute;
- market exclusivity for the first qualified ANDA filer.

In the US, both the NDA filers and the holders of approved NDA are required to submit patent information that claims the drug or a method of using the drug, and with respect to which a claim of patent infringement could reasonably be asserted if a person not licensed by the owner of the patent engaged in the manufacture, use or sale of the drug product.[11] However, only patents on approved active ingredients, formulations, compositions and method of use should be disclosed. Patent information, including the US patent number,[12] issue and expiration dates, and the name and address of the patent owner, should be listed on the 'Approved Drug Products with Therapeutic Equivalence Evaluations',[13] commonly called the 'Orange Book'. Since the submission and amendment of patent information are the responsibility of the originator companies, the FDA does not review the eligibility of disclosed patents or confirm the accuracy of patent information.

A mechanism for declaring patent status requires the ANDA filer to state its views with respect to each patent of the Reference Listed Drug (RLD) disclosed by the originator company. In general, the declaration of patent status can be categorized according to both the patent information itself and whether the launch of generic drugs would cause patent dispute or not. That is to say, an ANDA filer might declare that:

(i) patent disputes would not occur and the reasons would be as follows:[14]
   - the originator company did not provide any patent information;
   - the disclosed patent has already expired;
   - other reasons like the disclosed patent is valid and the right holder has given consent to the ANDA;

(ii) the patent will expire on a specifically identified date and patent dispute would not occur, since no marketing of the generic drug will occur before the expiration date of the patent;

(iii) the patent is invalid or will not be infringed by the manufacture, use or sale of the generic drug for which the application is submitted.

[11] 21 CFR §314.53(b)(1).

[12] In the context of patent on method of use, not only the patent number but also the claim number directly related to the approved drug should be identified.

[13] http://www.accessdata.fda.gov/scripts/cder/ob/default.cfm.

[14] 21 USC §355(j)(2)(A)(vii); Art 12A(1)-(2) of Medicines Act (Singapore), Art 23(1)-(4) of Health Products (Therapeutic Products) Regulations 2016 (Singapore); Art 50-4(1) of Pharmaceutical Affairs Act (South Korea); Art 48-9 of Pharmaceutical Affairs Act (Taiwan).

In the first circumstance, the drug authority can issue the approval immediately after the ANDA meets all applicable regulatory and scientific requirements. With respect to the second circumstance, the approval will not be issued until the disclosed patent expires, even if the regulatory conditions have been fulfilled by the ANDA. The third type of declaration leads to complicated possibilities. The core procedures of PL including notification, stay of market approval and market exclusivity of first qualified ANDA filer should be applied, in order to settle patent dispute before the generics company launches its product onto the market.

The main characteristics of PL in the US are summarized in Table 10.1.

Table 10.1 Main Characteristics of PL in the US

In Favour of Originator Company	In Favour of Generics Company
Declaration of patent status and notification	Disclosure of patent information
Stay of market approval of generic drugs by Drug Authority	Market exclusivity of the first qualified ANDA filer

B. Under the CPTPP

The CPTPP contains comprehensive IP provisions in Chapter 18, covering almost all areas of IP protection and enforcement. Article 18.53 mandates two options for CPTPP's members to adopt if they permit, as a condition of approving the marketing of a pharmaceutical product, persons other than the person originally submitting the safety and efficacy information to rely on evidence or information concerning the safety and efficacy of a product that was previously approved, such as evidence of prior marketing approval by the party or in another territory. The first option is to provide: (a) a system to provide notice to a patent holder[15] or to allow for a patent holder to be notified prior to the marketing[16] of such a pharmaceutical product, that such other person is seeking to market that product during the term of an applicable patent claiming the approved product or its approved method of use; (b) adequate time and opportunity for such a patent holder to seek, prior to the marketing of an allegedly infringing product, available remedies in subpara (c); and (c) procedures, such as judicial or administrative proceedings, and expeditious remedies, such as preliminary injunctions or equivalent effective

[15] Footnote 62 of the CPTPP explains: 'For greater certainty, for the purposes of this Article, a Party may provide that a "patent holder" includes a patent licensee or the authorised holder of marketing approval.'

[16] Footnote 63 of the CPTPP explains: 'For the purposes of paragraph 1(b), a Party may treat "marketing" as commencing at the time of listing for purposes of the reimbursement of pharmaceutical products pursuant to a national healthcare programme operated by a Party and inscribed in the Appendix to Annex 26-A (Transparency and Procedural Fairness for Pharmaceutical Products and Medical Devices).'

provisional measures, for the timely resolution of disputes concerning the validity or infringement of an applicable patent claiming an approved pharmaceutical product or its approved method of use (Article 18.53(1)).

Article 18.53(2) provides the second option:

> As an alternative to paragraph 1, a Party shall instead adopt or maintain a system other than judicial proceedings that precludes, based upon patent-related information submitted to the marketing approval authority by a patent holder or the applicant for marketing approval, or based on direct coordination between the marketing approval authority and the patent office, the issuance of marketing approval to any third person seeking to market a pharmaceutical product subject to a patent claiming that product, unless by consent or acquiescence of the patent holder.

In other words, members shall adopt a system other than judicial proceedings that precludes the issuance of marketing approval to a generic drug during the term of an applicable patent claiming the original drug or its approved method of use, unless by consent of the patent holder.

The first measure incorporates the main characteristics of the PL, including the mechanisms of 'notification to original drug company' and 'stay of market approval'. It is, however, unfortunate that Article 18.53 includes only the mechanisms that favour the original drug companies, and does not incorporate mechanisms that would benefit the generics industry, such as 'disclosure of patent information', or provide incentives for generic drug companies, such as 'market exclusivity of first qualified ANDA filer'.

III. Different Challenges under Different Domestic Circumstances in Asia

A. General Remarks

With regard to IP protection for pharmaceuticals, a 'one-size-fits-all' approach could not work in Asia. Each country faces different challenges under different domestic circumstances, including their health care system, pricing mechanism for medicines, development of the domestic pharmaceutical industry, and domestic market scale.[17] For example, in Japan, Singapore, South Korea and Taiwan, every citizen is covered by public health insurance, and the price of medicines is mainly determined or influenced by the public sector, namely the national health insurance agency. However, in some countries, such as India, where national healthcare is still developing and a certain proportion of the population cannot afford basic healthcare, the prices of the drugs are mainly controlled by market

[17] See paragraphs 2.1 and 2.2 of the 'Statement on Intellectual Property Protection for Pharmaceuticals and the Market Approval Mechanisms in Asia (n 9).

mechanisms, and accessibility and affordability of medical care at reasonable cost are still a big issue.

The development of the domestic pharmaceutical industry is also diverse in Asia. In Japan, the domestic innovative pharmaceutical industry is developed and capable of innovating new drugs. South Korea's pharmaceutical industry is becoming more capable of developing new drugs and biosimilars in recent years, and several locally developed innovative drugs have been approved.[18] However, in China, Malaysia and Taiwan the domestic pharmaceutical industry is mainly capable of manufacturing generic drugs and certain types of new drugs, such as new dosage forms and new administration routes of existing drugs. By comparison, the generics industry in India is competitive and capable of manufacturing generic drugs with high quality.[19] In Singapore, both original and generic drugs rely on foreign producers. To sum up, to date in the majority of Asian countries the demand for innovative and original drugs has been satisfied by foreign producers; Japan is the only exception. South Korea is trying to catch up with Japan.

Another important factor is the size of the domestic market. China, Japan and India are the top three countries in Asia in terms of pharmaceutical market,[20] and have attracted foreign pharmaceutical companies wishing to launch new products. By contrast, the domestic markets in Singapore and Taiwan are relatively small, and foreign original drug companies need extra incentives to launch new medications there. In these countries, ensuring the accessibility of innovative pharmaceutical products is one of the essential challenges for policymakers in the public health field.

Due to these differences, in Asia each country has different needs when seeking to strike a balance between the protection and enforcement of pharmaceutical patents and their citizens' right to health care, including access to medicines, innovative drugs and generics.

B. Singapore

Based on the FTA entered with the US, Singapore passed the Medicines (Amendment) Act and established the PL in 2004.[21] However, the laws and guidelines provided

[18] For more details, see Korea Drug Research Association, Overview, http://www.kdra.or.kr/english/03web01.php; International Trade Administration, 2016 Top Market Report Pharmaceuticals: Country Case Study, https://www.trade.gov/topmarkets/pdf/Pharmaceuticals_Korea.pdf.

[19] India Brand Equity Foundation (IBEF), India Pharmaceutical Industry, December 2018, https://www.ibef.org/industry/pharmaceutical-india.aspx.

[20] Industrial Development Bureau (Taiwan Ministry of Economic Affairs), 2018 Biotechnology Technology in Taiwan (in Chinese) 13 (2018), https://old.www.biopharm.org.tw/download/Biotechnology_Industry_in_Taiwan_2018.pdf; India Brand Equity Foundation (IBEF), India Pharmaceutical Industry, December 2018, https://www.ibef.org/industry/pharmaceutical-india.aspx.

[21] Health Sciences Authority, Legislative Changes and Implementation of Patent Linkage, 30 June 2004, https://www.hsa.gov.sg/content/hsa/en/Health_Products_Regulation/Industry_Engagement_Activities/Industry_News/archive/Legislative_Changes.html.

little instructions in its operation. For instance, before 2016 it was not clear whether the PL in Singapore included the 'stay of market approval' mechanism, one of the most important mechanisms of PL, according to which the drug authority shall not issue market approval within a certain time period in order to allow the litigation to play out. This issue and the details about the operation of PL were finally clarified by the Health Products (Therapeutic Products) Regulations 2016, which came into effect in November 2016.[22]

In Singapore the market scale is small, and both original and generic drugs rely on foreign producers. It is then no surprise that protection of domestic industry was not a crucial factor when Singapore introduced the PL. That is to say, the legal framework is beneficial to the original drug companies and encourages the launch of new medications into Singapore's market. Singapore's PL does not include provisions giving an incentive for generic drug companies to challenge the originator companies' patent rights.

C. South Korea

The KORUS-FTA[23] became effective in March 2012. The PL issue stipulated in Article 18.9 of the IPRs Chapter was implemented by a two-phased approach. Disclosure of patent information and notification procedures were in the first stage, which began in March 2012. The other mechanisms of PL are included in the second stage, which took effect in March 2015. It is worthy of mention that South Korea adopts a unique PL. The Ministry of Food and Drug Safety (MFDS) took account of the domestic legal system, national health insurance and the capability of domestic industry, and introduced 'Chapter V-II Registration of Drug Patent and Prevention of Marketing, etc.' into the Pharmaceutical Affairs Act. Even though the main characteristics and features of the PL established by the Hatch-Waxman Act are included in the Korean legal framework, many details are different. For instance, the MFDS is involved in the operation of the PL and plays an important role in maintaining a balance between the originator and generics industries.

[22] In recent years there were two cases between AstraZeneca AB (SE) and Sanofi-Aventis Singapore Pte Ltd related to the application of PL. See *AstraZeneca AB (SE) v Sanofi-Aventis Singapore Pte Ltd* [2012] SGHC 16 and *AstraZeneca AB (SE) v Sanofi-Aventis Singapore Pte Ltd* [2013] SGHCR 7. According to Bloomberg (https://www.bloomberg.com/research/stocks/private/snapshot.asp?privcapId=383605), AstraZeneca AB researches, develops, manufactures and markets gastrointestinal, cardiovascular, respiratory and pain control drugs. The company was founded in 1913 and is based in Sweden. According to Bloomberg (https://www.bloomberg.com/research/stocks/private/snapshot.asp?privcapId=34536495), Sanofi-Aventis Singapore Pte Ltd manufactures consumer healthcare products, generics and animal health products to patients and residents in Singapore. The company was incorporated in 1997 and is based in Singapore. However, the two cases have been sealed and no further information is available. Supposedly, the cases should have been settled between the parties.

[23] KORUS-FTA is available at http://www.ustr.gov/trade-agreements/free-trade-agreements/korus-fta/final-text.

D. Taiwan

Compared with many other Asian countries, affordability of medication and health care does not seem to be a major issue in Taiwan, since the National Health Insurance (NHI) program was launched in March 1995. Every citizen is required to join the program and pay monthly NHI premiums. When seeking medical care, citizens basically pay only the registration fee, ranging from NT$150 to 450 (approx US$5 to US$15), and cover the co-payment cost for innovative pharmaceutical products not listed in the NHI program, which helps reduce the national expenditure on medication.[24]

With regard to the pharmaceutical industry, since the 1980s, Taiwan has designated biotechnology and pharmaceutics as key development areas and made efforts to establish domestic industry: launching the 'Action Plan for Strengthening the Biotechnology Industry' in 1995; legislating the 'Act for the Development of Biotech and New Pharmaceuticals Industry' in 2007; and promulgating the 'Diamond Action Plan for the Takeoff of Biotech Industry' in 2009. However, the domestic pharmaceutical industry has developed slowly due to the limited scale of the domestic pharmaceutical market, and is mainly capable of manufacturing generic drugs.[25] The country's demand for innovative medication is mainly satisfied by import from Germany and the US.[26] Nevertheless, it is worth mentioning that in recent years some domestic companies have been undertaking R&D, trying to establish patent portfolios, and are capable of launching new dosage forms of existing drugs.[27]

The introduction of PL has long been a major issue in the negotiation of the Trade and Investment Framework Agreement (TIFA) between Taiwan and the US. In 2016 the Taiwan Food and Drug Administration (TFDA) started to draft the legal framework of PL, after Taiwan had expressed interest in joining the TPP Agreement. On 29 December 2017 the Legislative Yuan passed an amendment to the Pharmaceutical Affairs Act and established the PL, which is quite similar to that in the US. Even though the President promulgated the Amendment of Pharmaceutical Affairs Act on 31 January 2018, the newly introduced 'Chapter IV-II Patent Linkage' has not taken effect, as the TFDA needs time to prepare enforcement rules and detailed execution plans. The TFDA announced the first and second drafts of the Implementation Rule of Patent Linkage in September 2018 and January 2019 respectively, and it is expected to be finalized soon.

[24] The global spending on medication reached US$1.1 trillion in 2016. Medication expenditures in the US, China, Japan and South Korea were US$461.7 billion, 116.7 billion, 90.1 billion, and 13.0 billion respectively. In contrast, spending on medication in Taiwan was only US$5.33 billion. Ibid 50; IMS, Outlook for Global Medicines through 2021 (2016), at 9. https://morningconsult.com/wp-content/uploads/2016/12/QuintilesIMS-Institute-Global-Outlook-FINAL.pdf.

[25] Industrial Development Bureau (Taiwan Ministry of Economic Affairs), 2018 Biotechnology Technology in Taiwan (in Chinese), at 54–59 (2018), https://old.www.biopharm.org.tw/download/Biotechnology_Industry_in_Taiwan_2018.pdf.

[26] Ibid 56. Notably imported medication is increasing in Taiwan. In 2016 and 2017 the growth rate was 9.84% and 6.84% respectively. Ibid 56.

[27] Ibid 57.

In addition, providing an incentive for foreign original pharmaceuticals companies to launch new drugs onto the domestic market might be another crucial reason for Taiwan to introduce PL.

IV. Implementation of PL in Singapore, South Korea and Taiwan

Modelled on the Hatch-Waxman Act, Singapore, South Korea and Taiwan have established PL. Even though the legal framework is similar to the mechanism in the US, especially the declaration of patent status, there are variations in implementation. It is worth mentioning that the PL in the US only applies to small molecule drugs. Patent issues of biologic medicines should be dealt by the procedure of 'patent dance' introduced by the Biologics Price Competition and Innovation Act of 2009 (the BPCI Act). By contrast, both small molecule and biologic medicines are subject to PL in Singapore, South Korea and Taiwan.[28]

A. Disclosure of Patent Information

In Singapore, neither NDA filers nor holders of approved NDA are required to submit patent information. That is to say, generics companies intending to enquire about patent information on original drugs have to conduct a patent search themselves. The exclusion of disclosure of patent information from PL is disadvantageous to generics companies. However, the establishment of a domestic generics industry is not prioritized by the Singapore government.

The mechanism for disclosing patent information in South Korea is principally similar to that in the US. However, not only the patent number but also the claim number are required to be submitted to the MFDS. The Pharmaceutical Affairs Act states that the listed patent must be 'directly' related to the approved matters of the relevant drug.[29] To ensure the implementation of this provision, the relevance of the patent claim with the drug is under the MFDS' examination, and the submission of patent information might be rejected. Furthermore, the MFDS

[28] The issue of whether PL should apply to biologic medicines is controversial in Taiwan. The draft Implementation Rule of Patent Linkage announced by the TFDA in September 2018 covers solely the small molecule drugs. However, the TFDA released a revised draft on 30 January 2019 which stipulates that the application for market approval of biologic medicines should follow the PL procedures too, which was deemed by domestic industry to be a complete surprise and led to strong opposition. See TFDA, Re-announcement of the Draft Implementation Rule of Patent Linkage (in Chinese), January 30, 2019, available at https://www.fda.gov.tw/TC/newsContent.aspx?cid=4&id=t448516. For opposing opinion expressed by domestic industry, see https://www.chinatimes.com/newspapers/20190201000357-260204; https://www.chinatimes.com/newspapers/20190131000259-260202; https://www.chinatimes.com/newspapers/20190131000261-260202 (in Chinese).

[29] Article 50-2(4) of Pharmaceutical Affairs Act (South Korea).

enjoys the authority to edit the patent claims so that they could 'directly' match with the approved drugs. Originator companies are entitled to file an opposition if they disagree with the decisions of the MFDS. To sum up, the MFDS is empowered to decide whether the patent number and claim number are eligible to be listed on the 'Green List' and what the final outcome of the disclosed patent information is. The strict requirement for the disclosure of patent information is presumably to achieve the policy goal of ensuring the competitiveness of domestic industry.

According to the first draft of the Implementation Rule of Patent Linkage in Taiwan, the mechanism for disclosing patent information is very similar to the procedure in the US. Principally, only the patent number needs to be identified. Also, the originator companies take the responsibility for reviewing the eligibility and accuracy of disclosed patent information.[30]

A comparison of the disclosure requirements for patent information is shown in Table 10.2.

Table 10.2 Comparison of Disclosure of Patent Information

	US	**Singapore**	**South Korea**	**Taiwan**
Patents eligible for disclosure	• drug substance • composition and formation • method of use	no	• drug substance • composition and formation • method of use	• drug substance • composition and formation • method of use
Disclosed information	• patent number • issue and expiration dates • name and address of patent owner		• patent number and claim number • issue and expiration dates • name and address of patent owner	• patent number • issue and expiration dates • name and address of patent owner
Drug Authority's Role	none	none	• substantive examination conducted by the MFDS *ex officio* • edition of the disclosed patent information	none
Post-approval amendment to patent information	originator company		• MFDS • originator company	originator company
Deletion from the list	originator company		• MFDS • originator company	originator company

[30] Articles 48-3, 58-4 of Pharmaceutical Affairs Act (Taiwan).

B. Notification to Originator Company

With regard to the mechanism of notification, both the originator company and the patent holder are informed about the act of filing for market approval and the possibility of dispute over patent infringement. According to the PL in the US, Singapore, South Korea and Taiwan, the ANDA filer needs to send the notification within a certain period of time. Also, the notification must include a detailed statement of the factual and legal basis of the ANDA filer's opinion that the patent is invalid or will not be infringed.[31]

C. Stay of Market Approval

i. Importance of Stay of Market Approval

A mechanism of stay of market approval provides the originator company and the ANDA filer an administrative procedure, to ensure the settlement of dispute concerning the validity or infringement of the disclosed patents. The originator company, namely the holder of patent right, has to decide within a certain time frame whether to file a lawsuit after receiving the notification. If it ignores the ANDA filer's notification and does not sue the ANDA filer for patent infringement, the drug authority can approve the ANDA immediately after the regulatory conditions are fulfilled. By contrast, a patent infringement lawsuit triggers the mechanism of stay of market approval, which prohibits the drug authority from approving the ANDA for a certain period of time, while the litigation is ongoing. That is to say, the evaluation of the ANDA before the drug authority goes forward in its normal procedure, but the final approval permitting market launch of the generic drug cannot be granted until the stay period expires, the patent expires, or a judicial or administrative decision in favour of the ANDA filer is rendered.

ii. Controversy Over Stay of Market Approval

The mechanism of stay of market approval is the most controversial part of the PL, since the facts deciding whether an ANDA can be approved rely not only on the safety, quality and efficacy of the generic drug, but also on the issue of potential patent infringement. However, the act of applying for market approval of the generic drug does not necessarily amount to patent infringement, particularly in countries where the experimental use exemption (the 'Bolar exemption') is provided by patent law. Under the framework of PL, it is deemed to be an 'artificial'

[31] 21 USC §355(j)(2)(B)(i); Art 12A(3)-(4) of Medicines Act (Singapore), Art 23(5)-(6) of Health Products (Therapeutic Products) Regulations 2016 (Singapore); Art 50-4 of Pharmaceutical Affairs Act (South Korea); Art 48-12 of Pharmaceutical Affairs Act (Taiwan).

act of patent infringement, if the ANDA filer claims that the disclosed patent is invalid or will not be infringed by the generic drug.[32] It seems that the establishment of PL enlarges the protection scope of pharmaceutical patent right. Another criticism is that the mechanism of stay acts in the nature of a preliminary injunction and prevents the generics company from marketing its proposed product,[33] as long as the patentee commences a patent infringement suit. Furthermore, the patentee is still entitled to seek a preliminary injunction when the stay period expires, in order to block generic competition until infringement litigation is resolved.[34]

iii. Differences between US, Singapore, South Korea and Taiwan

With regard to this core procedure of PL, there are significant differences among Asian countries. Singapore follows the US approach and applies the same rule. That is to say, the drug authority is prohibited from approving the ANDA for 30 months, as long as the patentee files a lawsuit.[35] By contrast, the duration of stay of market approval in Taiwan is 12 months,[36] after taking the duration of market approval of ANDA and the average length of a patent infringement trial into consideration. The procedure of stay of market approval in South Korea is particularly remarkable among Asian countries. First of all, this mechanism is not triggered automatically. Namely, the patentee's filing of a petition for trial or litigation within a certain period of time is required for the prevention of marketing approval of generic drugs.[37] The MFDS has the final say, as it is empowered to decide whether the stay of marketing approval should be granted or rejected. Second, the duration of stay is merely nine months,[38] which is the shortest among the countries which have established PL. The reason for the nine-month stay is that dispute over patent infringement could be solved within nine months by the scope confirmation action at the Intellectual Property Trial and Appeal Board (IPTAB).[39]

A comparison of stay of market approval procedures is shown in Table 10.3.

[32] 35 USC §271(e)(2); Art 60-1 of Patent Act (draft, Taiwan).

[33] John R Thomas, Pharmaceutical Patent Law 314 (2005).

[34] John R Thomas, Pharmaceutical Patent Law 314 (2005).

[35] 21 USC §355(j)(5)(B)(iii), 21 CFR §314.107(f)(1); Art 23(9) of Health Products (Therapeutic Products) Regulations 2016 (Singapore).

[36] Article 48-13(2) of Pharmaceutical Affairs Act (Taiwan).

[37] Article 50-5 of Pharmaceutical Affairs Act (South Korea).

[38] Article 50-6 of Pharmaceutical Affairs Act (South Korea).

[39] Apart from filing patent litigation with the civil court, the patentee may assert its right against the ANDA filer by filing a positive scope confirmation action before the IPTAB to clarify whether the generic drug falls within the scope of the patent right. From the perspective of the generics company, apart from filing for invalidation before the KIPO, the ANDA filer may file a negative scope confirmation action before the IPTAB to seek a decision that the generic drug does not fall within the scope of patent right.

Table 10.3 Comparison of Stay of Market Approval

	US	Singapore	South Korea	Taiwan
Requirement for stay of market approval	patent litigation filed by patentee	patent litigation filed by patentee	• patent litigation filed by patentee or scope confirmation action filed by patentee or ANDA filer • patentee's request for stay	patent litigation filed by patentee
Automatic stay	yes	yes	• no • MFDS's review and decision	yes
Length of stay	30 months	30 months	9 months	12 months
Reasons to terminate the stay	• Expiration of stay period • Expiration of patent right • A judicial or administrative decision in favour of the ANDA filer	• Expiration of stay period • Expiration of patent right • A judicial or administrative decision in favour of the ANDA filer	• Expiration of stay period • Expiration of patent right • A judicial or administrative decision in favour of the ANDA filer, including a positive or negative scope confirmation action	• Expiration of stay period • Expiration of patent right • A judicial or administrative decision in favour of the ANDA filer

D. Market Exclusivity of First Qualified ANDA Filer

i. Importance and Controversy of Market Exclusivity

A mechanism of market exclusivity encourages the generics companies to step forward to challenge patents or design around them. It provides an effective reward for the first qualified ANDA filer that successfully proves that the disclosed patent is invalid or that it is not infringed by the generic drug. From the perspective of public interest, ANDA filers are encouraged to challenge the patent right.[40] Furthermore, the policy goal of market exclusivity is to establish a competitive

[40] Young Sun Cho and Hyunsuk Jin, *Overview and Implications of the Drug Patent-Approval Linkage System in South Korean Regulation*, available at https://uk.practicallaw.thomsonreuters.com/3-557-9230?transitionType=Default&contextData=(sc.Default)&firstPage=true&comp=pluk&bhcp=1.

environment in the generics industry and promote the development of generics companies. However, market exclusivity can lead to monopoly effects, and delays the subsequent market entry by other generics companies, and therefore the length of such exclusivity should be carefully calculated when establishing PL.

ii. Difference between Singapore, South Korea and Taiwan

In the US, the Hatch-Waxman Act established a 180-day market exclusivity period for the first qualified ANDA filer.[41] After taking the pricing mechanism of medicine and the procedure for reimbursement of medical expenses into consideration, Taiwan provides 12-month market exclusivity.[42] In the US and Taiwan, the requirement for market exclusivity is merely that the first ANDA filer challenged the patent protecting the original drug.[43] However, if the patentee filed an infringement lawsuit and the court ruled that the patent infringement is indeed established, the first ANDA filer will be disqualified from market exclusivity.

Details about market exclusivity in South Korea are different and more complex. First, only a nine-month market exclusivity period has been recognized.[44] Second, the first ANDA filer challenging the disclosed patent must obtain a favourable decision in a petition for trial or a litigation. In other words, if the generics company does not file a negative scope confirmation action and the patentee does not sue the generics company for patent infringement, this ANDA filer is disqualified from enjoying market exclusivity.[45] Third, the meaning of the 'first ANDA filer' is as follows:[46] the first generics company that challenges the patent disclosed by the originator company; *and* the ANDA filer that challenges the patent within 14 days of the first challenge. That is to say, the first generics company submitting the ANDA and challenging the patent is the 'first ANDA filer' and would be qualified to enjoy market exclusivity. Apart from that, those generics companies submitting the ANDA and challenging the patent within 14 days of the first generic approval application are also deemed to be the 'first ANDA filer'. However, the mechanism of market exclusivity provides little benefit to generics companies, as there will be at least in theory a number of 'first qualified ANDA filers' to share the nine-month exclusivity period.

In contrast to PL in South Korea and Taiwan, Singapore does not include the mechanism of market exclusivity, probably due to the fact that a domestic generics industry has yet to be established.

A comparison of market exclusivity is shown in Table 10.4.

[41] 21 USC §355(j)(5)(B)(iv)(1).

[42] Article 48-16 of Pharmaceutical Affairs Act (Taiwan).

[43] When multiple generics companies submit the ANDA and challenge the patent of the originator company on the same day, all are treated as first ANDA filers.

[44] Article 50-9(2)) of Pharmaceutical Affairs Act (South Korea).

[45] Mee Sung Shim, Inchan Andrea Kwon, Garam Baek, Patent Approval Linkage System – One Year After, November 21, 2016, https://www.internationallawoffice.com/Newsletters/Intellectual-Property/South-Korea/Kim-Chang/Patent-approval-linkage-system-one-year-later.

[46] Article 50-8 of Pharmaceutical Affairs Act (South Korea).

Table 10.4 Comparison of Market Exclusivity of First Qualified ANDA Filer

	US	Singapore	South Korea	Taiwan
Definition of first ANDA filer	first generics company challenging the patent of originator company	none	• first generics company challenging the patent of originator company • generics companies filing ANDAs within 14 days of the first challenge	first generics company challenging the patent of originator company
Qualification for market exclusivity	lawsuit filed by the patentee	none	• lawsuit filed by the patentee • decision granted by the IPTAB or the court in favour of the first ANDA filer	lawsuit filed by the patentee
Length of market exclusivity	180 days	none	9 months	12 months

V. Suggestions: Turning Challenge into Opportunity

The establishment of PL is an unavoidable challenge for countries intending to enter bilateral FTAs with the US or join the CPTPP. This 'TRIPS-plus' mechanism might have negative impacts on public health systems. To turn this challenge into an opportunity for improving the competitiveness of domestic pharmaceutical industry, Singapore, South Korea and Taiwan might provide some useful experiences.

First, the relevant crucial factors such as the administrative and juridical procedures dealing with patent disputes, procedure for and duration of market approval, the pricing mechanism of medicines, the procedure for reimbursement of medical expenses, development of domestic pharmaceutical industry and market scale have to be taken into consideration.[47]

[47] See paragraphs 2.2 and 6.3 of the 'Statement on Intellectual Property Protection for Pharmaceuticals and the Market Approval Mechanisms in Asia' (n 9).

Second, under the Paris Convention for Protection of Industrial Property, the TRIPS Agreement, Asian countries retain regulatory options to fulfil the need for IP protection of pharmaceuticals as well as to implement public health policy. They should be cognizant of the importance of a proper balance between the drug originator and the generics companies.[48] The operation of PL is a trade-off between the originator and generics companies. The originator companies are provided with an opportunity to resolve patent disputes before the generic products' launch into the market. The generics companies should be provided with the benefit of the identification of the essential patents related to original drugs, as well as the reward of a market exclusivity period.

Third, both South Korea and Taiwan did not blindly follow the US approach of 30-month stay of market approval, and took the relevant factors into consideration, particularly the procedure for and duration of market approval of ANDA, the procedure for reimbursement of medical expenses, and the procedure for and duration of patent litigation.[49]

Lastly, for countries which desire to ensure the competitiveness of domestic originals and generics industries, South Korea might offer a reference model. While in the US, Singapore and Taiwan, the drug authority seeks to distance itself as much as possible from patent disputes and litigation, which will be decided by the patent authority or the courts, the MFDS in South Korea plays a pivotal role in the operation of PL, including the disclosure of patent information, stay of market approval, and market exclusivity of the first qualified ANDA filer.

[48] See preamble and paragraph 1.2 and 1.3 of the 'Statement on Intellectual Property Protection for Pharmaceuticals and the Market Approval Mechanisms in Asia' (n 9).

[49] See para 6.3 of the 'Statement on Intellectual Property Protection for Pharmaceuticals and the Market Approval Mechanisms in Asia' (n 9).

11

Intellectual Property in Plant Material and Free Trade Agreements in Asia

CHRISTOPH ANTONS*

I. The Expansion of Intellectual Property in Agriculture and the Role of Free Trade Agreements

This chapter will discuss the rise of intellectual property rights in plant material over the last few decades, the expansion of UPOV (UPOV being the French acronym for the International Convention for the Protection of New Varieties of Plants[1]) since the WTO Agreement on Trade Related Intellectual Property Rights (TRIPS), and the considerable impact of current Free Trade Agreements (FTAs) and negotiations on these trends. As a background to the discussion, it is helpful to recall how, since World War II, in developing countries the development policies of aid agencies and international financial institutions have been dominated by modernization theory, perhaps most famously expressed by Walt Rostow in his book on the stages of growth from 1961.[2] Although often criticized, much of our current thinking about development, 'traditional societies' and economic take-off

* Professor of Law, University of Newcastle, Australia; Affiliated Research Fellow, Max Planck Institute for Innovation and Competition, Munich, Germany; Senior Fellow, Center for Development Research, University of Bonn, Germany. Research for this chapter was supported under the Australian Research Council's *Discovery Projects* funding scheme (project number DP170100747).

[1] Mark D Janis, Herbert H Jervis and Richard Peet, *Intellectual Property Law of Plants* (Oxford, Oxford University Press, 2014) 69–71.

[2] WW Rostow, 'The Stages of Economic Growth (1960)' reprinted in Naazneen H Barma and Steven K Vogel (eds), *The Political Economy Reader: Markets as Institutions* (New York and London, Routledge, 2008). Rostow, a Professor of Economic History at the Massachusetts Institute of Technology (MIT) and in later life Professor of Political Economy at the University of Texas, was particularly influential in development policy making during the 1960s when he held high government positions, including that of National Security Adviser, in the Kennedy and Johnson administrations. On Rostow and Modernization theory, see Harold Brookfield, *Interdependent Development* (London, Methuen & Co Ltd, 1975) 36–39; Ulrich Menzel, 'Walt Whitman Rostow (1916–2003)' in David Simon (ed), *Fifty Key Thinkers on Development* (London and New York, Routledge, 2006); Peter W Preston, *Development Theory: An Introduction* (Oxford-Cambridge, Massachusetts, Blackwell Publishers, 1996) 166–78.

is still based on modernization theory. In the thinking of classical development economists, industrialization and agricultural transformation go hand in hand.[3] Technical progress in particular is responsible for a declining share of agriculture of both domestic output and the labour force.[4] Based on World Bank data of 2016, agriculture contributes 17.8 per cent and 17.5 per cent on average to the GDP of South Asian and Sub-Sharan African countries respectively, but as much as 59.4 per cent to the GDP of individual developing countries like Sierra Leone. This compares to only 1.6 per cent in the European Union and 2.6 per cent in Australia.[5] Economists point to a similar inverse relationship between a country's per capita income and the size of its rural population.[6] In the footsteps of the industrialized countries, economic development processes are designed to encourage the migration of the rural population to the cities and to radically transform agricultural technologies and practices in order to make them more efficient, and to enable them to feed a larger population working in manufacturing or services, rather than producing food. Hence, similar to Rostow's stages of growth is a development model for agriculture in which agricultural evolution moves from peasant farming (subsistence agriculture focused on staple crops), through mixed farming, to specialized farming, which is focused on one crop, capital intensive, growing for national and international markets, using advanced technology, and which is understood to be the most developed and sophisticated form of farming.[7] As a consequence of such models, there has been an 'urban bias' among development planners in developing countries.[8] Malaysia, for example, is regarded as a successful 'second tier newly industrialising country',[9] because the country succeeded in dramatically reducing the share of agriculture in the economy vis-à-vis other sectors within a few decades, from 43.7 per cent in 1960 to 8.7 per cent in 2016 according to the above mentioned World Bank data. New seed varieties and other forms of input such as fertilizer have been part of this process in Malaysia, as elsewhere in the developing world.

Until recently, such input factors of agricultural transformation were provided to farmers by their own governments and either free of charge or at very low

[3] W Arthur Lewis, 'Economic Development with Unlimited Supplies of Labour' (1954) 22 *Manchester School* 119, as quoted in E Wayne Nafziger, *Economic Development* (New York, Cambridge University Press, 2006), 221.

[4] Nafziger (n 3) 221–22.

[5] For the World Bank data, see The World Bank, 'Agriculture, Forestry, and Fishing, Value Added (% of GDP)', https://data.worldbank.org/indicator/NV.AGR.TOTL.ZS. 2016 also recorded a remarkable reversal of the long time downward trend, however, with the average worldwide share of agriculture rising from well below 4% to 4.6%.

[6] James M Cypher, and James L Dietz, *The Process of Economic Development* (London and New York, Routledge, 1997) 331.

[7] Nafziger (n 3) 226–27.

[8] Nafziger (n 3) 243–44.

[9] Rajah Rasiah, 'Manufacturing Export Growth in Indonesia, Malaysia and Thailand' in KS Jomo (ed), *Southeast Asian Paper Tigers? From Miracle to Debacle and Beyond* (London and New York, RoutledgeCurzon, 2003) 28.

cost. The Green Revolution of the 1960s introduced new high-yielding varieties in Asian developing countries, many of which were given to governments by the new international agricultural research centres that had been established by the Ford and Rockefeller foundations between 1960 and 1968. The International Rice Research Institute at Los Baños in the Philippines is the most important such centre in Asia. These centres have been collecting germplasm from all over the world, but saw their collections and activities as publicly accessible and free of cost.[10] With the new seeds came seed certification laws that were designed to promote scientifically developed and tested varieties over traditional and local ones.[11] As to the controversial effects of the Green Revolution, critics[12] stress the inequality and monocultures that were created with overuse of pesticides, making it now necessary to find solutions against increasingly invasive pests in very short time frames.[13] Proponents of the Green Revolution contend that food supply would not have kept up with population growth in countries like India without high-yielding varieties and technological input.[14] They argue that a new Green Revolution that includes biotechnological applications is now needed.[15]

Intellectual property in agriculture has grown in importance simultaneously as the role of the private sector in agriculture has increased and, similar to the Green Revolution in agricultural policy, it has been one of the most controversial topics in the intellectual property field for several decades. Proponents of intellectual property protection regard plant innovation as 'equally well suited for intellectual property protection as other areas of the life sciences' and stress the critical role of patents in the evolution of plant biotechnology.[16] Critics point to the dominant position of a very small number of corporations in the global seed market, the impact of this domination on farmers, in particular in developing countries, and the role of intellectual property in promoting these corporate interests, often at the expense of environmental and social justice concerns.[17]

[10] MS Swaminathan, 'Seeds and Property Rights: A View from the CGIAR System' in Jack R Kloppenburg, Jr (ed), *Seeds and Sovereignty: The Use and Control of Plant Genetic Resources* (Durham and London, Duke University Press, 1988) 231–34; Keith Aoki, *Seed Wars: Controversies and Cases on Plant Genetic Resources and Intellectual Property* (Durham, North Carolina: Carolina Academic Press, 2008) 64.

[11] Franditya Utomo, *Bersemi Dalam Tekanan Global: Kriminalisasi Petani, Inisiatif Benih Lokal, & Uji Materi UU No. 12/1992 tentang Sistem Budidaya Tanaman* (Jakarta, Yayasan FIELD Indonesia, 2013) 4.

[12] See the sources in Nafziger (n 3) 288–90; Adam Szirmai, *The Dynamics of Socio-Economic Development: An Introduction* (Cambridge, Cambridge University Press, 2005) 382–84.

[13] James J Fox, 'Fast Breeding Insect is Devastating Java's Rice – Thanks to Pesticides', *Jakarta Globe*, (Jakarta, 7 March 2014).

[14] Robert Paarlberg, *Food Politics: What Everyone Needs to Know* (New York, Oxford University Press, 2010) 56–57.

[15] Nafziger (n 3) 287–88 with sources; Szirmai (n 12) 384–88. See also Paarlberg (n 14) 172–73.

[16] Janis, Jervis and Peet (n 1) 7.

[17] Nora McKeon, *Food Security Governance: Empowering Communities, Regulating Corporations* (London and New York, Routledge, 2015) 37; Susan K Sell, 'Corporations, Seeds, and Intellectual Property Rights Governance' in Jennifer Clapp and Doris Fuchs, *Corporate Power in Global Agrifood Governance* (Cambridge, Massachusetts-London, MIT Press, 2009) 189–91, with further sources.

Given the strongly diverging views on the matter, it is surprising that provisions related to intellectual property in agriculture in FTA negotiations have not attracted the same kind of public attention as those related to other fields of intellectual property, in particular copyright enforcement provisions that impact on digital access to copyright protected works.[18] The following sections will draw attention to these trends in FTAs related to plant material and to the context of the discussions about them. The analysis will begin with an overview of the instruments of protection in this field and their historical developments. The expansion of UPOV since the World Trade Organization (WTO) TRIPS Agreement will be discussed, in particular the impact of Article 27.3.b. TRIPS and the limited options that it leaves to countries that want to avoid moving towards the use of patents for plant material. The chapter then shows the move to UPOV-style sui generis and further to patent protection, and asks the question why countries have been prepared to sign away even this limited freedom to design their own laws in recent FTAs. This section begins with an analysis of the two currently largest and most interesting multilateral agreements in the Asia-Pacific region, the Regional Comprehensive Economic Partnership (RCEP), which is still being negotiated, and the Comprehensive and Progressive Trans Pacific Partnership (CPTPP), in its amended form after the departure of the United States from the Trans Pacific Partnership (TPP). It then moves on to bilateral agreements, identifying those countries that have shown particular interest in upscaling the intellectual property protection of plant material. A further section focuses on agreements that emphasize cooperation and

[18] For example, *USA Today* in discussing industries that would have benefited from TPP intellectual property rules mentions drugs, movies and software, see The Editorial Board, USA Today, 'Donald Trump Could Revive TPP to Pressure China', https://www.usatoday.com/story/opinion/2018/05/06/donald-trump-revive-tpp-pressure-china-editorials-debates/513233002. Notable exceptions from this relative lack of attention have been *The Nation* (Alex Press, 'The Trans-Pacific Partnership will hurt farmers and make seed companies richer' (2016), https://www.thenation.com/article/the-trans-pacific-partnership-will-hurt-farmers-and-make-seed-companies-richer), *IP Watch* (Burcu Kilic and Hannah Brennan, 'Inside Views: The TPP's New Plant-Related Intellectual Property Provisions' (2014), http://www.ip-watch.org/2014/10/17/the-tpps-new-plant-related-intellectual-property-provisions) and NGOs such as GRAIN (GRAIN, 'New mega-treaty in the pipeline: what does RCEP mean for farmers' seeds in Asia?' (2016), https://www.grain.org/article/entries/5405-new-mega-treaty-in-the-pipeline-what-does-rcep-mean-for-farmers-seeds-in-asia; GRAIN, 'New trade deals legalise corporate theft, make farmers' seeds illegal' (2016), https://www.grain.org/article/entries/5511-new-trade-deals-legalise-corporate-theft-make-farmers-seeds-illegal) and Public Citizen (Public Citizen's Global Access to Medicines Program, 'The TPP's New Plant-Related Intellectual Property Provisions: Strengthening the Rights of Breeders and Seed Manufacturers at the Expense of Traditional Farming Practices and Food Security in the Developing World' (2014), https://www.citizen.org/sites/default/files/impact-of-the-trans-pacific-partnership-on-farmers-and-food-security.pdf). Researchers from such NGOs have also published in academic online journals (Burcu Kilic, Hannah Brennan and Peter Maybarduk, 'What is patentable under the Trans-Pacific Partnership? An analysis of the Free Trade Agreement's patentability provisions from a public health perspective' (2015) *Yale Journal of International Law Online*, https://cpb-us-w2.wpmucdn.com/campuspress.yale.edu/dist/8/1581/files/2016/09/kilic-brennen-maybarduk-final-04-07-2015-1cassc8.pdf; Hannah Brennan and Burcu Kilic, 'Freeing Trade at the Expense of Local Crop Markets? A Look at the Trans-Pacific Partnership's New Plant-Related Intellectual Property Rights from a Human Rights Perspective' (2015) *Harvard Human Rights Journal Online*, https://harvardhrj.com/2015/04/freeing-trade-at-the-expense-of-local-crop-markets-a-look-at-the-trans-pacific-partnerships-new-plant-related-intellectual-property-rights-from-a-human-rights-perspective/.

exceptions to intellectual property protection rather than a further strengthening of the system. The penultimate section presents policy options for developing countries. The conclusion reviews the trends and suggests that countries with significant smallholder agricultural sectors should resist current pressure in FTAs to increase intellectual property protection in this field by joining UPOV or, if already members, upgrading to UPOV 1991 standards.

II. The Origins of Intellectual Property Rights in Plant Material and the Development of the UPOV Convention

The origins of this field of intellectual property are to be found in the United States in the Plant Patent Act of 1930. Because it was assumed that the patent system had been developed for engineering and machinery, the Plant Patent Act had features of the patent system, but simplified protection and application requirements.[19] European countries followed with intellectual property style rights in the 1940s and 1950s with the 1941 Breeders Ordinance of the Netherlands and the 1953 Seeds Act of Germany.[20] Such European-style plant variety rights, as they became known, were less strong in both their requirements and their protective scope than patent rights. Plant variety rights apply only to a particular variety, not to the underlying genetic structure, and allow for the so-called 'farmers' privilege' to save and reuse seeds from a protected variety. They include an exception for research and experimentation, meaning that a protected variety may be used for further breeding without restriction. In addition, plant variety rights allow the sale of crops produced by using the protected variety.[21] They constitute an intellectual property right for plants, but a much less stringent version than patent rights by leaving both competing breeders and farmers a certain amount of freedom. Nevertheless, they still favour the commercial over the smallholder farming sector, which, as explained earlier, remains large and important in much of the developing world.[22]

The German Seeds Act of 1953 became influential during the drafting of an international convention that attempted to export the plant variety protection approach and to standardize protection among member countries: the UPOV Convention of 1961. The UPOV Convention began as a European club with ratification by Germany, the Netherlands and the United Kingdom on 10 August 1968 as the first ratifying countries. Denmark was the only other country to join during

[19] Aoki (n 10) 30–34; Janis, Jervis and Peet (n 1) 183–90.

[20] Janis, Jervis and Peet (n 1) 70.

[21] For the example of the US Plant Variety Protection Act of 1970 see Aoki (n 10) 36; Janis, Jervis and Peet (n 1) 5. See also UNCTAD-ICTSD, *Resource Book on TRIPS and Development* (Cambridge, Cambridge University Press, 2005) 395.

[22] Sell (n 17) 193.

the 1960s.[23] With ratification by France (1971), Sweden (1971), Belgium (1976), Italy (1977) and Switzerland (1977), other European countries followed during the 1970s. Uptake outside of Europe, however, was slow. The United States, because of its traditional preference for plant patents, became a member only in 1981, South Africa joined in 1977, Israel in 1979, New Zealand in 1981, Japan in 1982, Australia in 1989 and Canada in 1991. This circle of non-European members remained small until the conclusion of the WTO TRIPS Agreement in 1994. Developing countries, in particular, had understandable concerns about plant variety protection and its impact on their food systems and remained outside of UPOV, with the exception of South Africa and Israel. Prior to TRIPS, developing countries typically had no plant variety laws and excluded plants and animals from patent protection. Typical examples were the first Indonesian Patents Act of 1989[24] and the Indian Patents Act of 1970.[25]

III. The Influence of Article 27.3.B. TRIPS and the Expansion of UPOV

A. Article 27.3.b. TRIPS as a Patentability Exclusion that at the Same Time Establishes Plant Variety Rights

A fundamental change regarding intellectual property in plant material arrived with the TRIPS Agreement. In view of the reluctance of the developing world to engage in discussions about intellectual property for material essential for food production, TRIPS had chapters on patents, copyright and other intellectual property rights, but not related to plant variety rights. What TRIPS did include, however, was with Article 27.3.b. a clause covering biotechnology in the part of the agreement dealing with patents.

The starting point for the discussion was the requirement of Article 27.1 TRIPS that in future any inventions in all field of technology must be patentable, provided they fulfil the standard requirements of a patent in that they are new, involve an inventive step and are capable of industrial application.[26] As a strict

[23] On 6 October 1968. For the accession dates discussed here and in the following and the version of the convention to which a country acceded, see the current membership list of UPOV at Members of the International Union for the Protection of New Varieties of Plants 'International Convention for the Protection of New Varieties of Plants', http://www.upov.int/export/sites/upov/members/en/pdf/pub423.pdf.

[24] See Indonesian Patents Act of 1989, Art 7c.: 'No patent shall be granted for: … c. an invention concerning a new variety of plant or animal, or concerning a process of any kind, which can be used for the breeding of plants or animals and its results.'

[25] See Indian Patents Act of 1970, Section 3: 'The following are not inventions within the meaning of this Act: …(h) a method of agriculture or horticulture.'

[26] See TRIPS, Art 27.1: '… patents shall be available and patent rights enjoyable without discrimination as to the place of invention, the field of technology and whether products are imported or locally produced …'

application would make the exclusions of plants and animals from the patent system, as commonly seen in developing countries impossible, such countries were negotiating for such an exclusion. The Anell draft text from the negotiations from July 1990[27] shows the difficulties in these negotiations. There were so many brackets indicating controversial matters that almost everything in the text was controversial except that it concerned plants and animals and processes for their production.[28] After much discussion and the determination to review the matter four years after the entry into force of the TRIPS Agreement,[29] the current wording of the exclusion of Article 27.3.b. was agreed upon.[30] It is an interesting provision in the sense that it is an exclusion that at the same time manages to establish rights to plant varieties that otherwise would not be covered in the Agreement.[31]

Article 27.3.b. indeed excludes plants and animals and essentially biological processes for the production of plants or animals. However, in contrast to previous laws typically found in developing countries, the exclusion in TRIPS does not extend to microorganisms and non-biological and microbiological processes. It does also not extend to cells, genes and sub-cellular components, which are not 'microorganisms'. Further, in the second sentence of Article 27.3.b., TRIPS requires from member states the protection of plant varieties either by patents or by an effective sui generis system or any combination thereof. As TRIPS does not

[27] Swedish Ambassador Lars Anell was the Chair of the TRIPS negotiation group, see Antony Taubman and Jayashree Watal, 'Revisiting the TRIPS Negotiations: Genesis and Structure of this Book' in Jayashree Watal and Antony Taubman (eds), *The Making of the TRIPS Agreement: Personal Insights from the Uruguay Round Negotiators* (Geneva, World Trade Organization, 2015) 12. The Anell draft refers to the composite text of different proposals as a basis for the negotiations that was compiled by the Chair and the Secretariat and became available as an informal document in June 1990 (Antony Taubman, 'Thematic Review: Negotiating "Trade-Related Aspects" of Intellectual Property Rights' in Watal and Taubman (eds), *The Making of the TRIPS Agreement* (ibid) 46–47; Adrian Otten, 'The TRIPS Negotiations: An Overview' in Watal and Taubman (eds), *The Making of the TRIPS Agreement* (ibid) 65–66. For a complete text of the Chairman's Report and the draft text see Appendix 2,'Negotiating Group on Trade-Related Aspects of Intellectual Property Rights, including Trade in Counterfeit Goods: Status of the Work in the Negotiating Group, Chairman's Report to the GNG' in Watal and Taubman (eds), *The Making of the TRIPS Agreement* (ibid).

[28] '1.4.4 [Any] plant or animal [including micro-organisms] [varieties] or [essentially biological] processes for the production of plants or animals; [this does not apply to microbiological processes or the products thereof]. [As regards biotechnological inventions, further limitations should be allowed under national law]', see UNCTAD-ICTSD (n 21) 391.

[29] John Gero, 'Why We Managed to Succeed in TRIPS' in Watal and Taubman (eds), *The Making of the TRIPS Agreement* (n 27) 98; Piragibe dos Santos Tarragô, 'Negotiating for Brazil' in Watal and Taubman (eds), *The Making of the TRIPS Agreement* (n 27) 246; Jayashree Watal, 'Patents: An Indian Perspective' in Watal and Taubman (eds), *The Making of the TRIPS Agreement* (n 27) 309.

[30] 'Members may also exclude from patentability: plants and animals other than micro-organisms, and essentially biological processes for the production of plants and animals other than non-biological and microbiological processes. However, Members shall provide for the protection of plant varieties either by patents or by an effective *sui generis* system or by any combination thereof. The provisions of this subparagraph shall be reviewed four years after the date of entry into force of the WTO Agreement.'

[31] Former members of the Secretariat and TRIPS negotiators refer to it as an example of 'constructive ambiguity' (Matthijs Geuze, 'Some Memories of the Unique TRIPS Negotiations' in Watal and Taubman (eds), *The Making of the TRIPS Agreement* (n 27) 124–25) in an area that 'will keep the next generation of lawyers busy' Thu-Lang Tran Wasescha, 'Negotiating for Switzerland' in Watal and Taubman (eds), *The Making of the TRIPS Agreement* (n 27) 177.

otherwise cover plant variety rights, it is widely assumed that plant variety protection laws following the UPOV model will constitute a suitable sui generis system and, indeed, it is further assumed that it was UPOV-style plant variety rights that the drafters of the TRIPS Agreement had in mind.[32]

B. Freedom to Design Under TRIPS: A Missed Opportunity for Developing Countries?

Actually, however, the freedom for developing countries to design their own systems was much wider.[33] The only restriction given in Article 27.3.b. is that the system must be 'effective'. Nevertheless, the vast majority of developing countries introduced a system that closely followed the UPOV models.[34] In view of the concerns of developing countries regarding intellectual property rights in living matter, why was this opportunity to be more adventurous in their legislation missed? Three reasons are particularly relevant.

First, developing countries that are dependent on foreign investment may have been reluctant to establish a system that is regarded by their trading partners as not 'effective'. As contraventions of the TRIPS Agreement can be brought by trading partners to the TRIPS dispute resolution process and ultimately be penalized with trade sanctions and as there is competitive pressure to have investment-friendly intellectual property rights, rather than experimenting with their own designs, developing countries probably found it safer to adopt the established solutions that would not lead to any irritation among their trading partners.

Second, many of the larger developing countries and those among the so-called 'emerging economies', in particular, have their own ambitious plans for the biotech and commercial seed industries. An instructive example is Malaysia. The Malaysian government had set up 'Cyberjaya' on the outskirts of Kuala Lumpur in the 1990s to attract investment in the IT industries in a zone with particular tax exemptions and investment rules.[35] In the early 2000s, it tried to do the same for the biotech industries with a special enclave called 'BioValley'.[36]

[32] UNCTAD-ICTSD (n 21) 394.

[33] UNCTAD-ICTSD (n 21) 394; Daniel Gervais, *The TRIPS Agreement: Drafting History and Analysis* (London, Thomson Reuters, 3rd edn, 2008) 353.

[34] Rajeswari Kanniah and Christoph Antons, 'Plant Variety Protection and Traditional Agricultural Knowledge in Southeast Asia' (2012) 13 *Australian Journal of Asian Law* 1, 12–13; Carlos M Correa, *TRIPS-Related Patent Flexibilities and Food Security: Options for Developing Countries* (Geneva, Quaker United Nations Office (QUNO) and International Centre for Trade and Sustainable Development (ICTSD), 2012) 3; Rajeswari Kanniah and Christoph Antons, 'The Regulation of Innovation in Agriculture and Sustainable Development in India and Southeast Asia' in Christoph Antons (ed), *The Routledge Handbook of Asian Law* (London and New York, Routledge, 2017) 294.

[35] Tim Bunnell, *Malaysia, Modernity and the Multimedia Super Corridor: A Critical Geography of Intelligent Landscapes* (London-New York: Routledge, 2003) 90–116.

[36] Sandra Smeltzer, 'The Message is the Market: Selling Biotechnology and Nation in Malaysia' in Joseph Nevins and Nancy Lee Peluso (eds), *Taking Southeast Asia to Market* (Ithaca, NY-London, Cornell University Press, 2008).

More recently, it is continuing such strategies via a network of industrial parks across Malaysia.[37] Other countries such as India and Indonesia have also been drafting seed certification laws that help to promote commercial suppliers.[38]

A third and final reason in some countries could be a lack of expertise and experience in designing alternatives. For many years after independence, many countries practised what I have called, using a term coined by Japanese law expert John Owen Haley,[39] selective adaptation of their intellectual property laws to Western models.[40] In this approach, models from many foreign traditions have been selectively adopted and selectively enforced. Foreign trading partners could be quickly satisfied with new laws, which were then frequently not enforced or, in some cases, even secretly subverted. Until the arrival of the WTO, this kind of intellectual property law making was sufficient to safeguard national priorities. After TRIPS with its enforcement provisions, however, more creativity would be required.

As a result of the TRIPS provision promoting plant variety protection and the decision of developing countries to choose standard models rather than to experiment with their own laws, the membership of UPOV changed. Many countries presumably thought that if they already had UPOV-conforming intellectual property laws, then why not join UPOV right away? As for Asia, while there had been only two Asian countries in UPOV prior to TRIPS (Japan and Israel), that number has since increased to 14[41] and many other developing countries in Africa, Central Asia and Latin America have also joined. There are now 30 developing countries in UPOV out of a total membership of 75 countries, compared to only two prior to 1994. At the domestic level in the ASEAN countries, eight of the 10 ASEAN countries now have plant variety laws.[42]

Still, compared to other parts of the world, UPOV membership in Asia remains low. The UPOV Convention has also become stricter in its protection requirements since it was founded in the 1960s. The versions used by developing countries as models for their legislation are the 1978 and 1991 versions of UPOV. However, there are important differences between the two: first, double protection under

[37] Natalie Heng, 'Malaysia's biotech landscape finally starting to emerge' (2014), available at https://www.thestar.com.my/lifestyle/features/2014/11/13/malaysias-biotech-landscape-finally-starting-to-emerge.

[38] Kanniah and Antons (n 34) 290–92.

[39] John Owen Haley, *Authority Without Power: Law and the Japanese Paradox* (New York-Oxford, Oxford University Press, 1991) 29–32, 82–96.

[40] Christoph Antons, 'Harmonisation and Selective Adaptation as Intellectual Property Policies in Asia' in Christoph Antons, Michael Blakeney and Christopher Heath (eds), *Intellectual Property Harmonisation Within ASEAN and APEC* (The Hague, Kluwer Law International, 2004) 110–18.

[41] The new members are the Russian Federation (1998); China (1999); Kyrgyzstan (2000); Republic of Korea (2002); Azerbaijan (2004); Jordan (2004); Singapore (2004); Uzbekistan (2004); Vietnam (2006); Turkey (2007); Georgia (2008); Oman (2009).

[42] Kanniah and Antons (n 34). See the Plant Varieties Protection Act, BE (1999) of Thailand; Law No 29 of 2000 on Plant Variety Protection of Indonesia; the Plant Variety Protection Act of 2002, RA No 9168 of the Philippines; the Protection of New Plant Varieties Act of 2004 of Singapore; the Intellectual Property Law No 50/2005/QH11 of Vietnam; the Law on Seed Management and Breeders' Rights of 2008 of Cambodia; the Law on Intellectual Property of 2008 of Laos.

patent laws and plant breeders' rights laws was prohibited in 1978, but is no longer prohibited in 1991. As a result, many industrialized countries offer both forms of protection,[43] many of the industries involved have moved to patent protection, and the big agro-chemical companies have come to dominate the seed sector in industrialized countries.[44] As a further result, plant variety protection has somewhat declined in significance.[45] Second, since 1991 the important general exemption for farmers to reuse and exchange harvested seeds is merely optional and needs to be specifically introduced by countries. Reuse is also limited to farmers' own holdings. Finally, besides harvested material, the rights of the breeder under UPOV 1991 now also extend to material from 'essentially derived varieties',[46] a criterion that has been criticized as narrowing the breeder's exemption and expanding the exclusive rights of first-generation breeders.[47] The closing date for membership under the less strict 1978 version of the Convention was for developing countries on 31 December 1995 (Article 37(3) of UPOV 1991), so after this date all new members will automatically be members under the 1991 version. Countries that are not members but use UPOV models, however, often turn to the less restrictive 1978 version. In principle, therefore, the options other than patents for developing countries are as follows: they can use the maximum freedom provided by TRIPS and design their own systems,[48] they can use UPOV 1978 or 1991 as model or a combination of all of these or they can follow UPOV 1991 strictly and become a UPOV member.

IV. The Push for Patents on Plants and Plant Material

Importantly, however, from the viewpoint of the agro-chemical industry and as indicated above, plant variety protection was never going to be enough.[49] Patents is

[43] Aoki (n 10) 66 fn 28.
[44] McKeon (n 17); Sell (n 17).
[45] Dan L Burk, 'Patents and Related Rights: A Global Kaleidoscope' in Rochelle C Dreyfuss and Justine Pila (eds), *The Oxford Handbook of Intellectual Property Law* (Oxford, Oxford University Press, 2018) 485.
[46] Janis, Jervis and Peet (n 1) 71.
[47] Laurence R Helfer and Graeme W Austin, *Human Rights and Intellectual Property: Mapping the Global Interface* (Cambridge, Cambridge University Press, 2011) 383, for a detailed discussion see Jay Sanderson, 'Essential Derivation, Law and the Limits of Science' (2006) 24 *Law in Context* 34.
[48] Several studies have indicated what such *sui generis* systems outside of UPOV could look like, see eg Dan Leskien and Michael Flitner, *Intellectual Property Rights and Plant Genetic Resources: Options for a Sui Generis System*, Issues in Genetic Resources No. 6 (Rome, Italy, IPGRI, 1997), https://www.bioversityinternational.org/fileadmin/_migrated/uploads/tx_news/Intellectual_property_rights_and_plant_genetic_resources_497.pdf and Carlos M Correa, with contributions from Sangeeta Shashikant and François Meienberg, *Plant Variety Protection in Developing Countries: A Tool for Designing a Sui Generis Plant Variety Protection System: An Alternative to UPOV 1991* (Alfter, Germany, Association for Plant Breeding for the Benefit of Society (APBREBES), 2017).
[49] Susan K Sell (n 17) 192.

the preferred way of protection, in particular for the new tools used in breeding,[50] and the incompatibility of patents and plant variety protection under the earlier versions of the UPOV Convention was the main reason for the long absence of the United States as the country with the longest tradition of plant patenting.[51] With the previous UPOV prohibition of double protection under patent and plant variety laws now gone after the UPOV revision of 1991, in the flurry of FTA activities post-TRIPS, governments with strong agro-chemical industries are pushing their developing country trading partners further towards the acceptance of patents on plants and plant material for the more advanced economies and further towards the establishment of UPOV-style plant variety protection systems for developing countries at a less advanced stage.

A. The Problems with Plant-Related Patents

As has often been pointed out, plant-related patents are problematic, especially for agriculture in developing countries, because of the limited scope for experimenting with the material that they allow. The patent system began in the nineteenth century in relation to engineering and machines.[52] It is regarded as a social contract between the inventor and the government representing the public interest or, as Dan Burk[53] has put it, a bargain between the inventor and the public, where the inventor publicizes the invention and allows others to experiment with it and build upon it, and receives in return a monopoly on the product or process as described in the patent documentation for a number of years, after which the invention becomes part of the public domain.[54] The engineering origins of the patent system also become visible in the rules on infringement and in the difficulties in drawing the line between authorized and unauthorized use of the invention. In most advanced patent systems, it is possible to do research *on* patent protected material, but not *with* patent protected material.[55] Reverse engineering of patented machinery and coming up with new innovative solutions for components is a typical example of what would be allowed and in fact encouraged by such systems.

[50] European Commission, *Final Report of the Expert Group on the development and implications of patent law in the field of biotechnology and genetic engineering* (Brussels, Directorate General Internal Market, Industry, Entrepreneurship and SMEs, 2016) 17.

[51] Janis, Jervis and Peet (n 1) 71.

[52] Ibid 2.

[53] Burk (n 45) 463.

[54] See also Katherine J Strandburg, 'Users, Patents and Innovation Policy' in Rochelle C. Dreyfuss and Justine Pila (eds), *The Oxford Handbook of Intellectual Property Law* (Oxford, Oxford University Press, 2018) p 735.

[55] William Cornish, David Llewelyn and Tanya Aplin, *Intellectual Property: Patents, Copyright, Trade Marks and Allied Rights* (London, Sweet & Maxwell, 7th edn, 2010) 940–41; Viola Prifti, 'The Breeding Exemption in Patent Law: Analysis of Compliance with Article 30 TRIPS Agreement' (2013) 16 *The Journal of World Intellectual Property* 218, 219; Sven JR Bostyn, 'Patentability of Plants: At the Crossroads Between Monopolizing Nature and Protecting Technological Innovation?' (2013) 16 *The Journal of World Intellectual Property* 105, 132.

However, farmers or plant breeders who experiment with plants may often make use of patented traits and breeding methods and are thus frequently working *with* patented plant material.[56]

B. Limitations and Exceptions to Patents on Plant Material?

One solution here would be a wider interpretation of the research exemption under Article 30 TRIPS. It has been argued that it is unrealistic and wrong in developing country situations to confine such research exemptions to scientific research only, because much 'research' in the context of local adaptation of plant material is in fact carried out by farmers themselves as well as by researchers in local government institutions.[57] Agricultural material is not a turnkey technology – it has to be adapted to local soil and weather conditions and standardized technological solutions have mostly not worked or not worked in a satisfactory manner on the ground.[58] It has also been pointed out that it is unrealistic to exclude from the definition research with a commercial objective.[59] Court decisions in industrialized countries, however, exclude research aimed at the development of a new commercial product[60] and the current legislative practice in many developing countries requires private, non-commercial research and/or scientific research.[61]

Under Article 30 of the TRIPS Agreement, exceptions must be 'limited', not 'unreasonably conflict with the normal exploitation of the patent' and 'not

[56] Bostyn (n 55) 132; Prifti (n 55) 218; CG Trojan, *Problem-solving approaches to the issues of the overlap between patent law and breeders' rights in the plant breeding sector*. Report submitted to the Dutch Ministry of Economic Affairs, Agriculture and Innovation. Available at the website of the International Association of Horticultural Producers, http://www.aiph.org/wp-content/uploads/2015/04/27428-236_engl_report_trojan.pdf 5–6. On the problem for breeders with the uncertainty about the patented status of plant material and the freedom to operate, see also European Commission, *Final Report* (n 50) 17–18). See also the discussion of patents on so-called 'must have-traits' (European Commission, *Final Report* (n 50) 23).

[57] Christoph Antons, 'Article 27(3)(b) TRIPS and Plant Variety Protection in Developing Countries' in Hanns Ullrich, Reto M. Hilty, Matthias Lamping and Josef Drexl (eds), *TRIPS plus 20: From Trade Rules to Market Principles* (Heidelberg-New-York-Dordrecht-London, Springer, 2016).

[58] Michael R Dove, 'The Life-Cycle of Indigenous Knowledge, and the Case of Natural Rubber Production' in Roy Ellen, Peter Parkes and Alan Bicker (eds), *Indigenous Environmental Knowledge and its Transformations: Critical Anthropological Perspectives* (London and New York, Routledge, 2000) p 215; Michael R Dove, *The Banana Tree at the Gate: A History of Marginal Peoples and Global Markets in Borneo* (Singapore, NUS Press, 2012) 101–02; David Frossard, 'In Field or Freezer? Some Thoughts on Genetic Diversity Maintenance in Rice' in Michael R Dove, Percy E Sajise and Amity A Doolittle (eds), *Conserving Nature in Culture: Case Studies from Southeast Asia* (New Haven, Connecticut, Yale Southeast Asian Studies, 2005) 155–61.

[59] Antons (n 57).

[60] Niels Louwaars, Hans Dons, Geertrui van Overwalle, Hans Raven, Anthony Arundel, Derek Eaton and Annemiek Nelis, *Breeding Business: The future of plant breeding in the light of developments in patent rights and plant breeders' rights* (Wageningen, Centre for Genetic Resources, 2009) 17; Bostyn (n 55) 133–34.

[61] Carlos M Correa, *The International Dimension of the Research Exception* (Washington, DC, SIPPI Project, AAAS, 2005) 34–66, https://www.researchgate.net/publication/265320959_The_International_Dimension_of_the_Research_Exception.

unreasonably prejudice the legitimate interests of the patent owner', although the 'legitimate interests of third parties' may be taken into account. While patent experts are concerned about broad research and experimentation exemptions in this regard,[62] hope has been expressed for a specific breeding exemption as introduced in a number of European countries, although the introduced exemption has been limited and disallowed commercialization.[63] An interesting exception from the above mentioned stance cautioning against broad research and experimentation exemptions is Belgium, which apparently allows use of the patented invention as a tool to develop new products and, therefore, breeders may use patented material for the purpose of breeding new varieties.[64]

There is a further way to opt out of stringent patent requirements, by relying on Article 27.2 TRIPS. Under that provision, WTO members may prevent the commercial exploitation of inventions to protect the public order or morality, to protect human, animal or plant life or health and to avoid serious prejudice to the environment. Although this seems to be a very fitting provision in this context, governments again have not made much use of it. One reason is probably that it prevents the 'commercial' exploitation of the invention. It would, therefore, violate the TRIPS Agreement if a government prevented the use of an imported commercial technology, only to give at the same time its farmers the opportunity to also commercially exploit it and then allow them do so for free.[65] Another concern is that the approach shifts the responsibility to make such ethical decisions to the patent offices, which are not well equipped for this task, and in many countries are understaffed and starved of resources.[66]

This leave those that are looking for restrictions on patents to plants to turn to compulsory licences. Such licences can no longer simply be granted in the national interest, but have to comply with Article 31 TRIPS Agreement. For the

[62] Rochelle C Dreyfuss, 'Fostering Dynamic Innovation, Development and Trade: Intellectual Property as a Case Study in Global Administrative Law' (2009) *Acta Juridica* 237, 252–55; Annette Kur, 'Limitations And Exceptions Under the Three-Step Test – How Much Room to Walk the Middle Ground?' in Annette Kur with Marianne Levin (eds), *Intellectual Property Rights in a Fair World Trade System: Proposals for a Reform of TRIPS* (Cheltenham, Edward Elgar, 2011) 236–37, 239–40.

[63] Prifti (n 55) 132; European Commission, *Final Report* (n 50) 18. The limited breeders' exemption refers to an exemption that 'enables anyone to use the protected material, without permission of the right holder(s), for the purpose of breeding, or discovering and developing other plant varieties' (European Commission, *Final Report* (n 50) 46). In contrast to the full breeder's exemption, it does not extend to commercialization of the obtained varieties. European Union members in which the limited breeders' exemption has been introduced into national patent laws are France, Germany and the Netherlands, see European Commission, *Final Report* (n 50), Annex A1 at 61–82.

[64] Article XI.34(b) of the Code of Economic Law (European Commission, *Final Report* (n 50), Annex A1 at 79–81); Geertrui van Overwalle, 'The Implementation of the Biotechnology Directive and its After-Effects: The Introduction of a New Research Exemption and a Compulsory Licence for Public Health' (2006) 37 *International Review of Intellectual Property and Competition Law* 889, 907.

[65] Geertrui van Overwalle, 'Biotechnology and Patents: Global Standards, European Approaches and National Accents' in D Würger and T Cottier (eds), *Genetic Engineering and the World Trade System* (Cambridge, Cambridge University Press, 2008) 81.

[66] Lionel Bently, 'Exclusions from Patentability and Exceptions to Patentees' Rights: Taking Exceptions Seriously' (2011) 64 *Current Legal Problems* 315, 239, 338–41.

first decade of the TRIPS Agreement, little use was made of compulsory licences, but recently this has changed as far as health and pharmaceuticals are concerned. India, Indonesia, Malaysia, Thailand, Brazil and Ecuador are examples of developing countries that have used compulsory licensing to guarantee access to essential pharmaceuticals to their populations.[67] A similar use of compulsory licensing for patented subject matter essential for farming is certainly possible. Nevertheless, countries use the compulsory licensing mechanism sparingly for fear of a backlash from foreign investors and trade reprisals under mechanisms such as section 301 of the US Tariffs and Trade Act. Similar to Article 27.2 TRIPS, compulsory licences are likely to remain a last resort in cases of national emergencies, for example in situation of health crisis or crop failures on a massive scale.

Patents for plant material, therefore, considerably narrow the scope for governments, researchers and farmers to experiment with the material. All in all, it appears that developing countries are better off staying clear of the patent option. As discussed earlier, Article 27.3.b. TRIPS actually gives them the freedom to do so; however, as the following sections will show some countries have signed away that freedom of choice in bilateral FTAs.

V. Intellectual Property in Plant Material in the RCEP and TPP

In 2015 I co-authored a book chapter comparing the intellectual property chapters in the FTAs of Asia-Pacific countries.[68] We took a bottom up approach to the analysis, starting with those countries that barely mention intellectual property in their FTAs, or do not mention it at all, and ending with those with very detailed intellectual property chapters. Not surprisingly, the countries requesting very detailed chapters are the high-technology exporting countries of the United States, Japan and the European Union, the non-EU countries of the European Free Trade Association (Norway, Switzerland, Iceland and Liechtenstein), Korea and Australia. New Zealand also negotiates intellectual property chapters with developing country partners, but with a somewhat different content, as will be explained further below. At the other end of the spectrum are Indian FTAs, which often avoid intellectual property all together and Chinese FTAs, which have intellectual

[67] Ida bt. Abdul Ghani Azmi Madieha, 'Scope and Duration of Compulsory Licensing: Lessons from National Experiences' in Reto M Hilty and Kung-Chung Liu (eds), *Compulsory Licensing: Practical Experiences and Ways Forward* (Heidelberg-New York-Dordrecht-London, Springer, 2015) 212–13; Carlos M Correa, 'The Use of Compulsory Licences in Latin America' in Reto M Hilty and Kung-Chung Liu (eds), *Compulsory Licensing: Practical Experiences and Ways Forward* (Heidelberg-New York-Dordrecht-London, Springer, 2015).

[68] Christoph Antons and Dilan Thampapillai, 'An Overview of Free Trade Agreements in the Asia-Pacific Region with a Particular Focus on Intellectual Property' in Christoph Antons and Reto M Hilty (eds), *Intellectual Property and Free Trade Agreements in the Asia-Pacific Region* (Heidelberg-New York-Dordrecht-London, Springer, 2015).

property sections, but often stress the obligations of intellectual property owners besides requiring minimum protection standards.

A. The Regional Comprehensive Economic Partnership (RCEP)

So what do these FTAs have to say about intellectual property related to plants and what does this reveal about the concluding countries' positions in the current negotiations for the RCEP and in the most recently amended TPP without the United States? In contrast to the publication mentioned earlier, the order of examination in this chapter will be reversed, and will begin with those FTAs that have many provisions relevant for intellectual property in general and intellectual property in plant material in particular. I will begin with an examination of the leaked 2015 draft of the RCEP Agreement and what it indicates about negotiation strategies related to intellectual property and plant material.[69] A section requiring membership in UPOV and other international agreements is proposed by Australia, Japan and Korea, whereby Japan and Korea only require their trading partners to 'endeavour' to join such agreements.[70] However, the ASEAN countries, India, China and New Zealand are opposed to any such requirement, even in the modified form proposed by Japan and Korea. On patent exclusions, the draft of the RCEP intellectual property chapter uses the TRIPS text of Article 27.3.b. for the exclusion of plants and animals. However, China, India and New Zealand propose a review of the provision if there is a relevant TRIPS amendment. Australia and Korea are opposed to such a review.[71] On plant varieties, Australia, Japan and Korea propose the establishment of a protection system in accordance with UPOV 1991, but the ASEAN countries, New Zealand, China and India are opposed to this provision.[72] Therefore, with some minor variations in the individual positions, Australia, Japan and Korea are seeking a TRIPS-plus text on plant varieties, but they are facing formidable opposition from the ASEAN countries, China, India and New Zealand.

B. The Comprehensive and Progressive Agreement for Trans-Pacific Partnership (CPTPP)

An amended version of the TPP Agreement (the Comprehensive and Progressive Agreement for TPP, CPTPP) was recently concluded by the remaining

[69] The leaked draft is available at 'Chapter on Intellectual Property Regional Comprehensive Economic Partnership (RCEP) Free Trade Agreement', https://www.keionline.org/wp-content/uploads/RCEP-TNC6-WGIP3-ASEAN-Draft%20IP%20Text-10Oct2014.pdf.

[70] Ibid, Art 6.

[71] Ibid Art 5.1.3.

[72] Ibid Art 5.1.

11 countries[73] after the controversial decision of the Trump administration to pull the United States out of the agreement.[74] On the question of UPOV membership, the CPTPP adopts the more stringent requirement of membership in UPOV 1991, which is now also proposed by Australia for inclusion in the RCEP.[75] Interestingly, however, New Zealand negotiated an exception for itself in an annex, which establishes a different timeframe and even allows it to avoid UPOV membership all together, if it establishes a UPOV 1991 compliant legislation.[76] New Zealand further retains considerable flexibility in designing such legislation in accordance with the country's obligations to its indigenous population under the Treaty of Waitangi.[77]

On patent exclusion, the TPP in its original form changed the wording of the TRIPS Agreement in important ways. Both TRIPS and the TPP allowed for the exclusion from patentability of animals other than microorganisms and essentially biological processes for the production of plants and animals, other than non-biological and microbiological processes. According to a further subsection of the TPP, plants other than microorganisms may also be excluded; however, importantly, patents must be made available for inventions derived from plants.[78] This provision and the absence of a section on plant varieties show the preference of the United States, as the most powerful negotiator in the original TPP round, for patent protection. A leaked draft from October 2014[79] shows that the United States, Japan and Singapore, facing opposition from the other negotiating parties, proposed to make patents available for inventions for plants and animals or, alternatively, to make patents available for plant-related inventions. This alternative text was changed in the final version to patents for inventions derived from plants. While lawyers working for NGOs found the revised wording 'ambiguous',

[73] This so-called 'TPP-11' is formed by Australia, Brunei Darussalam, Canada, Chile, Japan, Malaysia, Mexico, Peru, New Zealand, Singapore, Vietnam and, with some exceptions, incorporates the provisions of the TPP. For details see https://dfat.gov.au/trade/agreements/in-force/cptpp/Pages/comprehensive-and-progressive-agreement-for-trans-pacific-partnership.aspx.

[74] More recently, President Trump has indicated a possible re-entry of the United States, see *The New York Times*, 'Trump Proposes Rejoining Trans-Pacific Partnership' https://www.nytimes.com/2018/04/12/us/politics/trump-trans-pacific-partnership.html, only to reconsider that position once again on twitter a few days later, see Charles Hankla, 'What is the TPP and can the US get back in?' (2018), https://theconversation.com/what-is-the-tpp-and-can-the-us-get-back-in-95028.

[75] See CPTPP, Art 18.7.2: 'Each Party shall accede to each of the following agreements, if it is not already a party to that agreement, by the date of entry into force of this Agreement for that Party: … (d) UPOV 1991.'

[76] See CPTPP, Annex 18-A: '(1) Notwithstanding the obligations in Article 18.7.2 … New Zealand shall: (a) Accede to UPOV 1991 within three years of the date of entry into force of this agreement for New Zealand; or (b) Adopt a *sui generis* plant variety rights system that gives effect to UPOV 1991 within three years of the entry into force of this Agreement for New Zealand.'

[77] See CPTPP, Annex 18-A (2)-(4).

[78] TPP, Art 18.37.3: 'A Party may exclude from patentability … (b) animals other than microorganisms and essentially biological processes for the production of plants or animals, other than non-biological and microbiological processes.' TPP, Art 18.37.4: 'A Party may also exclude from patentability plants other than microorganisms. However, …, each Party confirms that patents are available at least for inventions that are derived from plants.'

[79] WikiLeaks, 'Updated Secret Trans-Pacific Partnership Agreement (TPP) – IP Chapter (Second Publication)', http://wikileaks.org/tpp-ip2.

they nevertheless concluded that it was likely to mean patenting of genes and cell cultures, leading then to patent rights in any organisms into which such genes are inserted.[80] That this understanding is correct was confirmed by a report on the TPP by the Industry Trade Advisory Committee (ITAC-15) to the United States Trade Representative, which concluded that '[t]he obligations set forth in this provision will ensure that processes, substances and articles that are used to impart improved characteristics into plants, as well as products derived from use of those processes, substances and articles, are eligible to be patented in all TPP parties'.[81] In view of the enthusiastic reception of this part of the original TPP by ITAC-15,[82] US-based agro-chemical companies must surely regret the decision of the United States to pull out of the TPP.

For some countries in the CPTPP or considering membership, the issue of patents had been settled in earlier bilateral FTAs with the United States, in which they had promised to introduce patents for plant material. As will be discussed in detail below, this concerns in particular Singapore, but also South Korea, which is reportedly close to joining the CPTPP.[83] However, the TPP in its original form would have raised the bar on plant intellectual property rights substantially for developing countries that had only promised to 'endeavour' to introduce such protection, such as for Peru and Chile, along with Mexico – which at the time was only bound under the older and more lenient previous NAFTA Agreement – and Southeast Asian developing country members of the CPTPP that do not yet have FTAs with the United States, such as Malaysia and Vietnam. Only Vietnam was granted the option to apply for a grace period of one year for the implementation of patents on pharmaceutical and agricultural chemical products with the possibility of a further two-year extension.

With the United States now no longer part of the agreement, at least for the time being, the remaining countries have followed up on a Ministerial Statement from the APEC Conference in Danang and signed in Chile a modified agreement with a list of provisions that are for now suspended. Of the three provisions in the intellectual property chapter related to plant intellectual property, the one requiring patents for inventions derived from plants was promptly suspended. Only the first sentence of the original Article 18.37.4 TPP remains.[84] This restores, therefore, the TRIPS position of Article 27.3.b. in this matter. The provision requiring UPOV 1991 membership and a provision on test data protection for agricultural chemical

[80] GRAIN, 'New trade deals legalise corporate theft, make farmers' seeds illegal' (n 18); Press, 'The Trans-Pacific Partnership will hurt farmers and make seed companies richer' (n 18).

[81] Industry Trade Advisory Committee (ITAC-15), *The Trans-Pacific Partnership Agreement*, Report of December 3, 2015, to the United States Trade Representative, 12, https://ustr.gov/sites/default/files/ITAC-15-Intellectual-Property.pdf.

[82] Ibid: 'ITAC-15 believes the objective of comprehensive patent protection for plant-related technology has been advanced by the TPP Agreement.'

[83] Hankyoreh, 'South Korean government consults with various industries about its accession to CPTPP', http://english.hani.co.kr/arti/english_edition/e_business/858098.html.

[84] The new version of Art 18.37.4 with the second sentence suspended now simply reads as follows: 'A Party may also exclude from patentability plants other than microorganisms.'

products have, however, remained in the amended document. As far as UPOV is concerned, if the CPTPP now requires Mexico (where the agreement is in force since December 2018) to upgrade from UPOV 1978 to UPOV 1991. If ratified in these countries, it requires Malaysia and Brunei to join UPOV 1991 and Chile and Peru to also upgrade from UPOV 1978 to UPOV 1991. New Zealand, where the agreement came into force in December 2018, as explained earlier, will now have to upgrade to UPOV 1991 or establish UPOV 1991 conforming legislation.

VI. Intellectual Property in Plant Material in Bilateral Free Trade Agreements

Apart from the two major multilateral initiatives in the Asia-Pacific region, there are of course many bilateral agreements between Asian countries and high-technology exporting and industrialized nations such as the United States, the EU, the EFTA countries, Switzerland, Japan, Korea and Australia. As is to be expected, these high-technology exporters are generally interested in an upgrading and upscaling of the international intellectual property system and they try to push for their interests in international negotiations. As far as plant varieties are concerned, there are several typical provisions used by countries interested in stronger plant intellectual property laws to require law reform in countries that do not yet have such laws.

A. FTAs that Rewrite Article 27 TRIPS and Require Patents for Plant and Plant-Related Inventions

The most far-reaching new regulation of plant intellectual property occurs in FTA provisions that rewrite Article 27 TRIPS. Such provisions, after mentioning the broad protection of Article 27.1., simply either delete the entire Article 27.3.b. from the list of possible exclusions or they rewrite Article 27.3.b. so that it no longer extends to plants. Such provisions have been used in many United States FTAs and in the Australia-Korea FTA. Under the US-Singapore FTA, signed in 2003 and in force since 2004, Singapore is precluded from excluding inventions under Article 27.3.b.[85] As the earliest FTA with the United States in the region, the US-Singapore FTA was widely regarded at the time as a blueprint for US negotiations with similar high protection countries, such as Australia and Korea.[86]

[85] See US-Singapore FTA, Art 16.7: '1. Each Party shall make patents available for any invention … in all fields of technology … Each Party may exclude inventions from patentability only as defined in Articles 27.2 and 27.3(a) of the TRIPS Agreement.'

[86] Wee Loon Ng-Loy, 'IP and FTAs of Singapore: Ten Years On' in Christoph Antons and Reto M Hilty (eds), *Intellectual Property and Free Trade Agreements in the Asia-Pacific Region* (Heidelberg-New York-Dordrecht-London, Springer, 2015) 351.

As Ng-Loy has pointed out, however, with regards to the patenting of plants and animals, it merely confirmed legislative steps that Singapore had taken as early as 1994.[87]

Similar as with the US-Singapore FTA, the Korea-US FTA also eliminates Article 27.3.b. TRIPS with its choice of patents or plant variety protection (PVP) systems and only leaves the exclusion options of Article 27.2 and Article 27.3.a. TRIPS untouched.[88] The Australia-Korea FTA follows this pattern[89] as do the US-Australia FTA[90] and the US-Jordan FTA.[91] The US FTA with Bahrain directly requires patents for plant inventions.[92] The US FTA with Oman also drops plants from the exclusion lists, but keeps the text of Article 27.3.b. for animals other than microorganisms and essentially biological processes for their production.[93]

FTAs of the EFTA countries with Korea, the Philippines, Hong Kong and Indonesia respectively have also altered the exclusion provision of Article 27.3.b. and brought it into accordance with the wording of Article 53(b) of the European Patent Convention, which clarifies that patent protection extends not just to microbiological processes but also to the products thereof.[94]

B. FTAs Requiring Countries to 'Endeavour' to Make Patents for Plant Material Available

There is a string of US agreements with countries in Central and Latin America that promise to 'endeavour' to make patents available in this field, including Chile,[95] Peru[96] and Colombia.[97] The Dominican Republic and Central American

[87] Ibid 343.

[88] See Korea-US FTA, Art 18.8(2)(a) and (b).

[89] See Australia-Korea FTA, Art 13.8(2)(a) and (b).

[90] See US-Australia FTA, Art 17.9(2)(a) and (b).

[91] See US-Jordan FTA, Art 18(a) and (b).

[92] See US-Bahrain FTA, Art 14.8.2: 'Each Party shall make patents available for plant inventions.'

[93] See US-Oman FTA, Art 15.8(2)(a), (b) and (c),

[94] See EFTA Agreement with Korea, Art 2(2)(ii), which provides that 'this provision shall not apply to microbiological processes or the products thereof'. See also EFTA-Hong Kong Agreement, Art 5(b) of Annex XII; EFTA-Philippines Agreement, Art 3(b) of Annex XVIII; Comprehensive Economic Partnership Agreement Between the Republic of Indonesia and the EFTA States, Article 5 of Annex XVII.

[95] See US-Chile FTA, Art 17.9(2): 'Each Party will undertake reasonable efforts, through a transparent and participatory process, to develop and propose legislation within 4 years from the entry into force of this Agreement that makes available patent protection for plants that are new, involve an inventive step, and are capable of industrial application.'

[96] See US-Peru FTA, Art 16.9(2): 'Nothing in this Chapter shall be construed to prevent a Party from excluding inventions from patentability as set out in Articles 27.2 and 27.3 of the TRIPS Agreement. Notwithstanding the foregoing, a Party that does not provide patent protection for plants by the date of entry into force of this Agreement shall undertake all reasonable efforts to make such patent protection available consistent with paragraph 1. Any Party that provides patent protection for plants or animals on or after the date of entry into force of this Agreement shall maintain such protection.'

[97] See US-Columbia FTA, Art 16.9(2) of the Agreement, which uses the same text as the US-Peru Agreement.

Countries in their FTA with the United States also state that they will 'endeavour' to shift to patent protection.[98] As an interesting further sign that plant variety rights are indeed only of secondary interest to the United States, this Agreement provides that for those that introduce patent protection, UPOV membership becomes optional. For those that do not, they were required to join UPOV 1991, with clear timelines to do so for all of them who were not yet members.[99] Costa Rica and the Dominican Republic have since joined Nicaragua as UPOV members.

C. FTAs and UPOV

i. FTAs that Require Accession to or Ratification of UPOV 1991 or Compliance with UPOV 1991 Standards

With their focus on patents for plant material US agreements have relatively little to say about UPOV-style plant variety protection. Many of them, however, do require accession to, or ratification of, UPOV 1991. Examples are the US FTAs with Singapore,[100] Korea,[101] Bahrain,[102] Colombia[103] and Oman.[104] Membership of, or compliance with, UPOV 1991 is also a focus of European, Japanese and EFTA countries' FTAs and, to a lesser extent, of Korean and Australian FTAs. This push for UPOV 1991 comes in, basically, five different forms. The most common form is for membership in UPOV 1991 to be required, sometimes with a deadline by which this has to be achieved. Examples are the EU-Korea FTA,[105] the Japan-Chile Economic Partnership Agreement (EPA)[106] and the Australia-Chile FTA.[107] Chile has been a UPOV member since 1996; Korea took this step in 2002.

A second form and variant of this push towards UPOV with similar results is the Japan-Indonesia EPA, which asks Indonesia only to 'endeavour' to become a UPOV member (Article 106(3)(c)), but this soft requirement related to membership is combined with a hard obligation in Article 116 to introduce UPOV

[98] See CAFTA-DR, Art 15.9(2) of the Agreement, which uses the same language as the US-Peru and US-Colombia Agreements.

[99] See CAFTA-DR, Art 15.1.5: '(a) Each Party shall ratify or accede to the *International Convention for the Protection of New Varieties of Plants* (1991) (UPOV Convention 1991). Nicaragua shall do so by January 1, 2010. Costa Rica shall do so by June 1, 2007. All other Parties shall do so by January 1, 2006. (b) Subparagraph (a) shall not apply to any Party that provides effective patent protection for plants by the date of entry into force of this Agreement. Such parties shall make all reasonable efforts to ratify or accede to the UPOV Convention 1991.'

[100] See United States-Singapore FTA, Art 16.1(2)(a)(ii).

[101] See United States-Korea FTA, Art 18.1(3)(g).

[102] See United States-Bahrain FTA, Art 14.1(2)(c).

[103] See United States-Colombia FTA, Art 16.1(3)(c).

[104] See United States-Oman FTA, Art 15.1(2)(e).

[105] See EU-Korea FTA, Art 10.39.

[106] See Japan-Chile EPA, Art 162.

[107] See Australia-Chile FTA, Art 17.4(1)(c).

1991 standards.[108] This means that, similar to the requirements imposed on New Zealand in the CPTPP, Indonesia has a choice of direct UPOV membership or the use of UPOV standards in its domestic legislation. Indonesia's obligations differ from those of New Zealand, however, in that it has to follow UPOV 1991 principles strictly and has not negotiated the freedom to design laws in accordance with its obligations towards indigenous or other communities.[109] A softer version of the same variant appears in the Comprehensive Economic Partnership Agreement between Indonesia and the EFTA states, which requires in Article 2.2. of Annex XVII that a party, which is not yet a party to the 1978 UPOV Act shall comply with the substantive provisions of the 1991 UPOV Act. This requirement is modified, however, by a footnote stating that this provision shall be without prejudice to the rights of Indonesia to protect its local plant varieties.

ii. FTAs that Accept UPOV 1978 Membership, but Prescribe Some UPOV 1991 Standards

Some agreements (especially those involving China) accept membership in UPOV 1978 or have no membership requirements, but use some modified and softened UPOV 1991 standards in the part on plant varieties. Examples for these types of agreements are in particular the FTAs of Korea and Switzerland with China. Both are content with UPOV 1978 membership, because this is the version of UPOV that China had acceded to. The China-Korea FTA reaffirms commitments from UPOV 1978,[110] but uses on the rights of the breeder somewhat modified language of UPOV 1991 without the extension to essentially derived varieties that UPOV 1991 offers.[111] The Switzerland-China FTA is also content with UPOV 1978 membership.[112] It also uses, however, important parts of the 1991 UPOV text for the rights of the breeder,[113] with acts done for experimental purposes and for breeding other varieties and their commercialization excluded from such extended rights.[114] The right of farmers to use farm saved seed on their own holdings is confirmed 'within reasonable limits and subject to the safeguarding of the legitimate interests of the breeder'.[115]

[108] Japan-Indonesia EPA, Art 116: 'Each party shall provide for the protection of all plant genera and species by an effective plant varieties protection system which is consistent with the 1991 UPOV Convention.'

[109] See the discussion under 5.2.

[110] See China-Korea FTA, Art 15.3(k).

[111] See China-Korea FTA, Art 15.18(3): 'At least the following acts in respect of the propagating material of the protected variety shall require the authorization of the breeder: (a) production or reproduction (multiplication) for the purposes of commercial marketing; (b) conditioning for the purpose of commercial propagation; (c) offering for sale; (d) selling or other marketing; (e) importing or exporting.'

[112] See Switzerland-China FTA, Art 11.3(1)(j) and Art 11.10(1).

[113] See Switzerland-China FTA, Art 11.10(2).

[114] See Switzerland-China FTA, Art 11.10(4)(a).

[115] See Switzerland-China FTA, Art 11.10(4)(b).

The protection granted for plant varieties under the Switzerland-China FTA extends immediately only to genera and species listed in an Annex of the Agreement, which in turn refers to the listing of the Chinese Ministry of Agriculture and State Forestry Administration and mentions that Switzerland already protects all genera and species in accordance with the UPOV Convention.[116] However, in accordance with the principles of national treatment and most favourite nation treatment, if a party grants further protection to genera/species not mentioned in Annex IX, that protection must be granted to any plant breeder of the parties.[117] A further expansion is envisaged in Article 11.10(6), according to which each party after two years can request discussions about the inclusion of additional genera/species in the protection regime and about a further expansion of Annex IX. The parties further agree after a period of two years to exchange information about the protection for essentially derived varieties 'with a view to extend the possibility of a more comprehensive protection regime, also with regard to essentially derived varieties'.[118]

iii. FTAs that do not Prescribe UPOV Membership or Standards, but have a Detailed Part on Plant Varieties

An example of a fourth category of agreements, which do not prescribe UPOV membership, but have a detailed part on plant varieties, is the EFTA-Philippines Agreement, which gives a choice of joining UPOV or complying with standards listed in the Annex on intellectual property protection, which are, with some modifications, the UPOV 1991 standards.[119] Importantly, and different from the agreements concluded by China discussed above, the EFTA-Philippines FTA extends also to essentially derived varieties and to harvested material from protected varieties.[120] The farmers privilege to farm saved seeds is restricted in this FTA to 'small farmers', defined in a footnote to Article 7(6)(d) as

> natural persons dependent on small-scale subsistence farming as their primary source of income and whose sale, barter or exchange of agricultural products do not exceed a gross value of one hundred eighty thousand Philippine pesos (P. 180,000.00) per annum based on 1991 constant prices, subject to adjustment by the authorities.[121]

[116] See Switzerland-China FTA, Annex IX Referred to in Art 11.10 – Lists of Protectable Genera/Species of the Switzerland-China FTA.

[117] See Switzerland-China FTA, Art 11.10(5).

[118] See Switzerland-China FTA, Art 11.10(6)(b).

[119] See EFTA-Philippines Agreement, Art 7(1) and (2) of Annex XVIII.

[120] See EFTA-Philippines Agreement, Art 7(4) and (5).

[121] At current value (as of 19 August 2018) this is an annual turnover of US$3377. This reference is taken from Section 4(1) of the Philippines' Republic Act No 7607 of 1992 Providing a Magna Carta of Small Farmers.

iv. FTAs that Require Countries to 'Endeavour' to Become a UPOV Member or to Comply with UPOV Standards

A softer and rather vague version of the push towards UPOV 1991 can be found in agreements that require countries to 'endeavour' to become a UPOV member or to comply with UPOV standards or simply to improve their plant variety protection systems. Examples include the Japan-Vietnam agreement, which requires the parties to 'endeavour' to provide for the protection of all plant genera and species in accordance with UPOV 1991 as early as practicable.[122] The Japan-Malaysia agreement requires from parties to provide adequate protection for 'as many plant genera or species as possible … within the shortest period of time' and 'in a manner consistent with an internationally harmonised system'.[123] The Japan-Brunei EPA requires parties to 'endeavour' to become a party of international agreements, but does not mention UPOV specifically or set a date.[124] The Japan-Philippines EPA requires parties to 'endeavour' to increase the number of protected plant genera and species and to consider the concerns of the other party.[125] The Japan-Thailand FTA requires protection of as many plant genera or species as possible 'as early as practicable' and 'in a manner based on international standards'.[126]

VII. Agreements that Stress Exceptions and Cooperation

The agreements discussed in the previous sections, which seek to strengthen plant intellectual property rights, can be contrasted with those agreements that specifically reaffirm the sovereignty of the parties and exceptions in relation to state regulation necessary for the protection of vital interests such as the protection of animals and plants – for example, the FTAs between former Russian republics.[127] The South Pacific Regional Trade and Economic Cooperation Agreement (SPARTECA) between Australia and New Zealand,[128] the Pacific Island Countries Trade Agreement (PICTA),[129] the Melanesian

[122] See Economic Partnership Agreement between Japan and Vietnam, Art 90.
[123] See Economic Partnership Agreement between Japan and Malaysia, Art 123.
[124] See Economic Partnership Agreement between Japan and Brunei, Art 97(c).
[125] See Economic Partnership Agreement between Japan and the Philippines, Art 127.
[126] See Economic Partnership Agreement between Japan and Thailand, Art 135.
[127] See the Free Trade Agreement between Azerbaijan, Armenia, Belarus, Georgia, Moldova, Kazakhstan, the Russian Federation, Ukraine, Uzbekistan, Tajikistan and the Kyrgyz Republic, Art 13(1).
[128] See SPARTECA, Art VI(1)(c): 'Provided that such measures are not used as a means of arbitrary or unjustifiable discrimination or as a disguised restriction on trade, nothing in this Agreement shall preclude the adoption or enforcement … of measures: … (c) necessary to protect human, animal or plant life or health.'
[129] See PICTA, Art 16(1)(b).

Spearhead Group Trade Agreement,[130] the Agreement on Trade and Commercial Relations between Australia and Papua New Guinea,[131] the FTA between India and Sri Lanka[132] and the Framework Agreement on Comprehensive Economic Co-operation between ASEAN and the People's Republic of China[133] also have similar provisions.

Chinese FTAs with developing countries often stress cooperation in the field of intellectual property rights rather than substantive standards, as in the agreement with Chile,[134] or the importance of genetic resources and traditional knowledge, as in the agreement with New Zealand[135] and those with Costa Rica[136] and Peru,[137] which also stress a mutually supportive relationship between the TRIPS Agreement and the Convention on Biological Diversity. The Republic of China-Panama agreement of 2003 requires the application of the UPOV principles, but leaves parties the choice between UPOV 1978 and UPOV 1991.[138] It also has detailed provisions on traditional knowledge, folklore and access to genetic resources and intellectual property.[139]

VIII. Options for Intellectual Property Policy Making in this Field and FTA Negotiations in Developing Countries

Given the role of agriculture in developing countries, discussed earlier in this chapter, most such countries are probably well advised to remain extremely cautious about the expansion of intellectual property rights in this field and to resist pressure to adopt positions and legislative models in FTAs that are potentially harmful to their economic interests as well as threatening their agro-biodiversity. This is especially true for those agreements that eliminate the flexibilities of Article 27.3.b. TRIPS and require patent protection of plant material. With the simultaneous expansion of patents and plant variety rights in this field and the technological advance in genetic engineering, an overlap of the protection systems has developed that is now of concern even in UPOV founding members such as France, Germany and

[130] See Melanesian Spearhead Group Trade Agreement, Art 15(1).

[131] See Agreement on Trade and Commercial Relations between Australia and Papua New Guinea, Art 8(f).

[132] See India-Sri Lanka FTA, Art IV.

[133] See Framework Agreement on Comprehensive Economic Co-operation between ASEAN and the People's Republic of China, Art 10.

[134] See People's Republic of China-Chile FTA, Art 111.

[135] China-New Zealand FTA, Art 165.

[136] China-Costa Rica FTA, Art 111.

[137] China-Peru FTA, Art 145.

[138] See Republic of China-Panama FTA, Art 16.01.

[139] See Republic of China-Panama FTA, Arts 16.05, 16.06 and 16.07.

the Netherlands. These countries have adapted the breeders' exemption of their plant variety laws to their patent laws in order to create badly needed space for conventional plant breeders to experiment.

However, the current push in FTAs to require developing countries to consent to UPOV 1991 conforming legislation or to join UPOV is no less problematic. Carlos Correa et al have explained the many problems that UPOV membership and UPOV standards create, especially for the small-scale farming sector, which is still of great importance in a majority of the countries.[140] Of particular concern here is the extension of the scope of protection to cover essentially derived varieties, which brings with it uncertainty in assessing what is an essentially derived variety, and this is problematic even for the smaller plant-breeding businesses in Europe and North America. Small farmers in the developing world are most certainly not in a position to make such assessments. Further, while the discussion about UPOV in industrialized countries is nowadays largely between large agro-chemical companies and 'classical' commercial breeders,[141] with farmers and consumers only in the role of 'the wider public concerned', in developing countries farmers may themselves be breeders and develop their own varieties and seed material.[142] In addition to that, of course, bartering and exchanging seeds in an informal manner continues to form an important part of their livelihood and an essential element in rapid local reaction strategies to changing weather patterns under conditions of climate change.[143]

Rather than focusing only on trade gains, these pressing socio-economic and environmental concerns must be taken into account by governments when embarking on FTA negotiations. This requires collaboration with all relevant government departments as well as information exchange with academic experts, NGOs and farmer organizations. For all these reasons, developing countries with considerable smallholder sectors should avoid binding commitments to UPOV membership or standards in bilateral FTAs, and avoid being drawn into such commitments as part of larger multilateral agreements, such as the CPTPP. If UPOV principles are required, the choice between UPOV 1978 and UPOV 1991 should be insisted upon and UPOV 1978 principles should be defended. Governments should further continue to emphasize the mutually supportive relationship between TRIPS and the Convention on Biological Diversity and, if possible, make reference to other important UN treaties and documents relevant for this field. Developing countries

[140] Correa (n 48).

[141] European Commission, *Final Report* (n 50); Jack Kloppenburg, 'Re-Purposing the Master's Tools: The Open Source Seed Initiative and the Struggle for Seed Sovereignty' (2014) 41 *The Journal of Peasant Studies* 1225.

[142] Yunita T Winarto and Imam Ardhianto, 'Tumbuh Kembang Benih-benih Pemuliaan Tanaman Padi di Ladang Petani' in Yunita T Winarto (ed), *Bisa Dèwèk: Kisak Perjuangan Petani Pemulia Tanaman di Indramayu* (Jakarta: Gramata Publishing, 2011).

[143] C (Kees) J Stigter, 'Climate Crises in the Livelihood of Indonesian Rice Farmers' in Yunita T Winarto (ed), *Krisis Pangan dan "Sesat Pikir": Mengapa Masih Berlanjut* (Jakarta, Yayasan Pustaka Obor Indonesia, 2016).

could further learn from the approach of New Zealand in insisting on freedom to design their laws in the interest of treaty obligations towards the country's indigenous communities. While New Zealand's Treaty of Waitangi is a rather special case of a country's relationship with its indigenous population, many developing countries have written obligations to recognize and respect the cultures and customs of their indigenous populations into their constitutions.[144] Governments could cite such constitutional obligations as important obstacles towards the acceptance of international obligations that concern traditional resource rights, with the aim of achieving greater freedom in designing their own laws to protect such rights.

IX. Conclusion

To sum up, the intellectual property system for plant varieties has expanded in an extraordinary manner since the conclusion of the TRIPS Agreement. While this initially concerned mainly UPOV membership and national plant variety laws in accordance with TRIPS, the United States, in particular, has recently expanded the protection in its FTAs to include patents. The TPP would have taken a further step in this direction, requiring patents for inventions derived from plants in developing country members Chile, Peru, Mexico, Vietnam, Malaysia and Brunei. The pull out of the United States from the TPP and the watered-down CPTPP which has meanwhile come into force for some of these countries (Mexico, Vietnam) have prevented this from happening, at least for now. However, even without the suspended patent provision, the CPTPP is still raising the bar for several countries to the higher standards of UPOV 1991.

With Indonesia committed to UPOV 1991 standards in bilateral FTAs with Japan and the EFTA countries and the Philippines accepting similar standards in a modified form in its FTA with the EFTA countries, once the CPTPP is ratified by all its ASEAN members, ASEAN would then have six countries basically committed to UPOV 1991 standards. This could also potentially shift the balance as far as UPOV-style plant variety protection is concerned for other negotiations, such as the one on the RCEP. China has agreed to 'UPOV 1978 plus' provisions in bilateral FTAs with Switzerland and Korea, perhaps indicating that its opposition to higher standards is softening. A further indication in this direction is the Australian FTA with China, which contains an interesting provision on cooperation with regards to plant breeders' rights between the two countries. Besides harmonization of administration and procedures, the provision also speaks of 'contributing to the

[144] See eg Indonesian Constitution of 1945, Art 18B(2) and 28I(3) and Brazilian Constitution of 1988, Art 231. For similar provisions in other Latin American constitutions see Carlos Frederico Marés de Souza Filho, 'Multiculturalism and Collective Rights' in B de Sousa Santos (ed), *Another Knowledge is Possible: Beyond Northern Epistemologies* (London-New York, Verso, 2007) 90–91.

reform and further development of the international plant breeders' rights laws, standards and practices, including within the Southeast Asian region'.[145] Since both countries are not actually situated within Southeast Asia or members of ASEAN and have different views in the RCEP negotiations about the extent of plant breeders' rights protection with Australia pushing for UPOV 1991, the provision from the Australia-China FTA is a bit surprising. It could possibly also raise eyebrows in ASEAN government circles and be interpreted as an attempt to encroach on regional policy making.

While the various agreements point to a further ratcheting up of UPOV-style plant variety protection towards UPOV 1991 standards, the departure of the United States from the TPP means the temporary end to the expansion of patents in this field. Of course, all of this could change again with a different administration in Washington, bearing in mind that the TPP provisions are only suspended and that the version negotiated by the Obama administration would have been a great advantage for US-based multinational agro-chemical companies. However, the extension of intellectual property rights in agriculture is now also facing increasing opposition from NGOs, environmentalists and associations of consumers or farmers, which take a more holistic view of food production and are less focused on yields.[146] Some of the NGOs active and influential in this field, such as La Via Campesina and Navdanya, are fundamentally opposed to any granting of intellectual property rights on seeds.[147] A movement arguing for 'food sovereignty' as opposed to 'food security'[148] also made its presence felt in the discussion in the UN Human Rights Council about the United Nations Declaration on the Rights of Peasants and other people working in rural areas,[149] which also deals with rights to seeds, and which was passed by the Council at the end of September and adopted by the UN General Assembly in December 2018.[150] This struggle between two camps representing very different visions of the future of agriculture and their respective influences on developing country governments may well be decisive for the future development of the precise form intellectual property rights to plant material will take in such countries. In the meantime, and for the reasons explained in this chapter, governments with substantial smallholder agricultural sectors should resist pressures in bilateral and multilateral negotiations to join UPOV or introduce UPOV 1991 standards. If plant variety protection

[145] See China-Australia FTA, Art 11.16(c).

[146] McKeon (n 17).

[147] For a discussion of these organizations and their policy positions see Kloppenburg (n 141) 1233–37.

[148] McKeon (n 17) 73–81.

[149] UN Doc A/HRC/WG.15/5/3 of 10 September 2018.

[150] Catherine Saez, 'UN Human Rights Council Passes Resolution on Peasants' Rights Including Right to Seeds' (2018), http://www.ip-watch.org/2018/10/01/un-human-rights-council-passes-resolution-peasants-rights-including-right-seeds; 'UN rights chief welcomes new text to protect rights of peasants and other rural workers', *UN News*, 18 December 2018, https://news.un.org/en/story/2018/12/1028881.

provisions cannot be avoided, the UPOV 1978 standards should be a baseline that countries should aim to defend, while also making reference to the CBD and other relevant UN treaties and documents. Finally, countries with constitutional and treaty obligations towards indigenous and other communities with traditional resource rights should refer to such obligations in international treaty negotiations to achieve the necessary freedom to legislate for the protection of such rights.

12

Pre-established Damages for Copyright Infringement and Trademark Counterfeiting

Suggestions for CPTPP/RCEP Based on Some Asian Experiences

KUNG-CHUNG LIU AND HAORAN ZHANG*

I. Introduction

Since the Agreement on Trade-Related Aspects of Intellectual Property Rights (TRIPS), free trade agreements (FTAs) have become more and more concerned with effective enforcement of intellectual property rights (IPR), such as the draft Anti-Counterfeiting Trade Agreement (ACTA) and Trans Pacific Partnership Agreement (TPP). The Comprehensive and Progressive Agreement for Trans-Pacific Partnership (CPTPP) and the pending Regional Comprehensive Economic Partnership (RCEP) all foresee pre-established damages for copyright infringement and trademark counterfeiting. However, it remains questionable whether such a regime is really justified and needed and how it can be interpreted and improved. This chapter will first, in section II introduce the origin of the regime from the United States (US), then examine in section III how major Asian jurisdictions, namely Taiwan, the People's Republic of China (PRC), Korea, Japan and Singapore, are dealing with it, before tackling the questions just raised in section IV.

* Dr Kung-Chung Liu is Lee Kong Chian Professor of Law (Practice) Director, Applied Research Centre for Intellectual Assets and the Law in Asia, School of Law, Singapore Management University/ Renmin University of China. Haoran Zhang is a PhD student at Renmin University of China. The first author would like to thank Weijie Huang and Kelvin Sum for their help in collecting the literature. Special thanks owed to Professors Masabumi Suzuki, Byungil Kim and Heinz Goddar for their invaluable help in studying the Japanese, Korean and German regimes respectively. All online materials were accessed on or before 6 March 2019.

II. The Origin of the Pre-established Damages for Copyright Infringement and Trademark Counterfeiting in the US

In the US, the 1909 Copyright Act first introduced statutory damages for copyright infringement. Under the Copyright Act, 17 USC § 504(c), a court can award statutory damages in a range between US$ 750 and US$ 30,000 per work infringed, and which can be ratcheted up to $150,000 per work infringed in cases of wilful infringement. In 1996 the Lanham Act followed suit and introduced two types of trademark statutory damages, one for counterfeiting (15 USC §1117(c)), and one for cybersquatting (15 USC §1117(d)).[1] It also mandates treble damages and statutory damages for use of a counterfeit mark.[2] 15 USC § 1117(c) provides that in a case involving the use of a counterfeit mark in connection with the sale, offering for sale, or distribution of goods or services, the plaintiff may elect, at any time before final judgment is rendered by the trial court, to recover, instead of actual damages and profits under subsection (a), an award of statutory damages in the amount of: (1) not less than $1,000 or more than $200,000 per counterfeit mark per type of goods or services sold, offered for sale, or distributed, as the court considers just; or (2) if the court finds that the use of the counterfeit mark was wilful, not more than $2,000,000 per counterfeit mark per type of goods or services sold, offered for sale, or distributed, as the court considers just.[3]

15 USC § 1117(d) provides:

> In a case involving a violation of section 1125(d)(1) of this title, the plaintiff may elect, at any time before final judgment is rendered by the trial court, to recover, instead of actual damages and profits, an award of statutory damages in the amount of not less than $1,000 and not more than $100,000 per domain name, as the court considers just.

Although statutory damages in the US Copyright Act have often been criticized as 'arbitrary, inconsistent, unprincipled, and sometimes grossly excessive', the US government has successfully exported this regime to other nations, along with the less criticized pre-established damages for trademark counterfeiting, through bilateral and multilateral FTAs.[4]

[1] David Llewelyn, 'Statutory Damages for Use of a "Counterfeit Trade Mark" and for Copyright Infringement in Singapore – A Radical Remedy in the Law of Intellectual Property or One in Need of a Rethink?' (2016) 28 *Singapore Academy of Law Journal* 61, 72.

[2] 15 US Code § 1117(b).

[3] The statutory damages were increased in October 2008 through the 'Prioritizing Resources and Organization for Intellectual Property Act (PRO-IP)' from the previous range of $500 to $100,000 per mark, up to $1,000 to $200,000 per mark. In addition, the statutory damages can also range up to $2,000,000 (up from the previous maximum of $1,000,000).

[4] Pamela Samuelson, Phil Hill and Tara Wheatland, 'Statutory Damages: A Rarity in Copyright Laws Internationally, But for How Long?' (2013) 60 *Journal, Copyright Society USA* 530–31.

A. ACTA, TPP, CPTPP and RCEP

Pamela Samuelson et al have famously asked how long the international rarity of statutory damages for copyright infringement will last. Unfortunately, it is here to stay, not the least in the two latest major multilateral FTAs.

i. From ACTA to TPP and CPTPP: From Covering Compensation Only to Also Including Deterrence

Article 45(2) of the TRIPS Agreement permits but does not require members to authorize payment of pre-established damages, even where the infringer did not knowingly, or with reasonable grounds to know, engage in infringing activity.[5] The notorious and eventually failed ACTA demanded that each Party should establish or maintain a system that provided pre-established damages at least for infringement of copyright or related rights and in cases of trademark counterfeiting; or presumptions for determining the amount of damages sufficient to compensate the right holder for the harm caused by the infringement; or at least additional damages for copyright.[6]

The TPP done at Auckland on 4 February 2016 has made progress in recognizing the importance of both ex ante ('expeditious remedies to prevent infringements') and ex post remedies ('remedies that constitute a deterrent to future infringements') for IPR infringement, and of the proportionate balance between effective enforcement of IPR and other legitimate interests of trade and third parties. Article 18.71(1) and (5) demands:

> 1. Each Party shall ensure that *enforcement procedures* as specified in this Section are available under its law so as to permit effective action against any act of infringement of intellectual property rights covered by this Chapter, including expeditious remedies to prevent infringements and remedies that constitute *a deterrent to future infringements*. These procedures shall be applied in such a manner as to avoid the creation of barriers to legitimate trade and to provide for safeguards against their abuse. [Emphasis added]

and

> 5. take into account the need for proportionality between the seriousness of the infringement of the intellectual property right and the applicable remedies and penalties, as well as the interests of third parties.

However, the experiences of the TRIPS Agreement with its general provisions, such as Articles 7 and 8, show that members tend to neglect these noble ideas of

[5] TRIPS Agreement 1995, Art 45 (Damages).
[6] ACTA 2011, Art 3(3).

proportionality and the interests of third parties in the actual design and implementation of the system against IPR infringement, as general clauses are often deemed declaratory in nature and can be satisfied by lip service.

The TPP then prescribes that pre-established damages or additional damages as civil remedies for copyright infringement and trademark counterfeiting be established or maintained by its members in addition to providing for the recovery of actual damages and the infringer's profits. The TPP has more flexibility, as a party does not have to adopt pre-established damages and can opt for additional damages, such as treble damages in cases of wilful infringement. Article 18.74.6 of the TPP provides:

> In civil judicial proceedings with respect to the infringement of copyright or related rights protecting works, phonograms or performances, each Party shall establish or maintain a system that provides for one or more of the following: (a) *pre-established damages, which shall be available on the election of the right holder*; or (b) additional damages. [Emphasis added]

Footnote 112/113 of the TPP explains: 'For greater certainty, additional damages may include exemplary or punitive damages.' Article 18.74.7 of the TPP provides the same for trademark counterfeiting. Article 18.74.8 (Pre-established Damages Serving Two Different Purposes) of the TPP expressly explains that pre-established damages serve two different but related purposes, ie *sufficient compensation with a view to deterring future infringements*:

> 8. Pre-established damages under paragraphs 6 and 7 shall be set out in an amount that would be sufficient to compensate the right holder for the harm caused by the infringement, and with a view to deterring future infringements.

The TPP almost became irrelevant when its main initiator, the US, withdrew from it under President Trump in 2017. The remaining 11 founding members[7] held together and transformed the TPP into the CPTPP, which took effect on 30 December 2018. According to Articles 1(1), (3) and 2 of the CPTPP, the provisions of the TPP are incorporated, by reference, into and made part of CPTPP mutatis mutandis, except for Article 30.4 (Accession), Article 30.5 (Entry into Force), Article 30.6 (Withdrawal), Article 30.8 (Authentic Texts), and those provisions suspended by the Annex of the CPTPP (Articles 18.74.6–8 and 18.71 of the TPP, mentioned above, have not been suspended); in the event of any inconsistency between this CPTPP and the TPP, when the latter is in force, the CPTPP will prevail to the extent of the inconsistency. Therefore, with regards to the issue of pre-established damages for copyright infringement and trademark counterfeiting, the stance of the TPP has been taken over by the CPTPP.

[7] They are Australia, Brunei, Canada, Chile, Japan, Malaysia, Mexico, New Zealand, Peru, Singapore and Vietnam.

ii. RCEP

Article 9*bis*.3 of the RCEP demands the establishment or maintenance of pre-established damages and unequivocally emphasizes deterrence first and then full compensation for copyright infringement and trademark counterfeiting. Article 9*bis*.3 stipulates:

> In civil judicial proceedings, each Party shall, at least with respect to works, phonograms, and performances protected by copyright or related rights, and in case of trademark counterfeiting, establish or maintain pre-established damages, which shall be available on the election of the right holder. Pre-established damages shall be in an amount sufficient to constitute *a deterrent* to future infringements and to compensate fully the right holder for the harm caused by the infringement.[8] [Emphasis added.]

B. Pre-established Damages for Copyright Infringement in Selected Asian Jurisdictions

i. Civil Law Jurisdictions

The four typical civil law jurisdictions in Asia – Japan, Taiwan, the PRC and Korea – have the following points in common when it comes to compensation for IPR infringement:

(1) The basic principle for torts as foreseen in the respective Civil Code is to recover the actual damages and the interests which have been lost.[9]
(2) This principle also applies to the compensation for IPR infringement.[10]
(3) Due to general lack of a discovery process to deal with the thorny issues related to the production and evaluation of evidence, other alternative remedies, such as the infringer's profit and royalty, and more recently pre-established damages, are widely employed, which mainly serve the purpose of reducing the IPR owners' burden of proving the loss they suffered from infringement of their IPR, with a gradual shift to emphasizing deterrence.
(4) Courts are empowered to recognize a reasonable amount of damages on the basis of the meaning of all pleadings and the result of the examination of evidence. Taiwan and the PRC are frequent users of pre-established damages (Taiwan limits it to copyright and trademark infringement, whereas the PRC also applies such to patent infringement). Korea and Japan have just adopted such a regime.

[8] RECP (15 October 2015), IP Chapter.
[9] Taiwanese Civil Code 2008, Art 216.
[10] Byungil Kim and Christopher Heath (ed),) *Intellectual Property Law in Korea* (Wolters Kluwer, 2nd edn, 2015); Llewelyn (n 1) 64.

ii. Frequent Users of Pre-Established Damages

a. Taiwan

Taiwan introduced presumption of damages and pre-established damages for copyright infringement in 1985 when amending the Copyright Act. Article 33(2) had provided that:

> The damages can be presumed based on the profit made by the infringer and the loss suffered by the copyright owner, which may *not be lower than 500 times the actual retail price* of the infringed work; if there was no actual retail price, courts can decide the damages based on the severity of the infringement. [Emphasis added.]

The1992 amendment revised how statutory damages are to be calculated. Article 88(2) provides that the injured party may make claim in any of the following manners: in accordance with the provisions of Article 216 of the Civil Code; provided, when the injured party is unable to prove damages, it may base the damages on the difference between the amount of expected benefit from the exercise of such rights under normal circumstances and the amount of benefit from the exercise of the same rights after the infringement. Article 88(3) further provides, if it is difficult for the injured party to prove actual damages in accordance with the preceding paragraph, it may request that the court set compensation at an amount of not less than NT$10,000 [approximately US$ 330] and not more than NT$500,000 [approximately US$ 16,500], depending on the seriousness of the matter. If the infringing activity was intentional and serious, the compensation may be increased to NT$1 million [approximately US$ 33,000], with the evident goal of deterrence. In 2003, the pre-established damages were raised to between NT$10,000 and NT$1 million and further to punitive damages of NT$ 5 million [approximately US$ 165,000] for intentional and serious infringement.

Clearly, pre-established damages for copyright infringement serve two purposes: (1) to alleviate the difficult situation of copyright owners not being able to prove the actual losses and (2) to deter and even punish intentional infringers. Pre-established damages are by far the most widely used method of calculating damages for copyright infringement. Between 2008 and 2013, out of the 112 cases in which courts rendered damages to the plaintiffs, 86 (76.8%) were based on pre-established damages.[11]

The Taiwanese Trademark Act started in 1972 to react to the difficulty of rights owners in proving their damages as a result of trademark infringement, and provided in Article 64 the presumed damages, namely the profit earned by the infringer as a result of trademark infringement and the reduction of the profit normally expected through using the trademark by the owner caused by the infringement. In 1985, the year in which the Copyright Act introduced pre-established damages 'no lower than 500 times *the actual retail price* of the infringed work' (emphasis added) as the floor of the presumed damages, the Trademark

[11] Kai-Chun Gao, *Empirical Research on Damage Award by Taiwan IP Court* (2015) (in Chinese) 135.

Act also introduced pre-established damages for trademark infringement in Article 64. This Article provided that:

> Damages demanded by the proprietor of a registered trademark may be calculated according to any of the following: (1) the method provided in Article 216 of the Civil Code; the proprietor is entitled to demand damages based on the amount of the balance derived by subtracting the profit earned through using the trademark after infringement from the profit normally expected through using the same trademark, if no method of proof can be furnished to prove the damage suffered; (2) the profit earned by the infringer as a result of trademark infringement; if no proof on costs or necessary expenses can be furnished by the infringer, the total amount of income from selling the infringing goods shall be presumed to be the amount of profit; (3) the amount not fewer than 500 times and not more than 1,500 times the unit retail price of the infringing goods; if over 1,500 pieces of infringing goods were found, the amount of damages shall be a lump sum of the market value of the infringing goods.

The damages floor of 500 times the unit retail price of the infringing goods has proven to be extremely harsh when high-priced products were involved, and therefore was deleted by the 2012 amendment, which also introduced (iv) to the newly numbered Article 71(1) as the fourth calculation method for damages: 'the equivalent amount of royalty that may be collected from using the trademark under licensing'. Pre-established damages is by far the most widely used method of calculating damages for trademark infringement. Between 2008 and 2013, out of the 60 cases in which courts rendered damages to the plaintiffs, 54 (90.0%) were based on pre-established damages.[12]

In the evolution of the pre-established damages regime for trademark infringement, the Taiwanese Trademark Act has pursued it solely in order to lessen the burden on the trademark owner to prove damages, and not as a deterrent.

The Taiwanese Patent Act follows the general principle for calculating damages, the profit earned by the infringer as a result of patent infringement, and reasonable royalties. It does not recognize pre-established damages, but provides for punitive damages of triple damages (three times the proven loss).[13] The profit earned by the infringer is by far the most widely used method of calculating damages for patent infringement. Between 2008 and 2013, out of the 79 cases in which courts rendered damages to the plaintiffs, 68 (60.8%) were based on the profit earned by the infringer.[14]

b. PRC

In the PRC, the Supreme People's Court introduced pre-established damages in 2000 through judicial interpretation, which has quasi-legislative effect. Article 10 of the *Supreme People's Court Interpretation Concerning Some Issues Concerning*

[12] Ibid 94.
[13] Taiwanese Patent Act 2013, Art 97 (Calculation of Damages).
[14] Gao (n 11) 53.

Applicable Law in Cases Involving Computer Network Copyright Disputes prescribes:

> When determining the amount of compensation for infringement, the people's courts may calculate the amount of compensation on the basis of the request of the infringed copyright holder, according to the economic damage and the lost expected profits suffered directly from the infringing activities, or may calculate the amount of compensation according to the profits received by the infringer due to the infringement. If the infringer cannot prove his costs or necessary expenses, income received due to the infringement will be taken as profit received. If the amount of damage of the infringed copyright holder cannot be determined, the people's courts may, on the basis of the request of the infringed copyright holder, determine an amount of compensation higher than 500 yuan [approximately US$ 72] and lower than 30.000 yuan [approximately US$ 432], according to the circumstances of the infringement, and at most may not exceed 50.000 yuan.

The pre-established damages were later codified into the Copyright Law and Trademark Law in 2001, and into Patent Law in 2008.

Article 49 of the Copyright Law stipulates:

> (1) Anyone who infringes upon the copyright or a right related to the copyright shall pay compensation for the actual losses suffered by the right owner, or where the actual losses are difficult to calculate, pay compensation to the amount of the unlawful gains of the infringer. The compensation shall include the reasonable expenses that the right owner has paid for putting a stop to the infringement.
>
> (2) Where the actual losses of the right owner or the unlawful gains of the infringer cannot be determined, the people's court shall, in light of the circumstances of the infringement, decide on a compensation amount not more than *500,000 RMB yuan.* [Emphasis added.]

Article 63(3) of the Trademark Law provides:

> Where it is difficult to determine the actual losses suffered by the right holder from the infringement, the profits acquired by the infringer from the infringement, or the royalties of the registered trademark, a people's court may award damages of not more than *three million RMB yuan* according to the circumstances of the infringement.

Article 65(2) of Patent Law provides:

> If it is difficult to determine the losses incurred by the patentee, the gains obtained by the infringer as well as the royalty obtained for the patent, the people's court may, by taking into account such factors as the type of patent, nature and particulars of the infringement, decide a compensation in the sum of not less than *10,000 RMB yuan but not more than 1 million RMB yuan.* [Emphasis added.]

In the ongoing fourth amendment of the Patent Law, the latest draft has increased the lower and upper range of pre-established damages by ten times and five times respectively: no less than 100,000 RMB yuan but not more than 5 million RMB yuan.

However, compared with the goal of pre-established damages in CPTPP, namely sufficient compensation with a view to deterring future infringements, the purpose of pre-established damages for IPR infringement in the PRC is solely to alleviate the difficult situation of IPR holders not being able to prove the actual losses or the unlawful gains of the infringer. No deterrence effect has been contemplated. As it turns out, pre-established damages have become the most common way of awarding damages. Statistics show that courts in Beijing have between 2013 and 2015 awarded the pre-established damages to 97.12% of copyright infringement cases, 99.59% of trademark infringement cases and 83.33% of patent infringement cases, and have seldom calculated damages by actual loss, infringer's profits or royalties.[15] Another empirical study shows that courts in Nanjing (from 2009 to 2015) and Changsha intermediate court (from 2010 to 2015) awarded pre-established damages to 97% and 98% of all IPR cases respectively, which is estimated to be the ratio even for the whole of the PRC.[16]

iii. New Adopters of Pre-Established Damages

a. South Korea

The Korea-US FTA (KORUS), concluded on 1 April 2007 and renegotiated and signed in early December 2010, requires the adoption of pre-established damages. Article 18.10.6 of the KORUS prescribes:

> In civil judicial proceedings, each Party shall, at least with respect to works, phonograms, and performances protected by copyright or related rights, and in cases of trademark counterfeiting, establish or maintain pre-established damages, which shall be available on the election of the right holder. Pre-established damages shall be in an amount sufficient to constitute a deterrent to future infringements and to compensate fully the right holder for the harm caused by the infringement.

As a result, Article 125-2 was added into the Copyright Act in 2011. Article 125-2(1) and (3) provide that a holder of author's economic right, etc may claim considerable damages within the scope of up to 10 million won [approximately US$9,235] (50 million won [approximately US$46,175] in cases of intentionally infringing rights for profit) for each work, etc whose right is infringed, in lieu of the actual amount of damages or the amount of damages determined pursuant to Article 125 (profit gained by the infringer shall be presumed to be the amount of damages or normal gain by an exercise of the infringed right by the right holder shall be made the amount of damages) or 126 (when it is difficult to estimate damages under Article 125, the court may acknowledge a considerable amount of damages), against a person who has infringed on rights intentionally or by negligence, provided that the works were registered before such an act of infringement occurred.

[15] Wan Di and Lu Cong, 'Analysing the Effects of and Ways to Improve Damages for Intellectual Property Infringement (I) – Taking Decisions of Beijing Court as a Sample' (in Chinese) (2016) 4 *China Trademark* 56.

[16] Song Jian, 'Discussion on Problems of Intellectual Property Damages – An Empirical Analysis' (in Chinese) (2016) 5 *Intellectual Property* 12–15.

Although the Copyright Act did not specifically mention deterrence, the level of damages for intentional infringement should suffice to deter future infringement. To date, there is no court decision that has applied Article 125-2.

With regards to trademark infringement in Korea, the proprietors of trademark can claim damages according to actual loss, infringer's profit or royalty,[17] and the court may recognize a reasonable amount of damages on the basis of the meaning of all pleadings and the result of the examination of evidence, to sufficiently compensate the proprietor for the harm caused by the infringement.[18] In addition, the proprietors also have options to claim pre-established damages according to Article 111(1) of Trademark Act, which prescribes that a trademark right holder or an exclusive licensee may claim compensation for a reasonable amount to an extent not exceeding KRW 50 million, in lieu of claiming damages under Article 109 against a wilful or negligent infringer.

In a 2016 decision the Korean Supreme Court applied Article 111 restrictively, where the trademark owner filed a trademark application for gene testing service in 2008 and obtained registration in 2010, but did not use the trademark in that business during that period. The trademark owner brought an infringement action, and sought statutory damages according to Article 111 against the defendant, who used similar marks on a gene testing business. The Supreme Court held that the defendant constituted an infringement of the plaintiff's trademark, but because the plaintiff had not been actually using its trademark, the defendant had not caused harm to the plaintiff. The court dismissed the plaintiff's statuary damages claim and ruled that a trademark owner may not file a claim for statutory damages if the owner has not in fact been using the registered trademark. In reaching its decision, the court noted that the statutory damages provision applies only exceptionally, in order to allow a trademark owner to receive a certain amount of compensation, even when the owner is not able to prove the amount of its damages.[19] Following this decision, pre-established damages mainly aim at providing sufficient compensation for loss suffered, but do not have deterrence or punishment in mind.

According to the Korean Patent Act, patentees can claim damages for actual loss, infringer's profit or royalty, but not pre-established damages.[20] When it is difficult to prove the facts necessary for the amount of damages, the court may recognize a reasonable amount of damages on the basis of the meaning of all pleadings and the result of the examination of evidence, to compensate the proprietor sufficiently for the harm caused by the infringement.[21] In practice, most plaintiffs

[17] Korean Trademark Act (amended 2016), Art 110(1) to (5).

[18] Ibid Art 110(6).

[19] Mi-Jeong Oh and Kurt Gerstner, 'Obtaining Statutory Damages for Trademark Infringement – A Cross Border Approach under the Trademark Act of the Republic of Korea' (2017), https://www.ilnipinsider.com/2017/08/obtaining-statutory-damages-for-trademark-infringement-a-cross-border-approach-under-the-trademark-act-of-the-republic-of-korea.

[20] Korean Patent Act (amended in 2017), Art 128(1) to (6).

[21] Ibid Art 128(7).

(54.4%) seek damages based on profits gained by an infringer as a result of the infringement, but most courts of first instance (64.6%) assess damages by applying Article 128(7) to grant a reasonable amount of damages.[22]

b. Japan

In order to implement its obligation under TPP, Article 114(4) was added to the Copyright Act on 9 December 2016, which took effect when the CPTPP came into force on 30 December 2018. Article 114(4) provides that if the holder of copyrights or neighbouring rights that is claiming damages for infringement is a copyright collecting society regulated under the Act for Copyright Management Service, it may assert *the applicable fees* for the use of works in its stipulation of tariffs (royalties) as 'the amount of money' [emphasis added]) provided in Article 114(3) (damages based on reasonable royalties).[23] Japan allows courts discretionary power to decide a reasonable amount of damages since Article 114-5 was introduced in the 2000 amendment. In a case where, from the nature of facts concerned, it is found that it is extremely difficult to prove the facts necessary for proof of the amount of damages, the court may award a reasonable amount of damages based upon the oral proceedings and the results of the taking of evidence. It is not rare that the plaintiff claims for damages based on Article 114-5. A recent decision applying that provision was made by the IP High Court in 2016 (Ne) 10029 (2 November 2016).

Taking the same approach as the Patent Act, Article 38 of the Japanese Trademark Act provides that the damages for trademark infringement can be calculated by multiplying the number or amount of products the infringer sold with a marginal profit the proprietor enjoyed,[24] the infringer's profits earned from the act of infringement,[25] or the amount the proprietor would have been entitled to receive for the trademark use.[26] According to Article 38(3) of the Japanese Trademark Act, Article 105-3 of Patent Act applies mutatis mutandis to trademark infringement. In addition, Article 38(4) was added in response to Article 18.74.6 of the CPTPP:

> Where the holder of trademark right or the exclusive trademark licensee claims against an infringer compensation for damages sustained as a result of the intentional or negligent infringement of the trademark right or the exclusive right to use, and the infringement is caused by the use of the registered trademark (including a trademark deemed identical from a common sense perspective with the registered trademark, including a trademark consisting of characters identical with the registered trademark

[22] Cheol Hwan Kim et al, 'Korean Courts Discuss Significant Changes to Patent Damages' (2017), https://www.lexology.com/library/detail.aspx?g=2c94f66e-ef07-481f-bc1a-8935bceafd49.

[23] Japanese Copyright Act (2016), http://www.bunka.go.jp/seisaku/chosakuken/hokaisei/kantaiheiyo_hokaisei/pdf/r1408266_02.pdf? (in Japanese).

[24] Japanese Trademark Act (amended in 2006), Art 38(1).

[25] Japanese Trademark Act, Art 38(2).

[26] Japanese Trademark Act, Art 38(3).

> but in different fonts, a trademark that is written in different characters, Hiragana characters, Katakana characters, or Latin alphabetic characters, from the registered trademark but identical with the registered trademark in terms of pronunciation and concept, and a trademark consisting of figures that are considered identical in terms of appearance to those of the registered trademark; the same shall apply in Article 50) in connection with the designated goods or designated services, the amount equivalent to *the cost normally required for the acquisition and maintenance of the trademark* right may be deemed to be the amount of damages sustained by the holder of trademark right or the exclusive trademark licensee. [Emphasis added.]

The Japanese Patent Act does not recognize pre-established damages. Article 102 of the Japanese Patent Act stipulates that the damages can be calculated by multiplying the number or amount of products the infringer sold with a marginal profit the patentee enjoyed,[27] infringer's profits earned from the act of infringement,[28] or the amount the patentee would have been entitled to receive for the working of the patent.[29] Article 105-3 of the Japanese Patent Act empowers the court, as the Copyright Act does, to award a reasonable amount of damages based upon all the oral proceedings and the results of the taking of evidence, if it is extremely difficult from the nature of facts concerned, to prove facts necessary for the proof of the amount of damages through mentioned ways.[30]

According to Professor Masabumi Suzuki,

> The Japanese government, particularly the Ministry of Justice, never thought of changing the compensatory principle in the Japanese damages system in response to the TPP/CPTPP. There was a view that such articles as Article 38 (3) (damages based on reasonable royalties) and Article 39 (incorporating Article 105-3 of the Patent Act, which is equivalent to Article 114-5 of the Copyright Act) of the Trademark Act, and Articles 114(3) and 114-5 of the Copyright Act could be regarded as providing 'pre-established damages' as prescribed in Article 18.74.6 of the TPP. In addition, the government thought that damages based on the compensatory principle still could have supplementary effects of deterring future infringement. Moreover, Article 18.5 of the TPP stipulates that '[e]ach Party shall be free to determine the appropriate method of implementing the provisions of this Chapter within its own legal system and practice.' Taking this article into consideration, the Japanese government was fairly confident that it would be able to convince other members of the TPP that the Trademark Act and the Copyright Act were already consistent with Article 18.74.6. However, in order to prevent any doubt about inconsistency (or any argument alleging inconsistency) between the Japanese law and the TPP/CPTPP, the government decided to introduce only non-substantive provisions to strengthen its position as consistent with Article 18.74.6. The results were Articles 38(4) of the Trademark Act and 114(4) and the Copyright Act respectively.[31]

[27] Japanese Patent Act (amended in 2006), Art 102(1).
[28] Japanese Patent Act, Art 102(2).
[29] Japanese Patent Act, Art 102(3).
[30] Japanese Patent Act, Art 105-3.
[31] Professor Masabumi Suzuki's email to the first author on 3 March 2019. Professor Suzuki is a well-respected IP law authority in Japan.

It seems to the authors that the Japanese stance on the CPTPP/TPP rules on pre-established damages is lax and more in compliance with the compensatory principle of the civil law traditional.

C. Common Law Jurisdictions: Singapore

Article 16.9.9 of the US-Singapore FTA signed in 2003 foresees the transplanting of the US system of pre-established damages to Singapore:

> In civil judicial proceedings, each Party shall, at least with respect to works, phonograms and performances protected by copyright or related rights, and in cases of trademark counterfeiting, establish or maintain pre-established damages that shall be available on the election of the right holder. Each Party shall provide that pre-established damages shall be in an amount *sufficiently high to constitute a deterrent to future infringements* and with the intent to compensate the right holder for the harm caused by the infringement. [Emphasis added.]

Subsequently, Singapore made the transplant to its Copyright Act and Trade Mark Act (TMA).[32] Since 2005, Section 119(2) and (3) of the Copyright Act has stipulated:

> (2) Subject to the provisions of this Act, in an action for an infringement of copyright, the types of relief that the court may grant include the following: (a) an injunction (subject to such terms, if any, as the court thinks fit); (b) damages; (c) an account of profits; (d) where the plaintiff has elected for an award of statutory damages in lieu of damages or an account of profits, statutory damages of (i) not more than *$10,000 for each work* or subject-matter in respect of which the copyright has been infringed; but (ii) *not more than $200,000 in the aggregate*, unless the plaintiff proves that his actual loss from such infringement exceeds $200,000. (3) In awarding statutory damages under subsection (2)(d), the court shall have regard to (a) the nature and purpose of the infringing act, including whether the infringing act was of a commercial nature or otherwise; (b) the flagrancy of the infringement; (c) whether the defendant acted in bad faith; (d) any loss that the plaintiff has suffered or is likely to suffer by reason of the infringement; (e) any benefit shown to have accrued to the defendant by reason of the infringement; (f) the conduct of the parties before and during the proceedings; (g) the need to deter other similar infringements; and (h) all other relevant matters. [Emphasis added.]

As of 2015, statutory damages had been considered by courts in only two copyright infringement cases.[33]

Statutory damages were introduced via the 2004 amendments to the TMA and are clearly aimed principally at providing trade mark proprietors with a more effective form of redress because the traditional process of assessing damages in IP infringement cases is too cumbersome and expensive in many cases to provide

[32] Ng-Loy Wee Loon, *Law of Intellectual Property of Singapore* (Sweet & Maxwell, 2nd edn, 2014) 199–200, 428.

[33] Llewelyn (n 1) 83.

a meaningful remedy against counterfeiters and pirates who will rarely, if ever, follow the detailed procedures for the submission and exchange of evidence that that process requires. Section 31(5) TMA provides that statutory damages are only applicable 'where the infringement involves the use of a counterfeit trade mark' and Section 31(6) TMA defines a sign as a 'counterfeit trade mark' if the sign '(a) is identical with or so nearly resembling the registered trade mark as to be calculated to deceive; and (b) is applied to goods and services (i) without the express or implied consent (conditional or otherwise) of the proprietor of the registered trade mark; and (ii) to falsely represent the goods or services to be the genuine goods or actual services of the proprietor or a licensee of the registered trade mark'. The court has the power to grant statutory damages 'not exceeding *$100,000 for each type of goods or service* in relation to which the counterfeit trade mark has been used; and *not exceeding in the aggregate $1 million*, unless the plaintiff proves that his actual loss from such infringement exceeds $1 million' [Emphasis added].[34] When awarding statutory damages, Section 31(6) TMA provides a list of factors that the court shall have regard to, namely, the flagrancy of the infringement of the registered trade mark, any loss that the plaintiff has suffered or is likely to suffer by reason of the infringement, any benefit shown to have accrued to the defendant by reason of the infringement, the need to deter other similar instances of infringement, and all other relevant matters. As of 2015, statutory damages had been considered by courts in only two counterfeit trademark cases.[35]

Pre-established damages are not available for patents and designs in Singapore.

III. Critiques of Pre-established Damages for Copyright Infringement and Trademark Counterfeiting

A. Under TPP/CPTPP

One fundamental challenge to pre-established damages under TPP/CPTPP is whether they are justified/needed. First, there are extremely few jurisdictions which have pre-established damages for copyright infringement and trademark counterfeiting.[36] Therefore, in and of itself, it does not make much sense for the members of the CPTPP, except Canada, which traditionally do not recognize such a regime, to adopt it, as no member is expert on this issue after the driver of the regime, the US, dropped out. At best, Article 18.74.6–8 should have been suspended until the US is back knocking at the door of CPTPP.

[34] Singapore Trademarks Act (2015), Section 31(5)(c).
[35] Llewelyn (n 1) 77.
[36] Samuelson, Hill and Wheatland (n 4).

Second, how do we define 'sufficient compensation'? The very reason why pre-established damages were put in place is that actual damages are hard to quantify. Given this, without knowing the suffered damages, how can one be sure that any compensation is sufficient or not? This is a tautology in reality.

Third, although TPP/CPTPP uses 'with a view *to deterring future infringements*', which might sound less strong than 'sufficient to constitute a deterrent' used by the RCEP and the US-Korea and US-Singapore FTA, there is still the issue of how to define deterrence. Is it to prevent a specific individual from again committing the same infringement, or to prevent the society as a whole from committing the same infringement? The former is easier to determine, as it is dependent on the one specific repeated offender, whereas the latter is in principle too abstract to ascertain.

Fourthly, in considering strategies for deterrence, one should look not only to civil remedies available, but also other remedies as a whole, especially criminal penalties. One of the features of Asian copyright laws is that many Asian jurisdictions are plagued by criminal sanctions. For example, in Taiwan, copyright infringement, whether for profit or not, can lead to up to three years of imprisonment, whereas manslaughter will result in only two years of imprisonment, and on average criminal cases against copyright infringement exceed civil cases by 300 per cent. Japan follows similar thinking and imposes even heavier punishment for copyright infringement: imprisonment for a term of up to 10 years, a fine of up to 10 million yen, or both.[37] Criminal punishment is rampant in Singapore, Malaysia, Korea and Japan. Substantial pre-established damages bundled with criminal punishment for copyright infringement and trademark counterfeiting can give rise to abuse and even troll activities. One recent incident happened in 2015, when Dallas Buyers Club LLC, which owns copyright on the movie of that title, issued warning letters to a large numbers of downloaders in Singapore and Australia, and asked the 'recipient to make a written offer within three days, failing of which proceedings may be commenced' ('speculative invoicing' as this practice is called). This led to public outcry, intervention by the Intellectual Property Office of Singapore (IPOS), and Attorney General's Chambers (AGC)[38] and raises policy questions about misuse.[39]

Last but not least, there are other proven ways of dealing with the issue of IPR holders' difficulty in showing the actual loss as a consequence of infringement, such as the imposition of duty on the accused infringer to provide relevant materials, or the recognition of the IPR holders' substantial right in requesting that the

[37] Kung-Chung Liu, 'Chapter 1 Introduction: Some Features of Copyright Laws and Cases in Major Asian Jurisdictions' in Kung-Chung Liu (ed), *Annotated Leading Copyright Cases in Major Asian Jurisdictions* (City University of Hong Kong Press, 2019).

[38] CNA, 'IPOS, AGC Applying To Intervene In Illegal Movie Download' (*Channel NewsAsia*, 20 September 2016), https://www.channelnewsasia.com/news/singapore/ipos-agc-applying-to-intervene-in-illegal-movie-downloads-case-7800838.

[39] Llewelyn (n 1) 63.

alleged infringer and even third parties provide materials in their possession,[40] and to structure the IPR infringement lawsuits into two phases:[41] the first stage is to determine whether indeed there has been copyright infringement or trademark counterfeiting; the second stage, after an infringement has been confirmed, is to determine the damages. Under the circumstances of a clear court decision, the parties will more likely reach consensus among themselves about the amount of damages and settle without the intervention of courts, which can avoid the actual amount of damages being disclosed.

B. Under RCEP

RCEP's regime on pre-established damages for copyright infringement and trademark counterfeiting is even more questionable, as James Love, Director of Knowledge Ecology International has pointed out: 'Some of the issues that negotiators did not understand in the TPP, such as the damages provisions, are also lurking in this text, creating risks that negotiators will do worse than they think.' RCEP even emphasizes deterrence over full compensation, clearly deviating from the original purpose of pre-established damages, namely to relieve the infringed IPR owners' burden of proving actual damages. Such emphasis will dramatically increase the risk of abuse and opportunism that has been described in section III.A.[42]

IV. Suggestions for TPP/CPTPP and RCEP

Given that Japan is now the leader of CPTPP and its pre-established damages regime for copyright infringement and trademark counterfeiting is lax and allows needed flexibility, it is suggested that CPTPP and its members should take Japan as a benchmark and not apply a high standard on 'sufficient compensation' and 'with a view to deterring future infringements'. In addition, the Singapore High Court decision could offer useful tip against the abuse of the regime. It held that

[40] Georg Benkard, Patentgesetz, 10 Aufl, 2006,§140b Rdnr 1.

[41] This has been the standard and common practice in the common law jurisdictions. German practice also follows this approach: In a patent litigation the court, if it finds infringement, first will pronounce that the defendant is liable for damages 'in principle', and request therefore the defendant to give details of the infringing actions etc. Only after these information (net turnover achieved with infringing goods, profit achieved, names of customers, names of suppliers, etc) have been given to the court, the patentee can request a specific amount of damages. Normally, the parties settle by then. Otherwise a separate, new damages complaint has to be filed by the plaintiff, in order to have the damages determined by court. The latter seldom happens. In fact, there is no special legal foundation for this practice in the Civil Procedure Law, which was developed by patent infringement chambers.

[42] Kimberlee Weatherall, 'Safeguards for Defendant Rights and Interests in International Intellectual Property Enforcement Treaties' (2016) 32 *American University International Law Review* 220–21.

the rationale of pre-established damages is 'to allow the proprietor of a trade mark or copyright owner to recover compensation in cases where actual losses arising from the infringement may be difficult to prove or an account of profits equally difficult to obtain' and 'the remedy of statutory damages is an alternative option to the traditional reliefs of damages or an account of profits, and is intended to enable trade mark and copyright owners to obtain compensation notwithstanding evidential difficulties'.[43] The court further held that:[44]

(a) Even though the successful claimant 'is relieved of his burden to prove his loss on a balance of probabilities as he would have had to do in the usual case', he 'will still have to adduce relevant evidence so as to establish an evidential foundation upon which the [court] can then assess the stipulated guiding factors in order to arrive at the quantum'.
(b) The court has a wide discretion hereunder and even though the quantum awarded 'cannot be arrived at with mathematical precision or exactitude', it 'will reflect the amount which the [court] feels is appropriate and proportional to compensate proprietor of the trade mark having regard to the stipulated guiding factors and the overall circumstances of the case'.

Furthermore, the insensitive application of pre-established damages can have abusive effects, as indicated by the Dallas Buyer's Club incident. Therefore, some procedural safeguards to check the copyright/trademark holder's exercise of rights should be put in place. In this regard, measures undertaken by the Australian Federal Court in the *Dallas Buyer's Club LLC v. iiNet Ltd* case, could offer good lessons for TPP/CPTPP, namely that courts should be allowed to ask the copyright/trademark holder to produce the draft of their proposed communications (warning letters) with alleged infringers and seek the court's approval before sending them to the alleged infringers.[45]

With regards to RCEP, it is suggested that it should refrain from adopting its current leaked text and at most follow TPP/CPTPP.

[43] *Louis Vuitton Malletier v Cuffz (Singapore) Pte Ltd* [2015] SGHCR 15 at [16].
[44] Ibid [17].
[45] Weatherall (n 44) 222–23.

13

Liberalizing Use of the Three-Step Test and Copyright Limitations in the Public Interest

HAOCHEN SUN*

I. Introduction

The resurgence of unilateralism worldwide has not brought negotiations for new trade agreements to a halt. For example, the withdrawal of the United States (US) from the Trans-Pacific Partnership (TPP) did not result in the death of that trade agreement as many experts had predicted and lamented. Rather, the TPP was later resurrected, with the 11 other participating countries deciding to go ahead even without US participation.[1] The Comprehensive and Progressive Agreement for Trans-Pacific Partnership (CPTPP) entered in force on 30 December 2018.[2]

Another mega trade agreement, the Regional Comprehensive Economic Partnership (RCEP), is also on the negotiation table. Launched in November 2012, the RCEP's aim is to conclude a comprehensive agreement that promotes free trade and investment among Australia, China, India, Japan, New Zealand, South Korea,

* Haochen Sun, Associate Professor of Law and Director of Law & Technology Center, University of Hong Kong Faculty of Law. This chapter draws on two previous publications: 'Statement of Public Interest Principles for Copyright Protection under the Regional Comprehensive Economic Partnership (RCEP)' (2017) 48 *International Review of Intellectual Property and Competition Law* 334 and 'Overcoming the Achilles Heel of Copyright Law' (2007) 5 *Northwestern Journal of Technology and Intellectual Property* 265. I am very grateful to the 76 scholars who have endorsed the Statement of Public Interest Principles for Copyright Protection under the RCEP.

[1] See A Chander and M Sunder, 'The Battle to Define Asia's Intellectual Property Law: From TPP to RCEP' (2018) 8 *UC Irvine Law Review* 331, 332 ('[w]hen the United States pulled out, the remaining nations suspended a number of its provisions, especially those involving intellectual property, and proceeded with a treaty now dubbed the Comprehensive Progressive Trans-Pacific Partnership (CPTPP)'); Patrick Gillespie, '11 countries sign TPP trade pact without the United States' (2018), https://money.cnn.com/2018/03/08/news/economy/tpp-trump-tariffs/index.html, accessed 15 April 2019; Ernesto Londoño and Motoko Rich, 'U.S. Allies Sign Sweeping Trade Deal in Challenge to Trump' (2018), https://www.nytimes.com/2018/03/08/world/asia/us-trump-tpp-signed.html, accessed 15 April 2019.

[2] Canada.ca, 'What is the CPTPP?' (2019), https://international.gc.ca/trade-commerce/trade-agreements-accords-commerciaux/agr-acc/cptpp-ptpgp/index.aspx?lang=eng accessed 15 April 2019.

and the member states of the Association of Southeast Asian Nations (ASEAN).[3] The 16 countries participating in the RCEP negotiations account for nearly 50 per cent of the world's population and 30 per cent of global GDP.[4] If successfully concluded, it will result in the world's largest mega-regional free trade agreement (FTA) to date.[5] The latest draft text of the RCEP's intellectual property (IP) Chapter, dated 15 October 2015, was leaked to the public via the Internet by Knowledge Ecology International.[6] As it stands, the Chapter provides out a comprehensive set of minimum standards for IP protection in the participating countries.[7]

As in previous negotiations on international IP protection standards, the draft of the RCEP's IP Chapter has given rise to a plethora of concerns over unintended effects such as the stifling of creativity, innovation and economic growth.[8] In this chapter, I argue that trade agreement negotiators should take limitations on copyright seriously by crafting them in the public interest. First, I caution against the direct inclusion of the so-called 'three-step test'[9] in future trade agreements, including the RCEP. Second, I propose that the test be altered in a liberal manner to allow it to be interpreted and applied in the public interest under future trade agreements. Last, I suggest that both professionalism and transparency are needed to guide the negotiating process of such agreements.

II. Overreach of the Three-Step Test

A. Critical Importance of Limitations on Copyright

Copyright law at the national, regional and international levels serves not only the private interest of copyright holders but also the public interest of society at large. For example, the Preamble of the World Intellectual Property Organization (WIPO) Copyright Treaty (WCT)[10] stresses 'the need to maintain a balance between the rights of authors and the larger public interest, particularly education,

[3] Association of South East Asian Nations, 'Regional Comprehensive Economic Partnership (RCEP)' (2016), http://asean.org/?static_post=rcep-regional-comprehensive-economic-partnership, accessed 15 April 2019.

[4] Ibid.

[5] See ibid.

[6] Knowledge Ecology International, 'Oct 15, 2015 version: RCEP IP Chapter' ('Draft RCEP IP Chapter') (2016), https://www.keionline.org/23060, accessed 15 April 2019.

[7] Draft RCEP IP Chapter, Art 1.3.

[8] See eg Asian Trade Centre, 'Fostering Innovation and Growth in Asia: IP, Copyright and Digital Trade' (2016), https://static1.squarespace.com/static/5393d501e4b0643446abd228/t/5752a6c2c2ea515ccf6d8f76/1465034436088/RCEP+IP+Working+Paper.pdf, accessed 15 April 2019; Malcolm Jeremy, 'Meet RCEP, a Trade Agreement in Asia That's Even Worse Than TPP or ACTA' (2015), https://www.eff.org/deeplinks/2015/06/just-when-you-thought-no-trade-agreement-could-be-worse-tpp-meet-rcep, accessed 15 April 2019.

[9] With respect to the nature and scope of the three-step test, see text accompanying nn 50–69.

[10] World Intellectual Property Organization Copyright Treaty, Dec 20, 1996, 36 ILM 65 (1997).

research and access to information'.[11] On the one hand, copyright law protects a range of exclusive rights over original works, rewarding rights owners both economically and morally for their creation and dissemination of such works. On the other hand, it carves out a variety of limitations on copyright, enabling the public to use copyrighted work for a multitude of purposes without the authorization of the rights owners.

To protect the public interest,[12] limitations on exclusive rights – such as fair use and compulsory licensing – are a necessary mechanism in copyright law. Such limitations are, by their nature, designed to ensure that users have access to copyrighted materials so that they can exercise their rights to freedom of expression, education and cultural participation. From this perspective, copyright law also protects users' rights.[13]

Take fair use as an example. It allows members of the public to use copyrighted work without obtaining authorization from, or paying remuneration to, the copyright owner. Fair use is of vital importance in a free and just society.[14] It encourages a wide range of freedom-promoting activities that involve the use of copyrighted materials, including news reporting, criticism, teaching and research.[15] As a result, fair use has been hailed not only as the 'engine of free expression'[16] but also as the engine of public interest protection.[17] Moreover, it also drives innovation in the form of new technologies designed to provide copyright owners with new ways to reach their audiences.[18]

[11] Ibid Preamble.

[12] See eg P Samuelson, 'Justifications for Copyright Limitations and Exceptions' in RL Okediji (eds), *Copyright Law in an Age of Limitations and Exceptions* (Cambridge, Cambridge University Press, 2017) 25 (arguing that protecting the public interest is one of the justifications for copyright limitations); RL Okediji, 'Reframing International Copyright Limitations and Exceptions as Development Policy', in *Copyright Law in an Age of Limitations and Exceptions* (Cambridge, Cambridge University Press, 2017) 440 (pointing out that '"public interest" tends to be identified with [copyright limitations] such as compulsory licenses or freedom of ideas and facts from a copyright owner's control').

[13] See eg H Sun, 'Fair Use as a Collective User Right' (2011) 90 *North Carolina Law Review* 125 (arguing that fair use should be redefined as a collective user right).

[14] See B Beebe, 'Does Judicial Ideology Affect Copyright Fair Use Outcomes?: Evidence From the Fair Use Case Law' (2008) 31 *Columbia Journal of Law & the Arts* 517, 522 (pointing out that the fair use doctrine defines 'the contours of the private and public domains of human expression and, in doing so, directly impact[s] our capability for human flourishing'); WW Fisher III, 'Reconstructing the Fair Use Doctrine' (1988) 101 *Harvard Law Review* 1661, 1661 (arguing that the fair use doctrine 'would contribute to the realization of a more just social order'); P Samuelson, 'Unbundling Fair Uses' (2009) 77 *Fordham Law Review* 2537, 2540 (arguing that the fair use doctrine protects 'the interests of the public in having access to new works and making reasonable uses of them').

[15] See 17 USC § 107 (2006).

[16] *Harper & Row, Publishers, Inc v Nation Enters*, 471 US 539, 558 (1985).

[17] See H Sun, 'Copyright Law as the Engine of Public Interest Protection' (2019) 16 *Northwestern Journal of Technology and Intellectual Property* 123.

[18] See DL Burk and JE Cohen, 'Fair Use Infrastructure for Rights Management Systems' (2001) 15 *Harvard Journal of Law and Technology* 41, 46 (pointing out that 'fair use adapts copyright to new technologies that pose challenges for the traditional copyright framework'); F von Lohmann, 'Fair Use as Innovation Policy' (2008) 23 *Berkeley Technology Law Journal* 829, 864 (concluding that 'the fair use doctrine may well be playing an increasingly critical role in U.S. innovation policy').

B. Vast Expansion of the Three-Step Test

There are, however, limits on copyright limitations. Although such limitations are of critical importance in protecting the public interest, their enforcement is not supposed to cause substantial harm to the interests of copyright owners. The major international copyright treaties, including the Berne Convention for the Protection of Literary and Artistic Works,[19] Agreement on Trade-Related Aspects of Intellectual Property Rights (TRIPS Agreement),[20] and the WCT have sequentially adopted the three-step test as a yardstick for measuring the validity of limitations on copyright.

By its very nature, the three-step test constrains countries from exercising legislative discretion to carve out limitations on copyright under domestic laws. For example, Article 13 of the TRIPS Agreement mandates that member states must 'confine limitations or exceptions to exclusive rights to certain special cases which do not conflict with a normal exploitation of the work and do not unreasonably prejudice the legitimate interests of the right holder'.[21]

Expansion of the three-step test at the international level has triggered the test's rapid incorporation into regional and bilateral treaties and national laws aimed at strengthening copyright protection.[22]

C. NAFTA

The North American Free Trade Agreement (NAFTA)[23] built the first systematic framework for IP protection under a regional trade agreement. On the one hand, NAFTA's inception gave momentum to the final conclusion of the TRIPS Agreement. On the other, as NAFTA provides broader IP protection than the TRIPS Agreement, it laid the foundation for the incorporation of TRIPS-plus standards in subsequent FTAs.

The three-step test is incorporated into NAFTA's copyright provisions.[24] Because NAFTA is a trade agreement, its inclusion of the three-step test produces the same results as the TRIPS Agreement. However, the scope of the exclusive rights provided for in NAFTA is broader than that of the rights in the

[19] Berne Convention for the Protection of Literary and Artistic Works, 9 September 1886, 828 UNTS 221 (last revised July 24, 1971) (the 'Berne Convention').

[20] Agreement on Trade-Related Agreements of Intellectual Property Rights, Art 13, 15 April 1994, Marrakesh Agreement Establishing the World Trade Organization, Annex 1C, 33 ILM 1197 (1994) (the 'TRIPS Agreement').

[21] TRIPS Agreement, Art 13.

[22] Okediji (n 12) 444 ('Today, building on the foundations established in the TRIPS Agreement, a slew of international economic agreements have fortified constraints on national copyright policy making, especially in the area of L&Es, by including the three-step test obligation.').

[23] North American Free Trade Agreement, United States-Canada-Mexico, Dec 17, 1992, 32 ILM 289 (1993) (NAFTA). NAFTA is scheduled to be replaced by United States-Mexico-Canada Agreement (USMCA) when the latter comes into effect.

[24] See ibid Arts 1705.5 and 1706.3.

TRIPS Agreement. Under NAFTA, therefore, the three-step test governs the imposition of limitations on exclusive rights that are not prescribed in the TRIPS Agreement, such as the right of importation.[25]

D. European Union

In 2001, the EU adopted the Directive on the Harmonisation of Certain Aspects of Copyright and Related Rights in the Information Society[26] with the aim of enhancing copyright harmonization within the EU and encouraging EU Member States to implement the WCT and the WIPO Performances and Phonograms Treaty (WPPT).[27] One striking feature of the Directive is its enumeration of the copyright limitations that may be carved out in each EU member's domestic copyright law. First, the Directive itemises an exhaustive list of specific limitations on copyright.[28] Second, it expressly prescribes that the three-step test should govern the imposition of those limitations under the domestic law of Member States.[29] Third, it channels the three-step test into the Directive on Rental and Lending Rights.[30]

The inclusion of the three-step test in the EU's Copyright Directive represents a considerable leap forward in strengthening the power of that test.[31] Unlike NAFTA, the Directive taps into the test's potential to constrain national legislative power to curtail digital copyright.[32] More importantly, it encourages the domestic courts of EU Member States to directly invoke the three-step test when dealing with any disputes associated with copyright limitations.[33] To date, the courts in both the Netherlands[34] and France[35] have directly applied the test.

[25] Under NAFTA, right holders have the right to authorize or prohibit 'the importation into the Party's territory of copies of the work made without the right holder's authorization'. NAFTA (n 23) Art 1705.2(a). This right, however, is not provided for in the TRIPS Agreement. See TRIPS Agreement, Art 6.

[26] See Directive 2001/29, Recital 44, [2001] OJ L 167/10, 13 (EU) (of the European Parliament and of the Council of 22 May 2001 on the Harmonisation of Certain Aspects of Copyright and Related Rights in the Information Society).

[27] Ibid preamble paras 1–15.

[28] Ibid Arts 5.1–5.4.

[29] See ibid Art 5.5.

[30] See ibid Art 11.1(b).

[31] See JH Reichman, 'The Limits of "Limitations and Exceptions" in Copyright Law' in RL Okediji (eds), *Copyright Law in an Age of Limitations and Expectations* (Cambridge, Cambridge University Press, 2018) 295 ('Technically, the dominant rule in Europe had become the three-step test, with its "exceptions should be narrowly construed" judicial mantra, and its built-in triple "yes" requirement that shrank the space in which positivist courts could apply any codified limitation or exception that might otherwise survive.').

[32] See J Oliver, 'Copyright in the WTO: The Panel Decision on the Three-Step Test' (2002) 25 *Columbia Journal of Law & the Arts* 119, 138 ('there is evidence that intention of the EC Directive is to further restrict existing exceptions, both at the level of EC law and the law of member states').

[33] Ibid 139 ('The wording in [the Directive's three-step test] is different and appears to refer to the application of the exceptions to an actual case, presumably by a domestic court.').

[34] De Nederlandse Dagbladpers/Netherlands, Court of the Hague, 2 March 2005, Case No 192880 (Neth), para 15 (holding that copyright limitation carved out in Dutch copyright law should be in line with the three-step test).

[35] Cass 1e civ, Feb 28, 2006, Bull civ I, No 824. For a comment on the decision as it stood before the Court de cassation quashed the motion, see C Geiger, 'The Private Copy Exception, an Area of

E. FTAs

The past couple of years have seen a proliferation of FTAs that enhance IP protection at the regional or bilateral level. Generally speaking, the US has played a leading role in capitalizing on FTAs to ratchet up copyright protection and enforcement standards. At the same time, however, the US has had to confront intense pressure from the international campaign against more stringent IP standards led by developing countries and NGOs.[36] As an alternative to the multilateral approach to copyright protection, the bilateral approach provides an efficient vehicle by which the US can exert maximum leverage to create more stringent IP standards than those set forth in the TRIPS Agreement and WIPO treaties.

The US has adopted such a bilateral strategy before.[37] However, it was not until it had concluded a proliferation of FTAs, with trading partners such as Singapore, Chile, Australia, Morocco and a number of Central American countries, that far-reaching and stringent standards of IP protection and enforcement were formally created.

Not surprisingly, the three-step test has found its way into those FTAs, all of which are designed solely for the protection of digital copyright. By tapping into the convergence of authors' rights and related rights and the simplified entitlements vested in rights holders, these recently concluded FTAs have simplified the legal framework for copyright protection to a significant degree. Drawing upon the WCT and WPPT, the copyright provisions set out in the agreements deal primarily with the cluster of exclusive rights that are core to the protection of copyright in the digital environment, including the rights of reproduction,[38] communication to the public,[39] and distribution.[40] Therefore, the three-step test governs the scope of the limitations on the rights enjoyed by authors, performers and phonogram producers. More importantly, these FTAs put forward WCT and WPPT-plus standards. For example, they mandate that temporary copies must be protected by the reproduction right under copyright laws of FTA member states.[41]

Freedom (Temporarily) Preserved in the Digital Environment' (2006) 37 *International Review of Intellectual Property and Competition Law* 74.

[36] This backlash can be epitomized by the campaign that sought to provide an increased access to patented drugs for the least-developed countries. See generally LR Helfer, 'Regime Shifting: The TRIPs Agreement and New Dynamics of International Intellectual Property Lawmaking' (2004) 29 *Yale Journal of International Law* 42, 45 (providing an overview of the major international events that contributed to the adoption of the Declaration on the TRIPs Agreement and Public Health).

[37] The US and Jordan entered into an FTA in 2000. This FTA, however, does not establish the basic framework for digital copyright protection as comprehensively as those contained in its progenies concluded in 2003 and 2004 respectively.

[38] See eg Free Trade Agreement, United States-Singapore, Art 16.4.1, May 6, 2003, available at https://ustr.gov/sites/default/files/uploads/agreements/fta/singapore/asset_upload_file708_4036.pdf.

[39] Ibid Art 16.4.2.

[40] Ibid Art 16.4.3.

[41] Ibid Art 16.4.1.

F. China

China's recently overhauled copyright law marks the first time that the three-step test has been embedded into domestic copyright laws. The Regulations for the Implementation of the Copyright Law (Copyright Regulations)[42] introduce a quasi-three-step test aimed at providing guidance to the courts when they consider the legality of the use of the limitations permitted by the Chinese Copyright Law.[43] Pursuant to Article 21 of the Copyright Regulations, the use of published work on the grounds of fair dealing exemptions or compulsory licences should neither 'conflict with the normal exploitation of the work' nor 'unreasonably prejudice the legitimate interests of the author'.[44] In light of the Chinese Copyright Law's embrace of a closed list of fair use exemptions and delineation of the specific circumstances in which the public can make use of copyrighted work,[45] copyright limitations are generally formulated in a manner compatible with the first condition of the three-step test, namely, 'in certain special cases'.[46]

G. Summary

As can be seen from the trajectory of the three-step test's expansion, the test has become a legal standard in international, regional and some national copyright laws. What the past few decades have witnessed is the transformation of the three-step test from a rule applied in the narrow sphere of the reproduction right, into a core standard governing the manner in which limitations on various categories of copyright can be carved out. Today, the test is widely used internationally to weigh the legality of all limitations on copyright.

III. New Approach to Crafting Limitations on Copyright Under Trade Agreements

The three-step test is poised to be further incorporated into new trade agreements. For example, the CPTPP has adopted the three-step test.[47] Furthermore, according

[42] Regulations for the Implementation of the Copyright Law of the People's Republic of China (as amended up to the Decision of January 30, 2013, of the State Council on Amending the Regulations for the Implementation of the Copyright Law of the People's Republic of China), available at http://www.wipo.int/wipolex/en/details.jsp?id=13428 (the 'Chinese Copyright Regulations').

[43] Copyright Law of the People's Republic of China (as amended up to the Decision of February 26, 2010, by the Standing Committee of the National People's Congress on Amending the Copyright Law of the People's Republic of China), available at http://www.wipo.int/wipolex/en/details.jsp?id=6062.

[44] Chinese Copyright Regulations, Art 21.

[45] See Sun (n 17) (discussing how the Chinese Copyright Law prescribes a closed list of fair use exemptions).

[46] See eg TRIPS Agreement, Art 13.

[47] Article 18.65.1, Consolidated TPP Text – Chapter 18 – Intellectual Property, https://international.gc.ca/trade-commerce/trade-agreements-accords-commerciaux/agr-acc/tpp-ptp/text-texte/18.

to the aforementioned leaked version of the RCEP's IP Chapter, participating countries have agreed to adopt the three-step test in defining the permissible scope of limitations on copyright.[48]

In this section, I propose an alternative approach to guiding application of the three-step test. This proposed alternative offers a constructive means of incorporating the test into future trade agreements with public interest considerations. It also provides a way for trade negotiators to craft provisions that protect the public interest primarily by carving out limitations on copyright. The proposal is that trade negotiators should adopt the following hybrid approach in crafting such limitations:

- **Liberal application of the three-step test**: New rounds of trade negotiations should make every effort to address concerns that the three-step test potentially rules out flexible, open-ended limitations and exceptions. It should be made clear that nothing in the test should prevent the introduction or retention of limitations and exceptions for such legitimate purposes as criticism, commentary, education, news reporting, parody, research and facilitating access for persons with disability.
- **Express recognition of certain limitations**: New rounds of trade negotiations should also acknowledge crucial limitations, including temporary reproduction, text and data mining, and regional exhaustion of copyright.

A. Liberal Application of the Three-Step Test

i. Problems with the Three-Step Test

A number of copyright scholars and policymakers have raised serious concerns over the three-step test, which, owing to its vague and potentially inflexible nature, may have disrupted the balanced protection of copyright by prioritizing the interests of copyright owners.[49] In particular, concerns have been expressed over the test's potential to rule out limitations and exceptions that have been carved out in open-ended and flexible fashion.[50]

aspx?lang=eng ('With respect to this Section, each Party shall confine limitations or exceptions to exclusive rights to certain special cases that do not conflict with a normal exploitation of the work, performance or phonogram, and do not unreasonably prejudice the legitimate interests of the right holder.').

[48] See Draft RCEP IP Chapter (n 6) Art 2.5.

[49] See eg C Geiger et al, 'Declaration: A Balanced Interpretation of the "Three-Step Test" in Copyright Law' (2008) 39 *International Review of Intellectual Property and Competition Law* 707, 708 ('The WTO Panel's interpretation of the test … was self-avowedly economic in focus and appears to leave limited scope for states to balance the interests of rightholders with countervailing interests of fundamental importance. Domestic courts have sometimes misunderstood the requirements of the test and, as a result, have applied it in a profoundly unbalanced manner.').

[50] See H Sun, 'Overcoming the Achilles Heel of Copyright Law' (2007) 5 *Northwestern Journal of Technology and Intellectual Property* 265, 283 ('The condition that requires copyright limitations be

In my view, the core problem with the three-step test lies largely in the inability of its 'authoritative interpretation'[51] to evaluate the legality of limitations in light of the public interest. For example, an authoritative interpretation rendered by the World Trade Organization (WTO) in 2000 failed to scrutinise public interest considerations, as discussed below.

The WTO Panel Report on Section 110(5) of the US Copyright Act[52] marked the international adjudicative body's first interpretation of the three-step test.[53] Its interpretation has shed new light on how the first two parts of the test should be applied. The first part mandates that limitations on copyright be 'confined to certain special cases'.[54] According to the Panel Report, this condition implicates two major requirements. First, the limitations on copyright afforded by national legislation should be 'clearly defined',[55] a requirement that 'guarantees a sufficient degree of legal certainty'.[56] Nonetheless, it is not necessary for national legislation to 'identify explicitly each and every possible situation to which the exception could apply, provided that the scope of the exception is known and particularized'.[57] Second, a limitation on copyright should also be 'narrow in its scope and reach',[58] which means that the limitation 'must be limited in its field of application or exceptional in its scope'.[59] Put differently, to guarantee a sufficient degree of legal certainty, a limitation should be maintained in both a quantitatively and qualitatively narrow manner.[60]

However, examination of the public policies underlying a particular limitation is not a necessary part of the inquiry into whether the first condition of the three-step test is met.[61] A finding that the two aforementioned requirements have been met suffices to demonstrate a given limitation's compliance with the first prong of the three-step test even if no public policy underlying the limitation in question can be discerned.[62] However, the avowed public policy purpose embodied in the

"clearly defined" and "narrow in scope and reach" calls into question whether the first prong of the three-step test will strike down copyright limitations that are by nature flexible and open-ended.').

[51] J Hughes, 'Fair Use and Its Politics – at Home and Abroad' in RL Okediji (eds), *Copyright Law in an Age of Limitations and Expectations* (Cambridge, Cambridge University Press, 2017) 245.

[52] See Panel Report, United States – Section 110(5) of the U.S. Copyright Act, WT/DS160/R (June 15, 2000) (the 'Panel Report') (in this dispute, the EU claimed that §110(5)(A)–(B) of the US Copyright Act violated, *inter alia*, Art 13 of the TRIPS Agreement, namely the three-step test).

[53] See J Ginsburg, 'Toward Supranational Copyright Law? The WTO Panel Decision and the Three Step Test for Copyright Exceptions' (2001) 187 *Revue Internationale Du Droit D'auteur* 3, 5.

[54] See eg TRIPS Agreement, Art 13.

[55] Panel Report (n 52) paras 6.108 and 6.112.

[56] Ibid para 6.108.

[57] Ibid.

[58] Ibid paras 6.109 and 6.112.

[59] Ibid para 6.109.

[60] Ibid para 6.109 ('In other words, an exception or limitation should be narrow in a quantitative as well as a qualitative sense.').

[61] Ibid para 6.112 ('The wording of Article 13's first condition does not imply passing a judgment on the legitimacy of the exceptions in dispute.').

[62] Ibid (pointing out that 'a limitation or exception may be compatible with the first condition even if it pursues a special purpose whose underlying legitimacy in a normative sense cannot be discerned').

limitation 'may be useful from a factual perspective for making inferences about the scope of a limitation or exception or the clarity of its definition'.[63] This means that public policy scrutiny is of 'subsidiary relevance' to the question of whether the first condition of the three-step test has been met.

Pursuant to the second condition of the three-step test, a limitation on copyright should not 'conflict with a normal exploitation of the work'.[64] The Panel Report first held that 'normal exploitation' involves 'less than full use of an exclusive right' by the copyright owner.[65] Moreover, normal exploitation 'should be judged for each exclusive right individually'.[66] The non-absolute nature of copyright and the severability of the exercise of rights are therefore seen as a premise for scrutinizing whether the second condition of the three-step test has been met. However, the Panel Report then concluded that a conflict would arise with the normal exploitation of a copyrighted work if a privileged user entered into 'economic competition' with its copyright owner. Such economic competition could prevent the copyright owner from 'normally extract[ing] economic value' from the work, thereby depriving him or her of 'significant or tangible commercial gains'.[67]

The WTO's Panel Report centres on the protection of rights holders' economic interests, paying no heed to users' interests. Therefore, public policy analysis simply plays no role in querying compliance with the second prong of the three-step test. According to the Report, that prong is violated if any given limitation on copyright causes the right holder to suffer 'significant or tangible' commercial losses in either the current or potential market. Because the term 'tangible'[68] is used, the threshold for violation is relatively low. As long as a 'noticeable effect'[69] on market substitution can be detected, the limitation can be taken as invalidated by the second prong. In other words, only a limitation that causes a *de minimis* economic loss to the copyright holder can survive the test's second prong.

ii. Liberal Interpretation and Application of the Test

The first aim of my proposed approach is to address concerns over the three-step test's potential to weed out certain public-interest-oriented limitations on copyright. Future rounds of trade negotiations should endeavour to make room for the test's interpretation and application in accordance with the public interest. To that end, negotiators should consider proposals designed to afford member states adequate discretion to carve out limitations for public interest purposes.

[63] Ibid.

[64] See eg TRIPS Agreement, Art 13.

[65] Panel Report (n 52) para 6.167.

[66] Ibid para 6.173.

[67] Ibid para 6.183.

[68] According to the Longman Dictionary of Contemporary English, one of the meanings of 'tangible' is 'clear enough or definite enough to be easily seen or noticed'.

[69] See *Sony Computer Entm't Am, Inc v Bleem*, LLC, 214 F 3d 1022, 1029 (9th Cir 2000). (The court infers that the defendant's allegedly infringing acts 'have no noticeable effect on' the plaintiff's ability to market their products.)

Hence, I suggest that future trade agreements include the following provision, or an equivalent, as a supplement to adoption of the three-step test:

> The Parties agree that the three-step test shall be interpreted and applied in a manner consistent with the objectives and principles of the intellectual property chapter of this agreement. Nothing in the three-step test shall exclude legitimate purposes such as criticism, commentary, education, news reporting, parody, research and facilitating access for persons with disability.

This proposed wording would subject the three-step test to a public interest inquiry. First, it would require the test's power to gauge the legality of copyright limitations to be exercised to further the objectives and principles of IP protection. Article 7 of the TRIPS Agreement states the public interest objectives of IP protection as follows:

> The protection and enforcement of intellectual property rights should contribute to the promotion of technological innovation and to the transfer and dissemination of technology, to the mutual advantage of producers and users of technological knowledge and in a manner conducive to social and economic welfare, and to a balance of rights and obligations.[70]

Moreover, Article 8 of the TRIPS Agreements adopts the public interest principle by stipulating that IP protection should 'promote the public interest in sectors of vital importance to [countries'] socio-economic and technological development'.[71] According to the draft RCEP, participating states are willing to adopt similar objectives and principles to those stated in Articles 7 and 8, as indicated at the outset of the RCEP's IP Chapter.[72] It thus clearly makes sense to those states that public-interest-oriented limitations on copyright, including criticism, commentary, education, news reporting, parody, research and facilitating access for persons with disability, are compatible with the three-step test.[73]

Second, the proposed wording reflects the extent to which the public interest considerations that undergird copyright limitations can be carved out under national copyright laws. This liberal approach to applying the three-step test is akin to the public-interest-oriented operation of the fair use doctrine in US law. Under US copyright law, the courts must consider four fair use factors in determining the public's invocation of a limit to copyright: 'the purpose and character of the use; the nature of the copyrighted work; the amount and substantiality of the portion taken; and the effect of the use upon the potential market.'[74]

[70] TRIPS Agreement, Art 7.
[71] TRIPS Agreement, Art 8.
[72] Draft RCEP IP Chapter (n 6), Arts 1.1 and 1.2.
[73] See PK Yu, 'The RCEP and Trans-Pacific Intellectual Property Norms' (2017) 50 *Vanderbilt Journal of Transnational Law* 673, 708 ('Among the negotiating parties, there was some effort – notably from Australia – to push for stronger language on copyright limitations and exceptions beyond the mere recitation of the three-step test in the TRIPS Agreement and the WIPO Copyright Treaty.').
[74] 17 USC § 107 (2006).

The US courts have made it clear that these limiting factors must be applied in the public interest. For instance, in deciding cases concerning the Google Books Library Project, both the Southern District Court of New York and the Court of Appeals for the Second Circuit injected public interest considerations into their interpretations of the four fair use factors. Following the Supreme Court's ruling on the nature of fair use in *Campbell v Acuff-Rose Music, Inc*,[75] the District Court defined fair use as a legal doctrine that functions 'to fulfill copyright's very purpose … "[t]o promote the Progress of Science and useful Arts."'[76] The Second Circuit also ruled that the four factors should be interpreted in the public interest. A judicial application of the factors is, by nature, an effort 'to define the boundary limit of the original author's exclusive rights in order to best serve the overall objectives of the copyright law to expand public learning while protecting the incentives of authors to create for the public good'.[77]

Akin to the fair use factors, the conditions set forth in the three-step test also serve as limits on limitations to copyright. For example, both the fourth fair use factor and second prong of the three-step test require adjudicative bodies to consider the impact of a copyright limitation on a work's market value. If the limitation is examined in light of the public interest by domestic courts, the interpretation and application of the three-step test should not deviate from the public interest approach. Supranational adjudicative bodies such as the WTO's Dispute Settlement Body and Appellate Body should endeavour to make inquiries into the relationship between a given copyright limitation and the public interest under the ambit of the three-step test.

B. Express Recognition of Certain Limitations

In addition to the liberal application of the three-step test, I also propose that future trade agreements make it clear that certain crucial limitations on copyright should be permitted by the parties to those agreements. Doing so would directly address concerns surrounding the test's vagueness and the consequent potential prevention of such limitations from being permitted.

More specifically, I recommend that trade agreements expressly recognize the following crucial limitations on copyright, among others. As noted at the beginning of this section, those limitations include temporary reproduction, text and data mining (TDM), and regional exhaustion of copyright. In the following discussion,

[75] *Campbell v Acuff-Rose Music, Inc*, 510 US 569, 575 (1994) ('From the infancy of copyright protection, some opportunity for fair use of copyrighted materials has been thought necessary to fulfill copyright's very purpose, "[t]o promote the Progress of Science and useful Arts …"' (alteration in original) (quoting US Const, Art I, § 8, c. 8)).

[76] *Authors Guild, Inc v Google, Inc*, 954 F Supp 2d 282, 289–90 (SDNY 2013).

[77] Ibid 213.

I will use the RCEP as an example to demonstrate why I believe future trade agreements should expressly recognize them.[78]

i. Temporary Reproduction

The temporary reproduction of copyrighted works is essential for the affordable and speedy transmission of information via the Internet. For example, caching is transient or incidental in nature, and technically required for the data transmission process to function efficiently. Therefore, the temporary reproduction of a copyrighted work (including its storage in electronic form) as a necessary part of the technical process of using that work should not be deemed an infringement of copyright.[79]

In the absence of a specific exception, the reproduction right applies to both permanent and transient copies of copyrighted materials. The duration of a copy's existence makes no difference to whether it constitutes a reproduction in the eyes of international copyright law.[80]

In today's information technology age, the temporary copying of data is fundamental to how computers and other digital devices work. Running a computer program or browsing an Internet webpage involves the automatic temporary copying of files by computers into their random access memory (RAM), and the streaming of videos requires the storage of buffer copies in RAM for reassembly. Copies of visited webpages are stored in a temporary 'Internet files' folder on users' hard disks, and browser cache files are stored on the servers of Internet service providers.[81] The copies generated in these activities are transient or incidental in nature, and are technically required for the transmission process to function efficiently. Temporary reproduction in computers and computer networks can save bandwidth, shorten transmission time, and lower transmission costs.[82] It is thus technologically indispensable for the efficient transmission of information via the Internet.

If the reproduction right applies in each and every instance of temporary copies being made in the course of the normal operation of computers and computer

[78] See Chander and Sunder (n 1) 360–61 ('If it includes an intellectual property chapter at all, the RCEP should create a new model of intellectual property agreement, devoted not to promoting intellectual property first and foremost and for its own sake, but to promoting health, education, and innovation.').

[79] For example, Art 5.1 of the European Copyright Directive (Directive 2001/29/EC) provides that '[t]emporary acts of reproduction referred to in Article 2, which are transient or incidental [and] an integral and essential part of a technological process ... shall be exempted from the reproduction right provided for in Article 2'.

[80] Article 9(1) of the Berne Convention provides that '[a]uthors of literary and artistic works protected by this Convention shall have the exclusive right of authorising the reproduction of these works, in any manner or form'.

[81] See C Waele et al, *Contemporary Intellectual Property: Law and Policy* (Oxford, Oxford University Press, 4th edn, 2016) 143–44.

[82] See PB Hugenholtz, 'Caching and Copyright: The Right of Temporary Copying' (2000) 11 *European Intellectual Property Review* 482, 482.

networks, the liability of end users and Internet service providers stretches too far. The European Court of Justice has ruled that on-screen copies and copies in the Internet 'cache' of users' hard disks made while viewing a website 'satisfy the conditions that those copies must be temporary … transient or incidental in nature and that they must constitute an integral and essential part of a technological process' as set out in the EU Copyright Directive.[83] Therefore, due to the harmonization of EU law, it has been established on a regional level that such copies may be made without the authorization of copyright owners. Similarly, in Asia a number of RCEP-participating countries, including Australia, Malaysia, New Zealand and Singapore, have already incorporated temporary reproduction exceptions into their national laws.[84]

However, if the RCEP fails to recognize the necessity of such exceptions, the broad reproduction right it confers will impede cross-border trade in information technology services, This will affect Internet and cloud services, in particular, which increasingly require the use of temporary copies,[85] eventually hindering the effective and efficient functioning of technology and stifling innovation in the digital environment.

ii. Text and Data Mining

In 2017, approximately 2.5 quintillion bytes of data were created every day,[86] 90 per cent of which had been generated over the two previous years. There is no doubt that the pace of data creation is accelerating with the launch of new digital devices such as Internet of Things products.[87] The data generated have potential economic and societal value that is yet to be unveiled.

Text and data mining (TDM) refers to 'the use of automated analytical techniques to analyze text and data for patterns, trends and other useful information'.[88] It generally comprises four stages: (1) identify potentially relevant documents; (2) convert those documents into a machine-readable format to allow structured data to be extracted; (3) extract useful information; and (4) discover new knowledge, test hypotheses and identify new relationships.[89]

[83] Case C-360/13 *Public Relations Consultants Association Ltd v Newspaper Licensing Agency Ltd and Others* EU:C:2014:1195.

[84] Copyright Act 1968, §§43A & 43B (Aust); Copyright Act 1987, Act 332, §13(2)(q) (Malay); Copyright Act 1994, §43 (NZ); Copyright Act, c 63, §38A (Sing).

[85] Australian Law Reform Commission, *Copyright and the Digital Economy (ALRC Report 122)* (2013) 251.

[86] See IBM Marketing Cloud, '10 Key Marketing Trends for 2017 and Ideas for Exceeding Customer Expectations' (2017), https://bizibl.com/marketing/download/10-key-marketing-trends-2017-and-ideas-exceeding-customer-expectations, accessed 15 April 2019.

[87] Ibid.

[88] Gov.uk, 'Exceptions to Copyright' (2014), https://www.gov.uk/guidance/exceptions-to-copyright#text-and-data-mining-for-non-commercial-research, accessed 15 April 2019.

[89] See Diane McDonald and Ursula Kelly, 'Value and Benefits of Text Mining' (2018), https://www.jisc.ac.uk/reports/value-and-benefits-of-text-mining, accessed 15 April 2019.

TDM is particularly important in the big data age, when massive computing power and a phenomenal amount of data are facilitating its application to the discovery of new relations, patterns and trends that could not have been revealed manually. TDM is becoming increasingly common in research in a variety of fields, including management, science, the social sciences, and the humanities,[90] offering numerous benefits. First, it allows the identification of relevant documents in record time.[91] Second, hidden information can be unlocked, and new knowledge developed.[92] Third, new horizons and research questions can be explored.[93] Fourth, the knowledge created by TDM can be easily interrogated and reused.[94] Fifth, the use of TDM greatly enhances the research process in terms of both quality and quantity.[95] Last but not least, it confers such broad economic benefits as cost savings, productivity gains, and innovative service and new business model development.[96]

The TDM process usually requires the copying of large quantities of material before data are extracted. If that material is subject to copyright, TDM constitutes an infringement of the copyright holder's exclusive reproduction right. One study revealed that a researcher had spent 62 per cent of his research time obtaining permission from publishers to mine thousands of articles on a single subject.[97] Excluding TDM from the scope of the reproduction right would benefit researchers by alleviating the need to seek permission from various publishers.

The UK introduced a TDM exception in 2014 that allows researchers to make copies of copyrighted material to perform TDM for non-commercial research, if they have lawful access to that material.[98] Singapore has proposed the inclusion of a similar exception in revisions to its Copyright Act,[99] although its proposed exception would permit TDM for both commercial and non-commercial uses.[100]

The use of automated analytical techniques to analyse text and data enables researchers to extract useful information from a massive quantity of text and data that cannot be detected through human reading or keyword searches. Such techniques thus foster information discovery and the creation of new

[90] See NK Herther, 'Mining for Gold: 21st-Century Search Arrives With Text Mining' (2014) 38(4) *Online Searcher* 38, 38–39; DR Hansen et al, 'Solving the Orphan Works Problem for the United States' (2013) 37 *Columbia Journal of Law & the Arts* 1, 21–22.

[91] See McDonald and Kelly (n 89).

[92] Ibid.

[93] Ibid.

[94] Ibid.

[95] Ibid.

[96] Ibid.

[97] A Guadamuz and D Cabell, 'Data Mining in UK Higher Education Institutions: Law and Policy' (2014) 4 *Queen Mary Journal of Intellectual Property* 3, 3–4.

[98] Copyright, Designs and Patents Act, 1988, c 48, § 29A (Eng).

[99] Ministry of Law and Intellectual Property Office of Singapore, *Public Consultation on Proposed Changes to Copyright Regime in Singapore*, 3.64 (2016).

[100] Ibid.

knowledge. Accordingly, I argue that TDM should not constitute an infringement of copyright as long as it is carried out for non-commercial research purposes and the researcher has lawful access to the data in question.

iii. Regional Exhaustion of Copyright

Exhaustion of copyright occurs where a copyright owner can no longer exercise control over subsequent dealings in a work embodying the copyright after the first sale of the work. This limitation removes the work from the copyright owner's proprietary control, allowing the purchaser to transfer ownership of the work or lend it to a third party without the consent of the copyright owner.[101]

The international community has yet to reach consensus on a global copyright exhaustion regime because of diverging national interests. International treaties currently impose no obligations concerning the application of national, regional or international exhaustion.[102] Article 6 of the TRIPS Agreement stipulates that '[f]or the purposes of dispute settlement under this Agreement, … nothing shall be used to address the issue of exhaustion of intellectual property rights'.[103] Countries are thus free to adopt one or a mix of the approaches to exhaustion of copyright.

Exhaustion of copyright is inextricably linked to the legality of parallel imports, which depends on which exhaustion regime a country adopts. Under such a national regime, the copyright owner can oppose parallel imports from any other country, whereas under a regional regime, the owner can oppose parallel imports from countries outside the region but not within it. Finally, under international exhaustion, the copyright owner cannot oppose any parallel imports irrespective of their source.[104]

The RCEP- and CPTPP-participating countries lack a common set of exhaustion rules for different IPR categories. For example, Singapore[105] and New Zealand have adopted the doctrine of international exhaustion in relation to some IPRs, but limit parallel imports in relation to patents and patented pharmaceuticals.[106] Japan employs international exhaustion with respect to copyrighted, trademarked, and patented goods.[107] India applies the doctrine of international exhaustion to trademarks and patents, and the doctrine of national exhaustion to copyrights

[101] World Intellectual Property Organization, *International Exhaustion and Parallel Importation*, http://www.wipo.int/sme/en/ip_business/export/international_exhaustion.htm, accessed 8 August 2018.

[102] See RL Vinelli, 'Bringing Down the Walls: How Technology is Being Used to Thwart Parallel Importers Amid the International Confusion Concerning Exhaustion of Rights' (2009) 17 *Cardozo Journal of International and Comparative Law* 135, 145–48.

[103] TRIPS Agreement, Art 6.

[104] Vinelli (n 102) 148–51.

[105] M LaFrance, 'Wag the Dog: Using Incidental Intellectual Property Rights to Block Parallel Imports' (2013) 20 *Michigan Telecommunications and Technology Law Review* 45, 86–91.

[106] See S Frankel and DJ Gervais, 'International Intellectual Property Rules and Parallel Imports' in I Calboli and E Lee (eds), *Research Handbook on Intellectual Property Exhaustion and Parallel Imports* (Cheltenham, Edward Elgar Publishing Ltd, 2016) 85, 102–04.

[107] See S Ghosh, *The Implementation of Exhaustion Policies: Lessons from National Experiences* (Geneva, International Centre for Trade and Sustainable Development, 2013) 41–42, available at https://www.ictsd.org/sites/default/files/downloads/2014/01/the-implementation-of-exhaustion-policies.pdf.

(with a few exceptions).[108] Moreover, some countries do not explicitly provide for exhaustion rules in their statutes. For example, China law statutorily allows parallel imports of patented goods, but it contains no explicit provision permitting such imports of copyrighted and trademarked goods.[109]

Parallel imports are thus both a cross-border trade and IP issue that needs to be addressed in the RCEP negotiations. If the aim is to promote regional market integration and free trade within the region, then adopting regional exhaustion as a copyright limitation within the RCEP-participating countries is likely to be the best way forward.

IV. Paths to Achieving Liberal Application of the Three-Step Test

In this section, I discuss the further actions that should be taken to bring my proposal for the liberal application of the three-step test to fruition. Using the RCEP negotiations as an example, I argue that trade agreement negotiations should promote both professionalism and transparency in protecting the public interest by setting minimum standards of copyright protection.

A. Professionalism

IP has become increasingly important in international trade, and most trade agreement negotiations therefore culminate in a set of provisions for protecting copyright as a part of IP. Given the importance of limitations on copyright, however, it is essential that negotiators diligently study the nature and scope of the public interest involved in the copyright standards they plan to create. First, they should scrutinize the current protection afforded the public interest in the use of copyrighted work. Take the RCEP negotiations as an example. A committee comprising negotiators and copyright experts should be set up to identify the myriad public interests involved in the use of copyrighted materials in the RCEP-participating countries. The committee should further consider whether and how the RCEP should promote those interests. In particular, it should reevaluate the potential positive and negative implications of copyright limitations for the economic, cultural and social development of the participating states.

Second, the proposed committee should examine the public interest mandates in international copyright treaties, and carefully consider the extent to which those treaties obligate the RCEP-participating countries to protect the public interest. For example, Articles 7 and 8 of the TRIPS Agreement mandate protection of the public interest in technological innovation and diffusion and market competition,

[108] See Ghosh (n 107) 39–41.
[109] See Ghosh (n 107) 43.

and the Berne Convention and WCT also contain provisions intended to protect the public interest.

Finally, the committee should also consider the public interest mandates in international human rights treaties. The Universal Declaration of Human Rights,[110] International Covenant on Civil and Political Rights,[111] and International Covenant on Economic, Social and Cultural Rights[112] all protect human rights with direct relevance to copyright protection, namely, the right to freedom of opinion and expression,[113] education,[114] participation in the cultural life of the community,[115] and enjoyment of scientific advancement and its benefits.[116] The proposed committee needs to consider the relevance of all of these human rights obligations to the RCEP.

B. Transparency

Procedurally, the transparency of further trade negotiations is key to ensuring adequate protection of the public interest by the RCEP in general and its copyright provisions in particular.[117] The RCEP will affect the lives and livelihoods of billions of people, not only in the participating countries but also across the globe. The international public therefore deserves a democratic right to know how the RCEP negotiating process has dealt with the issue of public interest provisions in the past and whether there are plans to adopt adequate such provisions in the future. However, the 24 rounds of RCEP negotiations that have taken place to date have resulted in the release of no substantive texts for public scrutiny.[118]

Against this backdrop, greater transparency is needed in the next round of RCEP negotiations, which could be accomplished through the following public consultation procedures. First, the RCEP should take proactive measures to ensure that all negotiating texts and other relevant documents are made publicly available

[110] Universal Declaration of Human Rights, Dec 10, 1948, GA Res 217A(III), UN Doc A/810 (1948).

[111] International Covenant on Civil and Political Rights, Dec 16, 1966, 999 UNTS 171.

[112] International Covenant on Economic, Social and Cultural Rights, Dec 16, 1966, S Treaty Doc No 95-19, 6 ILM 360, 993 UNTS 3 (1967).

[113] Universal Declaration of Human Rights (n 111) Art 19; International Covenant on Civil and Political Rights (n 112) Art 19.

[114] Universal Declaration of Human Rights (n 111) Art 26; International Covenant on Economic, Social and Cultural Rights (n 112) Art 13.

[115] Universal Declaration of Human Rights (n 111) Art 27(1); International Covenant on Economic, Social and Cultural Rights (n 112) Art 15(1)(a).

[116] Universal Declaration of Human Rights (n 111) Art 27(1); International Covenant on Economic, Social and Cultural Rights (n 112) Art 15(1)(b).

[117] See M Kaminski, 'The Capture of International Intellectual Property Law Through the U.S. Trade Regime' (2014) 87 *Southern California Law Review* 977, 995 (arguing that '[t]ransparency equalizes access to decision-making materials').

[118] See Reichman (n 31) 296 ('As that old world recedes before our eyes under the onslaught of new technological platforms for creating and distributing cultural artifacts, publishing intermediaries push legislatures to defend their interests by ever more restrictive measures, now typically negotiated in secret.').

as quickly as possible. In this respect, it can learn from the example of WIPO, which put in place transparency measures that facilitated the successful conclusion of the Marrakesh Treaty to Facilitate Access to Published Works for Persons Who Are Blind, Visually Impaired or Otherwise Print Disabled. WIPO publicly released the draft negotiating documents in timely fashion,[119] and also broadcast the negotiating process via a public webcast.[120]

Second, the RCEP should also strengthen stakeholder engagement. When considering critical issues, it should open up channels through which relevant stakeholders, including both business groups and civil society representatives, can submit their opinions concerning those issues. When necessary, the RCEP should also organize public hearings wherein various stakeholders can discuss the merits and demerits of draft proposals, and negotiators can explain the decision-making process.

C. Summary

Merely stating public interest considerations in copyright protection as part of the text of a trade agreement is a far cry from securing adequate protection of the public interest in practice. International organizations and national governments, as I have suggested in this section for RCEP negotiations, should adopt both professionalism and transparency as two procedural principles for making future trade agreements.

V. Conclusion

Copyright protection deeply affects the interests of authors, the creative industries, users of copyrighted works, and society at large. Therefore, the negotiators of trade agreements must endeavour to carve out copyright limitations sufficient to entitle the public to use copyrighted work in socially beneficial circumstances while protecting the legitimate interests of relevant stakeholders.

In pursuit of that aim, I propose in this chapter a liberal approach to interpreting and applying the three-step test, and recommend that the proposed approach be employed in future trade agreements to accommodate limitations on copyright that protect the public interest. If trade negotiators make concerted efforts to undertake the constructive measures outlined here, future trade agreements are more likely to win the hearts and minds of all global citizens in the digital age.

[119] See Toby McIntosh, 'WIPO Transparency Wins Praise, Gaps Remain' (2014), http://www.freedominfo.org/2014/01/wipo-transparency-wins-praise-gaps-remain, accessed 15 April 2019.

[120] Ibid.

INDEX

www.ingramcontent.com/pod-product-compliance
Lightning Source LLC
Chambersburg PA
CBHW071302180926
51613CB00001B/107
9781509922772